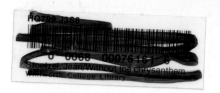

WITHOUT THE CHRYSANTHEMUM AND THE SWORD

The picture show

JEAN STOETZEL

WITHOUT THE CHRYSANTHEMUM AND THE SWORD

A Study of the Attitudes of Youth in Post-War Japan

A UNESCO PUBLICATION
NEW YORK : COLUMBIA UNIVERSITY PRESS
1955

Printed in 1955 by the IJsel Press, Deventer
for
The United Nations Educational, Scientific and Cultural Organization
19 Avenue Kléber, Paris-16e
and
The Columbia University Press
2960 Broadway, New York 27, N.Y.

CONTENTS

2060

LIST OF MAPS AND GRAPHS

FOREWORD

This book is the outcome of a decision by Unesco, at the end of 1951, to send a French sociologist and a Dutch expert on Japanese civilization to Japan to collect material for a report on the attitudes of Japanese youth. Very broadly, the division of labour was as follows: I was responsible for the general planning of the investigation, for putting together the documents collected or compiled and for drafting the report, while my colleague Vos (University of Leyden) acted as adviser on cultural points and as interpreter and also translated a considerable bulk of documents and texts. The working language of our two-man mission was English.

Our task proved to be very laborious and difficult. Even the modest results here presented could certainly not have been achieved but for the loyal and earnest co-operation which we received on the spot from Japanese colleagues, from the government and from a host of private persons, exalted and humble, but all well aware of the nature of the work in which they were co-operating. Where helpers are named in the text it is only for explanatory reasons, or because they are authorities; the number of such references gives only a feeble notion of the vast debt we owe to all concerned. That all are not thanked by name in no way diminishes the warmth of our gratitude.

It has been thought desirable to preface the report of our investigation with a kind of introduction, mainly cultural and sociological. This is both too much, and too little: specialists will readily discern gaps in our knowledge, crude simplifications and, despite the care taken by the author, in all probability errors too; whereas there is too much detail for the general reader, who will be inclined to give only the most cursory attention to what he regards as a vain display of undigested erudition—yet it is to him that it is directed, to give him an idea of the immense distance separating the Japanese and himself in character and culture.

The aim, basically, was to shorten this distance by providing a certain amount of accurate information to fill the gaps of ignorance and by trying to find a rational means of reducing it. Feeling as I do that, given the right approach, no culture is incomprehensible to a mind formed in any other culture, I should like to dedicate this book to the task, barely begun, of attaining to a full understanding of all peoples, beginning with the Japanese.

J. S.

Paris, October 1952.

NOTE TO THE READER

The transcription of Japanese words into Latin characters, as they will be found in these pages, follows Hepburn's rules, with the usual modifications. While there is no need to enter into details, the reader should note that vowels are pronounced as in Italian and consonants as in English. Vowels marked by a macron (ˉ) or a circumflex accent are long.

For practical reasons, all the tables are not presented in the same way.

In the body of the text, they are generally to be read horizontally, i.e. in lines across the page; this is particularly the case with tables indicating percentages for urban and rural age-groups. In the appendices, the tables are to be read vertically, i.e. in columns.

As regards percentages, the column 'Total: 100 percent' in the text and the cross-head 'Total: 100 percent' in the appendices, have been omitted. The total of the percentages indicated (usually in horizontal lines in the text and in the columns in the appendices) does not always add up to 100 percent: it is below that figure when all the replies are not indicated (e.g. when the 'no opinion' or 'vague' answers are omitted), and it is above it when the persons questioned gave more than one reply at a time. It should be noted that in some cases a question was deliberately framed in such a way as to elicit several replies. In all cases, however, the percentages indicate the proportion of persons giving the specific reply listed at the top of the column (in the text in general), or in the cross-head (in the appendices), out of 100 individuals belonging to the category specified in the cross-head of most of the tables given in the text and at the head of the column in the tables given in the appendices.

CHAPTER I

THE UNESCO ENQUIRY

The investigation organized by Unesco in 1951 and carried out between the end of that year and the first few months of 1952 was concerned with the attitudes of Japanese youth and the problems arising therefrom.

THE SPIRIT IN WHICH THE ENQUIRY WAS UNDERTAKEN

It will be agreed that an investigation of that kind, undertaken at that date, might, at least at the beginning, have aroused curiosity of a political nature. Whatever the respective degrees to which facts, which the historians can establish in due course, or mere propaganda have moulded ideas about Japan, it remains true that a profound and enduring impression has been made on the world by the arrogance and insolence with which militarist and imperialist Japan openly exhibited its thirst for power by its savage aggression on the Asiatic continent and in the Pacific region and by the almost superhuman ferocity of its resistance, physical and spiritual, when the tide of battle began to turn against it. As a result the notion has taken root and will long endure that the conflagration started in Japan, mastered in 1945 in circumstances with which we are all familiar, may still be smouldering under the ruins and the ashes, and that a suspicious watch must be kept on the country as on a volcano, inactive for the moment but liable at any moment to become again a menace.

Through SCAP[1] action has been taken by the Allied Powers to dry up the institutional sources of the totalitarian effectiveness of Japanese militarism and imperialism. The imperial régime, and everything stemming from or connected with it, have been profoundly altered; to all appearances all that is left is a façade without strength or substance. The Emperor survives indeed, but merely as a symbol of national unity. Sovereignty has been restored to the people. Family law and the legal

---

1. Supreme Command of the Allied Powers (later 'Commander').

status of women have entirely changed. Socially and economically a genuine revolution has been brought about by agrarian reform and the dispersal of the *zaibatsu*. The State religion, which was a tool of the State, has been abolished by a stroke of the pen. The nation's educational system has been recast in its entirety. By an explicit provision of the new Constitution, the army has been completely abolished forever, atomized as spectacularly as Hiroshima and Nagasaki, and no fragment survives of the incomparable metal from which the Samurai sword was forged; the chrysanthemum, the emblem of the imperial house, has disappeared entirely, as a glance at the new postage stamps will show.

With Japan on the eve of recovering her independence, what was going to be the frame of mind of a new generation deprived of its two national symbols, the sword and the chrysanthemum? How would it regard nations which, if no longer enemies, were at any rate its conquerors? Where would foreign affairs rank among its concerns? Would it, instead of withdrawing into xenophobic nationalism, show an interest in foreign countries? Would it prove capable of discriminating between them: if so how would its friendship and respect be apportioned among them? Would it accept disarmament imposed from without as a good thing or would it cherish thoughts of revenge? If it elected for a pacifist policy and ideology would it do so without reservations or would it set limits not to be exceeded? In view of the existing world situation, questions such as these obviously have their place in any enquiry into the attitudes of Japanese youth; obviously too they have direct political significance.

Furthermore, investigating what Japanese youth wants and thinks means seeking to determine its attitudes towards the country's institutions. What does it think of the economic system? What is its behaviour as regards political and administrative authority or the person of the Emperor? What positive steps is it prepared to take and in what respects can it be looked to for active co-operation? In the family domain, are the young, traditionally subject to the authority of the older generation, going to grasp the chance of liberty which is offered to them? How will they choose among the possibilities opened up to them by the new articles of the civil code? What are their ideas about the status of women in society, in the family and in personal relationships? On the threshold of the married state, what type of union do they wish to contract? What is their conception of the households they themselves will shortly establish? What weight do they give to traditional morality and, more broadly, what feeling have they for tradition in general? The political implications of such questions are as evident as their pertinence to an enquiry into the attitudes of Japanese youth; given sufficiently clear answers, tending frankly in one direction or another, we shall be able to assess the new Japan's chances of evolving on democratic lines or reverting to some form of totalitarianism.

Similarly, attempted analyses of personality among the young—which one cannot help wanting to undertake—should in turn enable political inferences of the same kind to be drawn: if individuals have become self-reliant and independent, if they show traits of realism and have a sense of security, the cause of democracy will be well guarded in Japan by the citizens of tomorrow; if the case is otherwise, the political inferences will be different. Hence the political interest of the enquiry is not in doubt.

It would however be a serious and in some respects a monstrous error, an unpardonable offence against subjects and investigators alike, to assume that this enquiry was essentially political. It is not sought to deny that political considerations enter into the matter, in two ways: as in all practical sociological research they constitute the inevitable background of the particular investigation; and secondly, the investigation itself brings to light subsidiary data, some of which is of political significance. It must, however, be repeated again and again that sociological research is not polarized in the field of values and that its principal requirement is an ascetical approach on the part of the research worker. As far as we ourselves were concerned, we can guarantee that we made it a first rule of intellectual honesty not to allow ourselves to be influenced by our attachments, and to make arbitrary choices, but to eschew every sentiment other than that of absolute respect for the right of an individual or a community to choose for themselves whatever values and cherish whatever attachments they liked. Some may think this rather solemn declaration superfluous; to others it will, we know, be shocking, affording yet another proof of the sociologist's lack of loyalty to the culture which bred him. I do not propose to waste time trying to remove the misunderstanding that clouds the vision of the latter. In answer to the former, however, I feel bound to point out, emphatically, that the line of conduct described above is easier to preach than to practise and that if we were to claim any merit for the present work, it would be on the grounds that it was carried out from first to last in a spirit of unqualified respect for the right of the Japanese to think and behave as Japanese.

Thus the motives prompting the Unesco investigation of the attitudes of Japanese youth must be interpreted quite otherwise, this particular study being in fact merely a part of a much vaster programme for the promotion of understanding between the peoples. By themselves, international goodwill and a spirit of co-operation are not enough to produce the happy results expected of them: with them must go accurate knowledge of one another on the part of the different peoples of the world. In the specific case of Japan, in so far as Westerners' minds are not a complete blank on the subject, their knowledge mostly boils down to a collection of arbitrary clichés, reflecting favourable or unfavourable judgments of uncertain origin, variously traceable to some irresponsible writer, to misleading propaganda or to the inflaming of passions and warping of judgment by political events.

American public opinion polls give an idea of the way the public in the United States of America pictured the Japanese during the war: it is only necessary to turn to the collection published in 1951 by Hadley Cantril.[1] A few examples taken from this collection will serve to bring out the significance of what was said in the preceding paragraph. An enquiry conducted by *Fortune* showed that in 1944 approximately 50 per cent of the American public thought that the Japanese could not read their own language or that not more than 50 per cent of them were able to do so; more than a quarter of the subjects in the upper income brackets who were questioned answered 'only a few can do so' (op. cit. p. 400). In an investigation conducted in 1942 by the Office of Public Opinion Research, adjectives chosen by the public to describe the Japanese people included 'two-faced' (73 per cent), 'crafty' (62 per cent), 'cruel' (55 per cent), and 'bellicose' (46 per cent) (op. cit. p. 501). A questionnaire circulated eight times at various periods between 1942 and 1946 by the National Centre of Public Opinion Research makes it clear that, while the Germans were, in the main, regarded as misled by a bad government, the most widespread view of the Japanese was that they had an ingrained love of war; the frequency of this opinion varied with the fortunes of the war and the prolongation of the war in the Pacific, rising to peaks in June 1943 (57 per cent) and December 1944 (56 per cent), and only becoming a minority view again (35 per cent) in May 1946 (op. cit. p. 501). As Bruner, who uses some of these results, puts it, the explanation of such stereotyped opinions is largely ignorance.[2]

Views of this kind are regrettable because, being charged with the emotions of those who expressed them—suspicion, hatred and anger—there is a danger of their bringing about equally undesirable reactions. But above all they are subjective and unrealistic—in a word, false; friendly reactions—which do exist—may be just as dangerous if of similar origin. Social relationships, like all other relationships, can be effectively pursued only if they have an objective basis, a statement which superficially seems a truism, but which, when its ultimate implications are thought out and when it is resolutely put into practice, clashes with many interests and shocks convention.

It is in that spirit that both this enquiry into the attitudes of Japanese youth and simultaneous enquiries in Germany and India have been conducted. The fact that several similar enquiries have been carried out concurrently will not only have the effect of enlarging our knowledge on many points but will also permit comparisons between the peoples concerned, without which the results secured, however objective they may be, remain inconclusive. Moreover, the twofold knowledge thus secured—first intrinsic, and then comparative—is not solely for the

1. Hadley Cantril (editor), *Public Opinion*, Princeton, 1951.
2. Jerome F. Bruner, *Mandate from the People*, New York, 1944, p. 136; French translation, *Ce Que Pense L'Amérique*, by Didier Lazard, Paris, 1945, p. 146.

benefit of outside observers. It is also intended for those who were originally the subjects of study and who co-operated in the hope that through having this opportunity to understand others better they would be able to understand themselves better, too. It is not only the foreigner who falls victim to the clichés of 'national psychology' and 'national character': a people's mental image of itself is no less a stereotype than its mental images of other peoples, for it is arrived at by the same irrational, arbitrary and irresponsible methods. With communities as with individuals, self-knowledge does not differ in nature from knowledge of others: it is deduced from clues and not from immediate acquaintance. The only notable difference is that one is more present to oneself, but that has never been a guarantee of objectivity. In point of fact the investigators have frequently had occasion to note the facility, and sometimes the complacence, with which the Japanese accept stereotypes of themselves suggested to them by foreigners.

Scientific works on Japanese culture and mentality are not, of course, entirely lacking. In the first place there are the writers of an earlier generation, such as Lafcadio Hearn, whose principal work—*Japan: an Interpretation*—was for long the West's best source of information.[1] Then there are the purely literary works which are valuable for their authors' great familiarity with the country and ability to view it in perspective; the most remarkable of these is probably *L'Honorable Partie de Campagne* by Thomas Raucat, which should still be put in the hands of all visitors to Japan. In addition to these two groups there is a selection of ethnographical studies which are worth perusal. The prototype—which will probably long remain a model for works of the kind—is the late Ruth Benedict's *The Chrysanthemum and the Sword*,[2] which should really be read in conjunction with a monograph to which its author often turned for guidance—*Suye Mura*, by John S. Embree[3]—though the latter is a work of sociology rather than of social psychology.

Klineberg [4] also very rightly draws particular attention to the studies of the Japanese character by Geoffrey Gorer, Weston La Barre and Haring.[5] The ethnographical documentation available will be further enriched in the near future by the results of the various kinds of research undertaken in the Okayama region in collaboration with the University of Michigan Center for Japanese Studies.

1. Published 1904; French translation—*Le Japon*—published by Mercure de France.
2. *The Chrysanthemum and the Sword*, Boston, 1946.
3. John S. Embree, *Suye Mura: A Japanese Village*, Chicago, 1939. A monograph bringing Embree's up to date is *The Japanese Village in Transition*, Tokyo, 1950, by Arthur F. Raper, Tamie Tsuchiyma, Herbert Passin and David L. Sills.
4. *Tensions affecting International Understanding*, New York, 1950, pp 18-19.
5. Geoffrey Gorer, *Themes in Japanese Culture* (Transactions of the New York Academy of Sciences) 1943, 5, 106-24; Weston La Barre, *Some Observations on the Character Structure in the Orient: The Japanese* (Psychiatry, 1945, 8, 319-42); T. G. Haring, *Aspects of Personal Character in Japan* (Far Eastern Quarterly, 1946, 6, 12-22).

The application of ethnographical methods to the study of literate cultures is undoubtedly a considerable advance. Paradoxically, until quite recently the only societies concerning whose cultural systems a body of scientific knowledge had been built up were those of the most simple civilizations, the implicit assumption being that the others had themselves an adequate knowledge of their own culture—an extension to the group environment of the classical psychologist's pre-critical trust in introspection. It has at long last been recognized that in this respect 'civilized' man differs in no way from the 'savage': he has as little comprehension, as little intuitive grasp, of his own culture as of his individual behaviour. It is fidelity to this principle that gives importance to the work of Ruth Benedict and Gorer and to that now being directed by Margaret Mead.

Unfortunately, the ethnographic method has limitations which are already clearly apparent to the social psychologist working among peoples of pre-literate culture, and which completely rule out any claim that it is by itself an adequate instrument for describing and interpreting the behaviour of members of the most complex civilizations. Even where 'primitives' are concerned, their behaviour, however uniform compared to our own, still admits of individual differences and a complexity of personal motivations, a kind of human solidity, made up of temperamental differences, psychological aptitudes, and intimate life stories, in sharp contrast to the social automaton which the beings described by the ethnographers so frequently suggest. When we come to what are called the higher civilizations, the standard behaviour-patterns of ethnography and the patterns of real life behaviour are as different as the phenomena to be described. Ruth Benedict is of course right to try out the validity, as a heuristic principle, of the idea that cultural behaviour-patterns form significant systems, configurations or *Gestalten:* that they are copies of quasi-platonic archetypes characteristic of the more or less ontological purpose of a given society.[1] But if these culture patterns and types of behaviour exist outside the mind of the ethnographer, it is as flexible figures which can be made to assume an infinite variety of shapes, as in topology; indeed — to continue the metaphor — in complex societies with a history and a past, they must be many-faceted models, and the problem of the research worker is not so much to hit on the more or less poetical formula which will explain the whole as to say with a certain degree of precision who does what: in other words the analysis of form must be abandoned in favour of quantitative evaluations. It must therefore be a matter for regret that Ruth Benedict not only neglected quantitative techniques—though indeed they were not available to her when she wrote *The Chrysanthemum and the Sword*—but also tried to justify this negligence methodologically.[2]

There is nothing personal in the above remarks. On the contrary they

---

1. Cf. Ruth Benedict, *Patterns of Culture.*
2. Cf. *The Chrysanthemum and the Sword*, pp. 17-18.

are in line with the consensus of opinion about Ruth Benedict's admirable work. Thus Klineberg in his critique remarks that the methods used by Ruth Benedict and her colleagues 'give us no idea whatever of the variations among the individuals making up the national group. They leave us with the impression of a pattern of behaviour common to the whole people which probably does not square with the facts .... The present writer can only ... urge that the ethnographers' reports be supplemented, wherever possible, by other methods, particularly quantitative methods' (op. cit. pp. 19, 20). A Japanese commentator writing a year before Klineberg's remarks were published and whom the latter had probably not consulted, expressed himself in very similar terms: 'What I have just said does not mean that quantitative methods are useless for the study of our country's culture. In a society going through changes as revolutionary as those being experienced by post-war Japan, measurements of the frequency and degree of regularity with which the various types of behaviour patterns and ways of thought recur is very useful, if not essential. Today, new types of behaviour and new modes of thought are growing up in the country in competition with the traditional forms. To determine in what manner, and how strongly, the former are establishing themselves against the opposition of the latter is of the utmost practical, as well as academic, interest. That is why we not merely confirm the need and value of quantitative methods in the study of everyday types of behaviour but feel it our duty to ask that they should be put into active use, and for this purpose we think that an enquiry into attitudes is of the first importance.[1]

One of our intentions in conducting the enquiry was therefore to try out methods that were at least partially quantitative, and appropriate to our purpose and the conditions in which we should be working. There could be no question of looking for new methods, nor indeed was there any special reason for harbouring an ambition of that kind. It was not even thought advisable to employ the most sensitive and complex methods. In the first place the investigators, as Occidentals, had to adapt themselves to a field of observation which was largely new to them, and they also had to allow for difficulties, possibly considerable, in collaborating with local experts. In this connexion, it should be made clear at once that the anticipated obstacles had been overestimated; the spirit of mutual understanding and goodwill informing our relations with Japanese psychologists and sociologists could not have been better: with the liveliest satisfaction and not—we admit—without some surprise, we constantly had the feeling of close intellectual kinship with our Japanese colleagues: the universality of science in human and social questions, as in others, is not an empty phrase but a precise fact. It

---

1. Takeyoshi Kawashima, 'Evaluation and Critique', *Japanese Journal of Ethnology (Minzokugaku-Kenkyu)*. Special number on the questions raised by *The Chrysanthemum and the Sword*, 1949, *14*, no. 4, 1-8, p. 3 (in Japanese).

should also be remarked that, as regards personal relationships, we met with hardly any difficulties: our status as Unesco's representatives, coupled with the fact that our nationalities were respectively Dutch and French, was enough to ensure us a favourable reception.

A second consideration affecting the choice of methods was our concern to ensure that the data collected should be comparable with the corresponding data for other countries; this meant selecting methods which were either directly transferable, or, at least, easy to transpose. The truly immense cultural differences between Japan and, say France, Germany or India, entirely precluded a satisfactory solution of this problem as regards the content of the enquiry: the actual questions asked and the cultural background of the projective test remained purely Japanese and would be meaningless outside Japan. But the methods of which these non-transferable elements form part are commonplace and can be practised anywhere with few resources, except of course in the case of the public opinion poll, which must be well organized in advance and would be difficult to improvise.

THE SCOPE OF THE PROBLEMS INVESTIGATED

Within the terms of the instructions given to the mission on its departure—reducible essentially to the directive—'to study the attitudes of contemporary youth'—three central themes of research clearly emerged: What were the attitudes of Japanese youth to foreigners? How did they comport themselves towards their country's institutions? What were their most important and significant personal characteristics? Exploration of the problems centred around these three themes could be expected to provide the answer to a great number of questions.

As regards attitudes towards foreigners the first question to be answered was how Japanese youth had accepted the fact of the 1945 defeat—whether the attitude adopted was one of withdrawal into themselves; whether they nourished feelings of revenge; or whether they were resigned to what had happened and were turning optimistically towards the future with the idea of co-operating sincerely and peacefully with the other nations of the world. If the last proved to be the prevailing attitude, how did they picture those other nations? What distinctions did they draw between them, both from the emotional and the rational point of view? What did they think about their chief conqueror and occupying power, the United States of America; their powerful neighbour, the Soviet Union; China, which they had sought to conquer; their former allies Germany and Italy; and the Western countries with which they had had extensive cultural relations in the recent past—Great Britain, France and the Netherlands—and what kind of interest did they take in each? What was their attitude to India; to Brazil, which provided an outlet for their emigrants; and to Australia, which was still forbidden territory? Were they specially interested in any other nations in East Asia, in the Pacific, in Western and Eastern Europe, in the Near and Middle East or in the Americas? This long list of questions, which was not expected to give conclusive results one way or the other, but rather to provide answers that could be classified, presented no particular methodological difficulties. One had only to take care not to provoke tendentious reactions by too peremptory questions; to choose for group or private interviews the type of questions that would call forth free and spontaneous replies, and above all not to try to probe too deeply or to ask for too precise (and therefore artificial) details. The fact is that in this field vague attitudes were to be expected on the part of most of those questioned, except, of course as regards the country with which the Japanese have had their most intimate contacts, the United States of America.

However, of the various problems relating to the attitudes of Japanese youth in the sphere of international relations, an emphatic exception to the foregoing rule must be made as regards questions dealing with war, pacifism and the recent decision to rearm. The war sufferings of the Japanese were greater than can be described or imagined. However, throughout the period of hostilities they do not appear ever to have questioned the rightness of their cause, their duty to be loyal to their country, symbolized by the imperial house, or their obedience to their leaders. Once they had got over the first shock, they accepted defeat as something inevitable, as already part of a past to which it was pointless to revert. Thereafter they received both from the highest Japanese authority and from the occupying power with all its prestige, new directives of which the tone was pacific, pacifist, anti-war and even anti-army. Today, though unobtrusively as yet, they are embarking on rearmament. A state of affairs of such complexity may well cause bewilderment in many minds, and here, it would be imprudent to be satisfied with superficial answers to stereotyped questions. We must go deeper and a public opinion poll will not suffice.

The question of young Japan's attitudes towards its national institutions is the kernel of the whole study. However important laws may be, institutions exist only through the men who make them work. The legal and administrative structure of Japan has undergone a profound transformation since the end of the war. The economic organization of town and country has been extensively recast and the empire has become a democracy with a strong bias towards decentralization in certain spheres. Women have been given equality with men, not only politically, but in the family and in daily life, while the principle of primogeniture, apparently strongly entrenched in the country areas, has been severely modified. The young are free to marry as they wish, and no longer need the consent of their families; at the same time attention has been drawn to the dangers of overpopulation and, to all intents and purposes, official sanction has been given to contraceptive practices and in some cases at least, to abortion. Lastly the 'established' religion has been abolished root and branch and freedom of worship has been granted to all faiths.

If these radical innovations are to be incorporated into Japanese culture, it will be primarily through the agency of the young and it is thus pertinent to ask what will be their attitudes towards economics, politics, the family and religion. The object of all the reforms mentioned was to reduce the excessive pressure of authority on the individual, in his family relationships, in his work and in civic and public life. What, in the result, is the attitude of the young towards authority in all its forms? Do they feel free? Do they want to be free? Do they feel what freedom is: in other words, do they intend to play an active part in the life of the community, with a full sense of their reponsibilities?

It is obvious that here, even more than in the case of international relations and the problems of militarism and pacifism, it is less important to form a general idea of the frame of mind of contemporary Japanese society than to try to analyse the elements of an infinitely complex psycho-social situation. Probably never before in the sociological history of Japan have the cultural options been so numerous or so contradictory; the traditional rules of life survive in the generations which never knew any other ways, but from the Meiji era onwards successive layers of new cultural traits have been added, sometimes giving rise to a bewilderment perceptible even in the remotest country areas. As long ago as 1936 Embree drew attention to such changes at Suye-Mura[1] and they have also been noted by many Japanese writers.[2] Nowadays, however, ambiguous values are, as it were, the rule; this is so glaringly the case that, as we have seen, in some instances the legislator has shirked a decision either way, leaving the responsibility of choice to the public itself. Hence in dealing with the main possible alternatives, research must endeavour to evaluate the strength of each current, to enumerate the frankly progressive and traditional attitudes, and, what is more, try to reveal the ambivalences and see how these work out in practice. Ultimately the analysis will narrow down to the authority-liberty antithesis: authority is given but liberty is achieved in more or less favourable circumstances; the question to be answered is whether and how far Japanese youth is capable of autonomy or whether it tends to eschew freedom.

Consideration of these points inevitably leads to the question of the personality of the young. What are the values by which they are governed? What traits do they exhibit most frequently? By what psy-

---

1. Cf. Chapter VIII *et passim*.
2. This is the essence of Tetsuro Watsuji's criticism of Ruth Benedict's work in his article Doubts on the Scientific Value of Ruth Benedict's Book, *Japanese Journal of Ethnology* (*Minzokugaku-Kenkyu*), no. 4, p. 23-7 (in Japanese).

chological processes do they solve the problem of adapting themselves to a society which presents them with such difficult and confused situations? Can various types of personality be distinguished among them and to what conditions do they correspond? Research along these lines can be only very modest and the conclusions arrived at will therefore be, at most, indicative. The use of psycho-analysis and ethnography in combination may produce brilliant syntheses at little cost, for instance under the heading of 'basic personality structure', but in the last resort, all reasoning depends on the weight of experience behind it; this kind of cultural psychology of the individual is little more than another way of presenting sociological data already available elsewhere and consequently conveys in a different language the same misleading impression of universality that is a weakness of synthetic sociological interpretations.

The attempt made in the present book is rather of a quantitative nature. It must not be thought, however, that it could be pushed very far. The study of a single personality trait alone requires considerable technical resources, well planned and carefully checked procedures and, in the preparatory stage at least, work on subjects about whom adequate information is available from other sources. None of this was possible and this study of the personality of Japanese youth is presented frankly for what it is—an attempt to make use of the subsidiary elements arising out of an investigation undertaken at several different levels, and dealing with the attitudes of several very heterogeneous groups of subjects, in domains where cultural changes are particularly keenly felt. We may, however, earn some thanks for having tried, for instance, to estimate by these means the numbers of genuinely autonomous subjects or to classify types of personal values by age-group and habitat.

From the very first, one of our main concerns was to make comparisons between significant sociological groups. Since we were concerned with the youth of the country, comparisons between age-groups were obviously desirable. It was therefore thought necessary to extend the investigation to adults as well as young people and this was the special function of the representative enquiry delegated to the National Public Opinion Research Institute. It proved possible to identify four age-groups—16-19, 20-24, 25-29 and over 30—whose attitudes very often revealed significant differences, in some instances successively throughout the range. A comparison of attitudes according to sex was no less indispensable. It was also necessary to distinguish between the attitudes of rural and urban subjects: social psychologists generally take the view that the town-dweller exhibits traits of cultural evolution which are not only quite opposed to those of the countryman but often foreshadow the direction in which the countryman will change. Regional differences also presented an interesting subject for investigation, but any attempt to study them systematically would have meant extending the investigation beyond the acceptable limits; we therefore decided to confine ourselves to two samples, as sharply contrasted as possible, for which purpose we selected a rural centre in the former province of Satsuma in South Kyushu, with a reputation for traditionalism, and the island of Hokkaido which is regarded as representing the exact opposite, socially and politically as well as geographically. Comparison between the attitudes of young trade unionists in industry with those of young peasants should give an idea of the differences arising out of social and economic conditions. Three groups of students were examined; the quite considerable effect of the level of education on the attitudes of the young has already been clearly demonstrated in the findings published by the newspaper *Asahi*, but the level of education is never an isolated factor and it is difficult to dissociate it from its social and economic correlatives.

On these lines, many comparisons between elements within the Japanese society have been sought out and made possible, but over the eminently desirable international comparisons envisaged in the original work plan we suffered what were probably our gravest disappointments. As similar investigations were already under way in Germany and India, it had seemed easy to incorporate at least some of the same elements in our own. As far as the Indian project was concerned we must report with regret that we were unable to secure any exact information either on our way out, in New York, from an adviser attached to the enquiry, or on our way back in Delhi, where we had arranged to break our journey especially for this purpose. The German investigation was much more ambitious and complex than anything we could hope to effect but in this case we did at least have Pipping's questionnaire available to us. This consists of a series of 10 simple propositions relating to authority, for rejection or acceptance, and keyed to a finely graded range of attitudes. Unfortunately the majority of these propositions relate to cultural traits common in the West but quite alien to Japan. For instance, it is pointless to ask Japanese whether they consider 'that a wise mother should let her children play unchecked, even at the risk of having the house turned upside down'. To all intents and purposes there is nothing in a Japanese house to turn upside down and no restraints are normally put on young children. However, we had thought that we could retain at least one item from Pipping's questionnaire; in the original text it reads: 'Wer Vorgesetzten nie widerspricht, ist feig' (he who never contradicts his superiors is a coward). The Japanese version, translated literally, reads: 'Some people have a saying, *nagai mono niwa makarero*, (never contradict a superior) or words to that effect; have you heard this said? If so, do you think this attitude is wrong or do you think it cannot be avoided?' The result was disappointing; of the Japanese interrogated, more than a quarter said they did not understand the phrase and in the 16-19 age-group the proportions who did not answer were 54 per cent in the towns and 52 per cent in the country. Here we put our finger, as it were, on the extreme difficulty of organizing accurately

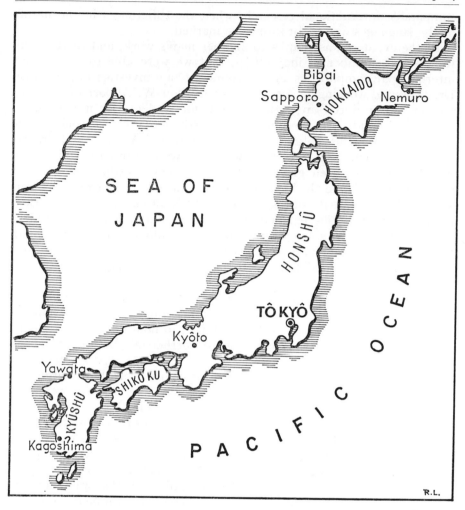

Fig. 1. Points or centres where investigations were carried out.

comparable international research, when the differences in the nature of the languages and institutions are marked.

In the event it was thanks to another man's work, and to the helpfulness of a number of individuals, that we were able to effect some international comparisons in the course of our investigation. In 1949 Dr. Gillespie, working under Professor Gordon W. Allport of Harvard University, produced an 'attitudes test' for students for use in an international study, to be published shortly, covering a considerable number of countries, notably the United States of America and France, as well as Japan itself. The test, which we were granted permission to use, had already been given to Tokyo students at the suggestion of Gillespie himself; and the kindness of Kiyohide Seki of Hokkaido University and Yoji Watanabe of the University of Kyoto in applying it in their respective universities enabled us to secure data concerning student groups differing in some degree from the Tokyo sample. It should, however, at once be noted that several questions (the same ones) in this test were misunderstood, both at Hokkaido, where it was given in English, and at Kyoto, where it was given in Japanese. As will be seen in due course, the Allport-Gillespie test was also drawn on for several items in the questionnaire used in a number of other educational establishments in Kyushu and Hokkaido—in this instance, to non-university students. Thus, when Gillespie's study is published, further international comparisons will be possible.

Besides the need to supply material for comparisons both within the Japanese society and between that society and others, we were also concerned to carry out our investigation on several levels. It was certainly a basic necessity for us to be in possession of representative data, otherwise we ran the risk of seeing things in a false perspective and accepting as important and typical phenomena which happened to make a strong impression on us, but which might in fact be merely fortuitous or local. An enquiry based on respresentative samples was therefore essential and an account of how this was carried out will be given in due course. However, if it is to be accurate, an investigation on these lines must be strictly standardized, and there must also be narrow limits to the number of themes to be explored, together with a certain rigidity, or lack of flexibility, in examining individual peculiarities of attitude.

This made it desirable to employ a method which would probe more deeply into the psychology of the young and our choice for the purpose was a combination of an exhaustive questionnaire and a specially designed projective test. Lastly, it seemed essential to us to acquaint ourselves at first hand with the psychology of young Japan and we were accordingly at pains to arrange a large number of interviews, both private and individual and on a group basis in public, at widely separated points, and with young people on very different intellectual and social levels. The opportunity at the end of our stay to use the Allport-Gillespie test was particularly welcome to us: in the final revision, which is the subject of the present report, it was of the greatest value in enabling us to cross-check and supplement our other data. That was also the purpose of the restricted and not very systematic, but extremely suggestive, enquiry carried out by Vos in Tokyo before my own arrival in Japan. Nor did we neglect the documentation already in existence: though it was out of the question for us to trace and sift it all, we have at least sought to profit by what was closest at hand.

Finally, to round off this account of the tasks we set ourselves and the conditions in which the investigation was conducted, attention must be drawn to a number of difficulties which prevented us from doing better. Something has already been said of our disappointments regarding international comparisons. In general, we felt that more could have been done had the time and the number of staff at our disposal been less limited. There is no question but that an additional three months in Japan, while not necessarily doubling the yield of the investigation, would at least have made it possible to clear up a fair number of uncertainties still subsisting. We should have requested, and probably received, still more assistance from the National Public Opinion Research Institute (its work in any case forms the skeleton of this report); we should have carried out exhaustive research at other points, notably in Tokyo itself and in central and northern Honshu; and lastly, we should almost certainly have visited Shikoku. But for this, personnel, even more than time, were lacking. The mission was composed of two persons: myself—a French social psychologist, who does not speak a word of Japanese—and a Dutch expert on Japanese language and literature. Both intellectually and personally our partnership was perfect, but the reader will appreciate how difficult it was for us to separate and work individually. The attempt was in fact made during the latter part of our stay, when Vos carried on alone in Tokyo and I went to Kyushu where I was to pick up a Japanese assistant. As this man was much occupied by work of his own, I found myself left to my own devices for much of the time and forced to rely on chance interpreters; a certain falling off in results, and also some practical difficulties, resulted from this. For the Hokkaido trip, I secured the services of Mario Schubert, a former member of the Unesco Tokyo office who gave me effective and valuable assistance. It would no doubt have been better if the mission had consisted of at least two teams working simultaneously on the separate tasks assigned them, under the direction of a head of mission. In the future this solution would seem preferable to extending the time of a one-team mission; in social psychology things change quickly, and a prolonged investigation may mean that later revisions lose much of their significance. This does not imply that the study of the changes taking place is unimportant—quite the contrary; but this is a separate problem which it is probably better to tackle by the method of interrupted observation.

It must also be acknowledged that our inexperience of Japan was the cause of some tardiness in starting work. We had to adjust ourselves to different ways of life—far more different than those accustomed only to the relatively minor dissimilarities between countries of the Western world could possibly imagine. Above all we had to get our bearings in the contemporary scene and among the sociological forms and mental trends which were to be the setting and the very subject of our investigation and which obviously could only be understood on the spot. It must also be admitted that, being uncertain what kind of welcome we should receive, we were cautious about making contact with our Japanese colleagues and with the country's administrative authorities. To give a specific example of the problems facing us: Should we tell them point blank that we wanted to study the attitudes of the young towards the imperial régime and the person of the Emperor? These doubts will be readily understood. We are therefore all the more pleased to pay tribute now to our colleagues' understanding and whole-hearted co-operation.

GENERAL ORGANIZATION OF THE INVESTIGATION

It was thanks to these specially favourable local circumstances that, despite our limited staff and resources, we were able, in a comparatively short time, to complete the enquiry described in this report. The general organization of the work was broadly as follows.

Relevant documentation from both Japanese and American sources was assembled. Eizo Koyama, Director of the National Public Opinion Research Institute, was kind enough to allow us to use the results of all the public opinion polls carried out by his organization since its foundation. We also had access through the kindness of the head of the company's research department, Mr. Takeshi Okamura, to the market research documentation collected by the Dentsu company (K. K. Nippon Dempo Tsushinsha). Professor Ayonori Okasaki, Director of the Institute for Research on Demographic Problems, at the Ministry of Public Welfare, gave us all the demographic information we needed and also put himself out in a thousand ways to facilitate our task. From the American Education and Civilian Information Services (CIE, SCAP) we met with the most friendly and helpful welcome; Colonel Nugent and Messrs. Bunce, Vogt and Neufeld, and later the State Department in Washington, supplied us with most valuable background material on education and youth movements either verbally or in the form of documents (including some for their own internal circulation). The Japanese Ministry of Education (Mombu-sho) was also most generous in giving us information about the progress of educational reform, particularly the new method of teaching history. The Centre of Japanese Studies of the University of Michigan, at Okayama, to which we made a special trip, gave us the run of its files, and the Director (Professor Robert Hall of the University of Michigan) and Edward and Maggie Norbeck, who had carried out research closely relevant to our investigation, were kind enough to authorize us to use their material. We were also able to utilize the results of investigations conducted by a number of newspapers, notably the *Asahi Shimbun*, and the Maruzen Publishing Company supplied us with a classified list of newspapers and periodicals.

Difficulties of co-ordination forced us to give up the idea of taking advantage of an investigation into moral ideas planned for March 1952 by the eminent sociologist Professor Takashi Koyama and to be carried out in a variety of habitats in the prefectures of Nara and Osaka; he would have been willing to include in his own enquiries questions of particular interest to us. Outstanding among the items in the documentation which we assembled is the Japanese bibliography on youth questions specially prepared for us by Professor Usui of Kyoto University. Unfortunately, we did not have time to make use of this bibliography, which is selected, classified and annotated for our purpose; but it is included in the present work as an appendix in the hope that it will prove of considerable service to other research workers. Vos had an important share in collecting the documentation I have just mentioned and also undertook the heavy work of translation in connexion with it, and at all other stages of our enquiry. Thanks are also due individually to the members of the Unesco Tokyo Office, Dr. Lee Shi Mu, the Director, and his colleagues Mr. Schubert, Mr. Ueda and Mrs. Fukai, for the active help they gave us by their knowledge and their contacts, and by the innumerable practical facilities they placed at our disposal.

The next step in our enquiry was the public opinion poll specially carried out at our request by the National Public Opinion Research Institute. This played so important a part in our work that it calls for special comment which will be found on a later page.

The help given by the Japanese Association of Cultural Science and personally by its chairman, Professor Tomoo Otaka of the Faculty of Law of Tokyo University, was immense, constant and covered many fields. At the very beginning of our relations, the Association agreed to postpone for two months the congress it had convened to study the results of the research on tensions in the Japanese society of today, undertaken at the suggestion of Unesco, so as to give us time to be present. This is not the place to deal with the congress at length; there is a note about it in the *International Social Science Bulletin*. Suffice it to say that the congress provided us for three days with an opportunity to absorb, in a lively and direct manner, a mass of first-hand documents which was a very great help in enabling us to find our way about.

In the course of the following week, we were given an opportunity of re-examining the principal themes of the congress privately and in small groups, and of getting explanations and amplifications from the various experts. We were able to hold eight such meetings, of two or three hours each, with three to seven people at a time. Those who took part are too numerous to be mentioned individually here but we consider that our conversations with them, marked as they were by complete frankness and objectivity, were of inestimable value in providing us with the necessary information.

We also received additional help from a number of members of the association. The contributions of Professor Feiichi Izumi of the University of Tokyo, and Professor Hirosato Fujiwara of the Meiji University, will be described in due course. Professor Jiro Suzuki of the Metropolitan University of Tokyo acted as our guide on a visit to an 'Eta' village in the country north of Tokyo, and explained the painful problem of discrimination which exists in Japan. We had access to a number of original manuscripts, particularly Morioka's report of a study, directed by Yuzuru Okada of Tokyo Bunrika Daigaku (university), into relations between parents and children in country areas. We were also able to visit the Tokyo Special Court for Juvenile Delinquents under the direction of Judge Morita.

A fundamental contribution to our work, that merits separate treatment—the exhaustive exploration of the attitudes of selected young people—stands exclusively to the credit of the Japanese Association of Cultural Science which supplied the funds and selected the staff and whose members guided our decisions by their advice and prepared some of the material we used in our enquiry.

Lastly it should be mentioned that Dean Otaka followed our activities throughout, used his influence to open all the doors we wanted to enter and prevailed on the government departments concerned—always, it must be said, extremely well disposed towards us—to give the necessary orders to the local authorities without whose goodwill nothing, or hardly anything, is possible in Japan. In this connexion, it must be recognized that a foreign mission wandering at large in any country with the avowed intention of ascertaining, by means as scientific as possible, what that country's young people think, seems at first sight, to be taking far too much on itself; we can well understand the occasional reticence and once or twice, even, the disagreeable obstacles we met with on the part of local authorities. We can only be the more grateful for the ready confidence and unreserved co-operation displayed at the highest levels.

The enquiry proper was supplemented—we think, very advantageously—from a number of sources. In the first place, as Vos was able to get to Japan nearly two months ahead of me and wanted to use the time to the best advantage, he decided to undertake a limited investigation of opinion in the Tokyo area only. As the matters for investigation had already been discussed in general terms in Paris, Vos drew up a questionnaire and managed, thanks to many contacts, to interrogate a total of 130 young people, of whom 84 were male and 46 female. The results of this enquiry are given as an annex to our report. Vos gives the following description of the way it was carried out: '112 subjects answered in writing and I interrogated 18 orally. The group I was dealing with consisted of students, mainly from the Meiji University, journalists, heads of youth movements, office workers in the Toyo Menka Kabushiki Kaisha Company and staff from Pakshimay (a Tokyo department store) and the PX (the special store for American personnel). They came from different layers of society, but the majority of them were well educated, to secondary or university standard. This is not a serious disadvantage, seeing that educated people will undoubtedly have more influence on public opinion than other groups . . . . For the preparation of the present report I chose at random 100 of the completed questionnaires, excluding those returned by heads of youth movements because their replies to certain questions would have produced misleading percentages.' Actually although the sampling method is not entirely to be recommended since the group was representative neither of the youth of Tokyo as a whole nor of a specific category of them, the investigation has an indicative value and is used in later pages, mainly for cross-checking.

In addition, as already mentioned, the Allport-Gillespie test was applied at Sapporo and Kyoto. The very satisfactory contacts we made with the sociology students of Professor Eitaro Suzuki and his assistant, Dr. Kiyohide Seki, during my visit to the University of Hokkaido emboldened me to ask them to write brief 'autobiographies of the future', i.e. how they pictured their lives over the next 50 years. The results (of which translations are given in Appendix III) struck me as extremely interesting, and I therefore asked Seki to have his students later complete the questionnaire which forms Part 2 of the Allport-Gillespie test.

This sociology class yielded eight 'autobiographies' and 17 completed questionnaires. Subsequently I asked Dr. Yoji Watanabe, of Kyoto University, a pupil of Professor Usui, to carry out the same procedure there. Whereas the Sapporo students (Sapporo is the seat of the University of Hokkaido) were given the questionnaire in English—which they completed in some cases in English and in others in Japanese—a Japanese version was available for the Kyoto students. A total of 220 questionnaires (of which six were unusable) was returned. The characteristics of the subjects and the details of their answers are given in an annex. Coding and analysis were carried out by Watanabe himself. At the same time, 194 'autobiographies' were secured but in view of the delay before they would have been available and the heavy work of translation and analysis involved, I have had to abandon the idea of utilizing them for the present report, but we hope that this valuable material may be put to some other use. A point to note is that both at Sapporo and at Kyoto, there were five questions which a large number of subjects misunderstood (questions 15, 16, 39, 40 and 46 in the Allport-Gillespie questionnaire); any attempt to analyse the answers to these particular questions had therefore to be abandoned.

Lastly, as indicated above, we considered it absolutely essential to secure as much direct personal experience as possible of the mentality of Japanese youth through group discussions and private conversations. Data of this kind may, if you like, lack scientific—or more accurately objective—value and unless the investigator watches himself carefully, there is even a danger he may be misled by them. However, in the case of Japan we are dealing with a society quite outside our ordinary experience so that its philosophy of life, its hidden motives and its emotional and intellectual mechanisms (its 'logic', if you prefer the term) are liable to be profoundly alien to us. The bare results of a test and the percentage tables showing the way a questionnaire has been answered—abstract data, dry and lifeless, devitalized, as it were, by the very process used to render them as clear to the observer as are slides under a microscope— must in the end be interpreted in human terms; and that, indeed, was in the last resort the real aim of our enquiry. We felt strongly that we could not find within ourselves the resources of thought and feeling necessary for such an interpretation unless we had acquired first-hand experience.

To deal with this point now, so as not to have to come back to it later: the lesson we drew from our contacts, in the course of which we sought to sympathize as deeply as we could while preserving a critical spirit, was, we would say, as follows: it seemed to us that, for a foreign observer, Japanese behaviour, like that of other peoples we have known of a different culture from our own, is on three different planes. First there is the exotic plane—the one that strikes the tourist, that Herodotus delighted to note in his descriptions of Egypt, and that appeals to the writer and the journalist.[1] The second plane is that of 'human nature', where is to be found the expression of the great biological needs and where the sociological institutions common to all men function: this is normally the plane on which relations with strangers are established and interchanges between peoples of different cultures are possible. Below these, however, there is a third plane, deeper perhaps than the others, where are situated the motivations, values and mechanisms of the

---

1. In *Japan in a Nutshell* (Yokohama 1949) the author, Atsuharu Sakai, takes an obvious pleasure in contrasting his country's culture with that of the West (which he identifies with that of the United States): Japanese strike matches away from them, wear white for mourning, write from top to bottom and from right to left, touch their own noses when they say 'I or me', beckon palm downwards, etc. (cf. pp. 255-8, for a list of 58 similar contrasts).

individual. While something very near to understanding can be achieved on the second plane, the true and full interpretation of conduct can be obtained only on the third. The ambition of the authors of this work was to penetrate that third plane. We cannot say that we have entirely succeeded.

It would be wearisome and pointless to describe in detail all our contacts with the young. Only the salient features of our conversations will therefore be recorded. Both in group discussions and in private interviews, we tried to get down to ordinary situations and typical cases. At Kyushu we talked to the son of a purged general, to a fatherless student of middle-class origin whose mother was employed as a labourer on municipal navvying work at a salary of 160 yen (160 francs) per day and to the secretary of a miners' union; while at Point Noshappu, the most easterly part of the Japanese archipelago which is in sight of the Kuriles and has to be reached by sledge across snow-fields, we met some young fishermen who had been captured by the Maritime Police in Soviet territorial waters. But we also met students of the classical type—comfortably off or poor—industrial and agricultural workers of both sexes. In the group interviews we saw socialist and pacifist students at Fukuoka, young people from a fishing and commercial port (Nemuro), most of them employed in commerce, and young municipal employees of a countrified township on the outskirts of Sapporo (Toyohira-machi); and we attended a kind of seminar on democracy arranged by the American Information Services of Sapporo. In some instances, when the people interviewed had sufficient command of English, we were able to have strictly private conversations. Generally, an interpreter was necessary but we did not notice that his presence made any difference: the atmosphere of most interviews was one of trust and relaxation. In a few cases, however, we were unable to get rid of observers from the administration and the constraint of the subject was painful to see; we recall a student of agricultural engineering in the University of Hokkaido who was so upset by their unwanted presence that the sweat ran from his forehead and dripped off his nose. In one instance, even—in a mining district—our request to interview the young people alone was met with a flat refusal; we never entirely succeeded in getting to the bottom of this incident.

In addition to our very frank and extremely useful contacts with our colleagues in various universities—particularly at Tokyo and Kyoto—we were able to have talks with prefectoral, municipal and university administrators, with secondary and primary school teachers and with leaders of youth groups; and often, behind an ostensibly favourable attitude towards new ideas and new institutions, we were able to measure at first-hand the obstacles put in the path of the young and in the way of any tendency towards change.

THE INVESTIGATION BY REPRESENTATIVE SAMPLING, AND THE
INVESTIGATION IN DEPTH

We must now go back and examine in greater detail the two essential elements of our enquiry—the public opinion survey carried out by the National Public Opinion Research Institute and the thorough investigation made possible by the Japanese Association of Cultural Sciences.

We have already mentioned the reasons why a survey of public opinion by means of representative sampling seemed a necessity from the start. In Japan conditions are favourable for an undertaking of this kind. The first requirement is obviously that there should already be at least one public opinion research organization in the country; the second is that enough research should have been carried out in the recent past for an investigation not to come as a surprise to the subjects interrogated; the third is that the local organization should be prepared to help. All these requirements are met in Japan. A count made in August 1951 showed that there are 25 public opinion research bodies, a good number of which are attached to newspapers. They are, moreover, very active and carried out at least 94 major enquiries in the 18 months from January 1950 to May 1951; thus the public opinion poll is an institution in Japan. Lastly, (in response to our request that he should undertake a special investigation on behalf of Unesco) the Director of the National Public Opinion Research Institute, Eizo Koyama, whose cosmopolitan outlook is well known and whom we had met a few months previously at Tunbridge Wells (England) at the congress of the World Association for Public Opinion Research (WAPOR), promised that he would submit and recommend the request to the institute's board of governors. The foundation of the institute dates from 1 November 1945, when a small body was set up with the help of the occupation authorities (CI and E) and placed under Cabinet control. Later, a law was passed, with effect from 1 June 1949, setting up a National Public Opinion Research Institute (Kokuritsu-Yoron-Chosajo), independent of the Cabinet office. Its function is to undertake scientific research with a view to advising the government on matters affecting public opinion. The law expressly forbids it to undertake any police or partisan activity, and consequently it refrains from asking questions about people's ideological preferences. Decisions regarding investigations and publications are taken by a board of governors appointed by the Prime Minister from the ranks of experienced scientists nominated by non-governmental organizations concerned with the study of public opinion. Technically, the National Public Opinion Research Institute, which we visited and saw at work, is a well-designed and well-equipped organization with a sizable staff. We had frequent contacts with its various department heads, particularly Messrs. Asano and Hattan, whose training measures up to the best international standards. We also had the luck to watch interviews being conducted: the interviewer adopts the attitude of a listener, while the subject expresses himself freely and at length. Occasional refusals to answer are accepted without argument—as, indeed, the institute is required by law to do. It is used to carrying out enquiries on a national scale.

The compilation of the questionnaire was long and troublesome. A first list of 63 questions, laboriously selected, worded and arranged in order, after days of effort, seemed to us, when completed, to miss the essential point of the investigation: the questions were centred too much on the individuality of the subjects and on their immediate environment. We therefore began all over again and drew up a fresh and almost completely different list of 86 questions. While this questionnaire was obviously too long for a survey of opinion, it was nevertheless an important step in the internal history of the investigation: it served as the basis not only for subsequent questionnaires submitted to NPORI but also for the questionnaire adopted by Sofue, which will be dealt with later. We also drew on it for almost all the themes of our personal interviews. In the next stage it was cut down to 31 main questions (58 queries to be answered) for use in the preliminary test and was again recast to obtain a better balance between the five main themes covered: attitude towards social changes, attitude towards authority, readiness to take part in public life, interest in and attitude towards foreign countries, and personal values. We had to leave out altogether a question about attitudes towards the Emperor, because it was regarded as too political and incompatible with the statutes of the institute; it is however included in Sofue's questionnaire.

Lastly, the questionnaire, as it finally emerged with 34 questions, was used as a basis for two successive trial tests carried out by the institute, at Tokyo and in the prefecture of Nagano, the first consisting of 31 main questions, and the second of 26. We were away at the time and on our return found that it had been felt better to disregard a question we had suggested, taking advantage of a current incident to study attitudes towards the police. Another question, too literally translated into Japanese from the English text we had submitted, was palpably absurd. However, Koyama's assistant, Asano, at once realized that these data were important to us and found a quick and satisfactory solution.

In the end, the questionnaire was reduced to the form in which it appears in Appendix I. It is still far from perfect: mention has already been made of the difficulty experienced in finding a Japanese equivalent for the notion 'never to contradict a superior'; a similar illustration of the cultural barriers encountered is our utter failure to arrive at an exact equivalent of the word 'happiness'—an idea that in its Western sense finds no expression in the Japanese vocabulary and probably not in the Japanese philosophy of life.

Truly representative answers were ensured by sampling the population according to various percentages, fixed in relation to sex, age, economic level, region and habitat, the general analysis to be in terms of age and habitat combined. Table I shows how the percentages worked out in connexion with our enquiry compare with the population percentages of the 1947 census.

TABLE I

Age group	Enquiry		Census Percentage
	Numbers	*Percentage*	
Urban			
16-19	133	5	4
20-24	145	5	6
25-29	153	6	4
30 and over	607	23	21
Rural			
16-19	200	8	9
20-24	255	9	9
25-29	224	8	7
30 and over	954	36	40
Total	2,671	100	100

We were unable to remain for the analysis of the results but before our departure we did see a number of sample replies. We also indicated the lines we thought it desirable to follow in codification—to subdivide the different categories of replies as much as practicable, so as to facilitate any regrouping that might later seem desirable; and to have, for each category, verbatim samples both of typical and of marginal cases. In the Japanese original, the code forms a volume of 86 pages; in our view it is of considerable interest and we cannot too strongly urge the reader to refer to the full-length translation given in Appendix I with the corresponding statistical tables.

The National Public Opinion Research Institute conducted the enquiry with the utmost goodwill and competence, and the result as it stands is a very suggestive approximation to the state of Japanese attitudes in 1952, particularly among the young, and, moreover, marks a step towards the solution of a number of problems in social psychology and sociology. It confirms the effectiveness of this method for carrying out research in the social sciences.

It is a method, however, that gains enormously from being used in combination with others, and that is why, as indicated above, we insisted on supplementing it by an investigation that would enable attitudes to be still more closely examined. We therefore hit upon a line of study which, while not strictly monographic and clinical, would deal with a limited number of individuals—about a hundred altogether—drawn from four or five geographically and socially contrasted groups, and evenly divided between the sexes, who would undergo a fairly exhaustive test. Each individual would be examined three times, in one-hour sessions on three consecutive days. The first session was to take the form of a projective test: a study of reactions to narrative themes (see example, Chapter VII, page 173), or preferably to visual themes, i.e. sketches and pictures designed and carried out *ad hoc*, on the same lines as H. A. Murray's T.A.T. The second session was to consist of a guided conversation, using a wide-ranging opinion questionnaire in the course of which the subject would have a chance of expounding his views and of giving his reasons freely. At the third session a study would be made, by a biographical method, of the subject's psychological evolution from childhood and youth to the present time.

It should be said at once that time proved too short for us to be able to consider submitting the subjects to the third test. However, it was possible to carry out the rest of the scheme fairly completely.

Reference has already been made to the leading part played in this investigation by the Japanese Association of Cultural Science. Indeed, our own part in it was confined to suggesting the scheme, submitting the 86 items of the questionnaire and indicating the themes we would like to have explored by means of an *ad hoc* projective test. Our general intention was also to embark on research in Kyushu and Hokkaido, without having any particular locality in mind. These plans were unhesitatingly and warmly approved. Our colleague Seiichi Izumi introduced a young assistant of his own, Takao Sofue, a member of the staff of the sociological laboratory of the Metropolitan University of Tokyo, who had already taken part in work on ethnographical psychology. The association's chairman, Tomoo Otaka, drew on its funds for the sum required to put the plan in operation. Several meetings, at which Mr. Hirosato Fujiwara, a political scientist from the University of the Meiji, was present, took place in Tokyo. The methods and materials to be used and the localities and types of subjects to be examined, were decided upon. Of the sketches and pictures, some were the work of Mrs. Kimiko Izumi and the remainder were either drawn by Sofue or selected by him from magazine illustrations. It was also Sofue who produced a questionnaire of some forty items, on the basis of the document mentioned above, with the help of Hirosato Fujiwara on the political science side; this questionnaire and replies to it are given in an annex. The 10 sketches and pictures used appear as illustrations at the end of Annex II. There is therefore no need to describe them here.

On the other hand, a social and geographical description of the points where our investigations were carried out will be useful. Here, we borrow from Takao Sofue's text, condensing it for our purpose. There were five points altogether: the village of F., the town of Yawata (or Yahata), the village of T., the town of Bibai, and the village of H.

F. lies on the outskirts of the town of Kagoshima, the headquarters of the most southerly prefecture in the Japanese archipelago, in the island of Kyushu. Kagoshima has two universities and the largest department store in the island, and enjoys a reputation as a tourist centre on account of the proximity of Sakurajima island. The population is about 230,000 and though 90 per cent of the town was destroyed by air-raids, it has been entirely rebuilt. F. is about twenty kilometres from Kagoshima, half an hour's journey by train. It consists of 934 houses with a total population of 4,376. Only 20 per cent of the agricultural land is under rice, the main crops being barley, sweet potatoes, millet and soya beans. Some families live on the coast and are also engaged in fishing. Part of the village population goes to work in Kagoshima, mainly the second and third sons of peasant families, and the young daughters; the investigation revealed characteristic differences between the opinions of members of this category and those of subjects who had remained in the village. The climate is sub-tropical but the soil is volcanic and very poor and yields are the lowest in Japan. Moreover, heavy damage is caused every year by typhoons.

The great interest of this region, which led us to choose it as one of the areas for our investigation, lies in its traditions, its past, and in the traces still to be found of both. On this we cannot do better than quote Sofue:

'In the Kamakura era (about A.D. 1200), Shimazu Tadahisa came to southern Kyushu as administrator appointed by the then shogun, Minamoto-no-Yoritomo. Thereafter, the power of the Shimazu clan grew and about 1600 Yoshihiro, the seventeenth prince, built a castle at Kagoshima from which the family ruled the provinces of Hyuga (the modern prefecture of Miyazaki), Osumi and Satsuma (now combined in the Kagoshima prefecture) for some three hundred years until the Meiji restoration (1868). The political philosophy of the Shimazu clan was marked by obvious militarism and even more by a caste system carried to the extreme, with absolute power in the hands of the Samurai. What was especially noteworthy was the kind of education given to the sons of the Samurai, which aimed essentially at inculcating the habit of unquestioning obedience and total self-abnegation in the service of the overlord, together with a soldierly spirit. To that end it was laid down that all sons of Samurai were to be trained on Spartan lines from the age of six, for which purpose the people of each area formed clans or units known as *gôju* and a disciplinary system known as *goju* training was introduced into these clans which quickly became famous.

'Needless to say, this system collapsed after the Meiji restoration; nevertheless its martial spirit, absolute obedience to elders and exclusion of all who did not belong to the clan persisted for a long time. It is said, for instance, that when the Hitler Youth from Germany visited Japan they made a special point of stopping at Kagoshima to see how this form of education functioned. However, with the introduction of democracy after the war, these traditions rapidly declined, and survive only among a fraction of the oldest generation. This region also long afforded the most remarkable example in Japan of "male domination", resulting from the absolute priority of men's rights over women's, which was the rule in feudal times. Outwardly at any rate, all this has now disappeared, so that to all appearances anti-democratic elements have been eliminated and democracy established. But has democracy really got into the people's bones? That is what our investigation tried to find out.'[1]

Yawata (also written Yahata) is an industrial town in the middle of a region known as 'the North Kyushu Industrial Belt'. It has a population of 210,000, 61 per cent of whom are employed in industry. There are nine companies in the town, of which the most important, largely overshadowing the others, is the Iron and Steel Company, Yawata being the metallurgical capital of Japan. In each of the nine companies, there are trade union branches, affiliated in the main to the left wing of the Socialist Party. The Metal Workers' Union has a membership of 37,000 and the subjects interrogated at Yawata were members of this union or of the union in a factory making electrical equipment, with a membership of 3,500.

The village of T. is in the neighbourhood of Sapporo, the capital of Hokkaido island, which is the largest prefecture in Japan as regards size and has the second largest population (the first being Tokyo). Sapporo with its population of 314,000, its university and its many huge department stores, is an important political and cultural centre of northern Japan. Industrially it is famed for its milk products, textiles, and breweries. T. village which lies in the administrative district of TY., is 20 minutes by bus from Sapporo, and comprises 1,636 houses and 7,714 inhabitants. Its sheep pasturage enjoys a national reputation and all the neighbouring areas are exclusively agricultural. The subjects interrogated in the course of our enquiry all worked on the land. The local crops are rice, oats, barley and wheat. The climate is decidedly cold and the snow does not disappear completely until the month of April. A point to be taken into account is the presence, in the neighbourhood, of an American garrison and airfield. As a result, the roads have been metalled and there is a continuous stream of military traffic over them day and night. In addition a unit of the National Police Reserve is also stationed in the vicinity.

Some supplementary details about Hokkaido, quoted from Sofue, may also be useful: 'Peasants and fishermen from the main island came to settle in this region during the early years of the Meiji era (about 1870).

---

1. Translated from Sofue's report.

Against them they had cruel cold, virgin forests and bears, and it was only at the price of a real pioneering effort that they gradually won the upper hand over the Ainu and achieved the prosperity of today. Consequently, they still retain the pioneering spirit and are extremely proud of being "Hokkaido men". Again, Hokkaido is notable for having as its present Governor Mr. T. a member of the left wing of the Socialist movement. Furthermore, the local youth movements are distinguished by their comparatively advanced stage of organization. All the groups in the region have combined to form a "Joint Council of Hokkaido Youth Associations". The annual congress of the associations is attended by delegates from all parts of the area and the headquarters' organization of the council publishes a monthly periodical and gives "short guidance lessons" both orally and by mail. The characteristics of Hokkaido as a whole are to be found in T., which was built by settlers at the beginning of the Meiji era. These facts must not be overlooked in any study of the personality of the inhabitants, particularly the young.'[1]

Bibai is a mining town, with the largest coal pits in Hokkaido, and the second largest in Japan (after Yubari). It is one hour by fast train from Sapporo and has a population of 87,000. The local trade union has a membership of about 3,000. Unfortunately, for a variety of reasons the investigation in Bibai and in H. village could not be carried out on the same scale as in the first three centres.

H. village is a small port of 800 inhabitants in the neighbourhood of Nemuro, to which we have already referred, on one of the eastern capes of Hokkaido. Fishing is very brisk between May and October when large numbers of fishermen, both from the main island and from Hokkaido, come to the port. The interest of this locality for the purpose of our enquiry was the proximity of the Habomai islands, reputed to have extremely rich fishing-grounds, and also the fact that these islands are occupied by the Soviet Union as part of the Kuriles, ceded to the U.S.S.R. under the Yalta Agreement. The boundary between Japanese and Russian territorial waters is the so-called MacArthur Line, over which the Japanese are not entitled to trespass. However, the fish seem to prefer the far side of the line and so the fishermen get as near to it as they can, at the risk, if they cross it unintentionally, of arrest by the Soviet coastguards and of being held in custody for an indefinite period. Sofue's opinion agrees with mine, formed when I visited this region by myself, as recorded earlier—that attitudes towards the Soviet Union are no different here from what they are elsewhere.

In all five localities, Sofue was entirely responsible for conducting the psychological examinations, which took place in February and March

---

1. Translated from Sofue's report.

1952. I was with Sofue at Kagoshima and at F., where I attended a number of sessions at which the questionnaire was used. I was unable to go to Yawata and though I visited the various centres in Hokkaido, it was not in Sofue's company; I rejoined him while he was working at Sapporo. However, we had frequent opportunities of discussing the work together as it progressed and of exchanging views. Unfortunately, I had to leave Japan when the analysis of the results had barely begun. Sofue alone was therefore responsible for this part of the work and is entitled to all the credit for it. It is regrettable that his extremely interesting report cannot be published in full; the English translation by the Ministry of Foreign Affairs runs to 104 foolscap pages. However, numerous extracts from it will be found in the following pages.

The subjects examined are divided among the various centres as follows: F. 1, 10 men, 9 women (total 19); Yawata, 11 men, 8 women (total 19); T., 7 men, 11 women (total 18); Bibai, 1 man, 1 woman (total 2); grand total, 63 (31 men, 32 women).

Those, then, are the main features of the Unesco enquiry into the attitudes of post-war Japanese youth. Its general purpose and the ideas behind it have been indicated, and the broad lines of the work and the conditions in which it was carried out have been described. There now follows a report on the results of this enquiry, which are given in full in Appendix I.

THE NATURE OF THE REPORT AS A WHOLE

A word of explanation is called for about the report itself. It was planned and drafted exclusively by myself and I must accordingly take full responsibility for it. The question is not whether its conclusions are correct or incorrect in relation to the real situation in Japan during the first three months of 1952; that is a question relevant only to the planning and execution of the various parts of the investigation. The report itself is strictly limited to the data collected. The real question that has to be answered is whether it is the right kind of report—whether it meets the requirements of a scientific survey. In any case, what I have tried to do

---

1. Two remarks should be made about the conditions of the investigation at F.: first, of the total shown, four subjects—three men and one woman—took the projective test only. Thus the total of those who filled in the questionnaire in all four areas is only 59 (28 men and 31 women); secondly, of the female subjects examined at F., three, who took both tests, work during the day-time in Kagoshima and exhibited attitudes and personality traits differing sharply from those of the six others. In his report Sofue therefore divides the subjects in F. into two groups—Group I which does not leave the village, and Group II which travels outside to work during the day-time.

is to evolve and present what philosophers call a 'theory'—that is to say, a more or less complex system, but one that would be intelligible, rational, and would take into account *all the facts within the limits of the experiment;* in other words I not only sought to refrain from selecting: I made it a rule not to do so, but on the contrary, to include in my account all the available data, often regretting not to have more detailed information on a particular point, but never, or rarely, yielding to the temptation to produce hypotheses in order to fill the gaps, and, above all, taking care not to pass over inconvenient facts contradictory to the main conclusions to be drawn from the other data.

The only kind of choice I have permitted myself, feeling that this was not exceeding my mandate and my responsibilities, has been in assessing the importance of the various facts collected and in deciding how exhaustively to analyse them and what emphasis to give them. This I have felt entitled to do as they are, after all, my own creatures: it was my researches that brought them to light, and indeed, actually produced them by means of the questions set; from this point of view, the mind must not be the slave of its own creations when the facts revealed include irrelevances.

One exception must be mentioned: it has not been felt necessary to draw all the inferences from the 'autobiographies of the future' by the Sapporo students. These are apparent at a first reading, and I felt, in any case, that the documents concerned are in line with my general interpretation of Japanese attitudes and that consequently any commentary, which would necessarily have to be fairly detailed, would burden the text to no real purpose. Moreover, as I am not an expert in psychoanalysis, I prefer to leave the task and responsibility of a detailed interpretation to others, better equipped than myself. However, the documents in question seem to me to be of great interest and while the reader must be warned that they are not representative, he is urged not to fail to read them.

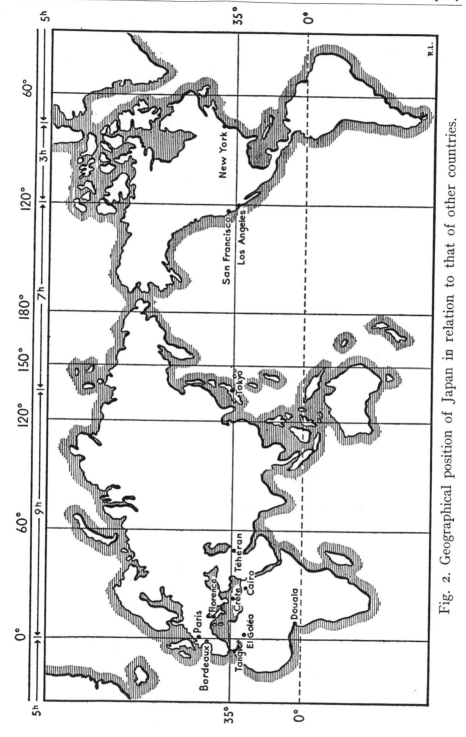

Fig. 2. Geographical position of Japan in relation to that of other countries.

CHAPTER II

FIRST ENCOUNTER WITH JAPAN

GENERAL DESCRIPTION OF THE COUNTRY AND THE PEOPLE

The situation of Japan, off the Eastern coast of Asia, calls up obvious comparisons with that of the British Isles, as the extreme Western prolongation of the Continent of Europe. The Japanese archipelago, however, is further from the mainland; it is more than 200 kilometres from Korea and more than 1,000 kilometres from China.

However, the analogy makes sense only on reflection. The earth is round only in the abstract, and the essential geographical characteristic of Japan, for the Westerner, is its vast distance away in terms of earthly dimensions. Lying on the 140th east meridian, Japan is really the Far East; solar time is 9 hours ahead of Paris, and shows a difference of 7 hours with San Francisco and 10 hours with New York. Even with the swift means of communication we enjoy today, Tokyo is two days' flight from Paris by the regular air services, whereas only half a day separates a Parisian from New York or from Doula in the heart of Africa. Even the swiftest liner takes a month to get from Yokohama to Marseilles. For dwellers on the Atlantic seaboard Japan is at the other end of the world, and the converse is obviously true for the Japanese.

In terms of latitude, the Japanese archipelago stretches from parallel 30 to parallel 45 north, approximately the same latitudes as Cairo or El Golea, Bordeaux or Florence, but average monthly temperatures rarely reach 27 degrees centigrade in summer in the south, while in the north the winter temperatures are as low as minus 5 or even minus 7 degrees centigrade. Off the coast of Hokkaido, there are sizeable ice floes as late as the middle of March. Though the latitude of Tokyo—35°41′N.—may be compared geographically with that of Teheran, Crete, Tangier or Los Angeles, in 1949 average monthly temperatures ranged from 5°5′C in January to 26°4′C in August.

The present area of Japan is about 370,000 square kilometres—greater than that of the United Kingdom (244,000 square kilometres) and Italy (301,000 square kilometres), but less than that of France (551,000 square kilometres). Today the archipelago consists of four main islands. Honshu, in the middle of the chain, is the largest, with an area of 230,000 square kilometres, and accounts for more than three-fifths of the total surface area of the empire. Hokkaido, in the north, with an area of 78,000 square kilometres, was opened up in comparatively recent times, and its geographical, economic and human characteristics differ noticeably from those of the rest of the archipelago. Kyushu, the most southerly island and the first to receive the impact of Europe, also has traditions peculiar to itself. Shikoku, 19,000 square kilometres in extent, shuts off the inland sea of Western Honshu from the open ocean.

The present population of Japan is about 84 million. Average density is thus about 220 to the square kilometre, but considerably higher if Hokkaido is excluded; since this island, though the second largest in size, has a density of barely 50 to the square kilometre. Thus population density in Japan is about three times what it is in France (75), one and a half times that of Italy and higher even than that of Great Britain (206), although Holland, with a population of 296 to the square kilometre, leaves the Japanese figure far behind.

Measurements taken periodically since 1948 in the course of sample investigations, yield the following anthropometric data; men, average height 1.6 metres, average weight 54 kilograms; women, average height 1.48 metres, average weight 48 kilograms. Even in ancient times Chinese chroniclers commented on the low stature of the Japanese. The present population of the archipelago is not indigenous. The original inhabitants, the Ainu, a people of proto-Caucasian type, were driven back towards the north, where a small number of them—reckoned at probably less than 20,000—still survive. There is much dispute as to the origin of the Japanese invaders. Experts discern in them a predominant Mongol (Tunguz) element but also Malay, Indonesian and Polynesian elements, as well as Caucasian (through intermarriage with the Ainu). But these crosses took place very long ago in prehistoric times, and today the Japanese do in fact present distinctive physical traits to the traveller in the Far East.

The physical features of the country, which is almost everywhere mountainous, make the exploitation of the soil difficult; in 1947 the total arable area was less than 5.5 million *cho* (a cho is approximately equivalent to a hectare), or 15 per cent of the total. More than half of this area is under rice, yielding nearly 40 hectolitres per hectare: the 1949 crop was 113 million hectolitres. Another extremely important source of food is fishing. The coastline, which extends to more than 11 thousand kilometres, is very indented and fishing conditions are good. In 1949 catches amounted to 2,350,000 tons. This compensates to some extent for the country's inadequate meat production—41,000 tons of beef and 12,000 tons of pork in 1949.

A major natural resource of Japan is its forests, which cover 26 per cent of the total land surface or 9.5 million cho. Timber is a raw material of the utmost value in a country where most of the building is in wood.

Before the war the Japanese were also large-scale manufacturers of wood-pulp (4 per cent of the total world production in 1935). The country is not badly off for coal and output in 1949 exceeded 3 million tons per month (against a French output of 4,267,300 tons). Water-power is also abundant and easily harnessed for the generation of electricity; in 1949 Japan produced 3,033 million kilowatt hours a month, i.e. three-quarters as much as the United Kingdom, nearly 30 per cent more than France and almost twice as much as Italy. In other respects, however, the country's natural resources are mediocre or worse. It is particularly poor in iron ore: its monthly output in 1949 was no more than 53,000 tons, which bears comparison with Italy's 43,000 tons per month but not with the United Kingdom's 1,135,000 tons and France's 2,619,000 tons (though in the two latter countries the iron content of the ore is lower).

HISTORICAL OUTLINE

These geographical and physical data—which can be found with many others in the statistical yearbooks[1]—are of course useful as an introduction to the study of a people's behaviour: they set the frame and the external limits of the environmental conditions to which individuals have to adapt themselves. It must however be recognized that the sociological conditions and the cultural traits peculiar to the people in question, are of still greater importance. They are in themselves an environment to which the individual must adapt himself, and, moreover, it is they which act as intermediaries between the individual and his physical surroundings. Making contact with Japan in order to study the attitudes of its population, or part of its population, therefore means getting acquainted, first and foremost, with its cultural characteristics. That is the main purpose of the present introduction.

But that is not enough. In addition to the physical and sociological conditions of the environment into which their members must fit, literate societies—those normally classed as civilized in the common meaning of the term—have a history and, more than that, a past. The explanatory role of history in sociology and social psychology is not confined to assisting in the study of genetics; history is something more than a description of the phases of development through which a country's institutions have passed and how values have emerged or changed. For a people with a history, its past is a living element of its present, enabling

---

1. *Japan, Statistical Yearbook*, Tokyo, 1950, from which, unless otherwise indicated, the statistics used in this report have been taken.

the individual to know himself better and endowing him with a rich source of motivations. On this score legends and even myths are no less important than scientifically established facts. Nor should it be thought that history is passed on exclusively through the schools or that if the teaching of history were abolished in the schools, contact with the past would be broken. A people's history is to be found in its theatre, its literature, its architecture and many aspects of its culture.

Hence it is impossible to get to know and understand the behaviour of the Japanese without studying their history. Unfortunately, geographical distance brings with it a kind of historical pluralism. Until recent times, the Japanese past unfolded itself in an historical universe that had hardly any more points of contact with the West than if it had been on a different planet. For us Japanese chronology is almost meaningless. The absence of common historical landmarks destroys the sense of perspective; and lack of actual experience of life in present-day Japan deprives the various epochs of the past of their ultimate meaning, or if you like, of their fertility. It is no use deluding oneself that a few brief historical paragraphs will make up for lack of information in this domain; their presence in this report is only symbolical.[1]

The official history of the Japanese empire begins with the arrival of Jimmu, chief of a number of Kyushu clans, in the Yamato (modern Nara) region, by way of the Inland Sea, and his settlement there. In his new home he built a palace and founded a cult of the Sun Goddess. This was merely filial piety on his part, since he was a descendant of Ninigi, the august grandson of the Sun Goddess, sent by her to Kyushu to reign over Japan. Going back still further, we discover that the Sun Goddess is one of the last-born children of Izanagi and Izanami, the god and goddess who were the seventh generation of the gods born after the Heaven and the Earth were drawn out of chaos. Izanagi and Izanami begot the islands which make up Japan, the sea, the rivers, the mountains and the trees, and only thereafter gave birth to the Sun Goddess, the Moon God, the Storm God and the Fire God. Thus nature is divine; Japan is divine; and the Emperor himself is an emanation of the divinity. The whole history of Japan is simply the tale of the vicissitudes attending the fulfilment of the august grandson's prophecy that his dynasty would endure forever. And has he not kept his word at least as well as the Sibyl of Cumae, who promised that Rome should be eternal?

Accordingly, it is, from certain points of view, unnecessary to correct the date of the Emperor Jimmu's expedition and place it, say, in the first century of our era. More important would be to trace in the details

---

1. Fuller details can be found in George Sansom's book, *Japan: a Short Cultural History*. This is a standard work to which the following pages owe much. A simpler book, also covering the contemporary period, is Edwin O. Reischauer's *Japan: Past and Present*, New York, 1951, which has also been drawn upon for the present report.

of mythology the amazing proliferation of gods, and thus come to realize that the primitive religion of the Japanese is a nature cult. No less interesting is to discover in a distant epoch—certainly before the sixth century of our era, when the impact of Chinese culture was reshaping society—features of social structure that have left almost indelible traces. In the Yamato era we find a society made up of patriarchal units, the *uji*, which were clans in the strict sense—i.e. communities of families sharing, or believing that they shared, a common ancestor. Each family had its own head, but over them all was the chieftain of the *uji* and also a tutelary god of the *uji*. The Emperor was a *uji* chieftain who had succeeded in dominating the others. The subordination of the clans meant the subordination of their cults: thus the cult of the Sun Goddess became the supreme cult of the national religion. Moreover, associated with the *uji* were communities of families having no common ancestor, but following a common occupation—something like guilds. Thus, at this remote period, there was a marked hierarchy, class distinctions and the handing down of living conditions from one generation to the next. With time the clans grew; younger branches broke away; Chinese and Korean immigrants found their niche in the guilds. Individuals sought to rise in the social scale, and invented family trees; and the great fought for power among themselves. However, until the revolution of 1868, Japanese history seems in the main a series of attempts by individuals to improve their relative positions within a social structure which outwardly remained unchanged.

In ancient times the imperial family had to face the rivalry of powerful clans, and in the sixth century a member of the Saga family became 'the Chief of Chiefs'. Not by overthrowing the imperial dynasty but by marrying its daughters to the Emperor's sons—a classical procedure—the Saga family in fact dominated the imperial throne for more than a century.

In the course of the succeeding centuries, power passed in turn to other great families whose heads took the title of 'regent', until 1192 when the term 'shogun'—generalissimo—was substituted.

The Kamakura period (twelfth-thirteenth centuries) named after the then capital, is marked by the growth of the feudal system, the idealization of the virtue of loyalty, and the cult of the sword and of military prowess. It is difficult to exaggerate the importance of the impression left on the Japanese mind by the history of the wars between the great families during that period, and by the examples of chivalry they provided; the struggle in the soul of the Samurai between the ties of family and the even stronger claims of his duty to his lord is an inexhaustible fount of inspiration for art and literature: even today there is hardly a *Kabuki* or *No* play to be seen in Tokyo or anywhere else which does not refer to that epoch.

The ending of internecine strife and the creation of a really effective central government in the second half of the sixteenth century was the work of three outstanding men, Nobunaga, Hideyoshi and Ieyasu. Nobunaga, who was called in by the Emperor to help him, had the good fortune to be served by a very great general, Hideyoshi, and by Ieyasu, a statesman of genius.

Nobunaga vanished from the scene in 1582, to be followed by Hideyoshi in 1598, and in 1603 Ieyasu was proclaimed shogun.

He installed himself far away in a remote corner in the east of the country, at the little village of Eto, later to become Tokyo. Ieyasu was of the Tokugawa family and the line of shoguns he founded was to govern Japan until the restoration of the Imperial family in 1868.

The history of Japan from the earliest days to the shogunate of Ieyasu may appear extraordinarily anarchic and turbulent. From one point of view it does undoubtedly look like an interminable record of attempts by the feudal lords who were the successors of the original clans to raise their social standing and to rival or replace the supreme authority. Yet one cannot but be struck by a state of affairs in which the nominal sovereign retains his throne while the real power is exercised by shoguns ruling in the name of the Emperor or by Hojo regents dominating the shoguns, still supposed to be governing in the name of the sovereign. Sometimes the situation is even more complex. What in fact happens is that the structure of society remains outwardly intact, even if internally it is turned upside down. This permanence of the social structure is all the more remarkable in view of the profound cultural influence of China on Japan.

As early as the first century, Chinese influences were at work upon Japanese society. Between the fifth and sixth centuries the Japanese borrowed the Chinese script, and in the sixth century they adopted Buddhism. Midway through the following century a mission of enquiry was sent to China and the outcome was the promulgation of the 'Great Reform' of Kamatari, which reorganized the whole administrative system on Chinese lines. Confucianism, the texts of which had long been imported into the country, took root from the eighth century onwards. Thus the political and administrative terminology of the Chinese, Buddhist morality, filial piety and ancestor worship, became a part of Japanese culture, not to mention literary and art forms. They were not, however, absorbed uncritically. Ancestor worship took its place in the national religion, but the Sun Goddess in her Ise sanctuary was kept informed of the building of the great Buddha of Nara. In administration the hereditary principle always outweighed the Chinese concept of appointment by merit. In the hierarchy of obligations, duty towards the chieftain— *chu*—always had priority over duty towards parents—*ko*. Thus imported Chinese ideas enabled Japanese culture to develop a wider variety of traits but left its original essence unchanged.

The efforts of Hideyoshi and Ieyasu were aimed at a final stabilization of the social structure by fixing the elements of its composition once and for all. It was made illegal for any man to leave his employment without the permission of his superior. The peasantry had to surrender their arms. No man was allowed to change from one class to another; class distinctions were firmly upheld, and the behaviour, moral, social and traditional, proper to each class was carefully codified. Finally Japan shut itself off completely from all foreign outside influences. The Portuguese made a chance landing in the south of Kyushu in 1542; St. Francis Xavier reached Kagoshima in 1549 and the Jesuits, following in his footsteps, began to preach the Gospel; the Dutch, in their turn, appeared in 1600. In a very short space of time, Christianity was proscribed (the first edict of banishment was issued in 1587), and foreigners expelled; by the middle of the seventeenth century, with the exception of the Dutch, who were confined to their small commercial concession in Nagasaki, and of a few Chinese, not a single foreigner remained in Japan. Travel by Japanese outside the empire on any pretext was prohibited and so was the building of any ship with a draught of more than 500 *koku* (92 tons).

With the Meiji restoration (Meiji means 'the order of light') in 1868, all was changed. The last shogun abdicated and the Emperor reassumed full powers; feudalism was abolished and the revolt of the feudal lords of South Kyushu was crushed. Thereafter Japan flung open its doors to the commerce, science, institutions and customs of the West, and at the same time, the population, which had remained stationary throughout the preceding epoch, increased rapidly. This country, which throughout the whole fifteen hundred years of its modern history had embarked on only one foreign war of aggression (the ill-starred Korean expedition under Hideyoshi, of 1592-98), now plunged headlong into military adventure—the Chinese war of 1894-95, with the annexation of Formosa; the Russian war of 1904-05, with the annexation of the southern half of Sakhaline; the annexation of Korea in 1910; participation in the first world war on the side of the Allies; and the acquisition of the German colonies in the Pacific; the attack on Manchuria in 1931, and the foundation of the puppet state of Manchukuo; the war against China in 1937, in which vast areas were occupied; the invasion of Indo-China in 1940; and finally Pearl Harbour in 1941, of which the final outcome was Japan's unconditional surrender on 14 August 1945.

The contrast is undoubtedly striking. But history is not only to be found in archives, for inspection by dispassionate scholars; it also lives in the minds of men. The Japanese today may often be heard to remark: 'the West taught us war; now it is for the West to teach us peace'. It is not Japanese militarism that strikes the foreigner as the most serious issue. We have seen the same people who waged savage war in the Pacific receive the news of their capitulation, if not without emotion, at least without any mass uprising. In the prison camps to begin with and later, even more markedly, in their own country, the Japanese set themselves courteously and diligently to conform to the wishes of the Americans. The occupation provoked no outbreaks of violence and there was no 'resistance'. Defeat, the law of the victor, far-reaching changes in the régime, and the trial and execution of Japan's military leaders caused even less protest than the Meiji revolution—which at least provoked Saigo Takamori's revolt on 1877—and there is a colossal statue of Saigo in a square at Kagoshima. Such docility is not merely suspicious after the determination shown by the people in its struggle against half the world; it is incomprehensible.

THE MAIN FEATURES OF JAPANESE SOCIETY

A study of the organization of society, where may be found in static form certain traits whose development is revealed by history, throws some light on the riddle of the public behaviour of the Japanese people. The fact is that many features of the organization and functioning of Japanese society undoubtedly make totalitarian behaviour on the part of its members possible and even easy.

This is clear from the outset, when we examine the position of women.[1] As distinct from Chinese practice, monogamy is the rule in Japan; but the position of women is no less inferior, in accordance with the Confucian maxim: 'a woman owes obedience three times in her life, to her parents when she is young, to her husband when she is married, and to her children when she is old'. This brutal rule is certainly not applied rigidly in all parts of the country. For instance it is relaxed in the town of Kawaguchi (Saitama prefecture), renowned for its cast iron stoves, where the traditional power of the women is well known: the men work in the foundry and the women look after the accounts. The same kind of situation is found in many villages, particularly fishing villages: while the men are out fishing, the women do the farm work; the men represent the family in the outside world but in the home the woman holds the purse strings.

However it does seem that, in many cases, the inferior lot of women is a reality, both established and sanctioned by law prior to the war, and recognized in the customs of today. Before 1945 women, of course,

---

1. Among the sources of information on all these questions readily accessible to the European reader, mention may be made of the following: Lafcadio Hearn, *Japan: an Interpretation*, 1904; Ruth Benedict, *The Chrysanthemum and the Sword*, Boston, 1946; John Embree, *Suye Mura: a Japanese Village*, Chicago, 1939; Arthur F. Raper, *Tamie Tsuchiyama;* Herbert Passin and David Sills, *The Japanese Village in Transition*, Tokyo, SCAT, Natural Resources Section, 1950. The last three works mentioned have been borrowed from frequently for the present report though without specific acknowledgment in footnotes.

had no right to vote, nor did they have the right to own property apart from their husbands; they could claim no share in the estate of their deceased husbands or fathers and could not initiate divorce proceedings. In everyday life, the wife takes her meals separately, serves her husband and stays at home, or, when she does go out with her husband, walks some paces behind him. It is only when a Japanese woman is wearing Western dress that she will walk beside a man in the street and precede him through doors; back at home, in her kimono, she will serve dinner to her husband and his European guests but will not eat with them herself. Her social status outside the home is governed strictly by that of her husband: if he is of high rank, his wife will receive greater marks of respect than are accorded to men of humble station. But this is a reflected honour, dependent on the standing of the husband and he is the one to whom deference is really being paid. Within the family, rank is determined by age and by relationship to the head of the family. The head of the family's wife, in particular, has authority over the other women and is entitled to respect from the younger men. Conversely, the position of the daughter-in-law is not an enviable one: living away from her own family, she is often the household drudge and butt of her mother-in-law. Some Japanese writers have protested at such a description, on the grounds that it takes too black a view of the situation and is too generalized.[1] However, it is probably true to say that in the country at least, women are rarely mistresses in their own homes before the age of 40. Nor should we overlook the threat of repudiation, far more often at the instance of the parents-in-law than of the husband himself, that hangs over the young wife, especially when she has no child.[2] Nowadays women have acquired the right to demand a divorce, but the men laugh heartily at the idea of a wife taking the initiative in breaking up the marriage.

The reasons for the social inferiority of women are not to be sought only in the prolonged influence of Confucian ethics. Ruth Benedict drew attention to a factor probably of considerable importance when she attributed it also to the sexual role of women. Despite the close analogy it is possible to draw in this respect with ancient Rome, Occidentals find it difficult to understand the separation of conjugal and erotic relationships. To the Japanese, love counts among the minor satisfactions and is kept quite apart from the serious things of life, in which the family is included. The unification of the marriage tie and of love, as accepted in the West, impedes understanding of a cultural system in which

1. Cf. Watfuji Tetsuro, 'Some Doubts regarding the Scientific Validity of Ruth Benedict's Book', *Japanese Journal of Ethnology* (*Minzo-kugaku-Kenkyu*), 1949, column 14, no. 4, pp. 23-7; the writer asserts that frequently it is the mother-in-law who is her daughter-in-law's victim.
2. See below, Chapter VII, p. 173, for the anecdote given by Ruth Benedict and the reaction to it by one of the subjects interviewed.

marriages are arranged and women are no more than instruments for the fulfilment of functions regarded as much more important than their individual destinies. Even in a man-dominated society, such as long existed in Europe and America, love as conceived in the West may lead men to think of their wives as persons. That is hardly ever the case in the Far East and reforms in this direction are not likely to come from the philosophy of life peculiar to that part of the world.

Nor must the economic factor be overlooked in accounting for the inferior status of women. It was largely the fact that they were able to earn their own living which gave Western women their freedom, and it is by a similar path that Japanese women who aspire to emancipation look to achieve it. That is the reason why so many country girls, both before and since the war, have wanted to go to work in the towns, either as factory hands or, if they were higher up the social scale, in the better paid employment of domestic service. Even so, however, the pace of emancipation is still slow; an investigation by the Japanese National Public Opinion Research Institute in 1948 showed that of 100 women in paid employment, more than half had accepted their jobs without knowing what the work was or what pay was attached to it. Politically, women have been granted equal rights with men and they do indeed crowd to the polling booths; but their participation in political life usually stops at that. An enquiry in a country area shows that women vote to avoid ridicule but take no real interest in the procedure; they follow the lead of prominent members of their own sex and refrain from asking advice of the men, who are amused at the idea of the new political rights for women; and, indeed, the women themselves think it is too early for them to take part in politics.

The status of women throws into relief the inequality characteristic of Japanese society, and the consequently dependent attitudes of some of its members. But that is perhaps saying too much: the inequality is organized, and has many gradations; relations between subordinates and superiors are very complicated, and the real conception behind the whole structure is hierarchical. Already in evidence in ancient times, and developed by feudalism to a point where, in the Edo era, there were as many as 360 recognized class divisions, hierarchy has left many traces of its survival in the Japan of today. It is to be observed above all in the structure of the family.

Let us consider, to begin with, the family in the limited sense: if we take as the centre of it a married couple whose children are not yet grown up, the family hardly extends beyond the couple themselves, the parents of one partner, a brother or two and the children; an idea of the average size of a Japanese family in this limited sense can be gathered from statistics for 1948, which show an average of four to six persons per household in the towns and seven to eight in the countryside. The traditional structure of such a family is strictly hierarchical;

authority belongs to the father or, more accurately, given the composition of the family suggested above, to the grandfather: at meals he is served first and he is the first to enter the communal hot bath. All the rest of the family bow to him; ownership of the family property is vested in him; he is the family priest and makes and unmakes the marriages of his children even when they are grown up with children of their own. His authority ends only with his death or voluntary retirement. Some Japanese, however, claim that for some decades now, their young compatriots have been free to choose their wives and their jobs.[1] It is unlikely that this is the general rule and it is certainly not the impression I got from my own enquiries. As regards divorce, a study of the archives of the family courts makes it clear that, in the recent past, the most frequent causes are not differences between the spouses but criticism by the parents-in-law.[2]

Immediately after the father in order of seniority comes the eldest son. Traditionally and under the old civil code, he was his father's heir and it was to him that the family property passed on his father's retirement. Since the occupation he has been deprived by law of this privilege, but a recent investigation in the countryside (cf. Raper, page 211) shows that, in the villages studied, the eldest son was still the sole heir in 78 per cent of cases, there was an equal division of the estate among the sons (but not the daughters) in 4 per cent of cases, and in 13 per cent of the cases, distribution varied according to age. Moreover, the majority of the villagers (67 per cent) replied that equal division of the estate among all the children would jeopardize the family's livelihood. Thus the privilege of the eldest son not only persists but is justified—or rationalized—by economic necessity. Against the privilege of the eldest son must of course be set the responsibilities: he inherits the expenses of the family cult and the family debts—both the material debts and the personal obligations which enmesh Japanese life with a network of commitments; and it is he who must care for his aged parents and look after his brothers and sisters when they get into difficulties. Just as the head of the family does not exercise his authority for his own advantage but in the interest of the family, his heritage having come to him more as a trusteeship than as a personal estate, so the privilege of the eldest son is offset by family duties: he knows that he cannot marry whom he likes, but must bow to the decision of the head of the family, who probably takes a longer and wiser view than himself; whereas his younger brothers may go elsewhere to seek their fortune, sometimes in the literal sense, he himself remains tied to his inheritance. This system, in appearance so intolerably authoritarian, does not, however, cause friction:

1. See Watsuji, loc. cit.
2. Report by Mrs. Hideko Ohama, arbitrator attached to the Tokyo Family Court, to the Congress of the Japanese Association of Cultural Science, January 1952.

between father and son there is no real competition; the father is the administrator of the household for a period—thereafter it will be the son. As there is no clash of interests between them it follows that there is no clash of wills; on the contrary they co-operate in the exercise of a function of great importance in their eyes, that of ensuring the continuance of the family.

The wife of a son who has remained in the family home, lives, as we have seen, in a state of real subjection, but she ranks no lower than the adopted son in a family without male descendants, i.e. the husband of the daughter of the house. No doubt the estate will pass to him in due course but meanwhile he has lost his own name and is regarded with some degree of contempt. In the family in the broader sense the 'extended' family, a meticulous etiquette traditionally regulated the status of each member. Even today the members of younger branches of the family are treated as poor relations; this is shown by the places allotted to them at banquets, and they enter the house by the back door. Out of 13 villages examined recently there were three in which these hierarchic customs still persisted.

Before going on to describe the hierarchy of the extended family, and of society at large, it would be well to give at this point an account of the way in which the patriarchial system is carried over into the professional and business sphere. Until recently, it was still the rule in trading and manufacturing concerns. The time is, of course, past when a business was regarded as an exclusively family affair, and business men recruited their young employees from their own families and set them up in branch undertakings. It would not even be true to say, as is sometimes done, that the majority of wage earners are employed in very small establishments; in 1939 the proportion of persons employed in manufacturing concerns with fewer than five workmen was below 23 per cent and in 1947 it was almost the same. However, the important fact is that, whatever the size of the business, large or small, its employees are organized in small family-like groups under what is known as the *oyabun-kobun* (quasi-father-son) system. The *oyabun* may be an older workman, or even a foreman, who takes newly recruited youngsters under his protection and acts as a real father towards them. The system in its most typical form is to be seen in the mining industry;[1] the *oyabun* helps the *kobun* at his work, instructs him in the traditions (often superstitious) of the pit, helps him in his private life and sometimes chooses him a wife; in a case quoted by the author referred to, an *oyabun* said that he loved his *kobun* better than his own children.

The *kobun* show their gratitude to the *oyabun* in the sentiments they express towards him. They call him *ototsan* (*otosan*, father) and his wife

---

1. See the paper on the position in the Ibaragi Mines by Shizuo Matsushima, 'Characteristics of the *Oyabun-kobun* system among Miners', *Japanese Sociological Review*, 1950, 1, pp. 61-7 (in Japanese).

okkasan (*okasan*, mother) and care for both of them in their old age. When the *oyabun* dies, the *kobun* go into the mountains and cut his headstone with their own hands, pay a priest to recite sutras in his memory, and look after his family.

These substitute family relationships are the more understandable among the Ibaragi miners, who come from remote areas, are cut off from their own families and need to find a substitute for family support. However, the *oyabun-kobun* relationship is to be found, in a general way, throughout Japanese society. Factory workers regard trade unions as necessary to protect their rights but they also expect their foremen to give them an *oyabun's* protection extending to their private life outside the factory; in some cases, moreover, the foremen recruited them. Similarly in the countryside, in addition to associations based on the extended family relationship (*dôzoku*), on relationship by marriage, or on neighbourhood, there are others based on the *oyabun-kobun* relationship.[1] The criminal gangs of the underworld are also organized on the *oyabun-kobun* principle: the *kobun* owe absolute obedience to their *oyabun*, who in return supplies them with all the necessities of life.[2] Changing techniques in industry are making the *oyabun-kobun* relationship increasingly difficult to operate; the absolute authority of the foreman over the workman is being replaced, in modern factories, by the authority of a personnel department which is making the protective function of *oyabun-kobun* increasingly meaningless. However, an intermediate system is conceivable, and that is the situation most frequently encountered in the factories of Japan today.

These extensions of the patriarchal system, eagerly adopted by the workers both for the security it affords them and, it must be said, for the prestige attaching to membership of *oyabun-kobun* groups, are to be found in other forms, but just as specifically, in the general organization of Japanese capitalism.[3] This patriarchal economic system is, indeed, so important an element of Japanese society that, although it was seriously weakened during the American occupation (notably by the anti-trust provisions of Law no. 207 of 9 December 1947), it has recently been reinstated under a law of May 1952, one of the very first laws adopted after the recovery of national independence. Indeed, the big Japanese trusts, the *zaibatsu*, are commonly known as *bôzoku-kaisha* (family businesses) and are precisely that. At the centre of each organization there is always a group of blood relations (*dôzoku-dan*) consisting of senior and collateral branches of the same family, with their various

---

1. Report by Tadashi Fukutake to the Congress of the Japanese Association of Cultural Science, January 1952; the study was of a village in Ibaragi Prefecture.
2. Iwai, ibid.
3. See Kizaemon Ariga, 'Ruth Benedict's *Assessment of the Hierarchical Element in the Japanese Social Structure*', *Japanese Journal of Ethnology* (*Minzokugaku-Kenkyu*), 1949, 14, no. 4, 13-22 (in Japanese), p. 19.

junior branches brought in to form subsidiary companies. The whole organization is conceived as an extended family (*shizoku*), and the subsidiary companies are affiliated in the literal sense; for, not only does the parent company levy a percentage (usually 10 per cent) of their profits, and handle the affairs of individual members of the firms in a family spirit; it also retains exclusive authority in all important matters and in the general policy of the trust, the directors of the other companies, in practice, having limited powers only. The rivalry between the different trusts is very similar to that which existed between the great feudal houses, and Japan's modern economic history bears a close resemblance to its political history since the earliest days.[1]

In point of fact, as Ruth Benedict rightly guessed, the whole social structure of Japan is dictated by a concept of hierarchy directly deriving from the kinship of the clan. Japanese society has of course undergone many far-reaching administrative changes since the remote epoch of the *uji;* without going back to the introduction of Chinese administrative models in the sixth to seventh centuries, we may point, in modern times, to the reforms of the Tokugawa and the Meiji restoration. The feudal system as a whole has been so far abandoned as to enable some writers (e.g. Watsuji, loc. cit.) to protest that neither they nor their fathers believed any more in hierarchy, or had any respect for it, nor were they content to remain unquestioningly in the station in society assigned to them. Similarly, with the emergence since the Meiji restoration of a semi-feudal capitalist system, there has developed a curious combination of self-interest and respect for superiors.[2] Nevertheless, hierarchy persists, fostered perhaps by a largely ideographic script which preserves the old ideas in the new terms. For instance though the word *shizoku* (family) expresses a notion of blood relationship widely different from the concept of the clan, thus *shi* (氏) is still the *uji* symbol; many features of contemporary Japanese culture bear the stamp of the hierarchical principle: it is for instance, the meaning behind the infinitely complex etiquette governing everyday relations in Japan, that unequivocally determines precedence at meetings and banquets and lays down, according to the rank of those concerned, the depths of the bows to be exchanged and the appropriate style of address. No individual initiative is permitted, and the egalitarian temptations to familiarity, so frequent in the West, would here be incomprehensible; everyone is conscious of having his prescribed, recognized and respected place in society guaranteed against any possibility of attack. In delicate situations, where accepted relationships between persons or families may be disturbed (as is typically the case in marriage), recourse is had to a go-between whose intervention

---

1. In this connexion the reader is referred to F. Barret, *L'Evolution du Capitalisme Japonais*, Paris, 3 volumes, 1945/47.
2. See Takashi Ota, 'Reform of Education', *Japanese Sociological Review*, 1950, 1, September, 17-23 (in Japanese).

allows face to be saved in all circumstances. Even in illicit sexual relations, when the absence of electric light made it possible for a country
boy to sneak into a girl's room at night, he used to take the precaution
of covering his face with a napkin so that, if he was repulsed, he could
pretend next day that he had not been recognized. Direct competition,
which questions the validity of rank, hurts feelings and jeopardizes
personal security and social stability, is avoided as much as possible;
thus the promoters of the recent educational reforms were being neither
as original nor, by the same token, as 'democratic'[1] as they thought
in taking such pains to abolish all competition in schools. At Suye-mura,
for instance, we found that the weaker pupils were not kept back and
that prizes were awarded to all the competitors in sports and events,
and not only to the winners.

The fact of the matter is that the individual has his predetermined
place in society just as in his family. This is not a mere metaphor: society
itself is no more than an organization of families and personal relations
are modelled on relations between kinsmen. This emphatically does not
mean that Japanese society excludes social mobility: the history of
Japan is enough to prove the contrary, and there are innumerable
instances to be seen of men striving and aspiring to rise in the social scale.
However, the psycho-social climate in which ambition and the desire
to get on develop, is one of stability, of the permanence of the general
structure. Just as certain Western countries, while professing a social
philosophy of mobility, competition and unrestricted access to all
employment, in fact have a camouflaged class system and are fairly
strict in keeping individuals to the station in which they were born,
so Japan, while professing a social philosophy of stability, presents a
social structure relatively flexible in practice. Ariga (loc. cit.) writing
from a historical standpoint, describes this situation admirably.

To understand the Japanese social structure, three ideas must be
brought into play, not separately, but together: (a) the idea of kinship,
by blood, marriage, adoption or service; (b) the idea of hierarchy, always
conceived more or less on the *oyako* (father-son) model; (c) the idea of
sharing in the protection offered by the tutelary deities, by a common
cult or at least by a common burying ground. These three ideas are
connected with each other, particularly the first two: wherever there is
kinship there is a hierarchical relationship, and the opposite, as we have
seen, is also true; as for the common cult, it is the symbol of the family
bond. In the rural areas investigated by Raper's team, a strict order of
precedence was observed at all full-scale family reunions; before the
war these invariably took place on New Year's Day, on the Day of the

---

1. See the remarks of the American Education Mission to Japan (*Report of the
United States Education Mission to Japan*, Washington, 1946, p. 10) and the
report of the Japanese Ministry of Education on the implementation of the
reforms (*Progress of Education Reform in Japan*, Tokyo, 1950, pp. 14-16).

Dead and on Ancestors' Day, with worship offered to the tutelary god of the family and to the family's ancestors. Conversely, when hierarchical relationships weaken and tend towards equality, the sense of kinship becomes dormant. The *shizoku* (which may be translated, roughly and provisionally, as 'family') relationship contains just these three elements —consciousness of common lineage, close hierarchical relationships, and an *ujigami* (clan-god) acting as intermediary.

The key institution is the *dozoku-dan*, or group of common ancestry. It consists of a *honke*, or senior branch, and *makke* or *bunke*, junior branches or off-shoots. The *bunke* are subordinate to the *honke*, to which they may be linked either by blood or by service (service *bunke*). The *bunke* may in their turn proliferate and form junior branches of their own. Extended families of this type are still a contemporary institution: Raper's investigation revealed one consisting of 20 closely related households, and another still extant, in a different village, numbering 60 closely related households within living memory. The formation of extended families is still proceeding steadily—for instance when a father sets up a younger son on capital from his own estate, or on land specially bought for him, or leased in the father's name and subsequently transferred to the son. Sometimes, for instance in fishing villages, the younger son may achieve financial independence as a fisherman, his father confining himself to providing him with a house.

Although the hierarchical system is modelled on the *oyako* (father-son) relationship, the essential factor in the subordination of the *bunke* to the *honke* is not the filial link, but the favour done them by the *honke* in establishing them; the *bunke* then incurred an *on*, an 'obligation', binding them indefinitely. The two notions of hierarchy and *on* are in practice inseparable: in principle an *on* can be received only from a superior, and the fact of receiving an *on* establishes the inferiority of the receiver. The peculiar logic of the hierarchical relationship, confused as it is with the *oyako* relationship, makes it possible to understand how, despite the undoubted borrowing from Chinese culture of the notions of *chu* and *ko*, Japanese culture should have reversed the order of priority which these two notions had, and still have, in China. For the Chinese, the fundamental obligation is *ko*, filial piety; in Japan *ko* takes second place to *chu*, loyalty to superiors. Repayment of *on* (*ongaeshi*) is the supreme obligation in the eyes of Japanese; hence the supremacy and universality of the hierarchical relationship in Japan, but as it is modelled on *oyako* it implies at the same time the notion of kinship.

A second remark should also be made. The creation of the *bunke* (related by blood or service) subordinate to the *honke*, is possible only in certain closely interrelated moral, legal and economic conditions; these must be such as to make it generally understood that a young man cannot enter into the category of adults by his own efforts, that he needs help to begin with, and that this will constitute an *on* for him and will establish a relationship of hierarchical dependence. In a wage-earning economy, for instance, there is little likelihood of a younger son having to look to his father for help to start life on his own: all he would need to do would be to leave the family home and keep himself and his own immediate household from his wages. It will undoubtedly be interesting to follow the course of the changes that the growth of this type of economy is bringing about in Japanese culture, both as regards the family and the hierarchical system in general. But the new economy is as yet far from having produced its full effects in Japan because salaries are low and in many cases are little more than pocket money. Thus young men who accept the new ideas of individualism and democracy, and feel the desire for independence run up against obstacles which keep them tied to the family. Conversely, it is possible that in the recent past the family bond, may, to some extent at least, have been responsible, together with the obvious pressure of overpopulation, for keeping salaries below subsistence level. The rates offered have nevertheless been acceptable to many workers because the family was still carrying out its protective function towards its members.

The hierarchical family relationship is not the only kind of group relationship conceived and existing in a Japanese community; there are also associations on a basis of equality, the *kumi*, having a very special character of their own, whose role in Japanese society is extremely interesting. However, for the moment we must follow the development of the logic of hierarchy in the *dozoku-dan*. The growth of *dozoku-dan* coincided with the expansion of the national economy; the *bunke*, and their own branch families, grew up around *honke*, the private *ujigami* of the *honke* being the public *ujigami* of the *dozoku-dan*. Where there were several *dozoku-dan* in one community, they co-operated as equals, if their *honke* were of the same strength; if, however, one *honke* was more powerful than the rest, it brought the remainder under its influence. It might then happen that the resulting relationships came to be regarded as those of common ancestry and it is in this way, according to Ariga (loc. cit.), that the basic structure of the *shizoku* is to be understood. (see page 57 above). Thus an intricate system of rank, with political as well as economic and religious implications, grew up within the general concept of the relationships of common ancestry—ancestry of course not necessarily meaning blood relationship. The extremely complex hierarchical system which then took shape naturally underwent frequent changes with the varying fortunes of the *honke;* it was considerably simplified by regulations of the feudal lords and as a system it vanished when the Meiji restoration put an end to feudalism. Nevertheless its spirit, as we have seen, still permeates Japanese culture. It should also be noted that, on occasion, intermediate stages in the hierarchical chain have been by-passed—e.g. when commoners have been placed under the direct authority of feudal lords (*daimyo*), or subjects under that of the Emperor. In these cases, direct family succession of the *shizoku* and *dôzoku-dan* type is lost sight of, but Ariga takes the view that the idea of common ancestry is then merely latent and can be inferred from the existence of a common cult; how otherwise is it possible to explain, for instance, why the cult of the sun goddess, in the great Ise sanctuary, should have been the tutelary cult of all subjects of the Emperor? In the last resort it appears that in Japan the hierarchical social and political structure, the common cult and the patriarchal principle are all indissolubly linked with one another, in detail as well as in general. In the coal mines of Northern Kyushu, the *oyabun-kobun* groups shout 'long live the Emperor' (*Tenno banzai*), thereby signifying that the Emperor, at the apex of the hierarchy, remains the supreme symbol and the supreme *oyabun*.[1] The real difference between Japan and the West is less a matter of social structure than of procedures and attitudes. Administrative efficiency, in particular, comes not only from gearing everything to perfection, but also from universal respect for the hierarchy.

We may perhaps have given the impression that hierarchy on the family model, as it exists in the *dôzoku-dan*, is essentially a rural phenomenon: that would be an error. Being of great antiquity, this system naturally came into being in an agricultural economy and the *dôzoku-dan* developed along with farming itself, around the large-scale agriculturalists, landowners and farmers; but they developed just as much in the towns, around the merchants and artisans. Moreover, in modern times, farms have grown smaller; fewer *makke* have been established without ties of blood, and the relations of the *bunke* to the *honke* have become less subordinate and are more on a footing of equality. Thus in the countryside, the hierarchical character of the *dôzoku-dan* has been appreciably lost, and with it has gone the sense of common ancestry. In the towns the opposite has occurred: merchant and artisan families, in expanding their businesses, have followed the *dôzoku-dan* principles of organization and have established many *makke* without the blood tie. As we have seen (page 55), a monopolistic economy, with the *zaibatsu*, was created on the same principles. The Meiji revolution was directed against the *Tokugawa shôgunate* by the Samurai and the merchants, but at the beginning these two classes allied themselves with the parties of the feudal lords which were based on the *shizoku* of the *daimyo*. As Ariga makes clear, the *daimyo* hardly suffered from the revolution: they lost their status as knights (*bushi*), but they kept a high political, economic and social position, for they were admitted to the House of Peers, became capitalists and received titles of nobility. Japanese industrialism of tomorrow will in all probability still be based, like that of yesterday, on the same hierarchical and family principles that were the foun-

---

1. Private report by Hirosato Fujiwara.

dation of the agricultural society in ancient and more recent times.

Nevertheless it would be dangerous and misleading to carry systemati-
zation too far. Vertical and hierarchical relationships, as we have already
pointed out, are not the only feature of Japanese society: there also
exist horizontal relationships, varying with the institution concerned,
which give rise to equalitarian associations or family co-operatives
known as *kumi*.[1] Typical of these associations is the *gonin-gumi* (group
of five persons), apparently of Chinese origin and brought to Japan by
the Kamatari reform (seventh century); this system still exists in most
agricultural areas, fishing villages and mountain villages.[2] Under the
leadership of a chief chosen from among themselves, the *gonin-gumi*
renewed every year, by solemn oath, a pact for mutual assistance and
the promotion of the common interest; the links thus forged between
families endured for centuries. A pyramid of local organizations long
rested on the *gonin-gumi*; two *gonin-gumi* made a *junin-gumi* (group of
10 persons), four a *nijunin-gumi* (group of 20 persons). The inhabitants
of an entire village would form an *isson-gumi* (village association) and
associations of five villages were also to be found. This whole organization
was legally dissolved in 1888, when a new municipal administration was
set up; but the idea certainly did not vanish altogether. After the great
Tokyo earthquake in 1923, *tonari-gumi* (neighbourhood associations)
sprang up everywhere, and they also flourished in every town during
the war. Thus, side by side with the hierarchical relationship, close and
widespread horizontal relationships exist in Japan, and in his monograph
on Suye-Mura, Embree lays much stress on this highly co-operative
aspect of Japanese society.

The existence of the *kumi* does not, however, diminish the hierarchical
character of that society: one might almost say the opposite. In the first
place, as Ariga has noted, when changes occurred in the circumstances
of the families concerned, hierarchical relationships developed within
the *kumi*, creating a sense of kinship—the reverse process from that
whereby the *dozoku-dan* degenerated into *kumi* when the *bunke* became
independent of the *honke*. Secondly, the central administration used the
kumi for its own advantage: the reorganization of the *gonin-gumi* by
Hideyoshi, in 1597, entrusted them with certain police functions, particularly the duty of denouncing any member of the group infringing the
laws (especially any member professing Christianity): all the members
of *gonin-gumi* were collectively responsible. Similarly during the last war,
extensive use was made of the *tonari-gumi* by the government in power.

---

1. See Japan-Handbuch, Nachschlagwerk der Japankunde, im Auftrag des Japans-
   instituts Berlin herausgegeben von Prof. Dr. M. Ramming, Berlin 1941, article:
   Fünferschaft; Shigeto Hozumi, 'The "tonari-gumi" of Japan'. *Contemporary
   Japan, A Review of East Asiatic Affairs*, Tokyo, 1943. *12*, no. 8.
2. Takeyoshi Kawashima, 'Evaluation and Critique (of *The Chrysanthemum and
   the Sword*)', *Japanese Journal of Ethnography*, 1949, 14, no. 4, 1-8, p. 3.

Every private person, whether Japanese or foreign, was required to belong to a *tonari-gumi*, and these groups were responsible for civil defence, and for the distribution of ration cards. They were also given a free hand in the matter of family assistance, and helped local administrations in distributing the texts of numerous rules and regulations. The horizontal organization of the Japanese society is thus anything but hostile to its vertical organization; although it is based on equalitarian relationships, it is just as effective in integrating the individual into society and in assigning to him his proper place, thereby adding the last touches of detail to the work of the hierarchical institutions. As one writer (Kawashima, loc. cit. page 3), judiciously remarks, the *kumi* were an invaluable tool of Japanese totalitarianism, which 'was able to use, reorganize and strengthen them and build on these foundations a powerful authoritarian system'.

Accordingly, the most distinctive feature of Japanese society is probably the way the individual is integrated into it. Beginning in the family, the institution upon which everything is based, this integration is evinced in all social relations and is encountered in all other institutions. This statement must not, of course, be accepted without qualifications, as this very summary introduction might tempt the reader to do.

The authority devolving from the summit encounters, before it reaches the base, a local administration presenting certain democratic features: but the democracy is a group, and not an individual, affair (it is significant, for instance, that the *kumi*, which are associations of families, call themselves groups of *persons*, *gonin-gumi:* associations of five *persons*). To take another example, it may be noted that freedom of speech and of criticism has always been a lauded and respected principle, even in the most totalitarian periods—but there was always one exception: absolute respect had to be paid to the Emperor as symbol and guarantor of the nation's unity.

CONCLUDING REMARKS

An important exception, in appearance at least, to the principle of the general integration of the individual into Japanese society, is the existence of marginal groups. One of these is the group of Korean immigrants, who are hated and despised, all the more because the occupation seemed to confer upon them a kind of superior status; but they are not nationals, and it is therefore not so surprising that they should be left outside the Japanese community. A second group is the Ainu: up to 1941-42, the government, which had been trying to turn these hunters and fishermen into farmers, maintained them in special schools. Today there are perhaps 20,000 of them, mostly living in isolation in their own villages in Hokkaido. At present the government has no active policy for protecting them. The gravest problem of discrimination relates to the eta, outcasts who work in leather and skins. Counting those who have been absorbed into ordinary Japanese society, they probably amount to 4.5 million; the vast majority live in quite separate 'special villages' and inter-marry. Official discrimination against the eta lasted rather more than two centuries and a half, from the Tokugawa era to 1871, but it actually began much earlier, probably before the introduction of Buddhism into Japan; it is still practised today, although the situation of the eta seems to be improving. It is not possible to discuss this problem here, but it should at least be noted that it does not impair the principle of social integration; on the contrary, it might be said that the more integrated a society is, the more it is inclined to discriminate.

We must beware of passing value judgments on such a society, and above all we must avoid evaluating it by Western standards. To call it oppressive would be to make use of a concept of individualism which grew historically out of the philosophy, ethics and religion of the West; and to say that individuals cannot be happy under the Japanese system assumes that happiness is a positive value. One of the great merits of Ruth Benedict's synthetical study is that it begins by examining the Japanese ethic. It is an ethic which imprisons the moral agent in a network of obligations and pluralistic values, and which, in its most elevated aspect, insists on a certain intensity and sublimity of action; but at no point does it include the notion of a system of conduct. It counts all pleasures as legitimate provided they are considered of minor importance, but it rejects as scandalous the pursuit of happiness as the serious purpose of life; indeed, the word 'happiness' has no exact equivalent in the Japanese language. In short, Japanese culture has no real place for the concept of individualism. Many of the antitheses familiar to the West—freedom or slavery, good or evil, happiness or misery, democracy or totalitarianism—are meaningless when applied to Japan. The distance between Japan and the West, not merely in space, but in the sphere of social psychology, has to be grasped; non-critical ideas of 'human nature' are liable to lead us seriously astray. Goodwill of itself cannot ensure mutual understanding; scientific data are indispensable, as is also a certain intellectual detachment.

It is true that, for seven years, Western ideas have been poured into Japan, but in seeking to discover what effect they have had on the population, particularly on what should have been the most receptive part of it, namely, Japanese youth, we must bear in mind that throughout the period when these influences were being brought to bear, Japan had not made a complete break with its traditions.

CHAPTER III

THE PLACE OF
YOUTH IN JAPANESE SOCIETY

DEFINITION OF 'YOUTH'

Japanese society recognizes and names various ages of life: *kodomo*, the child, from birth to 6 years old; *shonen*, the boy or girl from 6 to about 15; *seinen*, the young man or young woman; and lastly *otona*, grown-ups or adults. Terminologically, therefore, the subject of our study is clearly designated and identified as *seinen*, young men and young women.

However, the matter is not so simple when it comes to specifying the upper and lower age limits of the category. The dictionary is not very helpful: its definitions, when not vague, are rather arbitrary. One would welcome information that really threw light on the subject.

For this purpose, we might turn for help first to physiology. Clearly, the commonly accepted notion is that 'youth' begins at puberty and ends when the body has finished growing. In this connexion the measurements taken during the national enquiry on nutrition are of some interest.[1]

The graphs which can be plotted from these data (see figs. 3 and 4) need not be subjected here to an exhaustive biometric analysis. One need only look at them to see that the curve bends inwards between the ages of 11 and 13, marking the resumption of growth, and that the maximum height of the curve corresponds to the end of this growth. The increase in height does not keep pace with the increase in weight, and the graphs for the females only very roughly agree with those for the males and in any case are sharply divergent after the age of 14 as regards height, and after the age of 15 as regards weight, giving the impression that the young woman stops growing at an earlier age than the young man, with the result that as an adult she is shorter than he is. Maximum height is attained at the age of about 22 in the case of young men and at about 19 in the case of young women; maximum weight appears at about 23 in the case of young men, and at about 20 in the case of young women.

Observations of this kind, which are within the reach of all, undoubtedly constituted the original biological basis for the distinctions made by the

---

1. See *Japan Statistical Yearbook* 1950, pp. 456-7. Save where otherwise indicated the statistical data in the present chapter are taken from this reference book.

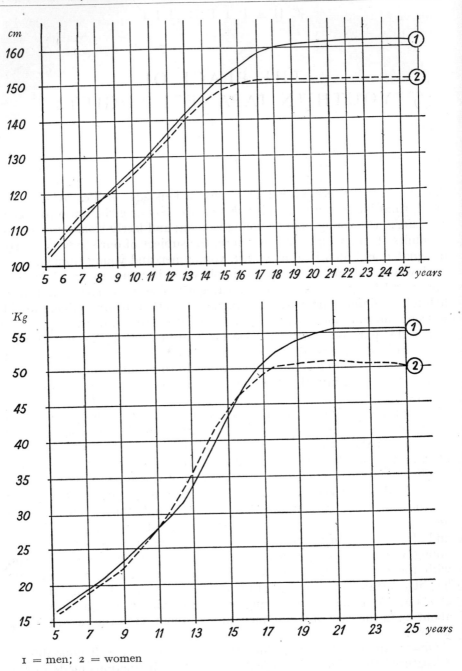

I = men; 2 = women

Figs. 3 and 4. Heights and weights of Japanese according to sex and age (*Japanese Statistical Yearbook,* 1950, p. 456)

language. However, the findings of physiology cannot be regarded as absolute. They vary with individuals, whereas the graphs have been plotted from averages only. Moreover, in the majority of cases, the changes are gradual and indeed almost imperceptible. But the conclusive reason for not relying only upon physiology is that, in essence, the distinction between the various ages of life is not biological but socio-logical; each society interprets the natural signs in its own way. The passage from adolescence to adulthood being still more important for society than that from childhood to adolescence, it is only natural that the rules governing the former should be particularly strict. In the time of the Samurai, legal majority was attained at the age of 15 in the country and at the age of 20 in the towns; indeed, at Suye-mura, we find youths of 14 or 15 doing a man's work on the farm (Embree, op. cit., page 193). The difficulty arises from the fact that a person does not legally attain majority in all respects at the same age. Marriageable age is fixed at 16 for girls and 18 for boys. Under the labour law 18 is the age at which a person may undertake adult employment. Smoking and the consump-tion of alcohol by minors are prohibited by law, and here the age limit is 20. The age at which a person attains majority under the Civil Code is also 20.

In fact, 20 is the official age for attaining majority in Japan, and is marked by a solemn coming of age ceremony newly instituted by the State. Coming Of Age Day (15 January) is one of the nine national feast days of the new order, and on that day ceremonies and meetings are held throughout the country at which young people are required to take formal cognizance of their new responsibilities.[1] Coming of age is un-doubtedly important in the eyes of the individual, and of his immediate circle. But at the age of 20, the individual is very far from being, in all cases, mature in the psychological and sociological sense, and adult in the full meaning of the word. The decisive line of demarcation between adolescence and adulthood is marriage, and, even more surely, in a country where marriages are often not registered until after the birth of the first child, parenthood. It is fatherhood that makes a man a full member of the community, and motherhood that converts the wife into a matron entitled to the privileges of smoking, drinking and of making, not merely laughing at, coarse sexual jokes, as Embree noted at Suye-mura (op. cit., pp. 182 and 215).

It should be remarked at once that many young men are in no hurry to get married and emerge from their 'adolescent' status. The age at which a young man wants to get married is nowadays 26, but sometimes even 30 (see Chapter VII, p. 181). What many young men see in the new legal freedom given them as regards marriage is not so much that they can choose their own wives as that they can themselves fix the date—

---

1. Cf. S. Uenoda, *Calendar of Annual Events in Japan*, Tokyo, 1951.

and fix it later—at which they enter into the category of married people. This is an interesting psychological fact; why do the young often seem so reluctant to assume adult status?

In the first place, there is probably the desire to avoid as long as possible the responsibilities and the expense of being adult. Marriage, in Japan, does not mean liberation from the family, as it does in the West. Having the status of an adult, through marriage and fatherhood, means above all being entitled to discharge all the responsibilities of a grown man in one's particular environment. It does not follow, however, that the young father thereby becomes his own master or the head of his household: as we have seen above, he will not attain these positions until they become vacant through the death or voluntary retirement of the present holder; and the young mother will become her own mistress only on the death of her stepmother. Thus marriage, and the consequent emergence from the category of the young, looks much more like the discharge of an obligation to the community than the exercise of a right to emancipation.

Possibly a second and additional reason is that many young people do not feel ripe for adult life, they do not feel able to stand on their own feet financially: as we shall see later, the economic position of the young is precarious and starting salaries are glaringly inadequate. But the young do not feel psychologically ripe either—as is made clear by much of the data quoted in the followings pages. One frequently gets the impression that Japanese culture, like Western culture, has become too complex, and for this reason psycho-social maturity comes late, and apprenticeship to social life must be prolonged; the position of the young is quite different from what it is in so-called primitive societies and this is an additional reason for not keeping rigidly to physiological criteria.

Thus, if we agree to the rather arbitrary choice of 15 as the lower age limit of youth, 20 can nevertheless not be regarded in all cases as the upper age limit; it marks a kind of subdivision, officially recognized by a coming of age ceremony, but the real dividing line between the state of *seinen* and that of *otona* must be drawn later, at the age of 25 or sometimes even of 30. In the pages that follow attention will therefore be focused on the section of the Japanese population that lies between the ages of 15 and 25.

DEMOGRAPHIC AND SOCIOLOGICAL DISTRIBUTION OF THE YOUNG

This section constitutes a large fraction—about one-fifth—of the total population, and numbers 15 million in all. Girls and women preponderate by a small margin: they represent 52 per cent, as compared with the figure of 51 per cent for females in the population as a whole. Of these

15 million young people, 35 per cent live in towns and 65 per cent in the country. Thus in speaking of Japanese youth, as of the Japanese population in general, we are speaking mainly of people living a rural existence. This is a fact which must be kept constantly in mind. In the sociological, psychological or economic description of a country, we must be careful to avoid concentrating exclusively or even mainly on the urban aspect, even when the town-dwellers have the advantage in numbers and prestige, or, if we may use the term, in vocation, as is the case in the great countries of the West: and there is therefore all the more reason to observe this rule when the country described is Japan. This is not easy, however, because the towns make a stronger impression by their size and variety; by the greater ease and subtlety with which town-dwellers express their culture and their psychology; by their subconscious but unshakable conviction of their own superiority; and by the fact that the observer exhibits the same urban bias in his own upbringing, interests and philosophy of life. We must therefore remember that almost two-thirds of Japanese youth consists of country-dwellers.

This proportion is in fact a little lower than it is in the population as a whole: here Japan has 67 per cent country-dwellers as against 33 per cent town-dwellers. It follows that the young form a slightly larger part of the population in the towns: in 1947 they accounted for 20.8 per cent of the total urban population and 18.7 per cent of the country population. Mainly because of the higher rural birth-rate, the under 15 age-group is relatively more numerous in the country areas, where it constitutes 36.6 per cent of the population (according to the 1947 figures), than in the towns, where it is 32.8 per cent. The higher proportion of adolescents in the urban population is the result of migration. In the absence (so far as the writer knows) of statistics or research on the question, it is difficult to reckon the extent of these migrations, the more so as we have no data on differential mortality. They probably occur as a rule after the age of 20. It can be worked out that a quarter of the 20-24 age-group lives in the most highly industrial prefectures, and represents 9.68 per cent of their population, while another quarter lives in the most markedly agricultural prefectures and represents only 8.32 per cent of their population.[1]

As it is impossible to calculate with any degree of accuracy, it can be estimated from the above data, and in the light of the difference in the relative proportions of children in town and country, that the number of former country-dwellers between 20 and 24 years of age to be found at any given time in the urban areas is 200,000.

---

1. The prefectures are the largest administrative divisions (*ken*); they number 46 in all. The most industrialized are Osaka, Tokyo, Kanagawa, Aichi, Kyoto, Hyogo, and the most rural, Tagoshima, Iwata, Aomori Shimane, Akita, Tottori, Kumamoto, Mei-Miyagi, Oita, Miyazaki, Ibaragi, Nagasaki, Saga, Chiba and Yamagaka.

Other statistical data about Japanese youth would also help to build up an objective picture. It would be particularly helpful to know what proportion of young people are married and how many are students. The common practice of delaying the registration of marriages prevents us from forming a precise idea of the distribution of marriages according to age. However, birth statistics according to the age of the mother throw light on the situation so far as young women are concerned. In the 15-19 age-group were registered 1.6 per cent of all the women who in 1949 had one child or more: as this age-group covers five years, we may assume that it produced about 8.5 children per 100 women, which means that there was a slightly lower proportion of mothers, as 0.2 per cent of the women had given birth to their second child. The 20-24 age-group included, in 1949, 18.8 per cent of the total number of women who had given birth to a child, equivalent to a birth-rate of 94 per cent for that age-group. As 6 per cent of the women gave birth to their second child, and 1.1 per cent to their third child, it may be reckoned that 79 out of 100 women in that age-group were mothers: hence most of the women of this age group are married, whether the marriage is registered or not.

For males, there is no comparable method of calculating percentages. However, some conclusions may be drawn from the investigation into personal salaries carried out in 1948. This shows that in the 16-20 age-group,[1] 9.4 per cent had dependents; and between the ages of 21 and 25 those having dependents amounted to 24.8 per cent.

The investigation deals only with men working in establishments employing more than 30 hands; moreover, a certain number of the dependents may be parents. The fact remains however, that, so far as it is possible to calculate, the number of married men in this age-group is considerably less than the number of married women.

It is also more or less by guesswork that we can arrive at some idea of the percentage of young people who are still continuing their studies. Under the previous law, school attendance was compulsory between the ages of 6 and 14.[2] The present law extends this period by a year, i.e. up to the end of the first cycle of secondary education in the new educational system.[3]

Thus the forms of education which normally affect the group to which this report relates are the second stage of secondary education, and higher

---

1. In this investigation ages are calculated in the Japanese fashion. A person is deemed to be one year old at birth and becomes one year older on 1 January of each succeeding year.
2. K. Yoshida and T. Kaigo, *Japanese Education*, Tokyo, 1937, p. 33.
3. Education (Organization) Law, 31 March 1947, Article 29. For these questions see *Post-War Developments in Japanese Education* two volumes, Tokyo, 1952 (published by SCAT and CI and ED); Volume 2 reproduces the text of the law and contains some statistics. The school statistics in this chapter of our report are taken from *Progress of Education in Japan*, Tokyo 1950, published by the Ministry of Education.

education, both of which are optional. In 1949, those in the second stage of secondary education were reckoned at 1,625,000, of whom 1,277,000 were studying full-time and 348,000 part-time. Assuming that all the students in question belonged to the 16-18 age-group, the proportion of the whole age-group continuing their secondary education would be 33 per cent to 26 per cent of them part-time—with males exceeding females by 42 per cent against 23 per cent. There are however, relatively more males continuing their education who do so on a part-time basis, that is to say, who, in many cases, are already in paid employment. We find in fact, still confining our calculation to the 16-18 year age-group, that among the males 31 per cent study full-time and 11 per cent part-time; for the females the corresponding figures are 20 per cent and 3 per cent.

Turning now to the position in higher education, we find that in 1949 there were about 400,000 students of university or equivalent grade in Japan, of whom one-eighth were females. While this proportion may appear very low, it will be remembered that university education for women is a recent innovation (cf. Yoshida and Kaigo, op. cit., p. 104). In the absence of statistics of the ages of university students it may be reckoned that, given four years as the normal length of the university course under the new system, the proportion of young people of both sexes now attending the universities is one in 20. Applications for admission are, of course, considerably higher. In 1949, total admissions to the new-style universities amounted to 50.8 per cent of the applications (49.6 per cent of which were from men and 69.2 per cent from women). Nearly two-thirds of the total student body is divided between the universities of Tokyo, Kyoto and Osaka—Tokyo University alone counting for more than 180,000 or 48 per cent.

Popular education, which has long been on an organized basis in Japan, continues to expand. Various enquiries have agreed in their conclusion that the education of the younger generation today has been carried to a more advanced stage than that of its predecessors. In particular, the investigation carried out by the National Public Opinion Research Institute, to which constant reference will be made in the pages that follow, supplies details of the average number of years spent in study by those at present falling within the various age-groups, with a breakdown of the figures for the total population according to sex and habitat.

It is a principle of social psychology, confirmed by observation, that receptivity to new ideas rises in direct proportion to the level of education; Table 2 gives an indication of the categories in which the most democratic attitudes should be found in the new Japan.

From an investigation of the working population by the bureau of statistics an idea can be gathered of the extent to which the young play a part in the economic life of the country. Out of 16,000 families picked at random throughout the country, comprising a total of about 56,000 persons aged 15 (Japanese reckoning) or above, 66 per cent are in paid employment (a percentage arrived at as a result of the enquiry made in December 1949), and of these 85 per cent are males and 52 per cent females.

TABLE 2.

| Present age-group | Average number of years of study effected | | | | |
	Population as a whole	Males	Females	Urban	Rural
16-19	10.88	11.01	10.74	10.92	10.86
20-24	10.91	11.18	10.75	11.38	10.64
25-29	10.37	10.55	10.31	10.99	10.37
30-39	9.76	10.53	9.72	10.40	9.78
40-49	9.02	9.99	9.33	9.71	9.37
50 and over	8.76	9.28	8.37	8.85	8.70

In the towns the general percentage in employment is 57 per cent (82 per cent for males and 34 per cent for females); in the country, it is 74 per cent (86 per cent for males and 63 per cent for females). As regards young people, in the country as a whole, among those in the 15-19 age-group, the proportion of those in employment is 47 per cent (49 per cent of the youths and 46 per cent of the girls); and in the 20-39 age-group the proportion for both sexes is 76 per cent (95 per cent of the men and 57 per cent of the women).

Thus, among young persons under 20 years of age, almost half are in work, with a slightly higher proportion of male than of female employment. In the tables consulted the 20-39 age-group is given without subdivisions; as far as men are concerned, however, since the proportion for the whole class is extremely high (95 per cent), that for any subdivision is unlikely to be much lower. For practical purposes it may be taken that practically the whole male population is in employment from the age of 20 onwards. Estimating the proportion of employed women in the 20-25 age-group is less straightforward. A Ministry of Labour enquiry into individual salaries may, however, provide some clues. The situation in this case is very different from that of the enquiry into the working population, because it relates only to workers in establishments with more than 30 employees; it thus covers rather less than 10 per cent of the population over 15 years of age. While the employment rate for men is shown to be more or less the same for all age-groups between 20 and 40, the position as regards women is quite otherwise, the proportion of employed women in the 21-25-year age-group being roughly four times that of the following 5-year age-group. If one assumes—and it is little more than a guess—that all the 5-year age-groups of employed women between the ages of 20 and 40 are divided in the same ratio, it follows that the proportion of girls and young women in employment between the ages of 20 and 25 must be very high—about as high as for men.

Nothwithstanding the many uncertainties, which, as we have seen, are due to the inadequate statistics available for each age-group, it is possible to arrive at a fairly clear idea of the place young people hold in Japanese society; in particular it is easy to see how youth forms the transition stage between childhood and maturity. Up to the age of 15, in principle all boys and girls attend school. From 15 to 20 about half the members of both sexes are already in paid employment; a small minority, decreasing with the increase in age, continues its studies. In both cases, most of the young people concerned still live at home. Less than 10 per cent are already married; a small flow of country-dwellers to the towns has already begun. After the age of 20 the whole picture changes. Before reaching the age of 25, many women (8 out of 10) become mothers and a quarter of the men have family commitments. Between 3 per cent and 4 per cent of the young people born in the country are now living in the towns. Further, 5 per cent of this age-group, mostly men, are attending institutes of higher education, half of them in Tokyo, either living there with their families or come up from the provinces and living alone. By now almost all the youths, at least 9 out of 10, have jobs. The proportion of women in paid employment cannot be determined but it is certainly high and will do nothing but decrease, steeply and rapidly, after the age of 25. Thus the two categories of young people who will be examined in the course of this report, the under twenties and the over twenties, offer sharply contrasted characteristics: the first is still turned towards childhood and has little social responsibility and few economic functions; the second leans strongly, both in the social and the economic sense, towards maturity.

It should not, however, be imagined that young people in the 20-25 age-group enjoy full adult status. It is quite clear that Japanese society continues to keep them in tutelage: the state of their salaries is not merely of symbolic significance but is also a causal factor. The investigation into personal salaries undertaken by the Ministry of Labour in 1948, which we have already quoted, yields invaluable information (see figs. 5 and 6). In the first place it shows that women's wages, beginning at the same low rate as men's (about 2,000 yen per month) do not rise to anything like the same level as the latter; the maximum pay for a woman is almost exactly half the male maximum. Further, while salaries for female office workers are markedly higher than the wages of female operatives, the difference in the wages of men is very slight. Another striking point is the decrease in earnings from the age of 45 onwards and even earlier in the case of women. The most striking conclusion of the investigation, however, and one of outstanding significance for the purpose of the present report, is that, until the age of 30 at least, young men are kept in an extremely precarious position financially: the wages

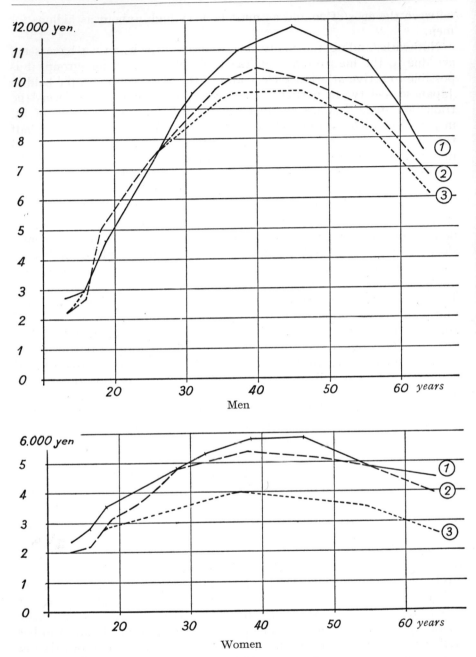

I = Executives; 2 = Office workers; 3 = Factory workers

Figs. 5 and 6. Monthly cash salaries in industry in 1948 (*Japan Statistical Yearbook*, p. 302)

are so low that it is not even possible to pay different rates according to ability—the three curves, for executives, office workers and operatives are practically identical and there are even indications that those who will later rise highest in the salary scale, i.e. the executives, are penalized. If it is true that in a given society remuneration is proportionate, not to the value of the services rendered, but to the esteem in which that particular culture holds the various sociological categories to which the wage relates, or—which comes to the same thing—to the social influence of those categories, it becomes apparent that in Japan not only are women held in very low esteem, but also that the status of youth is very low. The reader will recall the remarks made in the preceding chapter about the economic obstacles impeding the emancipation of the young. The salaries of young people, like those of women throughout their working lives, cannot be more than token wages—and the young therefore remain extremely dependent on their families. It is not surprising that, despite new policies and new laws, this dependence should be reflected in attitudes and personality traits.

THE INTEGRATION OF THE YOUNG INTO JAPANESE SOCIETY

Traditionally, young Japanese are organized in associations of their own.[1] Although the authoritarian administrations of modern times revived and strengthened these associations and reorganized them on nationalistic lines, they by no means created them: all they did, in fact, was to take advantage of a very ancient and enduring cultural feature of Japanese society. Associations of young people—known as *waka-renju* or by other names according to the region—can be traced historically as far back as the Kamakura period; the likelihood is that they are still older, and are analogous to the male associations of the Pacific and of Formosa. They had their own meeting places (*wakamono-yado*), where the youths often passed the night, particularly in fishing villages, and they formed special *kumi* (*wakamono-gumi*) in the country villages. They played their part in the activities of the local Shinto cult, undertook certain police tasks and carried out local relief duties in the event of natural calamities. One of their original functions was to protect the local association, and, hence, not only was any national federation of *waka-renju* impossible, but in the Tokugawa epoch relations between the associations were strained. Their membership consisted of the local youths from the age of 13 or 14 up to marriageable age.

---

1. Cf. M. Ramming, op. cit., article: *Jungmännerbunde und Seinen-dan;* the writer has also used information supplied verbally by members of the Japanese Association of Cultural Science (see Chapter I, p. 27).

The rapid Westernization of Japan at the time of the Meiji reform caused considerable disorganization of the *waka-renju*. However, about the period 1880-90, a revival of the old traditions, at the instigation of a schoolmaster, Yamamoto Takinosuke, led to the creation of the *seinen-dan* (youth organization). This organization rendered great service during the wars of 1894-95 and 1904-05, and attracted the attention of the government, particularly that of the War Minister, Tanaka. Under the régime which ended with Japan's defeat, the *seinen-dan* were closely linked with the local primary schools, whose headmasters were their leaders. At Suye-Mura, it was found that the difference between the *seinen-dan* and the *seinen-gakko* (youth school) was purely technical and the various *seinen-dan* of each prefecture came under the control of the director of education of the prefectorial government. Their activities were many-sided—cultural, physical and pre-military training, religious (Shinto), and social (relief service). They were the guardians of patriotic tradition, were responsible for the protection of monuments, and undertook civil defence in time of war. They were organized on a local basis, but there were federal organizations at county, prefecture, and national levels. A document of 1937 records that there were more than 15,000 youth associations of this type, with nearly two-and-a-half million members. The corresponding organizations for girls were of later date but almost as numerous in that year: over 13,000, with a total membership of one-and-a-half million.

As will be seen in the next chapter, the occupation authorities tried to put a stop to the regimentation of youth, but the institutions for organizing young people and absorbing them into the life of the community still survive and, moreover, they rest on such an ancient historical foundation and are so deeply rooted in the national culture at its most authentic, that there is not likely to be any modification of the collectivist spirit they imply.

There is no question but that this spirit—the feeling of dependence and of respect for hierarchy—is inculcated first of all in the family. Ruth Benedict laid great stress on these aspects of family life and early childhood education and her views have been approved by Japanese experts.[1] A child learns, from his babyhood, to bow to the father of the family and takes part in social observances even before he can walk: his mother, who carries him everywhere on her back, pushes his head down whenever she herself bows. Moreover, the child absorbs the idea that the world is full of danger and that he needs his family. In Takishima island (Okayama prefecture) children are not allowed to go to the beach alone and are never let out of sight; they are also forbidden

---

1. See for instance Takeyoshi Kawashima, *Evaluation and Critique* [*Japanese Journal of Ethnology* (Minzokugaku-Kenkyu)], special number on the questions raised by *The Chrysanthemum and the Sword*, 1949, 14, No. 4, 1-8, p. 7 (in Japanese).

to climb trees, though they are told that this is to protect the tree.[1]

Even the refuge of home has its share of dangers. It is lightly built on piles: one should not step on the threshold or even stand or sit over the joints of the thick mats (*tatami*) with which the floor is covered, for in the old days, the children are told, the Samurai used to thrust their swords up through the cracks and transfix the people inside. However, one is quite safe and comfortable on the *tatami*.

In the writer's view the most original features of a Japanese upbringing are the smooth assimilation of a strict system of discipline, adjustment without stress to an exacting society, and a combination of the sense of dependence and the sense of security. It is probably true, as Ruth Benedict asserts, (op. cit. p. 254) that, by contrast with the West, where the maximum degree of liberty is achieved in middle life, in Japan it is probably the children and the old people who enjoy the greatest freedom. However, a point which is probably of still greater importance is that a Japanese, on reaching man's estate, already has the habits of dependence and trustful respect thoroughly ingrained.

To understand how this can be possible, the discipline to which children are subjected should be examined in detail. In Takashima it is much commoner for children to be rebuked or praised than thrashed or rewarded; rewards are few because the people are poor; thrashing is infrequent— at first, because a baby is not a reasoning creature, and later on, because, if children are beaten they will beat other children. It is true that children are sometimes pinched or pricked with needles; the main physical deterrent however is the *moxa*, used more as a threat than in practice; but the *moxa* is a treatment rather than a punishment and the child knows that even the most obstinate disposition cannot hold out against three applications of *moxa*.[2] Hierarchy according to age and sex is accepted dogmatically. At Suye-mura, Embree noticed that when mothers go to the local shrine with their children they make the daughter walk behind because she is a lady and the boy is a gentleman, that the eldest son is better treated than his juniors, and that boys can hit their mother when they are angry and call her *baka* (idiot). However, the pattern of daily life is more complex and less rigid than certain writers would allow one to suppose. In Takashima, notwithstanding the privilege of age, mothers stand up for the younger children because they are the weaker. Again, daughters receive less money because they are only girls, and are, it is said, treated more strictly than the boys, because they will leave their

---

1. For these observations and a number of others which follow the writer is indebted to Maggie Norbeck, whose recent and still unpublished work he consulted in the files of the University of Michigan centre of Japanese studies at Okayama (cf. Chapter VI, p. 23).
2. The *moxa* or *mogusa* (same pronunciation) is a ball of vegetable tow taken from the underneath side of artemisia-leaves, which is placed on the back of the patient and lit with a stick of incense. When the flame dies out, the still smouldering tow is crushed out on the skin with the finger.

family in due course and must be better behaved to avoid disgracing their parents. However, it was also noticed at Takashima, that, despite the local practice of supporting the younger children, the mother took the daughter's part in quarrels with her brothers even when she was older than they. Lastly, the father, who is indulgent to his young children, becomes progressively stricter as they grow older and it is to the mother that the children give most of their affection.

An extremely interesting investigation undertaken as part of the programme of research on tensions, suggested by Unesco, provides detailed information on the position of young people in the family towards the beginning of adolescence.[1] It is not possible to say to what extent the village investigated—Kawabe-mura (Nagano prefecture)—is representative, but it seems at least that the observations made in the course of the enquiry do not conflict with the facts already known, and indeed in some respects amplify them. The method adopted was to start by studying a child and from there go on to study the child's whole family; 95 families in all were investigated. The children selected in the first instance were pupils in their second year at the Kawabe secondary school, who were members of the local youth association; there were 53 boys and 42 girls. In the first place this investigation makes it possible to form an idea of the way the family is built up. The average number of persons per family was 7.31 per cent; 16 per cent of the children had their grandfather living with them, 29 per cent their grandmother, 89 per cent their father, 98 per cent their mother; each had an average of 3.73 brothers or sisters; and finally, 7 per cent had uncles or aunts in the household, 10 per cent a sister-in-law, and 12 per cent had nephews or nieces.

The enquiry showed that the treatment of the young varied markedly with their sex. As regards physical well-being the boys were far better cared for; no boy looked after his own underclothing, whereas a third of the girls did their own laundry and dressmaking. Nineteen per cent of the boys got their own breakfast, compared with 33 per cent of the girls; for these services children relied mainly on their mother or elder sister; however, 2 per cent of the boys examined depended on their grandmothers for laundry and sewing, and in 5 per cent of the cases, the girls had their breakfasts prepared by their grandmothers. All the children in the group were given cakes from time to time, especially by their mother; this happened with 81 per cent of the boys and 78 per cent of the girls; cakes were also given by the grandfather or grandmother, father and elder sister, but male relatives gave cakes to the male children only, whereas 17 per cent of the girls got them from their grandmothers.

Parents introduce their children to the local community by taking

---

1. Here we have drawn on an unpublished report by Morioka; the investigation, under the direction of Yuzuru Okada, was carried out by Morita, Morioka, and Mrs. Ohama in December 1951.

them along when they go visiting, and on these occasions a clear-cut difference appears between the sexes: the boys count more for their visits on their fathers or brothers, and the girls on their mothers or sisters. In addition 21 per cent of the boys and only 2 per cent of the girls pay visits unaccompanied. The girls are helped with their studies a little more than boys are: here the role of the mother is least important; on the other hand that of the elder brother is extremely prominent, even more so than that of the father, and the eldest sister also does a great deal to help, though more with her younger sisters than with her brothers. In general, it is their mothers that young people regard as the most accessible; but in some cases the girls also mention their grandmothers and the boys their grandfathers or elder brothers, of course after their fathers, who come second.

The above data are set out in tabular form below:

TABLE 3.

				Rely on				
	No one	Grand-father	Grand-mother	Father	Mother	Elder brother	Elder sister	Others
Boys	%	%	%	%	%	%	%	%
Sewing and laundry	0	0	2	0	77	0	17	2
Getting breakfast	19	0	0	0	63	0	16	2
Gifts of cakes	19	2	7	2	82	0	6	0
Pocket money	19	2	0	60	34	0	2	0
Escort on visits	21	0	2	34	21	9	4	4
Help in school work	21	0	0	23	8	34	15	4
Approachability	21	2	0	26	68	2	2	0
Girls								
Sewing and laundry	31	0	0	0	57	0	12	0
Getting breakfast	33	0	5	0	52	0	10	0
Gifts of cakes	33	0	17	0	78	0	5	0
Pocket money	33	2	2	77	19	0	0	0
Escort on visits	2	0	0	36	48	0	12	0
Help in school work	2	0	0	24	14	29	24	2
Approachability	2	0	7	29	62	0	0	0

The exercise of discipline within the family also varies considerably, with correspondingly varied reactions on the part of the young people. Discipline is enforced mainly by the mother, the father, and the elder brother; the grandmother and the eldest sister also play a part, but mainly in respect of the daughters. The role of the mother is to praise rather than to blame whereas that of the father is the opposite; the eldest brother blames more than he praises, particularly when dealing with his sisters, and the tendency for the grandmother is to confine her rebukes mainly to her grandsons and to praise her granddaughters. Generally speaking, the girls appear to be treated on the whole slightly more strictly than the boys, but one's main impression is that the enforcers of discipline favour the young people of their own sex: except in the case of the father, the part they play in the upbringing of the young, by praising or blaming, is greater when they are dealing with the youngsters of their own sex, and in this case they also tend to praise more often than they rebuke; the partiality of the mothers, and still more of the grandmothers, is particularly evident.

The disciplinary agents who count most with the young are mostly those of the male sex; for instance, the number of children who are praised or blamed by their mothers is far greater than the number who are sensitive to the praise or the blame; the opposite is true where the father is concerned, whatever the sex of the child. The authority of the grandmother and the eldest sister is small; that of the eldest brother is higher with the boys, and that of the grandfather higher with the girls. Broadly, with the exception of their attitudes to their father and eldest brother, the boys bother far less than the girls about rebukes or praise and on the whole they appear a little less dependent, though the difference is not very great. Table 4, prepared from the data given in Morioka's report, gives a general picture of the situation:

TABLE 4.

	Grand-father	Grand-mother	Father	Mother	Eldest brother	Eldest sister	Others
Boys	%	%	%	%	%	%	%
Praise	6	4	26	49	9	2	2
Rebukes	6	8	32	21	23	4	0
Praise giving pleasure	2	0	38	43	8	0	0
Rebukes taken seriously	4	4	45	9	23	4	0
Girls							
Praise	2	12	24	57	0	5	0
Rebukes	2	7	36	17	29	7	2
Praise giving pleasure	5	5	26	50	5	2	0
Rebukes taken seriously	7	5	52	5	19	2	5

Lastly, when children reach the age of adolescence the order of preference in their family attachments becomes apparent. For boys and girls alike, the favourite parent is the mother; so far as the boys are concerned the grandfather comes second, the father third, and the grandmother fourth. Among the girls, second place goes to the grandmother, third to the father, and fourth to the grandfather. These of course are conscious responses only, as they were given to an investigator, and are valid both for the individual subject and for the group. The mother, who enjoys less prestige than the father, is at the same time the object of the strongest attachment on the part of her children of both sexes; on the other hand the symmetrical position occupied by the grandfather and grandmother in the affections of their grandsons and granddaughters probably reflects the children's identifications and hostilities in the matter of sex distinction.

The pattern of preferential attachments to brothers and sisters is equally interesting and likewise raises questions which one would like to see more thoroughly explored. On the part of the boys the strongest attachment is to the eldest brother, with the eldest sister second, the younger brother third and the younger sister fourth; among the girls the first place goes to the eldest sister, the second to the younger brother, the third to the younger sister and the fourth to the eldest brother. The same dissymmetry that was shown in the children's attachments to their parents and grandparents is observable here. The places occupied by the eldest brother and the eldest sister in the affections of boys and girls respectively suggests an identification of the subject with the privileged child of his or her own sex; that the boys put the younger sister last shows the double effect of the social hierarchy of age and sex; and that the girls put the eldest brother last probably reflects an hostility reaction: here the situation is analogous to that of the grandparents in the affections of their grandchildren of the opposite sex. Perhaps the most interesting fact that emerges from these observations is the subjects' choice of the person holding second place in their affections— the elder sister in the case of the boys and the younger brother in the case of the girls. With all possible qualifications, one is tempted to advance the hypothesis that these reactions express on the part of the boys a need to be protected and on the part of the girls a need to protect. It would be desirable to pursue the matter further, and also to make comparisons between different cultures.

DIFFICULTIES AND DEMORALIZATION OF THE YOUNG

Once the general characteristics of the place occupied by young people in Japanese society are outlined and what might be called the constants of their circumstances briefly analysed, an investigation dealing essentially with the present condition of young people would concentrate on defining the new problems facing them, particularly the difficulties arising out of the war and the defeat. The absence of the father, for instance, has given rise to serious problems. Up to the age of 10 (i.e. in the case of youngsters who were 16 years old in 1952) the effects of this absence were not serious, but they may have been far-reaching in the case of older boys and girls, who found it more difficult to get work, and in a more general way miss their father's support in the family and in society. Difficult situations have also arisen as a result of the migratory flux and reflux. Many children who were brought into the towns during the war and later taken back into the country, have only one desire—to get back to the town. This is also true of those evacuated from the towns because of the destruction of their homes; repatriated settlers from abroad (Korea, Manchuria and other lost territories); and second and third sons whose family property is so subdivided that it is no longer possible for them to wrest a living from the land if they want to set up independent households of their own. The disappearance of the black market has also done away with an important source of cash earnings.

The young undoubtedly have cause for anxiety, discontent and demoralization, for loss of confidence in the family and a lessening of interest in the family ideals; at Kawabe-mura, half the young people no longer accept parental decisions concerning their marriage, and the remainder do so grudgingly. It is very difficult, however, in the absence of accurate and representative data, to estimate how widespread this state of affairs may be. Many mistakes can be made by relying on limited personal observations or incomplete documentation collected haphazard. Some writers, for instance, point to an alleged recrudescence of suicides, but this is hardly borne out by the statistics for the last 20 years (it is a fact that the suicide rate goes down in wartime, and Japan is no exception; hence those who rely on limited documentation draw the wrong conclusions). The West continues to inveigh against the traffic in young people, but the confirmed official figures are very low and the real extent of the traffic is unknown (in 1951, 432 such cases were dealt with in one prefecture—Yamagata, in northern Honshu, an increase of 500 per cent over the preceding year, but the total number of persons proceeded against was only 34).[1]

As the investigations described in the present work were focused on other problems and detailed documentation is lacking, it would be rash to go further than the very general assertions made above. However, one well established fact is the considerable increase, both relative and absolute, in juvenile delinquency and crime. The proportion of young people among those serving their first term in prison, which long remained relatively constant, has risen considerably since the end of the war. Whereas in 1926 percentages were 3 per cent for the under 18, 6 per cent for the ages of 18 and 19 and 42 per cent for the 20-29 age-group, the corresponding percentages for 1946 are 6 per cent, 10 per cent and 44 per cent and for 1948—the last year for which statistics are available—5 per cent, 11 per cent and 53 per cent. In absolute terms, the number of crimes committed by persons under 25 years of age rose from 97,674 in 1943 to 267,494 in 1949, an increase of 174 per cent. Taking the 1943 figures as a basis, the indices of the principal categories of offences were the following in 1949 (1943 being taken as 100); general index 274; arson,

---

1. From the *Japan News* for March 1952. Recent information on this subject is contained in Jean Keim's *Mon Japon du demi-siècle*, Paris, 1952.

194; theft, 249; homicide, 530; rape, 458; robbery with violence, 1,280. There is more than the normal proportion of sexual crime among young people in the 14-19 age-group, while persons between 20 and 24 years of age account for more than their share of gambling offences, homicide and robbery with violence.

These objective facts are undoubtedly very significant and would be an interesting subject for discussion in themselves. In any case they are a reliable indication of the difficulties experienced by certain young people in adapting themselves to society, and of the demoralization they reflect and of which they are the victims. This aspect of the situation should be kept in mind, with the others outlined in this chapter, when we come to study recent attitudes of Japanese youth. However, before giving an account of the enquiry undertaken by Unesco in this sphere, it is necessary to give a rapid review of the peculiar features of the present situation in Japan, particularly of the more important reforms to which certain institutions have been subjected.

CHAPTER IV

THE RECENT REFORMS

GENERAL OUTLINE OF THE NEW SITUATION

The present situation in Japan shows the very deep impress of the war and of the defeat. The country is faced with serious economic and demographic problems. The average standard of living, always low compared to that of the West, has fallen considerably: on the basis of 100 in 1934-36, it sank to 58 in 1947 and was still no higher than 75 in 1950. The population, long stationary, and unwisely encouraged to multiply since the Meiji era, is now reaching a figure which alarms many Japanese. With the end of hostilities, the already heavy birth-rate was increased as a result of repatriation: not counting the return of about 3 million servicemen—who, indeed, would not have left the country but for the war—an almost equal number of Japanese had to quit the lost territories: these repatriations exceeded by 2 millions the number of foreigners leaving the country. Agriculture and commerce have absorbed many who would otherwise have been unemployed, but this is not a healthy solution: what is needed to secure a proper balance between the national economy and the growing population is that industry should find 720,000 new jobs a year for 10 years to come.[1] On the financial side the classical and disastrous phenomenon of inflation has made its appearance, bringing with it a giddy rise in prices (see fig. 7).[2]

However, although the economic and social position is still less than mediocre, it is improving, as even the most superficial study of all the statistics shows. After the collapse of 1944-45, the 1949 index of industrial activity was higher than that for 1930; the production and consumption of rice are rising; and over the last few years wages in industry have risen more than real prices (see figs. 8 to 11). This improvement is often felt by the Japanese public; while it would be out of place, after a shock as severe as that suffered by Japan, to speak of enthusiasm about the future, there is, at least, something approaching optimism.

---

1. Cf. Ayanori Okasaki's remarkable article 'Demographic Problems and Demographic policy in Japan', *Population*, 1952, 7, 207-26.
2. The reader is referred to Hyoye Ouchi: *The Financial and Monetary Situation in Post-war Japan*, Tokyo, 1948.

In 1950 the newspaper *Asahi* undertook a public opinion poll on the way the public was looking forward to the coming year, as regards both their personal prospects and those of the country; optimism and pessimism were evenly balanced in replies to the first question, whereas, in the second, optimism carried the day (see Table 5).

TABLE 5.

	Better	No change	Worse	No opinion
	%	%	%	%
Personal prospects	25	22	27	26
Economic prospects for Japan	31	14	6	39

Thus, disastrous though it was, the war seems to have meant no more to the Japanese than one catastrophe among others. The horror of the bombs that fell on Hiroshima and Nagasaki will not quickly be forgotten,[1] but there one is in the realm of feeling: on the realistic plane the Japanese are gritting their teeth and rebuilding the ruins, treating the whole incident as an item in the nation's profit and loss account.

Japan has suffered a much greater convulsion: the reforms enforced or suggested by the Occupying Power, and put into effect or accepted by the Japanese themselves, aim at nothing less than the complete overthrow of the traditional social structure. In its long history Japan has, of course, known far-reaching reforms, but the purpose behind these reforms was always to confirm the nation in what it deemed to be its vocation. Even the tremendous changes of the Meiji era were not, in intention at least, a recasting of society, but a restoration. For all practical purposes the reforms of today are tantamount to a revolution. That, in the early days at least, was what the Occupying Power wanted, and the Japanese themselves were under no delusion about it:

'(The problem was) to make it impossible for Japan to embark again on a war of aggression as it had done in the past. If the Japanese had been a people in whom confidence could be placed, the task would have been relatively easy. But seeing that the Americans as a whole looked upon the Japanese as a hopeless case, a nation of war-like fanatics, it followed that they had to abolish all means whereby Japan might prepare for war and all the country's industrial war potential. At the same time radical changes would have to be made in Shintoism and in the Imperial régime which were at the root of Japanese fanaticism; in the Zaibatsu, which were the stumbling block in the way of the country's democratization, and in the other Japanese organizations. Though the task might

---

1. See the special number of the *Asahi Picture News* (in Japanese), 6 August 1952, and the photographic album *Hiroshima and the Atom Bomb*, Tokyo, 1952 (in Japanese).

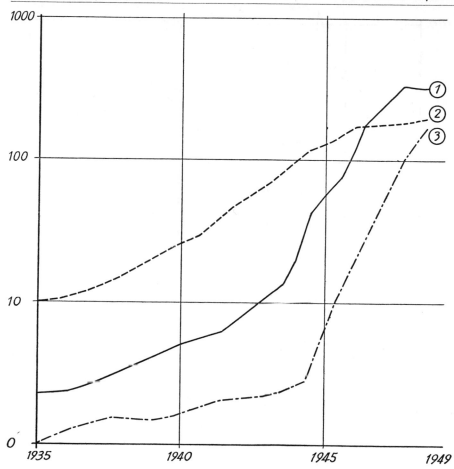

1 = Bank note issue (in 1,000 million yen) (*J.S.Y.*, p. 246).
2 = Treasury bonds outstanding (in 1,000 million yen) (*ibid*, p. 274).
3 = Index of wholesale prices at Tokyo (*ibid*, p. 285).

Fig. 7. Rate of inflation in Japan (semi-logarithmic scale)

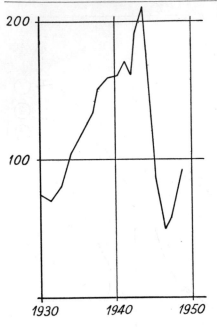

Fig. 8. Index of industrial
activity (*J.S.Y.* p. 174-5)

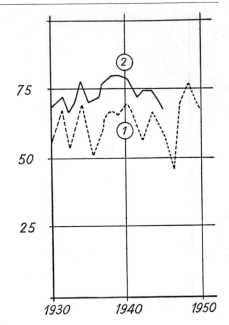

1 = Production
2 = Consumption

(in millions of *koku*)

Fig. 9. Rice production and
consumption (*J.S.Y.* p. 178)

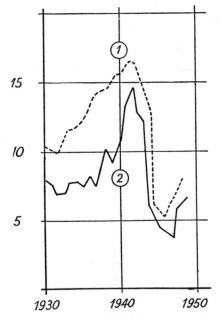

Fig. 10. Tea production and
consumption (*J.S.Y.* p. 178)

1 = Production
2 = Consumption
(in millions of *kan*)

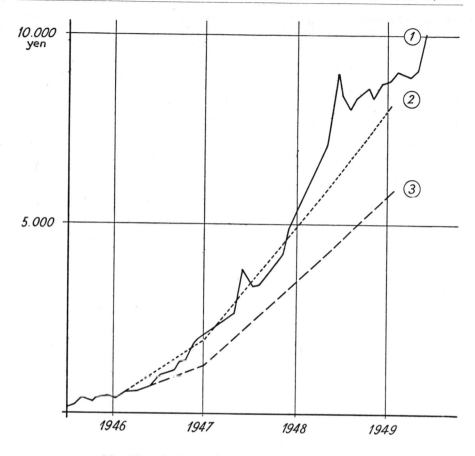

1 = Monthly salaries in industry (*J.S.Y.*, p. 312)
2 = Index of retail prices in Tokyo (*J.S.Y.*, p. 271)*
3 = Index of wholesale prices in Tokyo (*J.S.Y.*, p. 285)*
* Brought to the same scale

Fig. 11. Monthly salaries in industry and index of prices

take a very long time, Japan would have to be occupied until it was completed and its people entirely re-educated.[1]

In order to give a clear idea of the conditions in which the enquiry decided on by Unesco concerning the attitudes of Japanese youth was conducted, it is therefore essential to attempt to describe some at least of these reforms, just as it was also necessary to give a brief sketch of the traditional culture and to define the special place reserved in it for the young. It will not be possible to go into details, nor shall we try to draw up a balance sheet for its own sake. We shall, however, endeavour to define the new legal and social environment which presents itself to Japanese youth. The new arrangements frequently conflict, of course, with the traditional culture, since they were originally intended to supplant it. Accordingly the young, who have not so far found their final status in the community, will have to make choices, and their present position is essentially ambiguous.

The reforms carried out in Japan since 1945 are immense. To put them briefly: Japan renounces for ever the rebuilding of an army; the Emperor is now merely the 'symbol' of the nation, to which the sovereignty has passed; State religion has been abolished; the Zaibatsu have been dispersed and dissolved; there has been redistribution of the land in a vast agrarian reform; sex equality has been proclaimed; young people are free to marry as they will; the law of inheritance has been revised; there have been extensive innovations in education and youth organizations have been democratized. Statements such as these are however rather crudely over-simplified and require explanation and qualification. As it is not possible to enter here into an exhaustive study of the way the measures in question were introduced, of their precise significance and of their repercussions on Japanese society, we shall at least try to give a brief explanation of the changes that have taken place in the Imperial régime, the law of the family, and the school system, and also of what has been attempted with regard to youth movements.[2]

---

1. Toru Haguiwara, *Taisen no Kaibo* (analysis of the Great War) Tokyo, 1950, pp. 89-90 (in Japanese).
2. With reference to the armed forces the Constitution is concise and explicit: The Japanese people abjures war as a sovereign right of the nation and abjures threats or force as a means of resolving international differences. Japan will never maintain land, sea or air forces or any other warlike resources (Article 9). As regards religious questions, the reader is referred to Tadao Yanaibara's *Religion and Democracy in Modern Japan*, Tokyo, 1948; on agrarian reform see Shirokuro Yamaguchi's *Some Aspects of Agrarian Reform in Japan*, Tokyo, 1948. Reference should also be made to Raper, etc. *The Japanese Village in Transition*, Tokyo, 1950.

REFORM OF THE EMPEROR'S STATUS AND OF THE IMPERIAL SYSTEM

The terms of the Japanese surrender on 15 August 1945 virtually put an end to the absolute power of the Emperor, who accepted the Potsdam declaration requiring the 'revival and strengthening of the democratic tendeney among the Japanese people' and the 'adoption of a political structure based on the freely expressed will of the people.' As one writer puts it, since Japan had accepted this, it had no other means of regaining the confidence of the world as a peace-loving nation than by reforming the traditional political system and establishing a democratic political structure. Obviously in the course of these reforms it was inevitable that the status and power of the Emperor, who was the supreme head of the traditional political structure, would also have to undergo certain changes if the clauses of the declaration were to be faithfully carried out'. [1] In the event, after much discussion, the text of the revised Constitution, published by the Japanese Government on 17 April 1946, dealt with the status and powers of the Emperor in the preamble and in the first article. According to the English translation which appeared in the *Nippon Times*, these two passages read as follows: 'We, the Japanese people ..., do proclaim the sovereignty of the people's will and do ordain and establish this Constitution. Government is a sacred trust of the people, the contents for which is derived from the people, the powers of which are exercised by the representatives of the people, and the benefits of which are enjoyed by the people.' (Preamble.) Again, Article I reads: 'The Emperor shall be the symbol of the State and of the unity of the people, deriving his position from the sovereign will of the people.' These passages are clear enough: the Emperor has the status of a symbol, derived from the sovereign will of the people: Lincoln's democratic formula 'Government of the people by the people, for the people', is faithfully paraphrased, and for good measure the opening words of the American Constitution, '*We, the people of the United States* ...' have been copied. Earlier in the same year, the Emperor had solemnly declared in the Imperial Rescript of 1 January 1946: 'I am not a living God.' The bases of blind subjection to Imperial power, which the militaristic governments knew so well how to exploit, thus appear to have been done away with altogether.

In practice, and viewed from the Japanese angle, things are not quite so simple. In the first place, the writer to whom we are referring points out that the English translation is not strictly equivalent to the Japanese original; where the English text speaks of the 'sovereignty of the will of the people', the Japanese reads only '(We proclaim) that the general will of the people is supreme'; similarly in place of 'the sovereign will'

---

1. Genji Okubo, *The Problems of the Emperor System in Post-War Japan*, Tokyo, 1948, 87 pp., p. 19. The analysis which follows is in essence based on this booklet.

('holding his position by the sovereign will of the people') the Japanese text reads 'the supreme general will'. That is not the same thing, and in any case, for reasons not given, the translator has avoided rendering the original exactly into English. Moreover, the word 'people', used throughout in the translation does not appear in the original, where the word employed is not *jin-min* (people) but *kokumin* (nation), a word that commonly denotes the body of the people, transcending all classes, in its relations with foreign countries.

In Okubo's view there is not the slightest doubt that the use of *kokumin* instead of *jin-min* is responsible for much debate in the Diet, caused by uncertainty as to where sovereignty really lies; the use of the word *jin-min* would have defined the position clearly and unequivocally.

That, however, is not all. The new Constitution, for which the Yoshida government became responsible after the elections of 1946, had been drawn up by the outgoing Shidehara government, which had published its main provisions on 6 March. There was great surprise when it was seen that the Shidehara government had reduced the Emperor's status to that of a symbol and had considerably restricted his prerogatives, since this administration represented the same interests as the administration of Prince Higashikuni, formed after the defeat, which, having learned nothing and forgotten nothing, found it necessary to resign following the receipt of certain orders from the occupation authorities (SCAP). Tamon Maeda, Minister of Education in the Shidehara cabinet, had no hesitation in saying: 'Japanese democracy must be the new guiding principle of teachers now that hostilities are over. In other words it must be based on the idea that the relationship between the Emperor and the people, should be formally that of "sovereign and subjects" but in practice that of "father and sons". Teachers will not be permitted to criticize the Imperial régime in the classroom.' The final decision taken by the Shidehara government appears to have been dictated by the determination to limit the damage. In publishing its text on 6 March, the Government 'explained that it had to be as pacific and democratic as it was in order to protect the national régime by dispersing all doubts in the minds of the Allied Powers about a possible repetition of aggressive war by Japan. In other words, the Government wished to preserve the Emperor by any and every means'. If this is indeed so, the words of the Constitution, in so far as they prescribe the powers of the people, should be taken in as limited a sense as possible.

The attitude of the Yoshida government in the subsequent discussions is still more disturbing. At no point was it prepared to use unequivocal terms in reply to requests for clarification regarding the seat of sovereignty. Here, for instance, is an extract from a reply by Kanamori, Minister of State: 'If sovereignty is to be understood as signifying the real source of the motive power of the activities of the State, or the will of the State, it will be found to reside in the people as a whole, including the Emperor....

The source of the State's will is not to be found directly in the ideas of individuals, nor is it held that the ideas of individuals are the direct fount of sovereignty. It is only through the unity of the people that the ideas of individuals are associated in the will of the State. Looked at in this light, the essence of sovereignty may be said to derive from the will of the people organized in a community that includes the Emperor as one of its members. The unity of the people results, I think, from the ties of sentiment linking individuals together. In the accepted technical terminology, the individual wills of the people are represented by the will of the national co-operative entity.'

Thus the government takes refuge behind complicated theories—too complicated for someone merely wishing to acknowledge the sovereignty of the people. Yet that is what the Constitution is thought to mean. As Professor Shigeru Nambara, President of the University of Tokyo, pointed out in the House of Peers: 'It is quite clear, from the Preamble and Article I of the revised Constitution, that sovereignty now resides in the people. The Emperor is no longer the source of the supreme will of the Japanese people. Why does not the Government frankly state this obvious fact?' It may also be pointed out that in Kanamori's explanation, as in all those given by the Yoshida government, the interpretation of the terms of the Constitution always depends on the acceptance of a particular hypothesis ('if sovereignty is to be understood as signifying . . . '), leaving one with the impression that with a different hypothesis, the interpretation might also be different.

Lastly, in almost every instance government spokesmen are also at pains to introduce sentimental and moral considerations into their statements. In his answer to Nambara, Kanamori said: 'The fate of the national régime is indissolubly bound up with that of the State itself. The basic principle of the people's unity and the object of its adoration throughout the centuries, is the Emperor. In this sense the national character is unshakeable and unchangeable'. . . . As long as the Emperor exists as the moral centre of the nation and the object of its devotion, and as long as the identity of the State and the continuity of the laws are accepted, there can be no change in the national régime of this country. What changes is only the country's form of government.'

Thus the apparent explicitness of the terms of the new Constitution, particularly in its English translation, misleads ill-informed foreign readers. In reality, none of its provisions is decisive, because the desire was to avoid deciding anything. There will be complaints of duplicity and of machiavellism; people will say that what it was sought to do was to carry out the letter of SCAP's orders while at the same time confirming the ignorant masses in the impression that the Emperor, having been left on the throne, would continue to reign in the same conditions as emperors had done in the past, during that two thousand years or so of which so much is made. From the point of view of the present study the intentions

93

and responsibilities of the members of the government are of little importance; what matters is that these debates have given rise to a state of confusion and ambiguity in the country, compelling those individuals who are capable of it to make their own choice themselves. It hardly seems likely that this has been the aim of Japanese governments since the end of the war: nevertheless, thanks to them it will not be possible to say that, if real democracy succeeds in taking root in Japan, it will be as an importation pure and simple.

REFORM OF THE FAMILY AS AN INSTITUTION

The reform of the institution of the family is in some ways analogous to the reform of the imperial system. The motives of the authors of these two reforms appear to be very different and the results of their respective labours are in striking contrast: the new text of the civil code, in so far as it is prescriptive, does not allow for reading between the lines. But its authors, convinced of the importance of the family, and of the powerful values which the functioning of that institution calls into play, preferred in their turn to leave to the public the responsibility for making its own choice in certain directions.

As regards the family in particular, the revision of the Japanese civil code is a natural consequence of the revision of the Constitution.[1] Once this revision was accepted in principle (and this was not achieved without serious difficulties and the rousing of strong emotions, in which the imperial question was only one element), the tenor of the new code, conforming to the new democratic principles, gained wide approval. It should however be mentioned that the drafting of the new text also entailed lively discussions. In the course of this work, three trends became apparent: the conservatives were insistent on preserving the traditional co-operative character of the family; the young jurists were mainly concerned with ensuring the equality and dignity of all members of the family; and finally there was a party of compromise, which, while agreeing that radical reforms should be carried out as fully as possible, were still anxious to maintain continuity between the law and traditional practice. A typical example of the part played by this last section is their attitude towards family religion: they disapproved of it and refused to agree to legal measures designed to facilitate its official observance; but recognizing that this cult is still practised and that it might lead to litigation, they secured the inclusion of provisions for limiting or regulating litigation. During the course of the discussions

1. See Sakae Wagatsuma: 'Democratization of the Family Relation in Japan', *Washington Law Revue*, 1950, 25, 405-26. Professor Wagatsuma took part in the work of the sub-commission responsible for drafting the reforms.

another anxiety came to light—in this instance with no ideological implications: as agricultural land in Japan was already very subdivided, it was necessary to avoid any provisions that would cut up the land into such tiny portions that it would no longer be possible to farm it.

A first group of provisions deals with the family name and the family cult. In law these are two separate matters, but sociologically they are closely connected. Many families preserve a deep sentimental attachment for their name which they want to perpetuate, like the cult of the family ancestors. The problem which arises—a double problem in law but in practice often one and indivisible—is how the family name and the family religious obligations are to be handed on. If there is no male heir an answer is found in adoption, the adopted son being often the husband of the eldest daughter. On the other hand, ought a person to be at liberty to give up the family name, e.g. in the case of a widow wanting to remarry?

Article 750 of the new code provides that 'husband and wife shall adopt the family name (*uji*) of the husband or the wife as they shall jointly decide at the time of marriage'. Article 810 lays it down that: 'an adopted child shall take the name of the person adopting it'. Thus, despite the objections of those who see in its preservation a symbol of the continuance of the extended family, the *uji* is saved: the son-in-law can adopt the family name of his wife's family and the family name may be carried on by anyone, through adoption, provided he is not older than the person adopting him. On the other hand the *uji* can be abandoned in the event of divorce, widowhood or the dissolution of the adoptive relationship. The difference now is that abandonment of the *uji* has no material consequences. The rights of inheritance of a natural child or of a married daughter who has adopted another *uji* are not affected thereby. A woman adopting a different surname from that of her children after divorce or remarriage does not compromise her children's right to inherit from her; and a widow, whether or not she has changed her *uji*, must make a formal declaration if she wishes to break the links of her existing 'in-law' relationship. In short, what the legislature has sought to do is no more than to ensure that the *uji*, to which many people remain attached, can still be handed down and perpetuated.

Things are different as regards the cult of the family ancestors. The new law refuses it official support: it does not lay down that whoever inherits the family religious duties must also inherit the goods (apart from sacred objects) he requires to discharge them. However, the existence of the ancestor cult is legally recognized: Article 897 provides that the ownership of genealogical documents, the sacred objects of the cult, tombs and burial ground shall pass to a person nominated by the testator to be the head of the cult of the family ancestors. Essentially, the family religion becomes a matter of concern to the new law only in cases where it gives rise to litigation.

An adopted child or a son-in-law who has taken the *uji* of the adopting family or the wife's family and abandons it on the dissolution of the adopted relationship, or on divorce, is required, if he has inherited sacred objects of the cult, to hand them over to some person better qualified to exercise that cult. The purpose of this provision is to make divorce or termination of the adoptive relationship easier for the other party by reassuring them as regards the exercise of the cult. A similar purpose lies behind Article 897, which provides that a testator may nominate the heir to the cult: this is meant, in particular, to cover the case of a family where the eldest son has gone to seek his fortune in the town and the second son, who has stayed at home, is better placed to carry out the religious obligation. Thus is cannot be said that the law encourages the traditional family or ancestor worship; but neither, on the other hand, does it prevent either of these institutions from functioning.

The same caution is found in the new provisions concerning marriage and the status of women. Parental or equivalent consent is no longer required for marriage: the decision of the future marriage partners is enough (Article 24 of the Constitution). A couple can therefore, if they like, override parental objections or, conversely, a young man or young woman can always decline to marry. To begin with, though, one is bound to ask how young men and women can become acquainted in a country where the behaviour of youth is governed by the Confucian precept that boys and girls must not 'sit together after the age of seven'. There are, of course, people who hope for much from the newly introduced system of co-education; but against this, we have to set the entrenched habit of centuries, and in many rural areas there is not much respect for the will of the young. Lastly, the young person's moral obligations towards his or her own family subsist; eldest sons, in particular, are very conscious of the obligations falling on them and of their duty to marry when and as their family decides. In reality what the law provides is merely the chance of freedom; it is for the young to take advantage of it, if they so desire and if they want freedom badly enough. As Wagatsuma very justly observes, 'since family life is influenced by tradition, the Code, despite the compromises, brings no immediate changes'.

The wife of the eldest son no longer has any obligations towards her relations-in-law. Sex inequality before the criminal law in cases of adultery has been done away with and no criminal charge can now be brought against a wife for adultery, any more than against a husband; novel, indeed, is the tendency of the law to consider that the husband has the same obligations of fidelity as the wife. A widow can resume her maiden name, remarry, or take her children away with her, without any authorization by her late husband's family. A wife securing a divorce can claim a share of the joint property. All these measures make a high degree of emancipation possible for women but none of them automatically delivers the married woman from the almost complete subjection to mother-in-law and husband which is her traditional lot. Many Japanese women already know what their new rights are, but it remains to be seen whether they will wish to use them. This is more than a mere matter of will; it is first and foremost a question of imagination; one frequently gets the impression that the Western ways of life described to Japanese women strike them as idealizations, not merely outside the range of possibility for them, but not quite realized anywhere else in the world.

The third category of reforms affecting family law relates to the extended family and the laws of inheritance. It will be recalled that the traditional family structure of Japan (which some authorities go so far as to describe as a clan structure) consists of a head of the family who exercises authority over a group composed of his kinsmen and children, with their wives and children. After much heated discussion, Article 730 of the revised civil code now lays it down that 'immediate blood relations and other kinsfolk living together should help one another'. This Article appears to confirm the principle of the extended family championed by the conservatives and savagely attacked by the younger generation of jurists. Wagatsuma, who emphasizes the compromise nature of this Article, points out that little more can be read into it than an exhortation or a statement of a moral precept; nowhere is any obligation laid on anyone to submit to such a life in common. It could of course be retorted that this is a lawyer's argument and that, while legally free to go where they will, many young persons are obliged by material necessity to remain within the protective orbit of the family, and in that case a decision has to be taken as to the exact meaning of the kind of co-operation legally established by Article 730. In actual fact, the indications are that a clear-cut decision on this point has been deliberately avoided: the extended family system is still possible, while at the same time the option of organization on another basis has been provided.

As regards inheritance, the share of the estate set aside for the children is half the total, the testator remaining free to dispose of the other half as he sees fit (Article 1028). In practice it is reckoned that frequently the whole of the free estate goes to the eldest son. Moreover, the authors of the inheritance law are under no illusions: if a father dies intestate, the decision of the family will be to carry out his implicit wishes, and (an even more important point) it is customary for the daughters to renounce their part of the estate and for the second and third sons to content themselves with a minute share. The frequency of such renunciations can be gathered from the records of the courts; in 1949, of 286,156 cases dealt with by the family courts, more than half, 148,192, related to renunciations of inheritance rights, 32 per cent by men, 67.2 per cent by women and 0.8 per cent by both. There are grounds for thinking that many similar renunciations take place in the agricultural regions of the north-east without recourse to the courts.

In one respect the government itself goes further than this in limiting the scope of Article 1028, though less for the sake of the eldest son than in deference to the technical needs of agriculture. Farms are already very small and it would be dangerous to permit further subdivision, so in 1949 the government resurrected a 1922 Bill entitled Regulations for the Inheritance of Rural Real Estate, under which the family holding would pass in its entirety to the son farming it, subject to the payment by him to his brothers of the cash value of their shares. However, the Bill was rejected both on grounds of principle (it was claimed to be anti-democratic) and for financial reasons (in most cases it would be impossible for the farmer to discharge his debt).

In general, reforms in family law—some of them enormous when compared with the traditional model—nevertheless reveal much caution. The idea behind them appears to have been twofold; in the first place, not to oppose changes that are pronounced desirable and are already taking place, particularly in a section of the urban population, and secondly, not to outlaw the old customs hallowed by tradition, which it is thought would survive in any case and which one section of parliamentary opinion holds should be allowed to survive. The authors of the reform have borne constantly in mind the need to keep down the amount of litigation likely to result from it, and to provide a basis for the settlement of any cases which do arise; technically they have shown great skill. In so far as one of the functions of the law is to prescribe conduct, they have been more timid, and have frequently preferred to follow custom rather than to lead the way, and to leave the responsibility of choosing to the general public.

EDUCATIONAL REFORM

Educational reforms affecting Japanese youth were tackled in a completely different spirit, and the work accomplished in this field consists, not of a series of limited or ambiguous changes but of a complete recasting of the system.[1]

This came about as a result of a combination of circumstances. As Haguiwara has well observed, the Americans arrived in Japan with the firm intention of re-educating the Japanese people, a process which begins at school level. A completely new educational system had to be devised. The victors could not fail to be struck by the effect on their

---

1. Cf. K. Yoshida and T. Kaigo, *Japanese Education*, Tokyo, 1937; *Report of the United States Education Mission to Japan*, Washington, 1946; *Progress of Education in Japan*, Tokyo, 1950 (published by the Ministry of Education); *Post-War Developments in Japanese Education*, 2 vols., Tokyo, 1952 (published by SCAT, CI and EB); the writer has also used unpublished documents and manuscripts of the Mompu-sho (Ministry of Education), of the new teaching of history.

late enemies of a totalitarian education, which it was therefore necessary to sweep away. There was also the known belief of the American public in education, as evinced by their efforts in that direction in their own country during the last half century. This unwavering faith in education is part and parcel of a whole philosophy of life that, encouraged by the successes with which we are all acquainted, ranks technology well above nature and, in dealing with human beings, attaches much more importance to acquired than to innate qualities. The peoples of Europe, strong in their past, may feel the ties of tradition and history. The American, striking forward with cheerful boldness, unhesitatingly guided by his ethical and political principles, attaches less importance to the material than to the way it is handled.

If we look at the matter from the Japanese point of view, we shall understand why, in the educational field, the fight put up for the established order was bound to be less determined than in the case, say, of the imperial or of the family system. Compared with these, the educational system, as it existed at the end of the war, was a recent growth, the system of popular education having been introduced in 1872 by a Ministry of Education established only a year earlier. Hence the weight of tradition could not counterbalance the authority of orders and suggestions emanating from the occupying power. These were accepted docilely and respectfully by the Japanese officials (see the introduction to *Progress of Education*). As regards the basic principle—the obligation to adopt a new outlook—this had already been accepted by the politicians.

The American services in charge (CI and ED, and SCAP) proved extremely active and vigilant, and it is impossible to exaggerate the importance of the part played by the American Education Mission which arrived in March 1946 and spent nearly a month in Japan. Convinced of the inadequacy of the former system of education and of the danger it presented by reason both of its centralized structure and of its dogmatic moral attitude,[1] the mission drew up a detailed scheme of reform. Although its authors denied that they had any intention of practising cultural imperialism,[2] the mission's scheme was as faithful a copy as possible of the American system and it was in that spirit that it was put into force under the supervision of CI and E. In its final report for 1952,

---

1. The same reproach is levelled, incidentally but explicitly, at French education (see the report, p. 12). It is true that the spirit of French education is very different from that of American education, but there is much ignorance about the former. Attention must regretfully be drawn to the following passage by Ruth Benedict in her book on Japan: 'The State regulates every detail of the schools and, as in France, every school in the country is studying on the same day the same lesson from the same textbook' (*The Chrysanthemum and the Sword*, page 85).
2. 'We are not devoted to uniformity; as educators, we are not constantly alert to deviation, originality and spontaneity. This is the spirit of democracy. We are not flattered by any superficial imitation of our own institutions. Believing in progress and social evolution, we welcome cultural variety all over the world as a source of hope and refreshment.'

CI and E tries to find excuses wherever comparison with the position in the United States of America reveals any appreciable differences,[1] and there were few of its members who did not share its faith in the Americanization of Japan. However, one of the dissentients writes:

'For the most part, the United States has proceeded on the assumption that if we tell the Japanese "how we do it in America", that is all they need know to solve their problems. If they still have questions, we reply by telling them some more about "how we do it in America". . . . Actually, Japan's problems often resemble the problems of many—if not all—other United Nations democracies much more closely than they resemble the problems of the United States. . . . It would seem only sensible that information from and on countries like Britain, France, Sweden, Switzerland, Norway, Australia, New Zealand, Canada, Denmark, the Netherlands and Belgium be made available in liberal quantities.'[2]

While leaving to Mr. Textor the sole responsibility for his value judgments, one is bound to admit that his facts are correct, as regards educational reform in Japan. It is obviously impossible for us to deal in detail with the measures adopted, and we shall therefore confine ourselves here to the most important data about primary and secondary education. The first major change was to remove most of the schools from the authority of the central administration. Today, there are school boards elected by popular vote in the prefectures and at local level (towns and villages). Their powers are very wide, including, in particular, the appointment and dismissal of headmasters and teachers, decisions concerning school curricula and teaching methods, the choice of textbooks, and the training of teaching staff. An elected superintendent is responsible for administration and all State inspection of schools has been abolished, the inspectors being replaced by educational advisers who give guidance to headmasters and teachers, but do not issue orders and exercise no authority. The essential role of the Ministry of Education is now confined to providing the school boards with technical assistance and general guidance. The Ministry retains the right, however, to compile statistics and to work out norms for courses. It also draws up the list of authorized textbooks from which the school boards make their choice. In addition, the Ministry has sponsored numerous technical congresses and working parties and has brought out an abundance of professional literature for the use of teachers. In these tasks, it has received much help from the American services of the CI and E, members of which have also acted, in many cases, as educational advisers.

Instead of the complex structure of schools of different types formerly in existence, a standardized system—a kind of 'comprehensive school' (which we shall not, however, have time to consider here)—has been

1. *Post-War Development in Japanese Education*, I, p. 24.
2. Robert B. Textor, *Failure in Japan*, New York, 1951, pp. 150-1.

introduced up to university level. The full range of primary and secondary schooling is covered by 12 classes divided into 3 stages: 6 compulsory primary grades (the 'elementary school'); 3 advanced primary, or first stage secondary, grades, which are also compulsory (the lower secondary school, modelled on the American junior high school); and 3 second stage secondary grades (upper secondary schools, corresponding to the senior high school). Co-education, i.e. mixed classes of boys and girls, while not obligatory, is strongly recommended, and has been generally adopted at the first stage, but at the second stage it gives rise to difficulties and is less widespread.

Under the new organization, it is no longer possible to speak of programmes of study in the strict sense, since syllabuses are decided on locally by the school boards. Nevertheless, the Ministry of Education has made suggestions which have been generally followed, and has also laid down a number of prohibitions—the school boards do not enjoy unlimited freedom and democracy, too, can be dogmatic. As suggested by the Ministry, the primary education syllabus includes the following subjects: Japanese language, social studies, arithmetic, science, music, art and handwork, domestic economy, physical education and optional studies. The same subjects are repeated in the first cycle of secondary education, plus one vocational subject, a living language—almost invariably English—and *home room and club activities*. During the second cycle of secondary education the same studies are pursued, though with additional foreign languages (English, French, German and Chinese), but during these three years of their education, pupils have the right to choose between courses, on condition that the credits obtainable from the courses they select reach a prescribed total and that 45 per cent of the points, in specified proportions, are gained in five subjects—Japanese language, social studies, science, mathematics, physical education and health—which are thus to some extent obligatory.

A subject that has been suppressed—and this is nowhere mentioned in the official documents consulted by the writer, though it is much discussed among the Japanese—is the study of Chinese classics. This difficult subject served much the same purpose in Japanese secondary education that Latin and Greek did in European countries; it took the pupil back to the sources of his country's civilization; it was the essence of a liberal education and an adornment to the mind. It exercised the brain and it was an intellectual and emotional training for the appreciation of a way of thinking very different from that of the contemporary national society.

The teaching of Japanese ethics was stopped at a very early stage by the occupation authorities SCAP (directive of 31 December 1945), and all official religious instruction was forbidden even earlier (SCAP directive of 15 December 1945). The basic education law forbids all political teaching in schools. Extraordinary vigilance was exercised in putting a stop to the ceremonial recitation of the imperial rescript on education, and in a more general way it was indicated that the use of ceremonial marks for imperial rescripts must cease.[1] This does not mean that education is not to take sides; but it does so in new conditions. This point is brought out by the authors of the official American evaluation: 'The primary and secondary schools have not remained neutral in the conflict between democracy and totalitarianism, considered as ways of life. The premise has been propounded and accepted that one of the essential aims of the school is to train its pupils for participation, as democratic citizens, in the affairs of a nation which has proclaimed its intention to follow the democratic rather than the totalitarian model. University teachers belonging to left wing groups have from time to time charged that teaching which recommended democracy of the Western liberal type was a violation of the legal provisions prohibiting partisan political teaching in the schools. The answer to these critics is that democracy is neither a political party nor a political movement; it is a way of life which incidentally affects all the institutions used by the people in its community life, including political parties and the structure of the government. The schools of Japan have adopted, and now give, teaching designed to recommend the democratic way of life.'[2]

---

1. A translation of the famous rescript on education may be of interest to the reader. There are frequent allusions to this rescript in writings by foreigners and Japanese alike, but it is rarely found in works accessible to Westerners.

IMPERIAL RESCRIPT

Be it known to you, Our subjects:
Our Imperial ancestors established Our Empire on broad and eternal foundations and implanted deeply and firmly that virtue whose beauty has been demonstrated from generation to generation by Our subjects ever united in loyalty and filial piety. There lies the glory of the basic character of Our Empire and there too is to be found the source of Our teaching. Do you, Our subjects, be filial to your parents and affectionate to your brothers and sisters; as husbands and wives preserve harmony as between two friends; conduct yourselves with modesty and moderation; extend your benevolence to all; pursue learning and cultivate the arts and thereby develop your intellectual faculties and perfect your moral powers; moreover, further the progress of the common weal and promote the general interest; be ever respectful of the Constitution and observe the laws; in case of danger, offer yourselves bravely to the State; and thus safeguard and maintain the prosperity of Our Imperial Throne, co-eternal with Heaven and Earth. Thus not only will you be Our good and faithful subjects but you will also render illustrious the highest traditions of your ancestors.
The Way here mapped out is in truth the teaching handed down by Our Imperial ancestors to be observed alike by their Descendants and by their Descendant's subjects, infallible throughout the ages, true in all places. It is Our desire, jointly with you, Our subjects, to implant that teaching in all veneration in the hearts of men, that we may all attain to the same virtue.
Given on the 30th day of the 10th month of the 23rd year of Meiji (1890)

(The imperial sign manual)
(The imperial seal)

2. *Post-War Developments in Japanese Education*, I, p. 33.

It is impossible to explain in any detail the reforms introduced into the teaching of the Japanese language without becoming too technical. Japanese is beyond question a very difficult language. In the first place, there are four different ways of writing it: Chinese ideograms (*kanji*), almost unlimited in number (several thousand are required for everyday use); two completely different native phonetic (syllabic) systems, *hiragana* and *katakana;* and lastly the Latin alphabet (*romaji*), the use of which has given rise in practice to at least three different methods of transcription of Japanese sounds.[1] Secondly, four types of style are recognized, differing widely from one another either in some particular way or in almost every respect: the style of familiar speech, epistolary style, literary style and classical style. Finally, the grammar, particularly the conjugation of verbs and the agreement of adjectives, varies according to the respective rank of the speaker, the person spoken to and the person spoken about. The American Education Mission was greatly disturbed by this circumstance; it was specially struck by the waste of effort and the resulting inefficiency, and also by the undemocratic nature of the language, particularly in its spoken usages. The mission nowhere says that it would like the Japanese to give up their own language in favour, say, of English, but it does suggest the complete abandonment of the *kanji* and even of the *kana* in favour of a single system of *romaji* transcription (it does not indicate whether it prefers Hepburn's system). It also hopes that methods will be studied for promoting the growth of a more democratic version of the spoken language. What has actually happened is that the teaching of *kanji* in the primary schools has been cut considerably (about 500 characters to be learnt in the six-year course), and great official efforts have been made to teach and spread the use of the *romaji* script, though this was greatly impeded by the existence of three competing systems of transcription. Nevertheless, between 1948 and 1951 more than 25 million copies of textbooks were published in this script. In the secondary schools, the emphasis is no longer placed on calligraphy, grammar and literature, but has been shifted to the practical uses of reading, writing and speech. Thus 'the accent is now put on oral activities, such as conversation, using the telephone, school broadcast transmissions, "recitations" in class, class discussions, round tables and symposia, extempore speeches and participation in discussions conducted on parliamentary lines.'[2]

No educational reform was more radical than that affecting the teaching of history and the more or less closely associated subject of geography. Although the American Education Mission had regretted the spirit in which these two subjects had previously been taught in Japan and had stressed the importance of the study of the social sciences

---

1. It will be recalled that the method of *romaji* transcription followed in the present work is what is known as the modified Hepburn system.
2. *Post-War Developments in Japanese Education*, I, p. 19.

at secondary school and university level, it had not envisaged so drastic a change, which, indeed, it found rather embarrassing. But SCAP had already made up its mind: the teaching of history and geography was included in the regulation of 31 December 1945, suspending the teaching of ethics. The mission wrote: 'History and geography are normally designed to assist the student in orienting himself in time and space. They are expected to provide an objective basis, on which the student can develop an historical perspective, an acquaintance with his physical environment and a sense of the relationship between his own environment and the rest of the world.'[1] But the Japanese Ministry of Education went much further than this, as the quotation of a few passages from its *Guiding Principles for the Teaching of Japanese History*, of 9 December 1946, will show: ' . . . Efforts should be made to enable students to understand historical development synthetically and rationally. . . . Stress should be put on concrete aspects of the development of national life from social, economic and cultural viewpoints rather than on the history of peace and war, and the vicissitudes of the powers and struggles for political supremacy. . . . The excistence of Imperial families (the reader will note the plural) is of great significance in the development of our national history. Therefore, concerning this matter, teaching shall be conducted with the greatest care, firmly based on historical (i.e. not mythological) facts.'[2]

The most significant words from the above quotation are 'synthetically and rationally'. In point of fact, physical geography has been relegated to the science course, and history and geography, as such, have been abolished and absorbed into a new subject called 'social studies'. This subject is regarded as very important and is given a prominent place in the new curricula suggested or prescribed by Ministerial directives, being included among the compulsory studies at the second stage of secondary education, as Table 6 shows:

TABLE 6.

Subject	Total number of hours devoted to the study of each subject		Number of compulsory study units
	Primary Education (6 years)	Secondary Education 1st cycle (3 years)	Secondary Education 2nd cycle (3 years)
Social studies	980-1050	455-805	10
Japanese language	1250-355	410-770	9
Physical education	630	315-525	9
Mathematics	805-910	350-525	5
Science	525-95	385-525	5
A modern language	0	420-630	0

1. *Report of United States Education Mission to Japan*, p. 14.
   From *Development of the Teaching of History in Elementary and Secondary*
2. *Schools in Japan after the War*, unpublished documents of the *Mombu-sho*.

In teaching 'social studies' it is no longer a matter of requiring the pupil to learn in the old way, memorizing facts and reproducing them in written or verbal answers. Neither is he presented with separate subjects, formerly dealt with under the title of history, geography and civics; nor with an 'amalgam' of all these. The idea is to build up what are called 'study units' of related subjects (to the number of between four and six a year at first stage secondary level) around questions of significance to the pupils. A few examples will show how the new system works. In the first two years of primary education, the children study life at home and at school and the activities of the neighbours; in the third year, the life of the people in archaic and primitive societies; in the fourth year, everyday life in the past and present, including the growths of towns, villages and means of transport; in the fifth year, the growth of commerce and industry, and in the sixth year, the development throughout the world of communications and the means of information. The teaching of Japanese history is allowed at first stage secondary level, but repeated reminders are given that a synthetical approach must be adopted: the teacher is not to embark on a descriptive study by successive chronological periods, and 'history must not be studied for its own sake but as a component element in social studies'. Teachers are enjoined not to fail, as occasion arises, to 'give a reasoned criticism of mythology and traditions'; they are to emphasize the differences between the primitive, archaic and feudal societies of the past and the society of today, to note what still remains of them, and to pass judgment on them. At secondary education level, examples of the study units suggested in the 'Japanese history' subdivision are: How did primitive man achieve the mastery over nature in the Japanese islands? How did the contractual State take shape and what were the problems which confronted it? What was the nature of the society in which social rank and the master-servant relationship were established? How is Japan progressing along the path of modernization? In the 'world history' subdivision, units such as the following are found: How has the relationship between the 'nation' as a political entity, and the 'people' as a social entity developed? What part have the activities of the citizens played in social progress? Along what lines have attempts been made to secure world peace?

This brief account is necessarily incomplete and superficial. It may even be misleading, unless we point, in conclusion, to what is probably the essential feature of 'social studies' as a means of education—namely, that it is meant to exercise teachers and pupils in active methods. Both must respect facts, but not ready-made digests of them, still less cut-and-dried theories and value judgments. To answer the questions set them, pupils will have to consult books, illustrations and maps, and undertake sociological excursions to investigate social organizations on the spot. They will also have to form clear opinions of their own, so as to be able to explain them to others and submit them to the test of discussion. The new subject of 'social studies' appears to be aspiring in the main to become a technique which develops in the pupil a taste for information, a critical spirit and independent thought—results that in other countries are obtained by the expounding of prescribed texts and by the practice of essay writing.

It is not for us to try to evaluate this monumental reform nor to estimate the effect it may have produced on the mentality of Japanese youth. Nor is it possible to give a detailed review of Japanese opinion on the subject. Many conservatives hold that the reform went too far, but this is not the only kind of criticism levelled against it: there are others who think that the goal could have been set still higher.[1] They think that the reformers were quite right to overthrow a system of education based on blind faith in textbooks, in which things were carried to the point where, at the beginning of the Meiji era, school regulations often referred, not to the subjects to be studied but directly to the textbooks. Having recourse to active methods that put the accent on individual effort is not enough in itself, any more than merely expunging militaristic and totalitarian elements from the textbooks is enough. Well before the war, active methods were introduced in Japanese education, exploiting the children's individual interests to make them assimilate still more thoroughly what they found in the textbooks. Now (these critics continue), the children are merely being told to go to other textbooks and statistical tables to seek for truth and reality. Ready-made methods produced by and for a different society have been introduced into Japan. Homage is being paid to conventional democracy while at the same time everything is being done to preserve the traditional concept of life. The educational reforms have not gone to the root of the matter. As in the past, the *status quo* is accepted, and the structure of society is not questioned. Teaching by means of textbooks suited a feudal society: individualist teaching suits only middle-class children in the towns. What is now wanted is education on co-operative lines, better adapted to the tasks of social reconstruction, or, more probably, new forms of education not yet devised. In any case, school and society are interdependent and the new style of school is not a product of the Japanese society.

THE NEW YOUTH MOVEMENTS

As was to be expected, youth groups have also felt the effects of the occupation and the change of régime.[2] Regimentation reached its worst

---

1. See Takashi Ota, 'Reform of the Method of Teaching', *Japanese Sociological Review* (*Shakai-Gaku Huioron*), 1950, 1, no. 2, pp. 17-23 (in Japanese). We have drawn freely from this author in the following passages.
2. See *Post-War Developments in Japanese Education*, vol. I, pp. 303-16. Use has also been made of unpublished CI and E documents.

pitch in 1942 with the foundation of the *Dai Nippon Sei Shonen Dan*, the Youth Association of Greater Japan, a totalitarian body under Ministry of Education control, in which all youth associations were federated. In September 1945, a Ministerial circular sent to all prefectures, on 'the establishment and promotion of youth organizations', dissolved the previous centralized organizations and encouraged the fullest freedom in the formation of local groups.

Thus, the youth movements were reorganized. The most important of them is the *Seinen-Dan* which in 1951 had nearly 4 million members, of both sexes. This body is 90 per cent rural and concerns itself mainly with work of local public interest. Next comes the Children's Club with a membership of over 1 million, followed by the Junior Red Cross whose membership includes entire classes from the primary schools and first-grade secondary schools, with their teachers as leaders. In addition to its health aims, the Junior Red Cross provides a training in citizenship and promotes international friendships; it had more than 500,000 members in 1951. A new association which has lately taken root among the country population is analogous to the American 4-H Club movement and its local branches often use that name. It is supported by the Ministry of Agriculture and Forests and had a membership of 330,000 in June 1951; its object is to improve agricultural methods and to raise the standards of community life. A further 75,000 young people are accounted for jointly by the Boy Scouts, Girl Scouts, YMCA and YWCA. Thus over 6 million young people and children between 7 and 25 or 30 years of age belong to youth associations, or one in every five on the average, the proportion being certainly higher in the country.[1] Thus the interest with which the Ministry of Education and the occupation authorities have followed the rebirth of the youth movements is readily understandable.

As early as the beginning of 1947, joint consultations took place, as a result of which an advisory committee on youth organizations was set up at the Ministry of Education. It is an officially recognized body and includes representatives of children's and youth movements, private persons with an interest in these questions, university teachers and officials of the central administration. It meets regularly to examine general problems connected with the young and issues recommendations; in particular, it helped to draw up the training course scheme for youth leaders.

This training is mainly provided by the Institute for Educational Leadership with a mixed American-Japanese staff. Originally designed for the training of school inspectors and educational advisers, the institute now provides six types of specialized training courses, including

---

1. The investigation by F. Vos carried out in Tokyo at the end of 1951 showed that of the 100 young people examined, 12 belonged to some organization or club.

the one for youth leaders. It holds two 12-week sessions a year, preferably at one of the great universities. However, in 1948-49, in addition to a national conference, the institute organized seven regional conferences for youth leaders. It should also be pointed out that a number of schools now provide instruction which can serve as a technical training for the professional staff of youth movements.

A number of factors led to still further action by the occupational authorities. They were disturbed by the young people's need of spiritual guidance, and by the lack of resources and goodwill available for this purpose. They were also uneasy at the tendency of officialdom to mix in the affairs of youth movements—at prefecture level in the case of the *Seinen Dan* and nationally as regards the 4-H Club—and were frankly worried by the activities of the *Nippon Sokoku Sensen* (the Japanese Patriotic Front: a body of Communist tendency). Accordingly, they set up an organization of their own, first under the aegis of the Civil Affairs Service (CAS) and later under that of the Civil Information and Education Service (CI and E). An American youth affairs officer was appointed in every region, and each prefecture was provided with a Japanese youth expert appointed by the Japanese Government and paid partly from American funds, but dependent administratively on CAF (and later on CI and E).

The 1951-52 programme for youth leaders included the following among its aims: (a) planning and putting into effect a training scheme for leaders of youth movements; (b) working out programmes for the young, organized in small democratic groups for the pursuit of educational, recreational or civic activities, which would enable young people to become familiar with democratic forms of organization; (c) preserving the local autonomy of youth groups and their freedom from official interference at all levels; (d) safeguarding them against loss of liberty through the infiltration of Communist or Fascist elements out to gain control of the group for their own ends; (e) establishing contacts and co-operating with youth groups and other appropriate local organizations; (f) helping to spread understanding of youth activities among the adult members of local communities. These new youth affairs officers and youth experts have played an important part among the young; every month they have received thousands of requests for assistance, and during 1951 they made contact with more than 1 million young people at conferences, working parties and in training establishments.

CHAPTER V

CONTACTS WITH THE WORLD

Human life is primarily a matter of the everyday and the familiar. Most men, in the overwhelming majority of circumstances, cannot see beyond the visible horizon or, to put it more precisely, since it is far more a social than a physical environment to which they are conditioned, they rarely look further than the very limited circle of individuals with whom they have personal relationships. It follows that in most cases it would be purely academic to ask oneself questions about the contacts of a group with the outside world. Public opinion polls provide proof of this; questions of foreign policy arouse very little interest and the 'no opinion' percentage, even on the most topical subjects, is very high. In the autumn of 1951, the question that really interested the public in France was the price of meat; the reaction to the Abadan affair was one of indifference.

The Westerner attempting to study Japan would make a real mistake at the outset and run the risk of harbouring costly illusions if he failed to grasp this point. He is, nevertheless, in some danger of forgetting it, because he is in a very special situation himself: in his own person he introduces a disturbing element into the society he has come to study. Either from politeness and the desire to take advantage of an opportunity for easy contact, or more often because his presence has awakened quite new interests or made people aware of vague, half-conscious preoccupations, he will be asked innumerable questions about his own country and the outside world in general, with which he is identified as a non-Japanese, and apparently forgotten items of knowledge will be recollected for his benefit. It is a healthy scientific practice for the social psychologist consistently to play down whatever information he may have acquired himself about his foreign interlocutors' contacts with the world.

It must, however, be accepted as a fact (after the first cautious reactions) that the eyes of Japan are turned towards the outside world and this is especially so in the case of the young. The National Public Opinion Research Institute has discovered that 58 per cent of Japanese 'want to know all that goes on abroad'; even among those aged 25 or more the proportion is as high as two-thirds (66 per cent), but among the young it rises to 73 per cent. This high degree of interest is found just as much in the country as in the towns and is certainly not merely an expression of intellectual curiosity; indeed, it is among country-dwellers below 20 years of age that the maximum interest—76 per cent—is shown. Japan is a country wide open to the world.

It is not too difficult to see why this should be so: A good deal of anxiety is mingled with this desire for knowledge. Taking the nation as a whole, 65 per cent of Japanese hold the view that today foreign countries 'can prejudice the Japanese way of life' and this is the opinion of nearly 8 out of 10 of those who 'want to know', the proportion being more or less constant for all age-groups. If war does more than peace to bring the nations closer together, defeat opens the windows still wider and, while stimulating national self-examination and the feeling that reforms are needed, leads to comparison with other nations and inspires a search for examples to follow. The direct or indirect action of the conqueror impels the conquered in the same direction.

Such experiences are not only collective; they are embodied in the life-histories of individuals and are revealed in the individual reactions of young people to the questions that affect them, personally, the most. A Hokkaido village youth recalls that what frightened him most in his life were the false rumours about the American Army at the end of the war; a Yawata girl says that what upset her most was the harsh treatment she received during her repatriation from the mainland of Asia. The unhappiest memory of a young married woman of Bibai is of the anxious days she spent in China after Japan's capitulation. A Hokkaido village girl was never happier in her life than when she saw the kindliness of the American armed forces as they entered the district where she lived. Asked to name what they consider the three most important or significant happenings or situations in their lives, 71 per cent of Kyoto students instance happenings of the second world war and 20 per cent situations arising directly out of the war; the proportions among the Sapporo students are approximately the same—65 per cent and 29 per cent respectively. Thus it can be no matter for surprise that young Japanese of both sexes, despite the personal difficulties (to be discussed later) through which they are struggling, should be constantly thinking about what is going on far from their native land and should repeatedly ask questions about foreign or international affairs. Out of eight 'autobiographies of the future' collected in Hokkaido University, only one—the dullest and showing exceptional lack of imagination—makes no mention of world affairs. In the others, personal, national and world affairs are more or less inextricably interwoven.

For instance, a 20-year-old student writes: '... At the age of 24 I shall graduate from the Hall of Graduate Studies, and by recommendation of the professors I shall obtain a position in the Ministry of Labour. In pursuance of my long cherished desire to go abroad, I shall take an examination for students who are candidates for study abroad; but I shall fail. Both in the free and in the Communist countries, the development of industries using atomic energy is spurred on; the world is facing a critical situation. At the age of 25, the problem of love arises. My partner is an office girl working in the same section. She has a round face and is 5 *shaku*, 2 *sun* and 5 *bu* (C. 1.57 m.) tall. She is lively and has talent for music and dancing. At 23 she is at her best. Her mother and relatives, however, object to our free relations, and a *miai* (formal confrontation with a view to marriage) is arranged. The reason is that the girl was born in the same region as myself, and is an accomplished young lady who has attended college. In the same year (1957) there is a report that Stalin seems to be ill; but as this is reported so often, the world is not very much surprised. In America, the Republican Party gradually strengthens in power. 26 years old. I marry the girl mentioned above, in the traditional way. Japan's population surplus becomes ever greater, and the country now has nearly 100,000,000 inhabitants. Suddenly Stalin dies. The cause of his death is a special kind of heart disease in an acute form. As a result of this, insurrections break out in the U.S.S.R. The countries of Eastern Europe seize the opportunity, and escape from Soviet pressure; insurrections occur; in Eastern Germany and Czechoslovakia, liberal governments are already established. . . .'

In a more general way, when the students were asked what two things they would most like to know about the future up to A.D. 2000, the most frequent answers related to the international situation, particularly to the relations between communist and capitalist States, or the third world war; but they also dealt with the international situation in relation to the future of Japan, the personal affairs of the subject, the affairs of his family, or the industrial development of the world, including the development of atomic energy. Replies of this kind were made by 68 per cent of the students interrogated at Kyoto and by 76 per cent at Sapporo. Only afterwards in order of frequency came personal affairs—marriage, occupation, etc.—and national affairs, political and social; the proportion of students whose replies fell into either of these two categories was respectively 48 per cent and 22 per cent at Kyoto and 24 per cent and 47 per cent at Sapporo.

The young themselves are fully conscious of their lively interest in international affairs. The following question was put to them: 'Do you expect to be more interested in the local affairs and problems of your own community, in national affairs and problems or in international affairs and problems?' The majority of votes went to international affairs and problems—53 per cent at Kyoto (males 59 per cent, females 49 per cent) and 76 per cent at Sapporo. We should not, however, overestimate the importance of young people's concern with questions of foreign policy. In the question quoted above, the choice was confined to public affairs at three different levels. It was the questions at the highest level which aroused the most interest, and this is undoubtedly significant.

On the other hand, when there is a choice between private and public activities, the preference of students goes markedly to the former. This emerges clearly from the replies to the question: 'Of the following activities which are the three from which you expect the greatest satisfaction— your career or occupation, your family relationships, your leisure time, recreational activities, participation as a citizen in the affairs of your community, participation in activities directed towards national or international betterment, your religious beliefs and activities?' National and international activities came only third at Kyoto, being placed after family relationships and occupation, and second at Sapporo, where they came after occupation and on the same level as family relationships. The whole data available seems to warrant the conclusion that the interest which students are aware of taking in world affairs is less lively than the effect this interest has on their psychological behaviour.

In any case it is quite certain that to the youth of Japan, 'abroad' is something real, something of which they are very much aware. As to how they differentiate among foreign countries, which they respect or like most, how they judge them, and where they look for inspiration or influence, we can attempt to answer these questions with the help of the data which the investigations have made available to us.

ADMIRATION AND FRIENDSHIP FOR FOREIGNERS

The Japanese do not mind admitting that there are foreign countries ahead of Japan. When this question was put to the sample as a whole, only 13 per cent of the subjects interrogated named no such country, and the percentages were even smaller among the young—11 per cent and 6 per cent respectively in the 16-19 and 20-24 urban age-groups and 8 per cent and 12 per cent respectively among the youth of the countryside. Analysis of the answers according to sex shows that this circumstance is due to differences found among the women but not among the men. The percentage unable or unwilling to name any country is more than twice as high among the older women as among the younger women. This is probably to be accounted for by variations in the degree of general knowledge or differences in education; abstentions from this question are much more frequent among the less educated: 6-8 years of schooling, 30 per cent; 9-11 years, 9; 12-13 years, 5; over 13 years of schooling, 4 per cent.

A wide variety of countries were named—the United States of America, England, France, Germany, the Soviet Union, Switzerland, Denmark, Sweden, India, China, Italy, the Netherlands, Norway, Brazil, Australia and Canada. Some replied that all countries were superior to Japan; others, all countries of Europe and America. Thus the youth of Japan regards the outside world primarily with admiration.

However, there are degrees to the esteem in which foreign lands are held. The country that stands far and away highest on the list is the United States of America. Taking the Japanese public as a whole, 81 per cent of those interrogated named the United States as superior to their own country, and America's prestige stands still higher among the young, being respectively 84 per cent and 86 per cent among the two age-groups of young people in the towns, and 89 per cent and 79 per cent in the country. Their admiration is not entirely unalloyed, as will be seen later. However, the balance is strongly on the credit side; the vanquished nation nourishes a vast respect for the victor, and this is an important element in the psychology of Japanese youth.

Among the public as a whole, England is named superior to Japan by 18 per cent of the subjects interrogated, France by 7 per cent, Germany by 6 per cent, the Soviet Union by 5 per cent, Switzerland by 2 per cent, Denmark by 1.5 per cent and the remaining countries by fractions lower than 1 per cent. Low though these percentages may seem, they nevertheless represent numbers of individuals which are far from negligible. One per cent of the population aged 15 or over is equivalent to some 500,000 persons. In almost all cases, the figures for town-dwellers are above the averages just given and the opinions of the young are still more favourable. Thus 30 per cent of the town-bred youth in the 16-19 age-group name England, 12 per cent the Soviet Union, 10 per cent Germany and 9 per cent France; among the subjects examined by the National Public Opinion Research Institute the highest percentage picking France—15 per cent—is in the 20-30 urban age-group.

General knowledge and basic education undoubtedly play an important part in these judgments. The answers vary, indeed, appreciably according to the level of education, as Table 7 shows.

TABLE 7.

Countries deemed superior to Japan	Sample as a whole	Number of years schooling			
		6-8	*9-11*	*12-13*	*Over 13*
	%	%	%	%	%
United States of America	81	68	85	86	79
Great Britain	18	5	5	16	31
France	7	2	6	11	21
Germany	6	2	3	11	24
Soviet Union	5	3	4	7	19
Switzerland	2	1	2	4	8
Denmark	2	*	2	2	5

* Below 0.5 per cent

The detailed list of the respects in which foreign countries are held to be superior to Japan is long. Let us therefore begin by considering it, as codified by the National Public Opinion Research Institute:

Science, medicine and dyestuff chemistry, etc., 34 per cent of the public.

Industry, technology, machinery (heavy industry, industrial techniques, precision machinery), 24 per cent.

Standard of living and domestic arrangements (greater efficiency achieved in this sphere through rationalization of housework and the introduction of domestic appliances; high standard of living), 15 per cent.

Culture, art: literature, fine arts and music, 11 per cent.

Commerce, economic power, wealth of natural resources, planning, organization, capital, 7 per cent.

Civilization, in the sphere of industry, 7 per cent.

In politics: vast but united territories; handling of foreign affairs, maintenance of public order, 5 per cent.

Agricultural techniques: mechanization, methods of organization, 5 per cent.

Social system: thoroughgoing democracy, full acceptance of equal rights for men and women, 3 per cent.

'Breeding', education, social morality: sense of public duty, morality based on spiritual values, 5 per cent.

Military matters; scientific production of the atomic bomb, tactical superiority, 4 per cent.

Philosophical and social doctrines; democracy, respect for human rights, 4 per cent.

Education, higher level of education, 4 per cent.

Means of transport: motor cars, traffic, shipping, 3 per cent.

Manners and customs: kindliness, humanitarianism, 2 per cent.

Health and hygiene, 2 per cent.

Inventions, discoveries: inventive power, 1 per cent.

Clothing: they wear Western clothing which is simple and does not hamper movement, 1 per cent.

Diet, 1 per cent.

Housing: ultra-modern architecture, 1 per cent.

Strength of character, perseverance, 1 per cent.

Social institutions: social service, welfare of the old, homes for the aged, reclamation of juvenile delinquents, 1 per cent.

Peaceful outlook: the people love peace and are taking practical steps to ensure it, 1 per cent.

Superior in all respects, 5 per cent.

It will be seen that what the Japanese public most appreciates in foreign countries are factors that make for material power, particularly technological factors; the 2,671 persons questioned by the National Public Opinion Research Institute gave a total of 2,393 replies of this type: an average of 0.9 per person. The remaining answers, tending rather to indicate the perception of some intellectual, moral or aesthetic superiority, were given only in 837 cases: an average of 0.31 per person. These results clearly reveal the idea which Japan entertains of the West and allow us to infer Japan's own opinion of how it compares with Christian industrial civilization, which it regards as powerful materially and thereby enviable, but not truly cultivated and a little lacking in soul. From this it will be understood that the countries compared favourably with Japan, in terms of the latter's own values, enjoy a prestige perhaps less overwhelming but of a different kind.

In this respect, the attitude of the young does not differ in essentials from that of their elders, except that their replies are slightly more frequent: an average of 1.26 for subjects below 24 years of age, and 1.18 for those 25 years of age or over. Replies naming points of actual superiority average 0.94 per person among the young and 0.87 among the remainder; replies of the other type work out at 0.32 and 0.31 respectively. Thus the material superiority of the West carries a little more weight with the young but the difference is really very slight.

It is also interesting to see the proportions in which these forms of superiority are ascribed to the foreign countries most frequently named. This is shown in Table 8.

TABLE 8.

Nature of superiority over Japan	U.S.A.	U.K.	France	Germany	U.S.S.R.	Switzer-land	Denmark
	%	%	%	%	%	%	%
Science and technology	71	55	38	77	63	42	26
Intellectual values	14	23	55	17	14	12	10
Standard of living	18	16	19	18	5	14	12
Political evolution	7	22	10	3	19	29	14
Economic evolution	11	11	7	8	14	15	67
Spiritual values	5	14	7	11	5	6	2
Other particulars	6	3	4	2	3	0	0

The table shows that those naming the United States of America have uppermost in their minds the level attained by science and industrial technology in that country, but those naming Germany are thinking even more of this aspect of the superiority of a foreign country over Japan. This is, moreover, the form of superiority most frequently mentioned in support of the choice of a country, with about two exceptions—Denmark, where reference is most frequently made to economic development, and France, whose superiority in the sphere of intellectual values is mentioned above all.

Several countries—the United States of America, France and Germany—run level as regards the relative frequency with which their high standard of living is given as a reason for conceding their superiority. Switzerland, the United Kingdom and the Soviet Union, in that order, are the countries most frequently regarded as superior from the point of view of political development, while the highest percentages for 'spiritual values' (i.e. 'manners and customs', 'politeness' and 'strength of character') go to Great Britain first and Germany second.'[1]

For nearly a century past Japan has shown herself highly receptive to Western culture and skilful at borrowing from other peoples the cultural traits that seemed to give them an advantage over herself. One is justified in asking whether the Japanese attitude remains the same and the answer is that on the whole it does: the Japanese say they would be disposed to welcome new borrowings. However, they do not follow the same order of preference for their proposed borrowings as for the qualities they admire in other nations. Thus, 34 per cent consider that the superiority of foreign countries comes from the development of applied science but only 5 per cent consider that Japan should follow their example. Twenty-four per cent instance industrial and technological evolution but only 6 per cent consider that Japan should imitate this. Eleven per cent mention the literary and artistic achievements of foreign countries as reasons for their superiority, but no more than 2 per cent would like Japan to learn from them in this respect. The main types of borrowing regarded as desirable by the Japanese are first and foremost, better domestic organization, based on more mechanical aids in the home, which would make housework more efficient (19 per cent); social ethics— punctuality, and a scrupulous training in public morality (11 per cent). Other features thought desirable are certain ways of behaving, such as showing respect for women, and taking pains to secure harmony and co-operation in the family (5 per cent); industrial and technological development (6 per cent); the development of science (5 per cent), and of health techniques (4 per cent); legal and ethical principles, respect for human rights and democracy (3 per cent). It is also suggested that the West could be imitated in the matter of clothing (4 per cent), diet (3 per cent) and housing (2 per cent). In the course of the enquiry 91 persons said that the superiority of foreign countries was due to their military science but only five were found who wanted Japan to learn from them in this domain.

It thus appears that the borrowings the Japanese have in mind are mainly in practical matters and are very limited in scope. One never gets the impression that, comparing themselves with foreigners, they have lost confidence in their own society as a general system. All that can be said is that, in passing judgments on foreign countries admissions of superiority in the practical sphere are three times as numerous as in the cultural and ethical spheres. When it comes to the possible adoption of foreign traits the difference shrinks. Suggestions for the adoption of

---

1. This analysis has been made possible by a new condification and sifting undertaken by NPORI. See Appendix I for additional details.

material traits average out at 0.50 per person, compared with 0.32 per person for the non-material traits.[1]

There is little discernible difference between the attitudes of the young and those of their elders in any of these respects. Suggestions for adopting the material traits of a foreign country reach a frequency of 0.51 per person among young people under 25; as regards cultural traits the average frequency is 0.31. It does, however, appear that the desire to borrow from abroad is most frequently encountered in the 20-30 age-groups, particularly in the towns: 20-24 years, 0.55 (material traits), 0.38 (non-material traits); 25-29 years, 0.53 (material traits), 0.41 (non-material traits).

Four per cent of the Japanese consider it unnecessary to follow the example of foreign countries. In addition, however, a considerable number of traits of conduct are specifically indicated as undesirable for importation. The percentages are small in each case, but the remarks are significant and even tend in the same direction; they would appear to have been inspired, in part at least, by the actual experience of Westerners which the Japanese have acquired from the presence of the occupation forces and services. We find from the investigation conducted by the National Public Opinion Research Institute that 8 per cent of those interrogated mentioned, as one of the things which should not be imitated in Japan, the behaviour of Westerners with women—walking in the streets arm-in-arm or hand-in-hand, and over-crude (i.e. over-free) relations between the sexes; 3 per cent mentioned the exaggerated esteem in which women were held and the humiliating position of men; 5 per cent considered women's dresses too brightly coloured and make-up excessive; 1 per cent expressly picked on permanent waving; and dancing, kissing and divorce were disapproved of by 5 per cent, 6 per cent and 2 per cent respectively. This gives a total of 30 per cent of subjects disapproving of foreign sex customs.

Curiously enough, there were in all the categories, taken together, a total of 100 persons who disapproved of the eating habits of foreigners: they do not understand the art of good living; they are constantly eating and chewing, at work and in the street (4 per cent). Takao Sofue elicited a similar condemnation of the habit of chewing gum in the street when he asked what faults were seen in the Americans. As Western readers have forgotten the importance, in many societies, of restrictions and rules relating to food, other comments may perhaps strike them as more perti-

---

1. Asano, to whom a résumé of this passage was submitted, has sent the following comment:

'During our pre-test we found a proportion of subjects who could not answer this question because they had no views about it. We therefore added to the question the introductory phrase: "You can reply 'style of life' or anything else." I think the replies have been influenced by this phrase up to a point. However, it is not possible to say precisely how much distortion has resulted from it.'

nent: too much laxness in family relationships (5 per cent); the outlook of foreigners is too materialistic and they attach too much importance to money (1 per cent); they bother too much about social morality and not enough about morality within the family (1 per cent); in real life as in films, they allow too much prominence to be given to gangsterism (2 per cent); they are too addicted to pleasure and do not keep their feelings enough under control (1 per cent): thus we again find a total of 14 per cent of criticisms relating to customs and morality.

Lastly, the ideologies and political behaviour of foreigners come in for some criticism; too much individualism and liberalism, too many democratic notions (2 per cent); too imperialistic and aggressive (1 per cent); danger of the communistic ideology (5 per cent). Finally, a good half (53 per cent) of the Japanese public had nothing to say about Western traits which Japan must be careful to avoid.

The particular attitude of the young emerges fairly clearly from a regrouping of the replies: as regards political affairs, their behaviour is no different from that of their elders; in the sphere of ethics and manners, they are rather inclined to want to preserve the original features of Japanese culture; but in the sphere of sex, opposition increases in direct proportion to the age of the subjects. In general, opposition to changes would seem to increase with age. It must, however, again be pointed out that the replies of town-dwellers differ from those of country-dwellers; the more frequent absence of replies in country areas is not due to readier acceptance of Western culture, but to a less extensive personal experience of Westerners.

TABLE 9.

| Age-group | Features of foreign cultures which Japan should not imitate | | | |
	Political comportments	Ethics and behaviour	Inter-sexual institutions	No reply
Urban	%	%	%	%
16-19	6	14	21	60
20-24	6	16	19	59
25-29	3	21	30	47
30 and over	6	15	41	43
Rural				
16-19	7	16	16	65
20-24	7	11	16	63
25-29	7	12	23	59
30 and over	10	13	32	51

Thus, despite the very widespread admiration for certain foreign countries—the United States of America first and foremost, but also England, France, Germany, the Soviet Union, etc.—which is expressed even more strongly by the young than by the rest of the Japanese public, and which is based principally on the material and technical progress of those countries (with an exception, it is true, in the case of France and its intellectual and artistic culture), there would undoubtedly be strong resistance to total cultural assimilation with the West, if there were ever serious question of such a thing. This conclusion emerges quite clearly from the replies to the preceding questions, which were framed in a rational and impersonal way. It can be checked by a more emotional approach.

Confirmation, from this angle, of the results of the investigation carried out by the National Public Opinion Research Institute, is provided by the answers to two items in the questionnaire used by Takao Sofue. The first was: 'Do you think it a good thing that you were born Japanese or would you have preferred to have been born of another nationality?' The other was: 'What nationality would you have liked to have had at birth, if you had not been born Japanese?' In reply to the first question, the majority of the young people interrogated answered that they preferred to have been born Japanese. A young man from Yawata said: 'I am proud I was born Japanese'; a Bibai girl answered: 'I would kill myself if I were not Japanese.' Of all the persons interrogated, only 14 per cent said they would have preferred not to be Japanese. Although it may be risky to carry any further the analysis of results secured from so small a number of subjects, it is at least significant that the percentages for males and females are equal and that the replies are the same, whether they come from the industrial town of Yawata or from a district in Hokkaido.

Before examining the replies to the second question, we may usefully compare them with the results of a somewhat similar question put to students at Kyoto and Sapporo, who were asked, not whether they would have liked to have been born elsewhere, but whether they would like to live the greater part of their lives in their native land or in a foreign country. At both places the replies received were in the same proportions: 82 per cent of those questioned preferred to live in their native country and 18 per cent abroad. At Kyoto, would-be emigrants were a little more numerous among the men, since the proportion rose to 22 per cent, against 15 per cent for the girls. Among the countries in which the 18 per cent at Kyoto said they would prefer to pass most of their lives, were the United States of America (5 per cent), Switzerland (4 per cent), France (3 per cent), China (2 per cent), and also Great Britain, Germany and Brazil.

The second question in Sofue's investigation ('What nationality would you like to have had at birth, if you had not been born Japanese?') was not given as a rider to the first but followed it in the questionnaire. Fourteen per cent of those interrogated declined to reply or gave vague answers. Of the remainder, more than half (52 per cent) said that they would like to be Americans; this reply was given most frequently in the agricultural village of Kyushu and least frequently at Yawata. Other choices were divided among the following nationalities: French 8 per cent, British 8 per cent, Swiss 5 per cent, German 3 per cent, Swedish 2 per cent, Italian 2 per cent, Brazilian 2 per cent. Comments on the motivations of these replies, and the explanations given, merit quotation from Sofue's report:

'As regards Japanese who have been in contact with Americans only as members of the occupation force, the answer "American" was given by an overwhelming majority of men and women alike, and the women in particular show their interest in Americans. In the trade unions, interest in Americans (particularly among the men) decreases very appreciably whereas interest in other nationalities increases. One of the reasons most frequently given for interest in Americans is that they are a civilized people. The other reasons alleged are: "Democracy is well developed in America", and "The resources there are abundant". Two men in the village of F. answered: "Mechanized agriculture is well developed there"; the answer of a woman in the village of T. is also interesting: "Americans are physically attractive". With regard to the people of other countries, the reasons for replies are as follows. The French: "As the French excel in music and the arts there are some who are deeply attracted by them", "The French know human nature", (these two comments may have been inspired by the influence of French films); the Germans: "They have great vitality"—"they are clear-headed", the English: "We feel friendly towards the English people, who look as if they are thinking and keeping in touch with reality even when they are walking"; the Swedes: "They know human nature"; the Brazilians: "The climate of Brazil is pleasant and restful". An interesting point is that trade unions of socialist tendencies are drawn towards the English people, which may be the result of their contacts with the British Labour Party.'[1]

It is undoubtedly extremely fortunate for Japan that the percentage of young people who would like to settle abroad or would be willing to renounce their own nationality is not very high: if it were, that would be a very serious indication of national demoralization. It might even be estimated that, if Sofue's investigation were really representative (which it did not set out to be), his figure of 14 per cent for those who would have preferred not to have been born Japanese would be equivalent to more than 2 million young people and would constitute some grounds for alarm. However that may be, the question of the morale of Japanese youth will be discussed later.

---

1. Extract from Takao Sofue's report.

THE ATTRACTION OF 'ABROAD'

Confining ourselves, for the moment, to our analysis of the interest taken by Japanese youth in foreign countries, we should notice that the idea of foreign travel is undoubtedly attractive to many of them. Asked what they would do if they unexpectedly received a large sum of money, 8 per cent of the students at Kyoto and 29 per cent of those at Sapporo could think of no better way of spending it than on foreign travel. Of the 100 young people (including many students) questioned by F. Vos at Tokyo, only two said that they would not like to go abroad to study or to work. The representative investigation of the National Public Opinion Research Institute also shows that the percentage of young people who would like to go abroad if they had the chance is very high—distinctly higher than in the case of persons over 30 years of age. The figures are: *urban* 16-19 age-group (87 per cent), 20-24 (83 per cent), 25-29 (80 per cent), 30 and over (70 per cent); *rural*, 16-19 age-group (87 per cent), 20-24 (79 per cent), 25-29 (71 per cent), 30 and over (64 per cent). The sample as a whole showed 72 per cent.

Many subjects (24 per cent of those who say they would like to go abroad and 17 per cent of the sample as a whole) have pure tourism in mind: 'I only want to go somewhere'; 'I should visit famous places'; 'It would provide me with subjects of conversation and would enable me to spread knowledge'. Those in the youngest age-groups are particularly apt to give reasons of this kind for wanting to travel abroad; among the under-twenties, this is true of 26 per cent in the towns and 25 per cent in the country. Even more frequently (in 19 per cent of cases for the sample as a whole) we find the attitude expressed is that it would be interesting to travel in order to observe conditions of life in foreign lands, to be able to compare the status of women, standards of life or the state of a particular branch of trade in which the subject was personally interested; this kind of reason is given most frequently by young people between the ages of 20 and 24. These two types of answer show the lively interest taken by the Japanese, particularly the young, in what goes on in the rest of the world, especially in the West, but we are certainly not dealing here with prospective emigrants. That is very probably true also of those who say that they would like to go abroad to study, although the study is not necessarily of an academic nature and the wish is found in all age-groups; its average frequency for the public as a whole is 2 per cent.

Some, on the other hand, are quite explicit about wanting to emigrate: 2 per cent say that they would like to go abroad to work and 2 per cent that they have personal reasons for wishing to do so—they were born abroad, they have lived abroad, they have relatives living abroad. However these percentages are small, and it is probable that we should greatly underestimate the number of those wishing to settle abroad if we were to reckon only this 4 per cent.

Leaving aside a group of replies, whose frequency, in any case, does not exceed 2 per cent, and which relate primarily to countries formerly linked to Japan politically or economically, particularly Germany[1]—and probably of sufficient interest on that account for Japanese to want to visit them—we find a collection of reasons which are difficult to explain psychologically because they relate not to the intentions of the subjects but to the characteristics they ascribe to the country they desire to visit. We find such phrases as: 'It is a country with rational ways of life'; 'It is a very advanced country from the point of view of mechanization'; 'A country which is easy to live in, with a climate like that of Japan'. These replies are very frequent (25 per cent of the whole) and their frequency is in inverse ratio to the age of the subject. Probably they reflect a desire, vague perhaps, and conceivably timid and hopeless, to go and settle in some foreign paradise.

If these conjectures have any foundation in fact, a regrouping of the reasons for which the subjects interrogated would like to go to foreign countries brings out interesting differences according to age (Table 10).

TABLE 10.

Age-group	No desire to travel	Unlikely to emigrate	Might emigrate	Would probably emigrate
	%	%	%	%
Sample as a whole	28	38	25	4
Urban				
16-19	13	48	31	2
20-24	17	46	29	2
25-29	20	36	27	7
30 and over	30	35	24	4
Rural				
16-19	13	45	33	4
20-24	21	49	22	2
25-29	29	38	25	5
30 and over	36	33	22	4

It is the men and women in the higher age-groups who most frequently declare that they have no desire to travel abroad; but they also show a tendency to produce the largest percentage of 'probable' emigrants, particularly in the 25-29 age-group, which has reached the age of adult responsibility but has not yet achieved economic and social standing. It is the young who display the greatest curiosity about foreign countries,

---

1. Of the subjects expressing a wish to travel in Germany, 22 per cent gave it as their reason that this country had links with Japan.

and the most platonic interest in them, although they also yield the highest percentages both of 'unlikely' and of 'possible' emigrants; this, in fact, results from a psychological characteristic of the young: their immaturity. Other instances of it will be found in later pages of this report.

On the whole, the list of countries which those interrogated would like to visit if they were able to travel abroad freely, corresponds to that of the countries regarded as superior to Japan. However, comparison of the two tables prompts a number ot comments. The countries with the highest percentages of admirers do not attract as many prospective visitors; there is a single exception to this rule: France, which now moves up to second place, according to the investigation carried out by the National Public Opinion Research Institute, though still far behind the United States of America. On the other hand, a number of countries, placed low or even not mentioned in the list of countries regarded as superior to Japan, are named with varying degrees of frequency in the second list. This happens in the case of China, Brazil, Hawaii, Italy, India, Formosa, Manchuria and the Philippines.

The 10 countries most frequently mentioned are the following (the percentages are calculated on the basis of the sample as a whole): United States of America (48 per cent), France (8 per cent), Great Britain (6 per cent), Germany (3 per cent), the Soviet Union (3 per cent), Switzerland (3 per cent), China (2 per cent), Brazil (2 per cent), Hawaii (2 per cent), Denmark (1 per cent).

The great majority of these are Western countries. Brazil is mentioned not merely because of Japanese emigration there before the war, but also because it has lately organized a small-scale immigration of Japanese farm workers and this has been given generous publicity. At the present time, the Pacific countries have little attraction for the Japanese: the 15 countries or territories in this category which are mentioned (including Hawaii and China) account for barely 10 per cent of the replies of those naming a country they would like to visit, or about 7 per cent of the sample as a whole.

The reasons given by those who would like to travel in the six foreign countries most frequently mentioned may be divided as follows:

TABLE II.

Reason	U.S.A.	France	U.K.	Germany	U.S.S.R.	Switzerland
	%	%	%	%	%	%
High civilization	32	19	33	26	31	19
Fine country	6	11	2	0	2	37
To study the country	29	34	34	30	56	22
Sight seeing	24	25	19	12	5	15
For educational purposes	3	7	6	7	1	3
Business, employment	2	1	2	4	0	4
Links with Japan	2	2	3	22	3	1

The attitudes of the young are not clearly differentiated, probably because the number of replies is too small and the fluctuations due to sampling are too considerable. This at any rate is what seems to have happened in the case of the Asiatic and Pacific countries. Rural inhabitants of all ages are more attracted by the United States of America than are town-dwellers. The opposite is true as regards the countries of Europe, particularly France and the Soviet Union. The interest which the Japanese feel for France is greatest in the young (1 in 5 among young people in the towns).

Table 12 sums up the essential data at our disposal in the matter of countries subjects would like to visit.

TABLE 12.

Age-group	U.S.A.	France	U.K.	Germany	U.S.S.R.	Asia and Pacific
	%	%	%	%	%	%
Sample as a whole	48	8	6	3	3	7
Urban						
16-19	54	21	8	4	4	14
20-24	50	21	6	3	8	9
25-29	43	17	11	6	3	12
30 and over	45	7	7	3	3	3
Rural						
16-19	59	13	8	3	1	5
20-24	53	11	5	1	2	5
25-29	53	5	3	2	2	7
30 and over	46	4	5	2	3	6

TABLE 13.

Country	Kyoto		Sapporo	Tokyo
	Men	Women		
	%	%	%	%
U.S.A.	70	66	53	11
France	63	76	65	30
U.S.S.R.	39	11	41	8
U.K.	31	29	35	14
Switzerland	22	50	18	
Germany	14	13	12	14
China	14	9	29	5
Italy	7	11	18	
India	6	2	12	
Denmark	5	2	0	

Appreciably different results were obtained with groups of students or selected subjects, though the questions were not in fact identical. At Kyoto and Sapporo, the question was put in the following form: 'If you could travel, what other three countries would you most like to visit?' At Tokyo it was: 'If you could study or work abroad, to what country would you like to go?' The substance of the replies secured is given in Table 13.

There can be no question of making a comparison, item by item, between the percentages shown in the two preceding tables; the difference in the wording of the questions would alone make this impossible. It can however be asserted, from a general comparative survey of them, that the interest of students in various foreign peoples differs greatly from that of young people as a whole. France and the Soviet Union in particular, and for very different reasons, arouse sympathies among the future leaders of Japan that are found only to a much smaller degree elsewhere.

INTERNATIONAL CULTURAL RELATIONS

The expression of the wish to travel in foreign countries, and the value judgments on the people of other countries, constitute behaviour that is admittedly symbolic, but real, and absolutely objective psychologically; they provide incontrovertible factual data for interpreting the relations of Japanese youth with the rest of the world. They do not themselves, however, constitute these relations, but are only the expression of them, and consequently whatever significance they may have is open to discussion. There is more than one example in the earlier pages of the degree to which some of the data obtained from investigations can be ambiguous or obscure.

The study of cultural behaviour is not of this character: the facts disclosed may be fragmentary but they provide direct information about the contacts of the Japanese with the outside world. That is why it is interesting to complete an investigation of opinion by carrying out research on the behaviour of the young in the sphere of reading, films and radio.

The Japanese are great readers. Illiteracy (if the term is permissible, in view of their complex system of writing) is practically non-existent and the taste for reading, both in order to acquire knowledge and for amusement, is very marked. Newspapers are very numerous and the most important of them enjoy circulations which are among the highest in the world; monthly and weekly reviews are also to be found in abundance, and the output of books is considerable—60 million volumes were published in 1949. Of the group of 100 young people interrogated by F. Vos in Tokyo, only three did not read newspapers and 18 did not read monthly or weekly reviews; 52 read books. The proportion of those interested in foreign publications, mainly in Japanese translations, was high in this particular group—38 out of 100; 9 read *Life* in English, 5 the *Nippon Times,* 9 the Japanese edition of *Reader's Digest.* Of foreign books the most frequently read are French, especially the works of Romain Rolland, André Gide and Camus.

Subjects from rural and urban areas, from Hokkaido and Kyushu, read large numbers of periodicals. *Reader's Digest* is mentioned once, and, in addition to technical works on agriculture, 19 titles of favourite books are mentioned, 11 of which are foreign—*La vingt-cinquième heure,* by Gheorghiu; *The Good Earth,* by Pearl Buck; *Little Women,* by Louisa M. Alcott; *Les Thibault,* by Roger Martin du Gard (twice mentioned); *La Peste,* by Albert Camus; *In the Depths,* by Maxim Gorki; *The Idiot,* by Dostoievski; *L'Etranger,* by Albert Camus; *Gone with the Wind,* by Margaret Mitchell (twice mentioned); and *The Naked and the Dead,* by Norman Mailer.

Foreign dominance is also to be seen in film preferences, as noted by Vos in Tokyo: out of 100 persons questioned, 12 said they preferred foreign films in general; 11, French films; 7, American films; 7, English films; and 7 said they preferred Japanese films. The preferences noted by Sofue are, in the villages, for Japanese films, historical and otherwise, and American Westerns; whereas in the towns young workers of both sexes prefer French and Italian films. Visits to cinemas are frequent, two or three times a month on the average. In his report Sofue writes: 'Generally speaking, Japanese historical films and typically Japanese films of other kinds, and American Westerns, are in favour with the lower classes of the population and French films with the upper. It is permissible to say that the most popular amusement of the young is cinema-going.'

Two investigations by the Dentsu Company into the preferences and habits of radio listeners also point to the conclusion that Japanese youth is more interested in programmes of foreign music and less in Japanese programmes than their elders are. The younger the subject the less he wants to listen to Japanese music and the more he wants to listen to classical or light music, i.e. Western or Western-type music.

TABLE 14.

| Age-group | Listener preferences in broadcast music | | |
	Classical	Light	Japanese
	%	%	%
18-25	45	68	13
26-35	32	55	19
36-45	21	33	37
45 and over	6	21	47

In actual listening behaviour, a tendency is discernible on the part of the young to take less interest in broadcasts of traditional music, but the difference between age-groups is less marked as regards listener habits than it is in their declared preferences; in other words, the young picture themselves as even more interested in foreign culture, and less interested in Japanese culture, than they actually are.

TABLE 15.

Age-group	Choices between two programmes broadcast simultaneously in 1951		
	Famous Japanese songs	'The joke box' (riddles)	Proportion of subjects listening in
	%	%	%
17-25	13	47	60
26-35	11	39	50
36-45	13	39	52
45 and over	22	35	57

Thus, for the third time in the history of Japan, the country is wide open to Western influences. She eagerly evinces her desire to multiply contacts with the outside world and her young people give proof of even more clear-cut intentions. We must not forget, however, that the two previous occasions did not produce particularly happy results. The economic and religious infiltration which began by chance in the middle of the sixteenth century ended, a century later, in the complete self-isolation of the country. The Westernization of the Meiji era led to the development in the Japanese of contempt for the other Asiatic nations along with hatred and envy of the peoples of Europe and America; it was thus directly responsible for one of the most brutal attempts at aggression in modern history. In the years following the second world war the military and industrial power of the United States of America has given rise to a wave of respect and admiration: in 1950, the newspaper *Asahi* asked, in a public opinion poll, 'which will be the strongest Power in 20 years' time?'; 39 per cent of the replies named the United States of America and only 5 per cent the Soviet Union. The moderation of American policy, after the fears fostered among the public by the Japanese military government, has awakened gratitude and sympathy; 61 per cent of the subjects interrogated by Sofue think that Japan will get most help from the United States of America. The presence of the occupation troops and services has enabled the Japanese to acquire direct knowledge and better understanding of these 'strangers'—in Japanese as in many other languages a 'foreigner' (*ijin*) means a 'strange' or 'different' man (*i*:異). As the *Asahi Shimbun* was able to show, after its 1950 investigation, 10 per cent of Japanese have had direct dealings with Americans and 93 per cent have at least seen some; 61 per cent think that they now understand them; in the sample as a whole 32 per cent declared that they now like Americans (of these 44 per cent had received a higher education,

72 per cent had come into official contact with Americans and 79 per cent had met them socially).

In view of the geographical, demographic and human importance of the Japanese empire, the world may well rejoice at these propitious circumstances. But we must also remember that the situation can change. The data set out above were collected before the end of the American occupation and some of them before the conclusion of the peace treaty; many Japanese warn us that when the public grasps the real content of that treaty, the cordiality of their relations with the Americans may diminish. In that case we must simply hope that friendship with the West, based not on political considerations, but on the disinterested cultural message so readily accepted by Japan from countries such as France and Great Britain, will suffice to keep her within the concert of the nations. At a moment when Japanese psychology is perhaps on the point of changing, it is an encouraging sign that the youth of Japan is showing special interest in French and European culture—the young people in the towns even more than those in country areas, and the students, the future leaders of the nation, more than either.

PACIFISM AND ITS LIMITS

At the moment, in any case, the Japanese would certainly not be inclined to embark on any sort of war of revenge and the youth of the country is even further removed from any such intention. We have seen earlier what deep scars the second world war has left in the consciousness of the Japanese. To a traveller journeying through the country, Japan appears one of the most passionately pacifist nations in the world today. The work of Unesco is hailed there with enthusiasm, mainly because Unesco is regarded as an international undertaking aimed at regrouping the pacifist forces of the world. On innumerable occasions in the course of our travels about the Japanese archipelago, individuals or delegations came to welcome us, to tell us of the hopes they placed in Unesco viewed in this capacity; to inform us that they would resist conscription, and to ask us to intervene with the government in order to prevent unconstitutional rearmament. In this connexion as in others, we make no generalizations from our personal impressions, however vivid. But the objective investigations bear one another out and indicate that these are powerful tendencies.

It is a fact that the Japanese have conceived a deep fear of war and that their fear finds expression on every possible occasion. The following question was set by the National Public Opinion Research Institute: 'What is the thing—personal or otherwise—which most worries you and makes you most unhappy at the present moment?' The second most frequent answer, coming immediately after economic and financial worries, which, as we know, are serious in war-devastated Japan—is fear of war, to which must be added the question of rearmament, whether approved or disapproved. Economic worries were mentioned by 21 per cent of the sample as a whole, fear of war by 11 per cent and anxiety about rearmament by 6 per cent. Retabulation of these last two replies shows that this kind of anxiety is even stronger among the young.

TABLE 16.

Age-group	Causes of worry		Figure for the two preceding columns combined
	War	Rearmament	
	%	%	%
Sample as a whole	11	6	17
Urban			
16-19	12	11	23
20-24	14	12	26
25-29	16	3	19
30 and over	13	3	16
Rural			
16-19	11	11	22
20-24	13	9	21
25-29	10	7	17
30 and over	8	J	13

These percentages are all the more significant inasmuch as the subjects interrogated were allowed to name only one cause of worry. It is probable that if answers listing a number of worries had been allowed, fear of war would have been instanced much more often. This did in fact occur in the investigation carried out among the Kyoto students, who were asked: 'What are the two worst things that could *conceivably* happen to you during your lifetime?' Fifty-five per cent of the men and 39 per cent of the girls answered 'war', and their fear of it was such that, when they were thereupon asked: 'What are the two worst things that are *likely* to happen to you during your lifetime?' the percentages of those who replied 'war' rose to 57 per cent and 45 per cent. At this point it is worth mentioning that the Sapporo students, who were even more pacifist than those of Kyoto but exhibited more marked traits of immaturity, much less frequently included war among the things likely to happen to them: the percentages are respectively 18 per cent and 35 per cent.

The pacifist, and even anti-militarist, views to which their fear and hatred of war give rise in the Japanese, particularly in the young, will be dealt with later. Meantime, we should like to make a more detailed analysis of the attitudes exhibited on the subject of war and to examine the results of the projective test applied by Takao Sofue in Kyushu and Hokkaido.

Three of the plates used in the test illustrate wartime situations—Plate 5 shows the departure of soldiers from a station, Plate 6 a wartime review of conscripts by General Tojo, Plate 7 three *kamikaze* pilots ready to leave on an attack mission. The reactions to these plates can be stated in general terms; they are of three types.

Type I. Positive opposition and active hatred of war. Example: woman, F. village, Plate 5: 'This picture reminds me of troops leaving for the front. It makes me shiver. That was the time when militarism was at its height. People used to see the soldiers off and cheer them loudly. The two men on the right of the picture were democrats—progressive at that time. The artist has tried to draw men who were against the war and uneasy about the future of our country.'

Type II. Consciousness of the miseries of war, but in a sentimental and negative way with nothing convinced or positive about it. Example: man, F. village, Plate 5: 'It is a scene showing the departure of troops for the front. The expressions of the two people on the right of the picture reveal the sadness felt by those who watch their relatives leaving for the front with many others who are going to the war only to sacrifice their lives for their country.'

Type III. No sign of aversion to war. Example: man, F. village, Plate 5: 'The picture is of recruits going off to a barracks to join up. I don't like it that two people should be holding aloof and not saying goodbye to them when many have come to do so. Those two have an anti-social look.'

The 63 subjects studied by Sofue may be divided as follows: 35 per cent belong to Type I (active opposition to war), 25 per cent to Type II (sentimental opposition), and 40 per cent to Type III (acceptance); on the whole, therefore, the young people studied are pacifist (60 per cent), but the intensity of their attitudes varies. What is more, if a detailed analysis is made (always bearing in mind that the number of cases in each group is very small and that this is in no sense a representative investigation), it will be found that distribution between the types is very uneven: the men are much more positively pacifist (43 per cent) and it is noticeable in the tests that they identify themselves much more definitely with the young soldiers; in the case of the women there is no clear-cut identification and they fall more frequently into Type II, i.e. they exhibit a sentimental and ineffective pacifism (31 per cent). Among the rural population of both sexes, Type III (passive acceptance of war) predominates and this type, moreover, is much more frequent in the south of Kyushu than in Hokkaido. On the other hand, Type I predominates among the industrial workers of both sexes in Yawata and Bibai. The results of the investigation and number of subjects questioned are shown in Table 17.

TABLE 17.

Location	Sex	Type I	Type II	Type III	Number of subjects
F. village (Kyushu)	M.	1	1	8	10
	F	1	4	4	9
Yawata	M.	8	3	0	11
	F	4	2	2	8
T. village (Hokkaido)	M.	3	0	4	7
	F.	1	4	6	11
Bibai	M.	1	1	0	2
	F.	2	0	1	3
H. village (Hokkaido)	M.	0	1	0	1
	F.	0	0	1	1
Total	M.	13	6	12	31
	F.	9	10	13	32
Grand total		22	16	25	63

This analysis by Sofue makes it possible to interpret the attitudes towards military service and the rearmament of Japan. There is not the slightest room for doubt that Japanese youth is against military service. In support of this assertion we are not relying only on our personal experiences: for instance, a young man from a busy port in Hokkaido told us in public, quite calmly and spontaneously, that he was firmly determined to disobey his call-up notice; the man fully appreciated the gravity of his decision and was ready to accept all the consequences. But apart from numerous personal observations of this kind—some of them striking—we also have the questionnaires completed by the Kyoto and Sapporo students. At Kyoto 84 per cent of the men and 93 per cent of the women said they were against military service for men, as did also 94 per cent of the students at Sapporo; opposition to the idea of military service for women was still stronger—95 per cent, 98 per cent and 94 per cent respectively. We are dealing here, it is true, exclusively with intellectuals, who are inclined to go to extremes in such matters; nevertheless, the percentages are so high that they indicate beyond doubt the direction in which the opinion of most young people is tending.

At the time of writing, Japan is starting out along the path of rearmament. The 1946 Constitution contained an Article solemnly renouncing war, and as a result of this the only armed forces left at Japan's disposal were the National Police Reserve Corps and the coastguards. In January 1952 an investigation undertaken by the *Yomiuri Shimbun* revealed that 57 per cent of the public was in favour of Japan's rearmament, 37 per cent preferred the strengthening of the National Police Reserve Corps, but 47 per cent considered that the Constitution needed revision. Here we have a fresh situation, revealing a great change in public sentiment. In May 1946, immediately after the promulgation of the Constitution, an enquiry by the *Mainichi Shimbun* covering 2,000 intellectuals revealed that a large majority (69 per cent) of the men and 73 per cent of the women, or 72 per cent of the group as a whole) thought that the Article of the Constitution renouncing war was 'necessary'. A number of investigations carried out during the intervening years enable us to trace the evolution of public feeling (Table 18).

TABLE 18.

Date of investigation	For rearmament	Against rearmament	Body responsible for the investigation
	%	%	
August 1950	39	33	Yomiuri
March 1951	47	24	Yomiuri
August 1951	51	32	Yomiuri
January 1952	57	24	Yomiuri

Sofue's study shows that a majority of the young are opposed to rearmament—46 per cent, compared with 41 per cent in favour. The enquiry in question was not representative, but it may be taken as a fact that the young are consistently more pacifist than their elders. For instance, according to an investigation carried out by the newspaper *Asahi* in September 1950, which yielded results appreciably different from those obtained by the *Yomiuri Shimbun* (probably because, in the *Asahi* enquiry, the question of rearmament is more or less linked with the Korean incident, then in its opening stages), the strength of opposition to rearmament varies in inverse proportion to the age of the subjects interrogated and reaches its peak among those who have had a higher education. In the age-groups 20-29, 40 per cent were against rearmament; 30-39 (32 per cent); 40-49 (26 per cent); 50-59 (19 per cent); and in the age-group 20-29 of those who had had a university (or equivalent) education, 51 per cent.

This attitude in the young of opposition to rearmament deserves closer study. In almost all cases we find that girls are more against it than young men. It is also noticeable that, among the men, the opposition comes much more from industrial workers than from peasants; indeed, in the villages of F. and T. a majority of 71 per cent of the peasants are in favour of rearmament. In any case, the pacifist opinions of young women should not be lumped together in the same percentage with those of young workers.

An extremely interesting comparison made by Sofue between the distribution of subjects in the three types analysed above, and their opinions on rearmament, points to the following conclusions: among the men, those against rearmament belong predominantly to Type I and those in favour to Type III. Sofue's comment is worth quoting: 'Most supporters of the anti-rearmament movement base their views on "very severe criticism of the army" as it used to be', which is well justified. On the other hand it is clear that most of those who support rearmament do so on the strength of an 'uncritical attitude towards the former Japanese army and failure to appreciate its crimes'. There are, nevertheless, some subjects who support rearmament despite the fact that they belong to Type I; these are 'against it in principle' but they look at it from an angle that 'may make them accept it as inevitable having regard to the present situation'. The position as regards women is quite different: the majority of those who belong to the anti-rearmament group make no criticism of the old army. Here again Sofue's report should be quoted: 'It is therefore conceivable that their opposition is based more on sentiment than on principle; that they are influenced by their environment, i.e. by the opinions of others, and especially by the propaganda they absorb in the group organizations to which they belong; that they harbour little "criticism or hatred toward the army", and that their hostile views do not go below the surface of their thoughts.' The consequence of this is serious in the case of the younger women, as Sofue clearly points out: 'If propaganda in favour of rearmament is strongly concentrated on these women, it is not difficult to imagine that they will be easily converted.'

Hence the forces of pacifism in Japan are perhaps less substantial and effective than may have appeared a few years ago and even than they appear now on a superficial examination. Indeed, it is already significant that the young people in the country areas, particularly in the former province of Satsuma, which had such strong military traditions in the past and played so important a part in the building of imperialist Japan, accept with equal calm the memory of the last war and the remilitarization of the country. But it is, perhaps, even more serious that, without those concerned (especially the women) being even aware of it, so many undoubtedly sincere pacifist opinions are seen, on analysis, to be superficial and sentimental, easy to upset, and probably fated to be so. The students, whose degree of psychological maturity we shall have to discuss later, are perhaps more decided in their opinions. The young trade unionists, in any case, are undoubtedly so—but is their pacifist attitude coloured by political considerations? In some instances this is not impossible, but the warmth of the anti-war convictions of many of them leaves no room for doubt. By way of illustration, I should like to refer to the reaction of a young Yawata workman to Plate I of the projective test, designed, it must be said, to arouse quite other emotions: 'This picture shows a woman who has come to visit her lover in prison. The man was arrested on a charge of organizing an anti-war movement. It is just like the French resistance against the Nazis. As he thinks himself justified in the eyes of God, there is no shame in his bearing. The woman feels no special uneasiness or fear although she appears to be very tired.'

The wave of pacifism which flooded Japan at the end of the war was not only the result of reflection about the evil wrought by military adventures; it was also a consequence of people's feeling that now the war was over, not only did they want no more of it but they need have no more of it—in other words, that war was not only avoidable but would be avoided in future. Even today this attitude is not exceptional in Japan—the National Public Opinion Research Institute has discovered that it is held by 30 per cent of the public as a whole—but it is not the majority view either, since 52 per cent of the people hold the contrary opinion. On this question, the young show greater optimism (as Table 19 shows).

TABLE 19.

| Age-group | War is | | No opinion |
	avoidable	unavoidable	
	%	%	%
Urban			
16-19	49	45	6
20-24	43	54	3
25-29	42	53	5
30 and over	33	59	8
Rural			
16-19	48	45	8
20-24	41	45	14
25-29	41	50	9
30 and over	38	52	10

The students are in principle still more optimistic (Table 20).

TABLE 20.

	War is useless and avoidable	War is a necessary evil	War is some-times useful	No opinion
	%	%	%	%
Kyoto				
Men	72	16	8	4
Women	58	37	4	1
Sapporo	88	6	6	0

Moreover, they regard the possibility of another war with a great deal of fear, as we have seen, and the majority believe that its outcome would be the complete destruction of civilization (Table 21).

TABLE 21.

| | Results of another war | | | |
	Total destruction	Check to progress	No change	No opinion
Kyoto	%	%	%	%
Men	52	38	10	0
Women	50	45	5	0
Sapporo	59	23	12	6

However, the majority—which is very large at Kyoto—expects another world war within a relatively brief period (Table 22).

TABLE 22.

| | Prospects of war | | | |
	Within 5 years	Within 15 years	No war	No opinion
Kyoto	%	%	%	%
Men	31	43	13	1
Women	24	55	5	1
Sapporo	18	35	41	0

The subjects interviewed by Sofue put the date of the probable outbreak even earlier: 61 per cent of the men and 55 per cent of the women think that there will be another world war in less than five years. Questioned on the use to which atomic energy will be put 25 years from now, 59 per cent of the male students of Kyoto, and 68 per cent of the girls thought it would be primarily military and destructive; against this, however, must be set the fact that an overwhelming majority (82 per cent) of the Sapporo students thought that atomic energy would be used mainly for industrial purposes.

The Korean war appears to have made a profound impression. The investigation sponsored by *Asahi* in September 1950, indicates that the opinion most frequently expressed (34 per cent) is that the Korean war has had a bad influence on Japan, and this view is still more strongly held by the young (36 per cent). Above all, however, and in a more general way, it is the overt hostility between the United States of America and the Soviet Union which haunts the minds of Japanese and, wherever their sympathies lie, it is there that they see the source of possible danger in the future. Several of the 'autobiographies of the future' produced by students of the University of Hokkaido centre on this theme. It is also the leitmotiv of the verbal answers to one of the questions in Sofue's interview: 'What do you think will happen in the world during the next five years? What changes will take place, and what will happen in Japan?' A verbatim quotation from Sofue's report on this point is very illuminating as regards the way in which the young think about the future.

'*F., T. and H. villages.* (In the world): Hostility between the United States of America and the Soviet Union; cold war; war between the United States of America and the Soviet Union; expansion of science. (In Japan): Communist riots; lining up with the United States of America through the rearmament of Japan; expansion of science; improvement of living conditions.'

'*Yawata and Bibai.* (In the world): Hostility between the United States of America and the Soviet Union; cold war; armaments race; war between the United States of America and the Soviet Union; survival either of capitalism or of communism; crash of capitalism and survival of socialism. (In Japan): A rearmed Japan will be used as a tool by the United States of America; Japan will be reduced to the position of a United States colony; democracy will be overthrown; the working classes will make progress.'

Many young people ascribe either to the Soviet Union or to the United States of America intentions dangerous to peace in general or to Japan in particular. In 1950 the newspaper *Asahi* asked the following question: 'Is it true that the Communists think peace is possible only after the triumph of Communism?' (Table 23).

TABLE 23.

Age-group	Yes	No	No opinion
	%	%	%
20-29	45	24	31
30-39	36	26	38
40-49	40	24	36
50 and over	24	21	55

This indicates that the young, even more often than others, see in Communism a source of international instability and an obstacle to peace; this view is commoner still among persons who have received a higher education (60 per cent for all groups) and reaches its maximum frequency among young people who have attended universities (67 per cent). A certain number of young people, however, are no less suspicious of the United States of America. Plate 8 of the projective test used by

Sofue shows Prime Minister Yoshida shaking hands with General Mac-Arthur. Most of the subjects to whom this picture was shown saw in the scene a symbol of the good understanding between Japan and the United States of America. But this was not invariably the case, as the following extract shows:

'Prime Minister Yoshida is giving MacArthur a friendly smile but in his mind is the thought that only submission to the United States of America can keep him where he is. MacArthur is asking him to collaborate in the future, as in the past, for the good of the United States of America, and is picking his words with great care. MacArthur is probably thinking that Japan must do the utmost possible because she is a strategic base for America.'

In all, Sofue collected seven replies on these lines, six from Yawata factory workers (19 per cent of the men) and one from a woman (3 per cent of the female group). He comments that all seven subjects belong to Type I described earlier, and are actively pacifist.

Although Soviet-American tension is a clearly marked obstacle to the new pacifist philosophy of the Japanese, which has taken particularly strong root among the young, and although it causes anxiety and dis-appointment, the reaction to it is not merely one of vain regret. Pacifism has its limits and, despite objections and even repugnance which no attempt is made to dissimulate and about which, accordingly, there is no need to keep silent, there is no doubt as to the side on which the Japan-ese have chosen to range themselves. In this respect the attitudes of the young are no different from those of the rest of the public. The tabulated answers to two questions set by the *Asahi Shimbun* in Septem-ber 1950 should set at rest any lingering doubts on this subject:

Question: 'It is said in some quarters that, to prevent the present situation from developing into a world war, it would be better to let all Korea become Communist provided a Treaty is signed whereby the Soviet Union undertakes not to expand its territory any further. Do you approve or disapprove of this view?' (Table 24).

TABLE 24.

Age-group	Approve	Disapprove	No opinion
	%	%	%
Sample as a whole	7	53	40
20-29	8	54	28
30-39	7	60	33
40-49	5	63	32
50 and over	6	43	51

Question: 'Do you think that it is best to keep out of war at all costs even if it means Japan would become Communist?' (Table 25).

TABLE 25.

Age-group	Yes	No	No opinion
	%	%	%
Sample as a whole	10	57	33
20-29	13	63	24
30-39	12	62	26
40-49	10	62	28
50 and over	10	47	43

Replies in the negative show practically the same percentages in both cases. The second question, which relates to what is still very much a hypothetical situation, whereas the first is concerned with actual events, produced rather more replies in the affirmative. The young are no different from the rest of the population, except that they seem to make up their minds more easily. The fact is that Japan has chosen her side. We must not however lose sight of the fact that a minority of about 10 per cent disagrees with the choice made.

CHAPTER VI

YOUTH AND PUBLIC INSTITUTIONS

THE ECONOMIC SITUATION

From the sociological, or the ethnographical, point of view institutions are simply the regular 'ways' of a society, its manners and customs, regarded as having a certain finality, as designed to meet certain needs and perform certain functions, which analysis reveals. Thus one can describe and, if one so desires, attempt to interpret, for instance, the economic, political, or family behaviour of the Japanese nation.

But for the individual member of the society concerned, institutions are not external phenomena. As, for him, the society in which he lives is the actual environment to which he must adjust himself, and the field of his activities, its institutions are, as it were, predetermined moulds in which he is called upon to shape his conduct—his emotional as well as his practical or symbolical conduct. Indeed, in principle there is no reason for him to refrain from doing what his social environment seems to expect him to do: it would generally be a mistake to suppose that his institutional behaviour is forced on him; on the contrary, he cultivates it in the course of his social training because it offers the easiest way of adapting himself to his environment; what is more, institutional behaviour has its scale of values, and bringing his own conduct into line with it not only ensures his social success but also gives him the inner satisfaction of feeling that he is doing right.

That, at least, is how it works in theory. In practice few societies lay down for their members models of behaviour that have to be followed with equal strictness at all stages. To use Ralph Linton's terminology, while there are in every society 'universal' cultural traits and 'specialities' restricted to certain categories of its members, there are also traits which are 'alternative', or optional. When confronted with the latter, the sociologist need only describe them without taking sides. But the individual who is a member of the society in question must choose, and for that reason pass judgments, take risks and resolve conflicts of values.

The Japanese society of today is, so to speak, a perfect example of a state of affairs in which the main institutional traits have become optional. Since the defeat, the new watchword, 'democracy', is applied not only in the political sphere but to family relations, to the respective status of the two sexes, to the economic structure and to education. The old social order subsists, nevertheless, because values are nothing apart from the men who harbour them; it can never be possible to carry out a complete blood transfusion on a society: the generations overtaken by events are continuous with the new generations. Thus several types of institutional behaviour may exist side by side. The law itself sanctions the optional character of many forms of behaviour which might have been made obligatory, as we have seen in the case of reforms relating to the family.

In circumstances of this kind, the young are particularly interesting to observe, not only because their personal values are not yet fully crystallized and they may therefore seem to be more pliable, but above all because they are just reaching the age of choice, and are beginning to accept responsibility. It is therefore proposed, in the present chapter, to study the attitudes of Japanese youth towards the principal institutions.

As regards the economic structure, we were faced with a dearth of relevant documents. Two series of major measures have been put into force, the dissolution of the *zaibatsu* (economic and financial trusts) and the parcelling out of the great landed estates. In both cases the present situation is confused and it is difficult to judge how far these reforms will be carried out in practice. It would have been particularly interesting to see what are the attitudes of the young to these reforms and how much attention they pay them. There are several allusions to them in the 'autobiographies' of the Sapporo students.

'In practice', writes one student, 'the democratization of Japan is very behindhand, and the Japanese farming villages are repositories of the feudalistic dust of Japan's backwardness. The post-war land reform and the democratization of the farming villages were only partial. Thus, even though the farming villages are at present modernized and "capitalistic", the relations between the landowner and the tenant, between the rich and the poor farmer, are the same as they were in the middle ages. The special features of capitalist society are to be seen in the process. The suffering and the aspirations of the poor farmers who form the lowest class of this society (these feelings are similar to those of the labouring class under the capitalist system) can only be dealt with in a positive sense if these farmers form co-operative associations in a logical way, based on economic science.'

Another student, giving his impression of the future, writes: 'With the completion of the fifth five-year plan in 1984 private ownership of land entirely vanished from Japan.'

Yet a third looks forward to a peaceful socialist revolution which he pictures as world-wide: '1972. . . . Japan has feared revolution but it is now relieved of these fears, because relations between the United States of America and the U.S.S.R. have become less strained. This improvement of Russo-American relations between the two powers is due to American socialization within a short period. . . . The era of planned economy has begun. . . . 1982. . . . In present-day Japan the working class has absolute authority. Over the past 10 years there have been some struggles between the working class and the capitalists but each time labour has gained in strength.'

It should not however be thought, on the strength of these quotations, that the young have all become socialist. F. Vos put the following question to the group of young people he was studying in Tokyo: 'Was the influence of the *zaibatsu* good or bad?' Thirty-eight per cent answered it had been bad, but 20 per cent said that it had been good and 26 per cent that it had been good in some respects—i.e. there were some 46 per cent who declined to condemn the *zaibatsu* out of hand in spite of the fact that these were being treated as scapegoats both by the occupation services and by the Japanese Government.

There is no doubt whatsoever that economic difficulties weigh heavily upon Japanese youth. This figures very frequently in their replies when they are asked what makes them most unhappy and causes them most anxiety. Economic security and a higher standard of living are regarded as the most important conditions for happiness by those who think that health alone is not enough (these, by the way, are in the minority, which is perhaps, in itself, significant). Lastly, of seven possible aims in life from which subjects were asked to make a choice, the one most frequently picked out by the sample as a whole is framed in the following terms: 'to achieve material security through your own work'; on the other hand, the aim least frequently picked in almost all groups is: 'to become rich by devoting every ounce of energy to your work' (in this case the explanation may of course be that wealth is a goal so distant and inaccessible that hardly anyone dares to dream of it).

The reply percentages to the above questions among the younger age groups, as obtained by the National Opinion Research Institute, are set out in Table 26.

TABLE 26.

	Urban		Rural	
	16-19	*20-24*	*16-19*	*20-24*
	%	%	%	%
Economic and financial problems are my biggest worry	11	12	10	16
Economic security, etc., is necessary as well as health (percentage taken from those considering that health is not enough)	29	30	36	40
Aim in life: to achieve freedom from material cares	27	34	24	27
Aim in life: to become rich	1	1	4	3

This sort of obsession with financial difficulties is extremely noticeable among the Kyoto and Sapporo students. Among the 'two things they most want and have not got', 35 per cent of the Sapporo students and 35 per cent of the men at Kyoto mention 'money'; the proportion of girls at Kyoto making the same reply is only 15 per cent, probably because their financial responsibilities are much less. Asked about 'the two worst things that could conceivably happen to them', the young people in question do not forget to mention 'destitution' (Kyoto: men 9 per cent, women 8 per cent; Sapporo: 6 per cent) and a fair number think that it is, indeed, likely to happen to them (Kyoto: men 6 per cent, women 6 per cent; Sapporo: 18 per cent).

It must, however, be realized that economic worries far less frequently take the general form of 'lack of money' or of a desire for material security, among the young than among their elders. The great preoccupation of the young is to learn a trade, or enter a profession. In all the above extracts from the investigation carried out by the National Public Opinion Research Institute, the percentages of answers on the lines indicated are much lower among 'the under 25s' than among those over that age. On the other hand, the young more often refer to worries about their career. (Table 27).

TABLE 27.

Age-group	Most serious worry		Condition of happiness, apart from health[1]	
	Economic difficulties	Career	Financial security	Success in career
Urban	%	%	%	%
16-19	11	11	29	9
20-24	12	3	30	2
25-29	24	3	39	7
30 and over	26	7	36	6
Rural				
16-19	10	12	36	6
20-24	16	6	40	3
25-29	18	6	47	8
30 and over	25	6	35	4

1. Percentages taken from the 30 per cent minority which considers that health is not enough by itself.

It will be seen that these are burning problems, particularly among the 'under 20s', i.e. among those who in fact have not yet got a trade or profession. Among the students at Kyoto and Sapporo, the fear of failure in their job is several times mentioned among the 'worst things that could conceivably happen' and among those that 'are likely to happen'. At Kyoto for instance, the proportions of young men giving replies in this sense are respectively 5 per cent and 17 per cent. It is also rather significant that, at any rate among the young men at Kyoto, the 10-year period from which they expect most satisfaction is the one immediately following, i.e. the period in which they become settled in their job; the same point emerges clearly more than once from 'autobiographies of the future', written by Sapporo students. From the answers of the Kyoto students it is easy to discern the extreme importance the young attach to their job, which is placed after family life but well before every other kind of activity as likely to provide the greatest satisfaction. Hence, unemployment frequently crops up among the unprompted answers of subjects about their fears: 11 per cent of the Kyoto students class it as one of the two greatest misfortunes that could conceivably happen to them, and 8 per cent think it will really be their lot.

However, these fears shut out neither hope nor ambition. One of the questions addressed by the National Public Opinion Research Institute to the Japanese public as a whole was: 'Is there any particular thing you hope to achieve during your lifetime?' The replies of 2 per cent of the subjects referred to their 'social position', which in many cases meant their hope of promotion in their employment ('I have been taken on by a company: I want to become a foreman with them'); 4 per cent said they wanted to become experts in some particular job or to achieve technical skill of some kind ('I should like to try to work out my own special stock-raising techniques'), and 11 per cent mentioned their ambition for success in their occupations ('I want to be the best man in Japan in my line of work'). The special ambitions of the young are brought out by Table 28, in which the replies are arranged according to age-groups.

TABLE 28.

Age-group	Social position	Technical skills, craftsmanship	Success in occupation
Urban	%	%	%
16-19	3	9	8
20-24	4	7	17
25-29	1	5	23
30 and over	2	2	13
Rural			
16-19	3	18	14
20-24	2	7	11
25-29	2	3	11
30 and over	2	1	7

In the opinion of many, higher education is the normal way of achieving social mobility and a better social position. The vast majority of the students interrogated intended to take up occupations different from those of their parents. (Table 29).

TABLE 29.

| | Kyoto | | Sapporo |
	Men	Women	
	%	%	%
Same occupation as father	12	6	12
Same occupation as mother	1	7	
Closely related occupation	19	13	18
Different occupation	68	74	71
No reply	0	1	0

On the whole, and despite very real grounds for apprehension, the Japanese are not pessimists. The majority think that living conditions throughout the world will become progressively better and the youngest age groups are frankly optimistic—an impression which not only emerges from documents such as the 'autobiographies of the future' written by the Sapporo students but is confirmed by the investigation of the National Public Opinion Research Institute. (Table 30).

TABLE 30.

Age-group	Conditions will get progressively better	There will be no change	Conditions will get worse	No reply
	%	%	%	%
Urban				
16-19	56	14	14	16
20-24	48	18	17	18
25-29	46	21	13	20
30 and over	36	22	25	17
Rural				
16-19	49	21	16	15
20-24	46	25	15	15
25-29	46	17	24	13
30 and over	32	26	28	14

However attached they may be to tradition, the Japanese waste no time on futile regret for the past. In the group interviewed by Sofue, barely 7 per cent said they would have preferred to have lived in some bygone age; 37 per cent preferred the future, while 41 per cent (54 per cent of the men) were satisfied with the present. The Japanese put their trust in their capacity for hard work and also, especially, in technology, which many of them call 'science'. As we have already seen, technology is what they most admire in foreign nations and what they most want to borrow from them. The chief cause of their difficulties, in their opinion, is over-population: in 1950 the National Public Opinion Research Institute asked what should be done to remedy the lack of food, houses and employment;

over-population was mentioned in 6o per cent of the replies, and although no analysis of answers by age-groups is available, the same investigation showed that the younger generation was considerably better informed on the population problem than their elders. According to the investigation carried out by Vos in Tokyo, 69 per cent of the young people interrogated said that an increase in the Japanese population would cause serious difficulties. Demography is therefore the scapegoat at the moment, so far as the country's economic difficulties are concerned. The investigation carried out in 1950 by NPORI shows that 79 per cent of the general public would support a policy of birth control. There are, however, other points of view—of which we have seen examples among the Sapporo students: these lay the blame on social inequalities and on reforms that seem to lead nowhere. It is significant that in Vos's group the percentage in favour of the official promotion of birth control is smaller than among the public as a whole—being no more than 66 per cent, although this figure is still very high. We lack the data to assess the strength of the opposite opinion, and especially to estimate its later development.

PARTICIPATION IN POLITICAL LIFE

So far as can be seen, then, Japanese youth on the whole is not inclined to criticize the country's economic system and seems more disposed to seek a solution for its material problems in individual effort. We now have to consider whether it adopts a more independent attitude towards political institutions or whether it follows the tradition of submission to authority. One is tempted to say that the second attitude is both more common and more deeply engrained, but this statement needs qualification.

It is indeed true that Japanese youth is sincerely trying to break with the political ideology of the past and wants to repudiate its heroes and teachers of yesterday. Vos put the following question to the group he was interrogating in Tokyo: 'Do you think that the ideas of Japan's military and political leaders between 1930 and 1940 were basically correct, in spite of the fact that those leaders were not able to achieve their aims?' Forty-nine per cent replied that the ideas were wrong, but 26 per cent thought that they were correct up to a point, and 15 per cent considered that they were basically correct. For instance, a 22-year-old office worker said: 'They tried to make Japan a great country but they went about it in the wrong way; it was a stupid idea to go to war with the United States of America and England.' A 22-year-old typist said: 'There was some good in their ideas but their methods were bad.' The young whole-heartedly welcome the new watchword, *freedom*, but in fact they do not find it so very new. In Vos's group 76 per cent thought it perfectly consistent with Japanese culture and several remarked that it had existed in the past: 'In the Heian era', said a 19-year-old sales girl, 'we tried to find it and now we are trying again.' These young people do not, however, think that a democratic régime like that of Great Britain, France or the United States of America would suit Japan. This is the view held by 53 per cent, against 22 per cent who are of the opposite opinion and 10 per cent who think that it would suit Japan up to a certain point. But this does not mean that they reject democracy; what they want is a 'Japanese democracy', which has still to be created. 'Every nation is different, so the system in each country must be different, too.'

Nevertheless, older people are often heard reproaching the young for having embraced the new ideal of liberty too hastily, without having given enough thought to it. The rector of a university told me that the young understood the forms of democracy but not its spirit; only a short while previously, a party of students from another university had come to us to complain: 'We have been given institutions which are democratic in form but not in spirit.' The juxtaposition of these two remarks, taken from one of my notebooks, is not ironical: it brings us face to face with a question already raised by the comparison with Vos's observations, namely, what is the Japanese conception of democracy?

Nothing much is to be expected from replies to the direct question: 'What do you understand by democracy?' Vos did ask it but all he got by way of answer were clichés such as 'freedom', 'individualism', 'respect for the individual', 'government by the masses', and 'all of us voting together.' A question tried by Sofue in his questionnaire proved rather too ingenuous: 'Since, in a democratic nation, the men in power have been elected by a majority of the people, do you think that responsibility for what happens in that nation falls primarily on those in power or on those who elected them?' The trap was obvious and none of the subjects fell into it, which is a tribute to their intelligence but casts no light on their political philosophy. Another of Sofue's questions did, however, secure the kind of answer we were looking for: 'Democracy is sometimes defined as "government of the people, by the people, for the people". If you were compelled to choose, where would you yourself place the most emphasis, on "by the people" or "for the people"?' The replies are certainly worth study. In the group Sofue examined, 64 per cent of the men and 74 per cent of the women replied, 'on *for the people*'. Sofue suggests that these replies were given at random. However, the question was repeated to the Kyoto and Sapporo students and the proportions replying 'for the people' were 59 per cent at Sapporo, and at Kyoto 57 per cent of the males and 64 per cent of the females.

It is possible, in Sofue's opinion, that these reactions to a formula which was after all unfamiliar to the persons interrogated, who may therefore have missed its full ideological significance, do not mean what they seem to imply. Yet the fact remains that in their replies men are more inclined than women to think of democracy in terms of government 'by the people', and the same tendency is to be observed in the industrial workers of Yawata as compared with the peasants; and even among the latter, so far as it is possible to draw conclusions from differences between groups so small numerically, the people of T. village in Hokkaido, chose 'by the people' more frequently than those of F. village, in Kyushu. From the data available, the most likely hypothesis is that the young Japanese, even the factory workers and students, choose democracy 'for the people'.

Besides, the notion that what matters to the citizen is not what he gets but how he gets it, the exercising of a right and not the benefits this brings him, the idea that even a bad decision, which a man will have to pay for, but which he has made himself, is preferable to measures taken 'for his good' in which he has had no voice—this point of view is not so very widely accepted and understood even in the West. How much less so, then, in Japan. Both the rector and the students we have quoted above might be surprised if we tried to point out to them the virtues of the democratic process as such, and were to explain to them that freedom subjected to reservations as to its ends, freedom to do a specific thing, is not freedom at all. Moreover, we shall see later, when we begin to analyse the personality of young Japanese, that the 'social' type greatly preponderates over the 'will to power' type, and we shall realize that the preference for 'government for the people' to 'government by the people' is an almost immediate psychological consequence of this fact.

To all appearances the youth of Japan does not show a very great, still less a very active, interest in internal politics. At several points of our journey, young people, notably students at Fukuoka and workmen from a Hokkaido village, came to complain to us of their members of parliament, on the grounds that they had not kept their promises about improving living conditions, organizing peace and bringing about disarmament. But on the whole the young are, as we have seen, much more interested in international than in domestic affairs. (Table 31).

TABLE 31.

	Kyoto		Sapporo
	Men	Women	
	%	%	%
Points about the future, up to A.D. 2000, mentioned by subjects as arousing greatest curiosity:			
International questions	79	58	76
National questions	20	24	47
Personal questions	42	53	24
Subjects considering they are more interested in:			
International affairs	59	49	76
National affairs	31	24	12

It need only be remarked in passing that the Sapporo students, who more frequently regard themselves as members of the working class, are more politically minded than those at Kyoto, most of whom consider themselves middle class (compare, in this connexion, the percentages of those in each group mentioning national questions and personal questions in the first part of the above table).

Active interest in politics is very rare indeed, as may be seen from the results of the investigation carried out by the National Public Opinion Research Institute, in which two questions were asked which throw a good deal of light on the situation: 'Is there any particular thing you hope to achieve in the course of your life?', and: 'If a society or a meeting of any kind interested you, would you be inclined to take a lead in it or to make a personal contribution to the proceedings? If the answer is yes, what kind of society or meeting have you in mind?' To the first question, 70 per cent of the sample as a whole replied that they had some such aim in life, but only 1 per cent mentioned political aims ('When I am rich I will try to do something to benefit the administration of the village'; 'I want to help bring in a government of such a kind that there will no longer be any men who cannot get a living for their wives and children'; 'As a woman I cannot become prime minister but I want to take part in political life'. Forty-one per cent said they would be inclined to take the lead in societies or meetings, but only 2 per cent had political or trade union associations in mind: the analytical code grouped these two kinds of associations together). Table 32 shows the distribution of replies according to age-groups.

TABLE 32.

Age-group	Having a political aim in life	Prepared to take the lead in societies and meetings of a political character
	%	%
Urban		0
16-19	3	2
20-24	4	2
25-29	1	1
30 and over	1	
Rural		0
16-19	1	*
20-24	0	2
25-29	1	1
30 and over	1	

* Less than 0.5 per cent.

It will be seen that young people in the towns take slightly more interest in politics than the others, but no one under 20 years of age thinks himself capable of taking the initiative or playing a leading role. The investigation carried out in 1948 by the National Public Opinion Research

Institute among women in paid employment provides data on behaviour that cross-checks these data on attitudes. It shows that trade union membership, which averages 47 per cent over the sample as a whole, is highest between the ages of 20 and 30 and falls off markedly after the age of 40, while on the other hand the proportion holding office in the unions increases with age. (Table 33).

TABLE 33.

Women in employment	Union members	Union officials
	%	%
Sample as a whole	47	12
Up to 17	46	0
18-19	57	3
20-21	56	14
22-23	61	14
24-25	63	22
26-27	52	13
28-29	56	20
30-39	45 }	23
40 and over	41 }	

It thus appears that political activity on the part of the young, though not very marked, is slightly greater than among the older citizens, even though the social structure offers young people fewer opportunities of taking on responsible positions. In spite of this fact, the young seem considerably more inclined to make use of their civic rights: in 1947 an investigation carried out by the Jiji news agency showed that the young were more willing than their elders to accept the idea of a strike of civil servants and schoolteachers. (Table 34).

TABLE 34.

Age-group	A strike is unavoidable	A strike is a bad thing
Men	%	%
Sample as a whole	36	59
21-30	39	56
31-40	41	56
41-50	30	66
51 and over	24	70
Women		
Sample as a whole	29	57
21-30	37	54
31-40	34	52
41-50	24	59
51 and over	19	62

ATTITUDE TOWARDS AUTHORITY

Japanese youth appears disposed to show more independence in face of the civil authority, but a study of the available data from investigations leads us to conclude that this attitude is still not very firm and is more the exception than the rule. The investigation of the Jiji agency, from which we have quoted above, provides additional information. In the first place, the circumstances in which this representative enquiry— covering 4,000 subjects—was conducted in February 1947, must be briefly outlined. In January 1947, as negotiations between the government and the civil service trade unions had broken down, and arbitration by the Central Labour Relations Office had achieved no results, the unions called their 2,600,000 members out on strike with effect from 1 February; the strike was avoided only by an order by General MacArthur, the Supreme Allied Commander. Thereupon the Jiji Tsushin organized its investigation, in the course of which the following question was asked: 'Although the general strike of civil servants and teachers has been avoided, which party, in your opinion—the government or the unions— has shown itself unreasonable?' Table 35 shows that the young blamed the government more often than the other groups. It may also be noted that the women more frequently abstained from answering the question.

TABLE 35.

Age-group	Government unreasonable	Unions unreasonable
Men	%	%
Sample as a whole	31	50
21-30	33	49
31-40	34	50
41-50	29	52
51 and over	21	56
Women		
Sample as a whole	22	38
21-30	25	44
31-40	26	38
41-50	21	36
51 and over	14	30

The investigation carried out by the National Public Opinion Research Institute provides some data that tend to confirm this more independent attitude of the young towards authority, the greater frequency of their desire to make their views heard, and their more critical attitude. Thus, when asked to express an opinion on the dictum, *never contradict a superior*, more than a quarter of the subjects interrogated said they did not know the dictum and the number of young people declining to answer was considerable (54 per cent in the towns and 52 per cent in the country, in the case of the 16-19 age-group, compared with 13 per cent and 22 per cent respectively for the over 30 age-group). The majority disagreed with the dictum (41 per cent against 32 per cent). The relative difference between approval and disapproval is markedly greater among the young and diminishes with age, until, when it comes to the over 30 age-group, the majority view is that the dictum represents an attitude inevitable in a subordinate. The large majority (70 per cent) of Japanese think that citizens should be able to discuss public affairs in general; the percentage holding this view is, in all age-groups, lower in the rural areas; the number of abstentions is more or less constant, and the view that public affairs are better left exclusively to the government is much more common in the country. In every case, however, the younger the subjects interrogated, the more frequently they maintain that it is better to express one's opinions as freely as possible.

When the investigation is pressed further, however, their certainty about freedom of speech and the right of discussion begins to crumble and authority recovers all its prestige. The question put by the NPORI was phrased in these terms: 'In recent years it has become a basic assumption that public affairs are the concern of everybody in the country, and all have the right to discuss and criticize them from every angle as you do when a building is being put up. How will this work out in practice? In the case of unusually complex and technical questions, do you think it is unavoidable that these should be left entirely to the authorities concerned?' This time, three-quarters of the sample as a whole thought that it was unavoidable and the young showed hardly more independence than the rest; on the other hand it is worth noting that the country-dwellers, perhaps because the illustration of co-operative house building meant more to them, were less ready to renounce the right of free discussion. (Table 36).

TABLE 36.

Age-group	It is unavoidable	Such questions should not be left entirely to the authorities
Urban	%	%
16-19	76	24
20-24	81	19
25-29	72	28
30 and over	81	19
Rural		
16-19	69	31
20-24	71	29
25-29	70	30
30 and over	72	28

One test of attitudes towards authority is to secure the subject's reaction to situations in which the police are involved. The investigation carried out by the National Public Opinion Research Institute included two questions of this type: 'Do you think that people examined by the police are all of doubtful character, or are some of them different?' 'Do you know anything about the recent incident at Tokyo University? If so, what do you think of the attitudes of the students and the police respectively? Which of the two explanations seems to you the more acceptable?' In reply to the first question, the classification code makes no distinction between the two answers 'don't know' and 'some are different'. Replies under this head accounted for 80 per cent of the sample as a whole. It is, however, clear that the young are much less inclined than the others to uphold the police on principle. In the under-20 age-group only 15 per cent of those living in the towns and 12 per cent of those living in the country answered that people suspected by the police are invariably bad characters: the corresponding percentages for the 20-24 age-group are 17 per cent and 15 per cent.

The second question alludes to an incident of a political character. In the middle of February 1952, the students of Tokyo University discovered four plain-clothes policemen in the university precincts during the performance of a play. The students took forcible possession of the notebooks of three of the officers, from which they discovered that the police had been shadowing instructors and students of advanced views day and night in order to find out about their opinions. The affair caused rather a sensation and was debated in the Diet. A very large proportion of the people questioned by NPORI declined to express an opinion as between police and students. Some said they did not know enough about the matter to judge, others that they did not understand the incident, and others simply that they did not know. In the final count those expressing a definite opinion either way did not exceed 32 per cent

TABLE 37.

Age-group	Version preferred		Ill-informed	Don't understand	Don't know
	Students	Police			
Urban	%	%	%	%	%
16-19	17	11.5	11.5	16	44
20-24	25	12	14	25	24
25-29	24	15	14	19	28
30 and over	16	17	10	18	39
Rural					
16-19	13	17	7	17	46
20-24	13	15	10	14	48
25-29	15	15	14	12	44
30 and over	10	17	10	15	43

of the sample as a whole. In the main, the replies of those in the towns favour the students and the replies of those of the country favour the police; the 20—30 age-group shows the most sympathy with the students and the least with the police, but the most striking feature of the replies is the ignorance, or caution, or both, of those interrogated. (Table 37).

It must be admitted that the above results lead to no clear-cut conclusion; these two questions proved perhaps the least satisfactory of those included in the NPORI investigation. They give some indication of the groups in which sympathy for the police is least lively, but a major element of uncertainty is introduced by the fact that too many of those questioned either could not or would not give an opinion.[1]

The essential function of investigation by sampling, which is to divide the public into significant groups and evaluate their relative numerical strength, is baffled in this case. This particular example enables us to put our finger on one of the most serious shortcomings of the sampling method: if the situation is delicate, or if the question asked threatens to commit the subject further than he is prepared to go in conversation with a stranger, he invariably finds a way of escape by professing ignorance or inability to understand.

From this point of view the projective test is very much better. A reply given in a public opinion poll is not really susceptible of interpretation but must be taken at its face value; it is a fact which, within the limits of the experiment, is largely irreducible. Indeed, that is why the answers obtained in opinion polls can be added up, and a quantitative technique becomes possible. In a projective test, on the other hand, the reactions

---

1. As regards the question about the Tokyo incident, it is quite probable that inadequate information, rather than fear of the police, limited the number of definite answers. The extent to which the police are feared is assessed in another NPORI investigation into 'the attitude of the public towards the police' (September/October 1951). Investigators were asked to indicate whether the person interrogated replied freely or not and the following results were obtained:

Category of population	Hesitated	Replied freely
	%	%
Sample as a whole	22	78
Sex		
Men	14	86
Women	29	71
Standard of education		
Primary (6 years study)	31	69
Senior primary (9 years total study)	21	79
Secondary (12 years total study)	16	84
Higher (over 12 years total study)	7	93
Economic and social level		
Upper	13	87
Middle	20	80
Lower	23	77

It should be pointed out that at the time of the 1951 investigation subjects had more grounds for fearing the consequences of their answers.

are not explicit but suggestive: they have an underlying significance, unperceived by the subject, who does not know the signposts, but perceptible to the psychologist, who works by analogy. In Sofue's projective test, Plate 10 shows a skirmish in which can be seen policemen with their chinstraps down, in the midst of a crowd that is standing up to them; a placard above the heads of the crowd reads 'Strike today'. Sofue distinguishes three types of reaction.

Type I. Attitude of hostility to the police. Example: woman from the town of Yawata. 'This shows, I suppose, a legitimate strike being suppressed by the authorities. The police, after all, is only a tool in the hands of the capitalists. Anyway, democratic police would not tackle people so roughly. There is no doubt that these policemen are ready to club any worker who stands up to them.'

Type II. Subjects in this category admit there is a strike but do not think the police are behaving brutally; they interpret the picture in a milder fashion. Examples: man, H. village. '. . . perhaps the workers have gone on strike to get a rise in pay or something of that sort. So the police have come to pacify them, to keep them calm and stop them running riot.' Woman, F. village. 'The workmen of a company have gone on strike and the police have come to find out why they had to go to that length.'

Type III. Critical attitude towards the strike. Example: man, F. village. 'This is a shocking example of the after-effects of the war. I am afraid these workers are in the pay of the Communist Party. There are certainly some Communists among them. Most of them are just kicking up a dust for nothing at all.'

The great majority (79 per cent) of the women belong to Type II; three women could not be classified because the picture conveyed nothing whatever to them. The men are more or less equally divided among the three types; Type I is drawn exclusively from the factory workers, whereas the villagers are divided between Types II and III. (Table 38).

So far as this plate is concerned, therefore, the most important emotive element is not the police but the opposition, with which the factory workers tend to identify themselves, whereas the villagers are inclined to dissociate themselves from it. Where there is neither of these reactions, the attitude adopted is neutral. Hence it would seem that the police in themselves awaken no tendency either way, positive or negative. As, in the group studied, those most inclined to assert their independence against authority appear to be the factory workers, it is a pity that no

TABLE 38.

Locality	Sex	Type I	Type II	Type III	Number of subjects
F. village	M.	0	6	4	10
	F.	0	7	1	9[1]
Yawata	M.	9	1	1	11
	F.	1	7	0	8
T. village	M.	0	2	5	7
	F.	0	9	0	11[1]
Bibai	M.	1	1	0	2
	F.	1	2	0	3
H. village	M.	0	1	0	1
	F.	0	0	1	1
Total	M.	10	11	10	31
	F.	2	25	2	32[1]
Grand total		12	36	12	63[1]

1. Including unclassifiables.

opportunity was given them to show their reactions to a picture of the police alone. All the same, it is noticeable that women tend not to take sides in situations where the civil authority is implicated; in other words, they tend to hold aloof from civic life. It is also possible to observe a tendency among members of the rural population, when they take sides at all, to side with authority.

Another plate, No. 2, presents a scene in which the theme is authority. Sofue describes it as follows: 'An outdoor scene in a country district. Outside the picture to the left someone wearing a foreign suit and with his hat on, must be standing: we see his shadow on the ground. Two people side by side are bowing deeply to the owner of the shadow. They seem young or youngish and they might be men or women. Behind them is a large tree on the other side of which a young man is hiding and watching them with disgust, his arms folded. On this side of the picture a little boy and a little girl are looking on.' The theme of authority is introduced by the very deep bow being made to the shadow by the two people in the background, and it is heightened by the fact that the shadow itself seems larger and heavier than life. It should also be added, for the benefit of the Western reader, that the bow is the normal type of salute in Japan and that, when an inferior is greeting a superior, bows as deep as in the picture, with the hands on the knees, are in no way an exceptional sight.

As regards identifications, reactions are of two types.

Type I. Identification with the person concealed behind the tree, approval of his annoyance at the mark of profound respect given by the other two. Examples: man, F. village. 'They are bowing deeply to the landowner who has come along while they were working. The man behind the tree is watching the scene with displeasure. Two children are also looking on and wondering about the difference in circumstances that causes such behaviour.' Man, town of Yawata. 'Three labourers are at their work in the fields. It is a hot day and they were going to take a rest in the shade of the tree, when their boss turned up. Two of them have hurried to greet him, because they are in the habit of flattering him. The man in the shade of the tree is thinking that it is reasonable enough for them to take a rest and there is no reason to fuss because the boss has come along. The children are laughing at the two men because they are overdoing the civility and making themselves ridiculous.'

Type II. Identification with the two men who are bowing and with their annoyance at the behaviour of the man behind the tree for keeping out of sight and not paying his respects. Example: man, T. village. 'A scene in a country area. They are greeting the village headman who has come along. The man concealed behind the tree appears to harbour ill-will towards them. Although the two children are paying their respects to the man behind the tree, they are thinking that he is apt to let his feelings get the better of him.'

The most frequent type of reaction is the second, which is met with in 64 per cent of the men and 78 per cent of the women. Type I is much more frequent among workers in the towns; whereas it is found in only 36 per cent of the men over the sample as a whole, among the Yawata factory hands it occurs in 55 per cent of the cases.

Reactions can also be classified in terms of the character ascribed to the person casting the shadow. Subjects saw him variously as the Emperor, the village headman, the teacher or schoolmaster, an official, a landowner, a rich man, a benefactor, an acquaintance, the boss or the foreman. Some, too, thought that the homage was being paid, not to the person casting the shadow but to the sun, or to a shrine. These two features of the reactions are far from being entirely unrelated. In nearly half the Type I cases, the person casting the shadow is thought to be the landowner or a rich man. In half the Type II cases, the shadow is thought to belong to the schoolmaster or to an official. Conversely, in eight out of nine cases where the landowner or a rich man is mentioned, the reactions are Type I; in 22 out of 25 of the cases where the schoolmaster or an official is mentioned, Type II reactions are found. It would seem, then, that certain attitudes of respect or revolt suggest specific objects, and conversely—for it is difficult to know which process normally comes first—that a particular object, or rather a particular category of persons or an institution, produces one or other of these types of reaction. The relationship between the attitudes of respect or disrespect and their objects is shown in Table 39.

TABLE 39.

	Number of cases		
	Type I	*Type II*	*Total*
Schoolteacher	1	13	14
Official	2	9	11
Landowner, rich man	8	1	9
Boss, foreman	3	5	8
The Emperor	1	3	4
Village headman	1	3	4
Benefactor, acquaintance	0	5	5
The sun	2	0	2
A shrine	0	2	2
Unidentified	0	4	4
Total	18	45	63

Table 39 shows that, in the main, disrespect is shown in circumstances where there is an economic relationship but not when the relationship is with the civil or administrative authority. It is, indeed, noteworthy that the official is one of the objects most frequently evoking an attitude of respect and that the one who evokes respect most of all is the school-master, who is not merely the dispenser of knowledge but also the spokesman of authority and of the official moral code. It is suggestive, but perhaps not significant, that veneration of the sun—the oldest and most respected cult of the Japanese—is linked with Type I reaction, whereas reverence for shrines goes with a Type II reaction. It is also worthy of note that identification of the shadow with the person of the Emperor is associated with Type II.

RESPECT FOR THE EMPEROR

Thus a situation awakening feelings of respect, but in which the object of the respect is not clearly identified, may, in a projective test, evoke the image of the Emperor. This fact in itself leads us to suspect that not a few traces of the traditional devotion to the Emperor are still to be found in the young. Several analogous features in the results of the investigations carried out by Sofue and Vos throw light on the attitude of the young in this respect.

In Sofue's questionnaire, one of the items was phrased as follows: 'Although Tojo has been sent to the gallows as a war criminal, the Emperor, who declared war on the United States of America, was not regarded as a war criminal. Do you think that this is reasonable or un-reasonable?' The vast majority—about 78 per cent—thought it reason-able: the commonest reply (73 per cent) was that after all, under the dictatorship of Tojo, the Emperor had no real power; in 5 per cent of the replies the point was also made that it was the Emperor who gave the cease-fire order over the radio. Fourteen per cent had no opinion, and a very small minority of 8 per cent thought that the decision was unreasonable. The attitude of the women does not differ to any appreciable extent from those of the men, except that they more often refrain from expressing an opinion (men 3 per cent, women 23 per cent). The most striking circumstance however, is that the dissident voices, unfavourable to the Emperor, all come from the industrial town of Yawata and even there, though they represent a quarter of the total replies received, they are still in a marked minority.

The Emperor remains, at the very least, the symbol of the nation, not merely on paper, in Article 1 of the new Constitution, but in the hearts and minds of the people. Vos found that this was the view of 74 per cent of the group of young people he questioned in Tokyo. As regards the Emperor-worship which existed up to the time of the capitulation and has since been abolished, 17 per cent of the same group had no opinion, about it, 37 per cent objected on one ground or another, but the majority, 46 per cent, still thought it good or even necessary.

That these are the feelings of the young towards the person of the Emperor is made even clearer by their reactions to Plate 9 of the projective test. Sofue says in his description that this plate shows 'the Emperor walking, with a soft hat in his hand. A crowd of people nearby are welcoming him. A middle-aged woman on her knees is worshipping him, and another is doing the same, standing, and with all her heart. In the background a man is waving his hand and shouting something. A young boy is glowering at the Emperor while another is smiling at him. The Emperor himself appears to be deep in thought and is turning his face slightly to one side.' Sofue notes three kinds of reaction to this picture.

Type I. Exhibition of feelings of hostility to the Emperor or criticism of the imperial régime. Following is an example: man, T. village. 'There are a number of people worshipping the Emperor, whom they look upon as a god, just as in the feudal period during the war, while some others are showing that they object to the belief that the Emperor is divine. The child at the bottom of the picture is intelligent and rejects the Emperor system.'

Type II. Rejection of Emperor-worship, but acceptance of the imperial régime and affection for the person of the Emperor. Example: man, Bibai. 'The long and the short of it is that this picture shows people in the presence of the Emperor—all of them seem happy to see him. The older people look on him as a god because they cannot yet rid themselves of their old habits instilled into them by the education they have had. I simply cannot understand why the children in the bottom right corner of the picture look so angry. It is very odd.'

Type III. The people belonging to Type III proffer no criticisms and accept the whole scene as entirely natural. Example, man, F. village. 'Ah! It is His Majesty the Emperor, isn't it? It is a joy to us that, as a result of our defeat, we now for the first time have the chance of seeing His Majesty. This picture shows that we, the people, all rejoice to see him. I should imagine that the persons at the bottom of the picture are Communists. . . .'

Half the group studied by Sofue exhibited Type III reactions, and the other half is evenly divided between Types I and II. More detailed analysis, however, brings out a number of interesting differences. Types II and III are much more common among the girls; while Types I and III are met with equal frequence among the young men, and have a clear preponderance over Type II. Type III predominates in the countryside, particularly in F. village in Kyushu; and Type I is in the majority among workers in the towns, where Type III is rare or non-existent. Table 40 shows the distribution of the types of reaction to Plate 9.

TABLE 40.

Locality	Sex	Type I	Type II	Type III	Number of cases
F. village	M.	1	1	8	10
	F.	1	3	5	9
Yawata	M.	8	2	1	11
	F.	2	2	4	8
T. village	M.	1	3	3	7
	F.	0	1	10	11
Bibai	M.	1	1	0	2
	F.	1	2	0	3
H. village	M.	1	0	0	1
	F.	0	1	0	1
Total	M.	12	7	12	31
	F.	4	9	19	32
Grand total		16	16	31	63

It is clear that, notwithstanding Japan's setbacks and political upheavals, attachment to the imperial house remains strong. This attachment, however, is much more political, or philosophical, than personal; in other words it is directed more towards the imperial régime than towards the person of the present sovereign, His Imperial Majesty the Emperor Hirohito. This is brought out by the replies to a question in Sofue's list: it will be remembered that this questionnaire was put to the same subjects as underwent the projective test, except that four subjects, three men and one woman, all from F. village, were subjected to the projective test only. This question was drawn up as follows: 'The King of England has just died. Do you think this is a great loss to every

Englishman? If the President of the United States of America were to die, do you think it would be a great loss to every American? If it were Stalin, in the Soviet Union, would it be a great loss for every Soviet citizen? And if it were the Emperor of Japan, would it be a great loss to you?'

The results, which at first sight seem very strange, were as follows: 49 per cent of the subjects said that the death of the Emperor of Japan would not be a great loss to them personally, and this was the highest percentage of negative replies. The next highest percentage, 41 per cent, was of those holding the view that the death of the King of England had not been felt as a great loss by the English; 32 per cent considered that the death of the President of the United States of America would not be felt as a loss by the Americans, and only 31 per cent, the lowest proportion, thought that the Russians would not feel the death of Marshal Stalin as a great loss.

We might try to explain these results by pointing out that in the United States of America and the Soviet Union the powers of the head of the State are more of a personal character, whereas in England and Japan they are more dynastic. The Japanese frequently refer to the analogy between their own imperial system and the English monarchy. Several of the young people questioned by Vos on their attitude towards the Emperor said that the Japanese ought to adopt towards him an attitude similar to that of the English people towards their King. In one of the 'autobiographies of the future' written by Sapporo students, the writer foresees the survival in the year 2002 of no more than 'five or six monarchies, including Japan and England.' This may explain why the young Japanese, being of the opinion that the death of the head of the State is a less personal matter in Japan and the United Kingdom than in the United States of America and the Soviet Union, are inclined to imagine that it would be felt less keenly by the citizens of the first two countries than by those of the other two.

One point, however, should be noted: the statement that the death of the present Emperor would not be felt as a loss is made more frequently by the groups which have also shown least favour towards the imperial régime, particularly the Yawata industrial group and the rural group of T. village in Hokkaido; moreover, replies of this kind are on the whole far less frequent among the girls. Replies that the death of the heads of the States under consideration is not or would not be felt as a loss are as in Table 41.

The most likely conclusion is that the motivation and significance of these replies are both ambiguous: in some cases they may indicate attachment to the régime and the dynasty, which are regarded as more important than the persons who at any given time hold the reins of power; in other cases they may imply hostility both towards the régime

TABLE 41.

Locality	Sex	England	U.S.A.	U.S.S.R.	Japan
F. village	M.	0	1	0	0
	F.	3	1	1	2
Yawata	M.	5	6	7	8
	F.	2	3	1	3
T. village	M.	6	3	3	6
	F.	2	1	2	5
Bibai	M.	2	2	2	1
	F.	2	1	1	2
H. village	M.	1	1	1	1
	F.	1	0	0	0
Total	M.	14	13	13	17
	F.	10	6	5	12
Grand total		24	19	18	29

and towards the heads of States. Used by itself, this question, which might have seemed likely to enable us to diagnose the attitudes of the subjects towards their own and a number of foreign régimes, would probably have led us far astray.

Leaving aside any question of political ideology, attachment to imperial and national traditions remains very strong. The great annual celebration of the foundation of the empire, on 11 February, is now omitted, by order, from the list of official holidays. However, 85 per cent of the subjects in the group interrogated by Sofue favoured the revival of Empire Day. The comments quoted by Sofue are worthy of note: 'Reviving Empire Day is a good idea. But all displays of fanaticism must be rigorously excluded. No attempt must be made to treat a myth as if it were the truth.' 'I have no objection to the revival of Empire Day. But we must be very careful not to let ourselves be exploited again by certain "god-inspired" persons.' 'I am in favour of reviving Empire Day but only as a way of marking the birth of the new Japan. For this reason it appears necessary to change the name of the day so as to distinguish it from the former Empire Day.' The qualifications contained in the above comments give us an idea of the sincere desire for reform which exists among some of the people. On the whole, however, the replies to Sofue's question confirm one extremely important fact—that the youth of Japan has preserved intact its sense of continuity with the country's most distant past and retains a most lively awareness of Japanese history even in its mythological aspects. For contemporary Japanese youth, Japan is still a nation with a past.

Another example of the attachment of Japanese youth to its traditions is the attitude it adopts towards the imperial rescript on education. From 1890 onwards this document played a considerable part in the ethical and civic life of the Japanese. Ruth Benedict regards it as constituting, together with the rescript to soldiers and sailors, 'the true holy writ of Japan'.[1] One of the first measures of educational reform adopted after the defeat was to do away with the ritual reading of the rescript in the schools (circular of October 1946). Nevertheless, the authors of *Progress of Educational Reform in Japan* (published by the Ministry of Education in 1950), who normally bow with complete docility to the wishes of SCAP, did not accept this sacrilegious measure without reservations. 'In the process of carrying out a major reform of educational aims and policy', they write (page 11), 'it was only to be expected that the imperial rescript on education, long regarded as the "Bible" revealing the basic ideology of Japanese education, should not be left untouched. It will be conceded that the rescript contained a number of admirable moral notions, common to all humanity. But it also contained many points which were obviously bound to disqualify it from serving as a charter of education in a new democracy, where sovereignty lies in the hands of the people.' The views of the young are more explicit than the latent nostalgia of this passage. 'Do you consider it preferable', Sofue asked them, 'that people should be guided by the imperial rescript on education?' and for those replying in the affirmative, he added a second question: 'In that case, do you think it unnecessary to revise the Rescript?' Seventy-six per cent of the replies to the first question were in the affirmative and 8 per cent of those interrogated thought revision unnecessary. The percentage of those wishing to retain the rescript, with or without revision, was lower among the men (64 per cent) than among the woman (87 per cent) and notably low among the Yawata trade unionists (45 per cent). Having regard, however, to the controversy roused by this document, its nature and, above all, the part it has played in the past, and having regard also to its close association with the fallen régime, the percentage of subjects desiring its preservation seems highly significant.

Hence, on the purely political side, the anxiety of people in Japan and elsewhere, who fear lest the youth of the country may plunge into an excessive form of liberalism appears, for the present at any rate, to be ill-founded. It is true that, in every case where it is possible to make comparisons, the young in general show more independence than their elders. For all that, they remain extremely attached to the person of the Emperor, and still more so to the imperial régime and to the symbols, memories, traditions and values which go with it. The display of authority is closely accompanied by reactions of respect, except when these are replaced by abstentions based on fear. Moreover, interest in national politics is still negligible; the urge to play an active part in them, though slightly more common than among older people, is still only very rarely exhibited. From the national standpoint, it is the economic

---

1. *The Chrysanthemum and the Sword*, p. 209.

problems which are regarded as the most urgent and it is in connexion with these that authority, when displayed, is most liable to be questioned. It is therefore not surprising that trade unionists should apparently be the most wide-awake section of the population, politically. But the young are not yet fully aware of the socio-economic problems and seem much more inclined to solve their own difficulties by individual effort than by co-ordinated political action. However, things may change, and the direction these changes are likely to take may be guessed, having regard both to the psycho-social and the economic situations. It is very easy to make mistakes when one starts to prophesy; the consolation in this case is that where the worst was foretold, the best is happening. It is to be hoped that, contrary to what now appear to be the most likely forecasts, Japan will not commit herself to either of the two forms of totalitarianism which today appear to threaten her in equal measure, and whose advent would add still further to the heavy problems with which Asia already confronts the West.

CHAPTER VII

PRIVATE RELATIONS

THE FAMILY

In their private relationships do the young people of Japan show more independence and initiative than they evince towards public authority? To what extent do they welcome the new opportunities offered to them? The answers to these questions are of great importance for our investigation: an impetus towards change has certainly been given as much in private as in public matters, and its effects are interesting in themselves; but in addition to this, the change brought about in personal relationships may well have repercussions on the relationship between the individual and the State. Changes of this kind in private attitudes might thus foreshadow changes in the conduct of public life.

We shall examine this question first in relation to the family, for in many societies the political organization reflects that of the family, and vice versa, or they tend to react on one another. From the cultural, if not from the individual standpoint, the same type of behaviour, whether liberal or authoritarian, may frequently be observed in both public and family relations. A study of the attitudes of Japanese youth towards and within the family, interesting enough for its own sake, should, therefore, also enable us to widen and deepen our earlier analysis of political life.

Now, in the family sphere, both the young and their elders feel that things are changing, that the new generation no longer wants to follow the example of the ones that went before. This was among the first comments we heard during our visit to Japan and it was frequently repeated. At the Congress of the Japanese Society for Cultural Science, Judge Merita of the Tokyo Family Court, speaking on the connexion between juvenile delinquency and family tensions, instanced, among other causes, the fact that the family 'no longer interests' many young people, 'has no more attraction for them'. A group of teachers with whom we had an opportunity of exchanging views in Sapporo, told us that conflicts between parents and children were increasing—not, they said, because moral training in the schools had been done away with, but because the idea of freedom had been misinterpreted: 'Democracy', they explained, 'is not properly understood.' Among the 100 young people whom Vos interrogated in Tokyo, he found 50 who thought that there was a gulf between themselves and the preceding generation; 14 others said the gulf existed, but was not very wide; and only 27 thought that the chain of continuity between themselves and their predecessors was unbroken. Furthermore, 35 accused the previous generation of not having behaved as they should; 20 said that they had behaved only 'up to a point' as they should; and only 21 had no criticism to make. The representative investigation carried out by the National Public Opinion Research Institute reveals that 66 per cent of the public consider that 'the number of children who pay no attention to their parents has increased of late'. This view was almost equally distributed among all age-groups, though it rose to 69 per cent among persons over 30 in the towns. Sofue included in his questionnaire an item worded as follows: 'Does your opinion sometimes differ from that of your parents and other older members of your family?' The question was answered unanimously in the affirmative; those with whom the young most frequently disagree are their fathers, then their mothers, brothers and sisters. The conflicts are usually 'between old-fashioned views and new ideas about social problems such as divorce, sex equality and the principles on which brothers and sisters should be brought up. . . .' Thus the first impression one gains from all these data is that the attitudes of the young towards the family are in process of changing.

Nevertheless, there is no doubt that the family still counts for much with the young. An interesting test of this was the question set by the National Public Opinion Research Institute: 'Is there any particular thing you hope to accomplish in the course of your life?' Two groups of replies relate to the family: group I, 'the home (filial piety)'; examples: 'I want to spare no pains to be a good child to my parents.' 'I want my parents to die with an easy mind about me.' 'I want to make my family life harmonious.' Group II is concerned with 'bringing up children'; examples: 'At the very least I want to give my children a first-class upbringing and make them into people who will exert themselves for the benefit of society.' 'If I have children, I want them to live their lives as free individuals who are not dominated by their surroundings.' 'All I want is to make my children straightforward and honest people.' The distribution of these answers varies greatly according to age, as Table 42 shows.

Family preoccupations increase with age and are centred on different things: the adults, heads of families, think primarily of their children while the young think primarily of the home in which they were brought up; with age, of course, status and responsibilities change. Nevertheless, in every age-group, both types of family preoccupation continue to occur: even among the youngest they are mentioned as an aim in life by about one-fifth of the subjects. In the minds of Japanese youth only

TABLE 42.

Age-group	Object in life		Total
	To be a good son or daughter	To bring up one's children properly	
	%	%	%
Urban			
16-19	12	9	21
20-24	6	12	18
25-29	3	27	30
30 and over	3	41	44
Rural			
16-19	11	8	19
20-24	5	18	23
25-29	6	35	41
30 and over	4	44	48

one aim in life can compete with family devotion—education (20 per cent of those in the towns and 14 per cent of those in the country).

The Kyoto and Sapporo students also manifest a very strong attachment to family values. For instance, in reply to the question: 'If you should get a large sum of money five years from now, what would you do with it?', the second most frequent answer is 'build a house'. Here again, education is the only serious competitor, receiving even more votes than family values. (Table 43).

TABLE 43.

	Use of a large sum of money	
	Would build a house	Would spend it on study, schooling
Kyoto	%	%
Men	20	28
Women	20	15
Sapporo	24	24

The weightiest evidence of the great importance which the family as an institution retains in the eyes of Japanese youth is to be found in the answers to a question put, like the preceding one, to the students at Kyoto and Sapporo. The number of students questioned at Sapporo was too small for us to be able to make a sufficiently detailed analysis, but at Kyoto it was possible to distinguish between the reactions of the youths and the girls, and this often led to interesting results. The question, borrowed like many others from the Allport-Gillespie questionnaire, ran as follows: 'Of the following activities, which are the three from which you expect the greatest satisfaction? (Number your answers 1, 2 and 3 in descending order of importance): your career or occupation, your

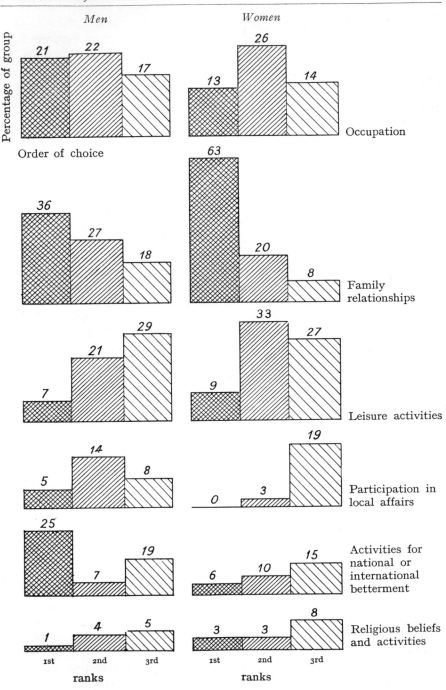

Fig. 12. Activities likely to afford most satisfaction (Kyoto)

family relationships, your leisure and recreational activities, your participation as a citizen in the affairs of your community, your participation
in activities directed towards national or international betterment, or
your religious beliefs and activities?' Although the classification is
incomplete, since there is a choice between six items and we are concerned
with the first three only, partial 'popularity graphs', at least, can be
constructed and are shown in the diagram facing this page.

It will be observed that not only do both youths and girls give family
relationships first place more often than any other kind of activity,
but that their choices may be graphed in the form of an 'L', clearly
showing the predominance of family relationships over all other choices,
and this does not occur in any other instance. To some extent, the
number of times family relationships are placed first by the youths is
reduced through competition with professional activities; this also
happens, in a male group interested in social problems, through competition with replies under the heading of 'activities directed towards national
or international betterment'. No such alternative choices presented
themselves to the girls, among whom family values come easily first.
Indeed, even among the youths it is quite clear that family relationships
are regarded as likely to bring the greatest happiness.

It will be seen in the next chapter how much young people depend
psychologically, on their families. At this stage, it should be noted that
the young rely completely on their families, through which alone they
obtain security. This emerges clearly from the replies of the Kyoto and
Sapporo students to the question: 'To what extent do you expect members
of your present family and your future in-laws to be of assistance to you
in life?' At least two-thirds expected to receive from their relatives
either regular assistance or assistance whenever they might need it.
(Table 44).

TABLE 44.

Kind of assistance expected from family	Kyoto		Sapporo
	Youths	Girls	
	%	%	%
Regular, indispensable	26	17	12
Whenever necessary	45	52	53
In the event of money difficulties only	22	26	12
None	7	2	23
No reply	0	3	0

The Sapporo students, who belong to an economically less privileged
class, and who also more frequently expect to rise above their parents'
standard of living, show more independence: 23 per cent of them expect
no help from their families. Even in this group, however, 65 per cent

had the idea that they could count on their families whenever they needed help. Thus the dependence of the young remains considerable.

However, as we have seen above, many people consider that in present-day Japan children no longer pay heed to their parents. It is indeed possible to discern, here and there, an attempt on the part of the young to emancipate themselves, but because of their economic dependence and above all, perhaps, because of the strength of tradition, since the moral climate has not changed, many of these attempt fizzle out. The following fragment of a conversation with a youth of 17, the son of a purged officer, provides an example of this psychological predicament:

'Do you think that when you are a man you will be happier than you were in your childhood?'

'Yes, I think so.'

'Do you think your children will be happier than you have been?'

'I will try to make them happier.'

'Will your wife be happier than your mother has been?'

'I think so.'

'What do you want to do in life?'

'I want to teach in a university. My father was an officer. I do not want to do the same thing as my father. Being a military man made my father *very hard with his wife and children.* Now that he is a farmer he is less hard. My brother was an officer as well and was also very hard. He, too, was purged and is not so hard as he was.'

'At what age do you think to marry? Will you follow your parents' advice?'

'I shall marry when I am 25—no, 26. I will ask my parents' advice and then decide for myself.'

'Do you approve of the traditional marriage by arrangement?'

'No, I disapprove of it, but I think that when one is older *one understands and approves of one's father's advice. My father's orders and advice to me were sound, I see it now. My mother was too soft; she spoilt me.*'

'But you have just said that your children would be happier than you have been. That means that you do not consider that you have been very happy. Now you say that you approve of the way your father brought you up. Does that mean you will bring up your children the same way? You know, you said the opposite.'

(Subject makes no reply. He sees the contradiction and does not know what to do about it.)

It is easy to guess how this subject was dragooned in his childhood, not only by his father but also by his elder brother; how he suffered from it; how he longs to emancipate himself now and—identifying himself with his future children—how much he wants to give them a more liberal upbringing. But the prestige of paternal wisdom still weighs with him and, although he may say he disapproves of the traditional marriage by arrangement, he admits that he will seek his father's advice before

getting married; he will perhaps go even further, for he grants the sound-
ness, not merely of his father's advice, but of his father's orders, and
blames his mother for not having been firm enough in bringing him up.

This example illustrates the situation, but is not necessarily representative. Not all young Japanese are sons of regular officers and not all
have been moulded by such an autocratic upbringing. Nevertheless, it
does seem that the tradition of respect and obedience remains strong
in Japan and this is confirmed by the investigation carried out by the
National Public Opinion Research Institute.

In the course of this investigation a question was put in two parts,
as follows: 'Do you think there is no harm in children obeying their
parents implicity? Is this still the case when the children have become
independent?' To the first part of the question, two types of reply were
given: 'There is no harm in it' and 'I can't say' (it depends on circumstances, I can't give a general reply, I don't know). There were three
types of answer to the second part: 'There is no harm in it in any circumstances'; 'When they are independent, it is different'; 'Once they
have become independent, I don't know'. Finally, taking the two questions together, four types of replies are obtained: 'There is no harm, in
any circumstances, in children obeying their parents implicity'; 'There
is no harm in children obeying their parents, but when they become
independent it is different'; 'I can't say about when they are independent,
but they should obey when they are small'; 'I can't say'. The distribution
of the answers is as in Table 45.

TABLE 45.

Age-group	Children should obey their parents			
	In all circumstances	*But not when they are independent*	*When they are independent, I don't know*	*No reply*
	%	%	%	%
Urban				
16-19	8	35	4	53
20-24	16	31	4	39
25-29	8	33	5	53
30 and over	11	38	3	47
Rural				
16-19	11	19	7	64
20-24	13	27	8	52
25-29	14	31	7	48
30 and over	12	35	6	47

The first point which will be noted is the extreme frequency with which
the question is avoided, especially among the young; a mean figure of
50 per cent of abstentions must be regarded as exceptional in opinion

polls, although we have come across other instances in Japan, notably when the question related in any way to the police. It might be thought that this reaction is the refuge of persons who, while not approving the tradition of obedience, do not want to commit themselves to an opinion about it; this is probably the case with some of the subjects interrogated, but not all. In this connexion, we would point out that town-dwellers in the 20-24 age-group are an exception to the rule applying in the other cases that abstentions are most frequent among the young; but in expressing an opinion, most of them, instead of affirming the freedom of young people who have achieved independence, insist that obedience to parents cannot be a bad thing in any circumstances. The average proportion of those who agree that independence releases children to some extent from their duty of obedience is one-third of the whole group and two-thirds of those expressing an opinion. These proportions are fairly high, but it will be observed that it is not the younger groups who speak up most frequently for emancipation: on the contrary, the proportion favouring it tends to increase with age. Particularly among the rural population, the percentages in favour of emancipation are low and one is certainly left with the impression that it will be difficult for the young to win emancipation in the family by themselves: it is more likely to be granted to them from outside.

On the other hand, when we come to relations between the children of the same family, where the father's authority no longer makes itself felt directly and where it is less a question of standing up to the will or personality of a particular individual than of fighting the strength of tradition, there is a greater weight of opinion among the young in favour of reforms that would ensure a nearer approach to equality; they are more frequently against the right of primogeniture and any special privilege for the eldest son. It is true that this attitude is not absolute. The right of primogeniture, abolished by recent legislation, is still favoured by the Japanese public; 66 per cent continue to support it and the percentage is even higher in the rural areas than in the towns. These attitudes undoubtedly stem from underlying economic conditions, particularly in the country: the equal sharing of an inheritance would mean that holdings would have to be split up still further—and this process has already gone too far. But even when it is merely the privileged status of the eldest son within the family that is called in question, there is no clearcut majority either way among the public as a whole: 48 per cent are in favour of special privileges for the eldest son, while 49 per cent favour equality. The distribution of attitudes according to age is as in Table 46.

The same caution in accepting new ideas is found among the young regarding the various ways in which the family, as an institution, functions. A case in point is the status of the mother-in-law in the family and her traditional treatment of the daughter-in-law. One of the items

Table 46.

Age-group	Right of primogeniture		Privilege of eldest son	
	For	Against	For	Against
Urban	%	%	%	%
16-19	53	45	35	64
20-24	51	48	39	59
25-29	54	42	39	56
30 and over	64	34	50	48
Rural				
16-19	57	37	37	55
20-24	63	33	40	55
25-29	68	28	46	50
30 and over	76	22	56	42

in Vos's questionnaire was: 'What do you think about the position of the mother-in-law and her attitude to the daughter-in-law?' Forty-one per cent of the young people interrogated in Tokyo said that a change was needed, against a mere 2 per cent who saw nothing wrong; but 30 per cent condemned the situation without, however, advocating any change, and 27 per cent had no opinion.

The fact is that family relationships make up a system which it is not easy to alter in any particular without imperilling the functioning of the whole, unless one is prepared to recast it completely. Westerners may be revolted by the traditional tyranny of the mother-in-law. Ruth Benedict gives a restrained account of the following distressing case: 'One "Modan" Japanese now in America took into her own rooms in Tokyo a pregnant young wife whose mother-in-law had forced her to leave her grieving young husband. She was sick and broken-hearted but she did not blame her husband. Gradually she became interested in the baby she was soon to bear. But when the child was born, the mother came accompanied by her silent and submissive son, to claim the baby. It belonged of course to the husband's family and the mother-in-law took it away. She disposed of it immediately to a foster home.'[1] This story, told to a Tokyo girl, aged 20, elicited the following comment: 'The husband was weak with his mother. It is not good for a man to live with his parents when he is married. Left with its mother, the baby might perhaps have been happy. But if we think of the future, he would have grown up into a boy without a family, so it was better for him to be claimed by his father's family. The young wife loved the child but she had no social position. The husband's mother loved her son. Her love was not social.' This is the opinion of a girl of 20, i.e. of one who will soon be married; can we really say that she wants a change in the status

---

1. *The Chrysanthemum and the Sword*, p. 121.

of her future mother-in-law? Can we even say that she conceives of the possibility that the family might be differently organized?

To the young, the family as an institution means two things which, though related, are nevertheless distinct: the home in which they were brought up and trained, and the home they will themselves establish. So far, we have not touched on the second aspect, but before going on to examine the attitudes of the young to the institution of marriage and to parenthood, we must glance at the problems raised by the status of women in general.

THE STATUS OF WOMEN

Traditionally, Japanese women are minors. Under the new régime, they now have equal rights with men. Personal status, however, is not determined merely by law: it depends far more on the attitudes prevailing in a particular society. Ostensibly, at any rate, the Japanese public, especially the young, have accepted easily and even with satisfaction the new equality granted to women.

A question set by the National Public Opinion Research Institute may serve as an introduction to our analysis: 'Asked their views about this or that, women often say, "I know nothing about it because I am only a woman. Are they right to take this attitude?' The answers and their distribution by age-groups were as in Table 47.

TABLE 47.

Age-group	They are right	I don't think so	No opinion
	%	%	%
Sample as a whole	8	88	4
Urban			
16-19	4	89	7
20-24	12	85	3
25-29	7	88	5
30 and over	11	86	3
Rural			
16-19	4	90	6
20-24	5	93	2
25-29	9	91	*
30 and over	9	88	3

* Less than 0.5 per cent.

Thus the vast majority of the Japanese think that the social inferiority of women is not a law of nature and the rural population is at least as positive on this point as the townsfolk; the young tend to be, if possible, even more emphatically of this opinion, with the rather inexplicable exception of the 20-24 urban age-group. We need not, in any case, labour the point: the Japanese, young and old, do not approve of women who profess their own inferiority.[1]

Sofue found that, of the 59 subjects to whom his questionnaire was submitted, all but two declared themselves in favour of sex equality; the two exceptions were both women, one from F. village, and the other from H. village. The first said: 'I am against it because women are inferior to men.' The second said: 'I am against it because women are happier when they obey men's orders.' But the same group of subjects were all, with two exceptions, of opinion that equality was not yet a fact. In the group interrogated by Vos, 88 per cent were in favour of giving women the same rights as men and only 10 per cent were against it.

It is also the majority opinion that girls should be given as good an education as boys: In Vos's group this view was taken by 53 per cent of the subjects and in Sofue's by 96 per cent of the young men and 84 per cent of the girls. Sofue's group was also in favour of co-education in the proportions of 75 per cent against 18 per cent of the young men and 48 per cent against 33 per cent of the girls. Young trade unionists were strongly in support of the idea, while the largest number of opponents was found among the farmers of F. village in Kyushu, who showed their conservative outlook in many other ways. It is also evident that the women's attitude is markedly more conservative, but in the final analysis, even in the most conservative groups, a substantial proportion is invariably found in favour of the idea of equality as between men and women and ready to approve measures for bringing this about.

---

1. Women, whom this question directly concerns, are also of opinion that their social inferiority is not a natural law; they are, however, a little less positive than the men on this point (Are women right to profess their own inferiority?).

Sex	Yes	No	No opinion
	%	%	%
Men	6	91	3
Women	10	86	4

The point is worth making since elsewhere—for instance in France, on the question of equal pay—the majority of women in favour is even higher than that of men.

In the Japanese investigation, the fact noted in this particular instance is of general significance. The women are more traditionalist, less 'social', less ambitious and demanding. This is illustrated by the following data:

Sex	In favour of the right of primogeniture	Want to do something for society	Want nothing in particular apart from health
	%	%	%
Men	65	57	62
Women	70	42	75

One of the factors which have contributed most to the emancipation of Western women is paid employment outside the home. Japanese youth is not against the employment of women. Thus among the Kyoto students, those against the employment of unmarried women did not exceed 6 per cent of the men and 5 per cent of the girls; and only 22 per cent of the men and 25 per cent of the girls were opposed to the employment of married women. Among the Yawata and Bibai trade unionists, only 4 out of 13 men and only 1 out of 10 women raised objections. Sometimes, one has the impression that the men would be more inclined to keep the women at home and that the women themselves are readier to lead an independent life outside. In an investigation carried out among women in employment by the National Public Opinion Research Institute in 1948, between 7 per cent and 8 per cent of the women under 25 years of age said that they were working in order 'to see life', and about 20 per cent said they were working 'for pocket money'. Thus the employment of women outside the home, which is not a new thing in Japan, is accepted without difficulty.

We still have to determine, however, whether young Japanese are prepared to promote sex equality actively and personally. In the group of young people he questioned in Tokyo, Vos found that 61 per cent were in favour, or very emphatically in favour, of the cultivation of specifically feminine accomplishments such as the tea ceremony or the technique of flower arrangement; he was told that these were occupations which 'put the soul into a state of repose' or 'refine the female character'. We had a chance of discussing the question of sex equality with a group of young men and girls from Nemuro. An extract from our conversation may throw some light on the situation. The discussion was directed to the question of co-education:

'What do you think of co-education?'

(Young man aged 19) 'It is a good thing. It brings about a better understanding between the sexes.'

(Girl aged 19) 'I am in favour of co-education.'

Young man aged 26) 'In the days when girls and boys were educated separately in different schools, if they went out together parents used to say: "That's a bad girl." Now all that is over and things are much more natural.'

'Of course, co-education means the same education for both sexes. In your view should girls be given the same education as boys?'

(First speaker) 'I am in favour of it. But co-education need not stop the girls having special instruction, for instance, cookery courses.'

'Should both sexes have the same rights?'

(A chorus) 'Of course!'

'For instance, should it be possible for a woman to become mayor of this town?'

(Laughter) 'Yes, if she is capable of carrying out the duties of the post.

'Could any of the girls here today become town councillors?'
(General burst of laughter) (Unanimously) 'No.'
'But would the men in the room be able to shoulder the responsibility?'
(Young man, aged 22, former fisherman, now in a company) 'I am in a company; I shall be able to get more experience and develop my personality.'
'Are you in favour of more equality between the sexes?'
(A chorus) 'Certainly.'
(To a girl aged 22, who works in a jam factory) 'And you?'
'I don't know.'

As may be seen, so long as the discussion is confined to matters of principle, no difficulty arises about agreeing on equality of status between men and women. But as the question becomes more practical and its implications more personal, it gives rise to astonishment, indecision and finally withdrawal: 'These are very fine principles and we admire them because we see others admiring them; but they have not yet been put into practice here, they are not for us; elsewhere conditions must be such as to make them possible; conditions here are not like that.'

It is interesting to see how students picture the practice of sex equality in their own future homes. The question put to them was: 'If you get married and have a family, who do you expect will be more influential in the direction and control of the affairs of the family?' (Table 48).

TABLE 48.

	Kyoto		Sapporo
	Men	Women	
	%	%	%
Myself	21	7	12
My wife (or husband)	13	16	0
Both equally	66	75	82
No reply[1]	0	2	6

1. And special cases replying 'I shall not marry'.

In all three groups, a clear majority of the students said that they intended to apply the principle of sex equality in their own homes; the Sapporo students, who were inclined to exhibit a more liberal outlook throughout the questionnaire, also proposed to apply the principle of equality in their own households. At Kyoto, in a relatively homogeneous environment, the girls appear to claim equality more often than the young men are ready to grant it. It also emerges from the Kyoto replies that some thought it was the wife's duty to run the household, and this view is held twice as often by the men as by the women. Replies of this type undoubtedly reveal a genuine cultural trait which, in Japan as in other man-dominated societies, exists side by side with male predominance. The most notable replies, however, are those expressing the opinion that the authority of the husband should continue as before. Even among these cultivated young people, who are absorbing the whole range of liberal ideas and are destined to be the leaders of the new democratic Japan, we find 12 per cent of the very 'left wing' students of the university of Hokkaido, and 16 per cent of the women students and 21 per cent of the men at Kyoto anticipating that the affairs of their own homes will be run by the husband.

Plate 4 of Sofue's projective test enables us to secure a still deeper insight into attitudes relating to sex equality. It shows a man, apparently in his own home, seated with his legs crossed under him—the Japanese way of taking one's ease—at a dinner table drinking wine; the members of his family—his wife and two children—kneeling one behind another, are bringing him his food; all of them have anxious expressions on their faces. Sofue classifies the reactions to this scene in two categories.

Type I. An attitude of lively criticism regarding the scene, the subject considering that it shows a 'feudal' domination of men over women. Example, woman, F. village, (employed in the neighbouring town of Kagoshima). 'This picture gives an impression of feudalism. It looks as though nothing had been changed since the war. The woman seems to be trying to serve her husband and please him. One feels that there are many instances of this kind of thing in rural areas. The suffering of women is enormous.'

Type II. The picture is thought to depict a peaceful scene. Example, woman, F. village (who has not left the village). 'This is a really peaceful scene. The father is drinking by himself. We feel that all families would do better to behave in this cheerful way, although that obviously depends on the family.'

Most of the reactions noted belong to Type I: these constitute 56 per cent of the whole; 25 per cent of the subjects gave ambiguous answers which are unclassifiable, and Type II reactions are found in 19 per cent of the cases. The women's reactions are more frequently Type II (22 per cent) or doubtful (31 per cent). None of the Yawata or Bibai trade unionists gave a Type II answer and there were fewer answers in this category from T. village, which is more liberal than F. village.

Thus more than half the subjects condemn what the Japanese describe as the 'feudal' character of this picture. Nevertheless Sofue, in his comments on what he observed, says that he is not satisfied: 'The proportion of those who regard the scene illustrated as "feudal" is low, contrary to what one might have expected; in particular, it is below 50 per cent for the women as a whole, and in the case of F. village, it goes down to zero, which is really surprising.' Indeed, in the first place, the picture was completely unambiguous, bringing out the strong contrast between the comfort of the father and the anxious servility of his family towards him. Further, it must not be forgotten that almost all the subjects to whom this questionnaire was put (see page 175 above) said they were in favour of sex equality, of which this picture is a glaring negation. Lastly, a third most important point which Sofue rightly emphasizes is that a proportion of the male subjects in fact identified themselves explicitly with the father and, to rationalize behaviour which they could not help realizing was unacceptable, suggested excuses for it. The following is an example of this reaction: man, Yawata. 'In this worker's house a father's authority is great and his only pleasure is drink. In his factory, he is thoroughly stamped on by his superiors and by way of reaction he gives free rein to his bad temper at home.' In seeking to absolve himself in his own eyes and those of the psychologist for behaviour of which he disapproves but for which he senses that he shares the responsibility, the subject provides a psychological analysis of rare subtlety: the relations between individuals in a family are not determined solely by the law, or even by tradition; there is also a connexion between them and the other phases of the individual's social life, particularly his personal relationships in his work. While it is true that family life is reflected in, and reacts on, the other forms of social behaviour, the converse is just as true and must not be lost sight of. As one of the functions of the family is the protection of the individual, it is natural that compensation for the frustration and aggression suffered elsewhere should be sought in the home. In other societies a similar outlet is provided by the political institutions, but, as we have seen, this is hardly the case as yet in Japan. It is thus apparent that the harshness of economic and labour conditions is one of the major obstacles to the democratization of the Japanese family.

The full distribution of reactions to Plate 4 is shown in Table 49.

TABLE 49.

Locality	Sex	Type I	Type II	Ambiguous answers	Number of cases
F. village	M.	5	4	1	10
	F.	2	3	4	9
Yawata	M.	9	0	2	11
	F.	6	1	1	8
T. village	M.	4	1	2	7
	F.	4	3	4	11
Bibai	M.	2	0	0	2
	F.	3	0	0	3
H. village	M.	0	0	1	1
	F.	0	0	1	1
Total	M.	20	5	6	31
	F.	15	7	10	32
Grand total		35	12	16	63

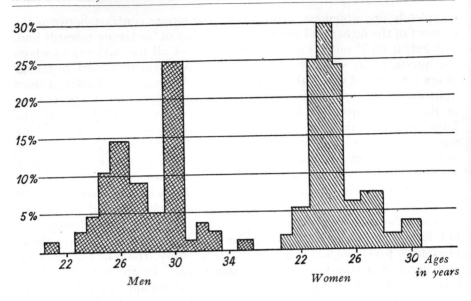

Fig. 13. Anticipated age at marriage (Kyoto).

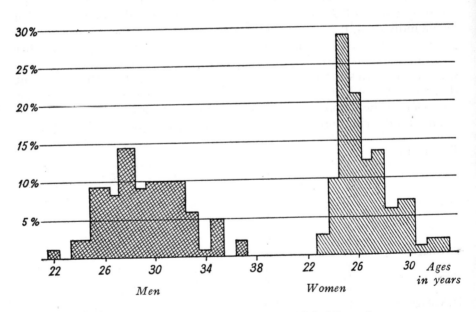

Fig. 14. Anticipated age at birth of first child (Kyoto)

Many women, moreover, while bowing to the fashion of the day and saying that they are in favour of the new principle of sex equality, have no great belief in it nor do they really want it put into practice. In Sofue's group 39 per cent of the girls interrogated said they would have preferred to have been men, as against 61 per cent who were contented with their lot. The point stressed by those who would have preferred to be men was male superiority: 'Men have more power than women'; 'Men can supply their own needs'; 'If I were a man, I could get a higher education'. Those who preferred being women stressed the social difference between the sexes or said they liked it better if they were subordinate: 'There are specifically women's activities such as housework or dressmaking which can only be carried on by women. I am used to that kind of work and also I like it'; 'I am glad I was born a woman because women are not expected to take responsibility'. Attention must be drawn, however, to the following remark, which is unique in Sofue's report: 'I think it is worth while being a woman, because it is the women who will over-throw feudalism.'

Despite all this, the women appear to be much more dissatisfied than the men; it is just that they do not attribute their dissatisfaction to their status as women. That this is the case is clearly shown from some of the questions in Sofue's list. Whereas 54 per cent of the male subjects, given their choice of the age in which they would like to live, would choose the present, the corresponding proportion among the girls is only 29 per cent; in the rural areas three-quarters of the youths want to stay in their own villages, whereas half the girls want to go elsewhere. A point brought out by Sofue is that, among the boys, one sometimes finds a feeling of regret at having been born in the village associated with a determination to stay there: 'I should have liked to have been born somewhere else, but since I was born in this village, I want to remain here in order to improve its living standards.' A diametrically opposite attitude is found among the girls: 'As I was born, and have passed many years, in this village, I feel an attachment for it. But now I am tired of living here and I want to go somewhere else.' In other words, the young men in Japan show a greater sense of reality, and the young women a larger measure of ineffective dissatisfaction.

MARRIAGE, LOVE AND HOME

The married state is not merely the most frequent and normal condition in Japan; it is to all intents and purposes universal. At Kyoto, the propor-tion expecting to get married was about the same among male and female students alike—97 per cent. Though it was a little lower at Sapporo, it still amounted to 94 per cent. The age at which they expected to marry was markedly higher among the men than among the girls. Without trying to illustrate this statement by figures, which would be misleading, it is fair to say that the ages usually selected were 29 at Sapporo, whereas at Kyoto the men chose 27 and the girls 24. But the distribution of ages in the replies calls for comment. As regards the girls, the distribution graph tends to be L-shaped, indicating general acceptance of a social obligation—to marry young. In the case of the men, the distribution can be shown in two distinct graphs; the first, approximating to the normal and averaging probably just under 26 years of age, reflects the expectations of those who attach no special importance to the age at which they marry and are not particularly conscious of pressure from those around them; the second is L-shaped, suggesting the existence of a norm at the age of 30, corresponding to the intentions of those who wish to postpone their marriage. In our conversations with young men we repeatedly had the impression that we were dealing with one or other of these types.

The minds of the young are not entirely unpreoccupied with marriage. At Kyoto, 1 per cent of the men and 7 per cent of the girls mentioned among the things they would do if they unexpectedly received a large sum of money, getting married, or spending some of it on clothes. In the NPORI investigation, marriage was mentioned as one of the most serious causes of anxiety in 2 per cent of replies; this referred, of course, to the marriage of their children in the case of subjects above a certain age, and to their own marriage in the case of the young. The frequency of these replies is as follows: marriage is a cause of anxiety to 1.5 per cent of the urban age-group 16-19 and to 4.8 per cent of the urban age-group 20-24; to 4 per cent of the rural age-group 16-19 and to 1.9 per cent of the rural age-group 20-24.

These figures would appear to reflect the fact that marriage takes place earlier in the country than in the towns, but it must be borne in mind that the percentages themselves are low, indicating that marriage is not the primary concern of the young, and not their main preoccupation. Moreover, in the same investigation, in reply to the question whether they had selected an aim in life, only three young men, all countrymen over 20 years of age, of the 733 interrogated thought of mentioning marriage. (The corresponding proportion among the adults was 12 out of 1,938 interrogated.) One is inclined to think, therefore, that marriage is not very important in the eyes of the young, or rather that they do not regard it as their personal affair and leave it to those adults who will arrange it for them.

What is, in fact, the attitude of the Japanese, particularly the young, with regard to the tradition of the negotiated marriage? A comprehensive answer is supplied by the NPORI investigation. The question was asked: 'Do you think that the choice of a husband or wife is a matter for the person concerned or for his or her family?' The replies were as in Table 50.

TABLE 50.

Age-group	For the family exclusively	Intermediate opinions	Exclusively for the individual concerned	No opinion
	%	%	%	%
Sample as a whole	14	39	44	3
Urban				
16-19	17	24	51	8
20-24	10	36	49	5
25-29	12	31	53	5
30 and over	14	39	45	2
Rural				
16-19	15	30	49	8
20-24	13	39	47	1
25-29	15	36	47	2
30 and over	14	47	38	3

These figures leave no room for doubt: the view most widely held is that marriage is exclusively the business of those immediately concerned. Moreover this is true not merely of the sample as a whole but of each separate age-group, with the exception of the over-30s in the rural areas, who do not consider, however, that marriage is exclusively the business of the family. This view, infrequent in all groups, does not reach its maximum with the group just mentioned. The opinions most commonly held by them are those shown, for the sake of simplicity in tabulating, under the general heading of 'intermediate opinions' and are of three different types: 'It is primarily the business of the two families'; 'The individuals and the families concerned should have an equal say'; 'It is primarily a matter for the individuals concerned.' The over-30 rural group generally expresses the first or second of these three opinions.

The attitudes of the young merit rather closer consideration. In town and country alike, the tendency to claim freedom for the individual is found more frequently in the youngest age-group (16-19) than in the others; but it is also this age-group which shows itself most in favour of the authoritarian approach. The inference would seem to be that, given two cultural alternatives, the very young are more ready to elect for one or the other and less apt to think of possible compromises. In any case, at this age opinions are still theoretic; only a minority get married before the age of 20 years.

The next two age-groups, on the other hand, are directly concerned, with the difference that 20-24 is the time of life at which men more commonly marry in the country, as compared with 25-29 in the towns. Taking these two most marriageable age-groups in town and country respectively, we find that it is in the towns that the demand for individual freedom reaches its maximum; in the rural areas support for this view is lower in the corresponding age-group than it is in the youngest age-group, there is less acceptance of the traditional procedure, and a compromise solution is more frequently sought.

It would seem, then, that marriage arranged by the families concerned without reference to the future marriage partners is no longer in favour with more than a small minority. Indeed, it is doubtful whether this has ever been the universal custom, at least in recent times. The young, especially in the towns, prefer the type of marriage in which the wishes of the couple concerned are the deciding factor. At the same time, it is certain that this latter type of marriage will have to compete with a type of arranged marriage in which both the interests and preferences of the two families and the wishes of the prospective husband and wife are taken into account. It can hardly be said, in this mid-twentieth century, that this particular type of marriage is a novelty in Japan.

The above conclusions, drawn from a discussion of the results of the NPORI investigation, agree with the other data collected elsewhere. Vos's investigation revealed unreserved acceptance of the traditional marriage arrangement by 10 per cent of the persons questioned, while 45 per cent suggested that it should be modified to some extent. Of Sofue's subjects, 58 per cent of the men and 45 per cent of the women preferred the love match, whereas 14 per cent of the men and 23 per cent of the women still favoured the traditional procedure. It was realized that the individualistic approach to marriage would not suit everybody. One of Vos's subjects said: 'In the modern world, the traditional arrangement is bad, unless a person lacks the opportunity to find a marriage partner for himself.' Sofue reports that several of the women interrogated gave him answers on similar lines, e.g.: 'My ideal is a love match, but since we have little opportunity of finding sweethearts or choosing husbands, insisting on love lessens one's chances, from the practical point of view.' We could quote many similar remarks from our own experience. At a meeting held in T. village, near Sapporo in Hokkaido, a number of young men told us that, in choosing their wives, they would be guided in the first place by their own inclination—love—but that they would try to secure their parents' approval; a youth who had lost his parents said that he would ask, but not necessarily take, the advice of his elder brother. As far as the girls were concerned, the difficulty was that, not having been brought up with boys, they did not know any; their inclination would therefore be either to use the services of a go-between or to ask their parents to help them. There is no point in multiplying examples. While large numbers of young people regard the love match as the ideal, it seems fairly certain that the intermediate type of marriage is, and will continue to be, the most prevalent.

Moreover, love does not seem to occupy a particularly prominent place in the life of young Japanese, at least, not so far as one can judge from their answers. In this respect the replies to the Kyoto and Sapporo questionnaires are typical. The students were told that their replies would be anonymous, and it was therefore expected that these would be given freely, which is indeed the impression one has from reading them. Now one of these questions asked the subjects to name the three events in their past life which struck them as most significant, making 300 possible answers per 100 subjects. Though the young people in question were at what is supposed to be the very age for falling in love, love seldom figured in their answers—it was mentioned by no more than 18 per cent at Sapporo and 10 per cent at Kyoto. It is true that the exceptionally small percentage at Kyoto is due to the fact that it represents the average for both male and female students, and only 5 per cent of the girls name love, whereas in the case of the men the proportion is 17 per cent (almost the same as at Sapporo). The attitude of the Sapporo students towards love seems, however, to be more positive than that of the students at Kyoto: in reply to a request to name two things they want and have not got, only 9 per cent of the men at Kyoto mention a girl friend, compared with 33 per cent at Sapporo (one of whom writes in French *la belle amie*). It should also be noted that when they were questioned as to their probable choice of confidant, it sometimes occurred to young men to name their fiancées (in 4 per cent of the cases at Kyoto). Among the greatest evils which could befall them, the subjects interrogated sometimes include the unfaithfulness of husband or wife, or of the betrothed. This reply was given by 5 per cent of both male and female students at Kyoto but not at all at Sapporo.

The data at our disposal hardly confirm Ruth Benedict's remarks about the absence of puritanism in sex matters among the Japanese and the small extent to which they associate love with marriage.[1] As we have seen, many young people think the love match the ideal form of marriage and it will not be hard to demonstrate that some of their attitudes towards sex are as puritanical as those of the Victorians. As a number of Japanese critics have pointed out, Ruth Benedict seems at times to generalize from observations which are only valid for the aristocracy or the wealthy middle class.

The Allport-Gillespie questionnaire, used at Kyoto and Sapporo, includes the following question: 'To what extent would you agree with the following proposition? "I would approve of an expansion of the idea of trial marriage i.e. of greater sexual freedom among young people, so as to enable them to discover whether they are compatible as marriage partners." ' Replies were as in Table 51.

The answers rejecting trial marriage are in a marked majority in all categories. The girls are much more strongly opposed to the idea than the men. It is true that they are younger and also that trial marriage does not mean the same thing to them as to the men, but in general, one is not surprised to find them less adventurous. As regards the men, the real

---

1. *The Chrysanthemum and the Sword*, pp. 183-4.

TABLE 51.

	Kyoto		Sapporo
	Men	*Girls*	
	%	%	%
Agree	17	3	6
Slightly agree	23	18	29
Slightly disagree	17	16	12
Disagree	43	61	53
No reply	0	2	0

significance of the disparity between the Kyoto and Sapporo figures becomes plain if we bear in mind that the Kyoto students come mostly from middle-class families, whereas the Sapporo students are mainly of working class origin; in Japan, sexual freedom appears to be greater in the upper classes.

Attitudes concerning the relations between the sexes are very well brought out by Sofue's projective test. Plate I was devised for that purpose. In a dimly lighted room a young woman wearing a sweater, who may perhaps be seated, is turning to look towards the door. The door is open, letting in the light. In the doorway a young man is standing, gazing at the woman. He wears an open-necked shirt, and there is a sombre expression on his face. Subjects described this couple in very different ways: as husband and wife, as lovers, as friends, as brother and sister, as father and daughter, as acquaintances and as strangers. Moreover, when they did not take the two persons for a married couple or a pair of lovers, they fairly frequently interpreted the scene either as an attempted rape on the part of the man or as a rejection by the woman of the man's advances. A sample of the first type of answer is the following: F. village, woman (domiciled at F. but working in Kagoshima). 'An unpleasant night incident. Fright of a woman who has found herself unexpectedly involved in such an incident. The picture shows a man suddenly appearing before a woman who was in her room and expecting nothing of the kind. It isn't necessarily a room: she might be on a road or in some lonely spot surrounded by pine trees. The man's intentions can be seen in his eyes: his aim seems to be to satisfy his primitive desires. You get the feeling that the room or road is not absolutely strange to the woman. She doesn't seem to find anything particularly frightening but just now she is startled.' The following may be quoted as an example of the other interpretation: woman, Yawata. 'A man seems to be talking to a woman. She stiffens as though something disgusting had just been said to her.' By combining the identification of the characters in the picture with the interpretation of what is going on between them, we get five different types of reaction:

Type I. The picture shows a married couple;

Type II. They are an unmarried couple, devoted lovers;

Type III. A man is trying to rape a woman;

Type IV. A woman is repulsing a man who loves her or is paying court to her;

Type V. Relations of another kind between people who may be father and daughter, brother and sister, two friends, acquaintances, or strangers.

Table 52 shows the distribution of replies.

TABLE 52.

Locality	Sex	Type I	Type II	Type III	Type IV	Type V	Number of cases
F. village	M.	5	0	4	0	1	10
	F.1[1]	2	1	0	1	2	6
	F.2[1]	1	0	2	0	0	3
Yawata	M.	3	6	0	1	1	11
	F.	1	1	2	2	0	7[2]
T. village	M.	3	1	0	1	3	7
	F.	2	1	2	1	3	9
Bibai	M.	1	1	0	0	0	2
	F.	1	0	0	0	2	3
H. village	M.	0	0	0	0	1	1
	F.	0	1	0	0	0	1
Totals	M.	11	8	4	2	6	31
	F.	7	4	6	4	7	29
Grand total		18	12	10	6	13	60

1. F.1 indicates women who spend their whole time in the village. F.2 indicates those who are domiciled at F but work at Kagoshima.

2. This figure represents the replies in the table plus one ambiguous and unclassifiable reply.

Comparing these results, we find that a picture of a man and woman together is most commonly taken to mean that they are married (Type I). Alternative interpretations, into which no sexual element enters, are also fairly common (Type V), but it is also thought that they may be lovers (Type II) and, less frequently, that a man is trying to rape a woman (Type III) or that a woman is repulsing the advances or courtship of a man (Type IV). Types I and II are commoner among men than among women, while the reverse is true of Types III, IV and V. If these results could be proved representative, one might conclude that the attitude of men towards women is more often than not peaceable and relaxed. The tension that may be suggested by the scene is less frequently ascribed to something in the relations between the couple themselves than to some external circumstance; thus, as we saw above (Chapter V, page oo), a young Yawata working man interprets this particular scene as representing the persecution of a pacifist. Another Yawata trade unionist

187

says: 'They seem to be a married couple. The husband looks very worried about life in general and about having been dismissed by the company he works for. His wife doesn't seem as worried as he is; she appears to be more easy-going, doesn't she?' The women, on the other hand, tend more frequently to regard the opposite sex with hostility, suspicion or at the least indifference. The inferior status of women, coupled with their need for a male helpmate to give them the social standing they require while at the same time they depend absolutely on the will of the man for satisfaction of that need, may perhaps explain this rather neurotic attitude. It must, however, be said at once that this is not the normal behaviour of all the girls and young women who took the test. One feminine reaction quoted by Sofue makes it clear that women are not incapable of reactions similar to those of the men illustrated above: woman, Bibai. 'The husband is a working man who has returned to the house to get something he forgot to take to work. His union is fighting the management for a wage increase. That is why they both look gloomy.'

We may attempt to carry the analysis further. In F. village, the commonest interpretation is that the scene represents a married couple. This is particularly the case among the men. The picture never suggests to them a peaceful irregular relationship between a man and a woman, but they do frequently interpret it as a scene of attempted rape. Sofue writes: 'What can be said, in the light of the above results, is that, in F. village, the men cannot see a couple together without thinking that they are probably married. There appear to be many cases in which the sight of a young man and young woman who are not married is associated more or less with the idea of something unsavoury, such as an attempted seduction. From the answers to the questionnaire we know that in this village the desire to make a love match is quite common, but we may well ask ourselves if a traditional psychological attitude towards sex relationship is not more firmly anchored in their minds. As far as the girls are concerned, the position is rather less serious: they have not the slightest sense of being tempted by men, but they cannot see a man and woman together without thinking they are married, nor can they conceive of social relations of any description between a man and a woman who are not married.' The position in T. village resembles that in F. village, though less clearly marked.

In the industrial town of Yawata, on the other hand, it is far less frequently inferred that this is a married couple; the men see them, instead, as a pair of lovers. Among the women the commonest reactions are either: 'A man is trying to seduce a woman or to commit a sexual offence against her, and she is afraid', or 'The man sees his love rejected by the woman'. Sofue notes that the girls from F. village who work in the town tend to react like the Yawata women and not like the rest of the women in their village. Regarding the reactions observed in Yawata, Sofue writes: 'The men interpret the scene as one in which a woman is welcoming a man's advances and as depicting their love for one another; most of the women, on the contrary, interpret it as a scene in which the woman is on the defensive against the man.'

We may, therefore, conclude that Japanese youth is far from adopting a uniform attitude towards sex relationships. The predominance in the country areas of the traditional pattern of sex relations legalized by marriage enables the girls to consider the whole subject calmly, but gives rise in the men to feelings of aggression and guilt; the disruption of this pattern in the industrial towns tends to make the men confident and relaxed and the girls, on the contrary, suspicious and hostile.

In their future life companion, both young men and young women look far more for qualities of character which will ensure that there is no clash of wills in everyday affairs than for guarantees of intellectual compatibility and similarity of outlook. This emerges clearly from the replies of the Kyoto and Sapporo students. (Table 53).

TABLE 53.

Qualities desired in the marriage partner	*Kyoto*		*Sapporo*
	Men	*Women*	
	%	%	%
Similarity of outlook	18	19	18
Intellectual ability	13	11	29
Good temper	68	68	47
No reply	1	2	6

The girls attach great importance to family life. Several investigations have revealed that one of the arguments advanced against paid employment for married women is that it is detrimental to family life. In the course of the investigation carried out in 1948 by the National Public Opinion Research Institute this explanation was offered by about one-seventh of the women in employment who said they were against the employment of married women (41 per cent of the subjects, on the average); but it is noteworthy that this point of view is three times as common among young women below the age of 28 as among the older women—as if the latter had lost some of their illusion.

The death of the marriage partner is regarded as a great misfortune and was mentioned spontaneously by about one in ten of the young people of Kyoto and Sapporo in reply to the question: What are the two worst things that could conceivably happen to you during your lifetime? About 12 per cent of the men and the same percentage of the girls thought that they might have to face a divorce, and about the same proportion thought they would marry more than once. The death of a child is often envisaged as a great misfortune, and was mentioned as such by about 1 per cent of the men at Kyoto and 4 per cent of the girls.

At this point we must again pause in our account of the attitudes of the young regarding their own homes, in order to consider the problem of children. Here we have at our disposal some data concerning the young men and women interrogated by Yoji Watanabe at Kyoto. The average number of children they want and the average number they actually expect to have, are as follows. Number of children wanted: men 2.68, women 2.62; number of children expected: men 2.78, women 3.02.

The first comment to be made is that these numbers are relatively low; we must however bear in mind that the young people in question are of middle class origin.

Secondly, a fact that merits discussion from more than one angle is the difference between the number of children wanted and the number expected; the first figure is throughout appreciably lower than the second—young Japanese think they will have more children than they want, and this attitude is typical of a society perpetually haunted by the spectre of over-population. It is also noticeable that the girls want fewer children than the men, and, above all, that the discrepancy between the number of children wanted and the number expected is much greater in the case of the girls than in that of the men; this suggests that the men have the impression that it will be easier for them to accomplish their desires, whereas the girls think they will be forced to have more children than they want.

A study of the age at which young people expect to have their first child serves only to confirm the foregoing observations (see graph on page 180). The women's replies may be plotted in an L-shaped graph reaching its maximum at the age of 25, which indicates that, over the birth of their first child even more than over their marriage, the girls are conscious of a social standard determining their fate and their conduct alike. In the case of the young men, on the contrary, their replies tend to form a normal, evenly distributed graph. The mean time interval in the women's replies is 2.12 years against 2.99 years for the men's. There seems to be no standard age at which the young men expect the birth of their first child. Indirectly—and this is all the more striking because it is unexpected—this analysis brings out the dependence of the Japanese girl not necessarily upon a particular person but upon social customs— a dependence which should be compared with the relative freedom felt by the young men.

RELIGION AND MORALITY

We are very unfavourably placed for studying the attitude of the young towards the institution of religion, since the investigation was not specially planned for that purpose, and the question is undoubtedly very complex. The generally accepted cliché is that 'the Japanese are not religious' and by Western standards this is probably true—but any ethnographical investigation in which only Western standards were applied could hardly be satisfactory. The number of Christians in Japan is very low, under 400,000, i.e. less than a half of 1 per cent. Moreover, religion is passing through a period of crisis; simultaneously with the proclamation of freedom of worship, State Shintoism has been abolished and denounced as pernicious. The clear-cut legal distinction made between the State cult and the Shintoism of the shrines is perhaps less evident to some of the faithful, and a special investigation would be needed to analyse the demoralization which the suppression of State Shintoism may have brought with it. It is not in fact sufficient to make an abstract distinction between the personal religious activities of subjects and whatever conformity they may show towards religious institutions that have remained intact, if we are to clear up the confusions and contradictions in the evidence at our disposal.

Of the group studied by Vos at Tokyo, only 31 per cent professed any particular religion, and of these 7 per cent at least were Christians (this shows fairly clearly that Vos's investigation cannot be regarded as covering a representative sample of the youth of Tokyo, where the proportion of Christians probably does not exceed 1 per cent. Within this professedly religious group, 58 per cent worshipped at the family altar. Of the people questioned by Sofue, 86 per cent of the men and 90 per cent of the women said that they had no religion. Nevertheless 32 per cent of the men and 13 per cent of the women believed in some kind of survival after death. It should also be noted that none of them acknowledged Shintoism as his creed; this hardly seems credible and is also inconsistent with the facts established by our investigation: it will be remembered that in one of our projective tests, in which the theme was authority and respect for authority (Cf. Chapter VI, page 156), four of the subjects said (two of them with approval) that the picture seemed to be about some religious topic. One is therefore inclined to think that direct questionnaires lead to the underestimating of religious attitudes.

In other cases, however, the impression conveyed is that these attitudes have been overestimated. The last question in the Allport-Gillespie list, used at Kyoto and Sapporo, was: 'Do you feel that you require some form of religious outlook or belief in order to achieve a fully mature philosophy of life?' The replies were as in Table 54.

Although the replies tending to indicate some need of religion are not very numerous, they still represent substantial minorities. But this impression is probably misleading. Another question in the same list, quoted earlier, was designed to show the relative interest taken by the subject in a given range of activities. What emerged quite clearly was that, both for the group as a whole and for almost all the individual

TABLE 54.

Reply	Kyoto		Sapporo
	Men	Women	
	%	%	%
Yes	36	37	47
No	26	14	35
Doubtful	38	49	18

members of it, religious activities played only the most negligible part (see graphs, page 168).

Indeed, it appears, that what we call religious needs, while not absolutely unknown to the Japanese, are an exceptional element in their psychology. Some traits of behaviour consistent with such needs can be found in the results of the investigation carried out by the National Public Opinion Research Institute, which seems to us the most interesting source of information on this point; but the list is not long. Thus, 11 people (out of 2,671) thought of mentioning religious experiences among the things which had made them happy; the following are a few examples: 'When I came to believe in salvation (through the power of Amida)'; 'During periods of meditation'; 'When I got a close view of His Imperial Majesty the Emperor' (it is significant that the Japanese investigators should have classified this reply here); 'When I felt the dawn of Buddhism upon me'. Four young people gave answers along these lines. Among the things necessary for happiness, four people, one of them young, mentioned religion (' should like to live a pious life with Buddha as its centre'; 'I should like to spread religion—Buddhism, or religion in general'; 'We find joy in our faith'). Sixteen people, one of them young, mentioned religion as their goal in life: 'My faith is extremely weak and I want it to become strong'; 'I want to win more people to the Tenri-Kyo'; 'I want to spread the life of Christian love in the world'. Lastly, two replies by young people, out of a total of 22, indicate an intention to work for the good of society through religion. All this amounts to very little; interest in religion is very poorly represented, especially among the younger generation.

Traditional morality is another institution passing through a crisis. The teaching of ethics has been suspended in the schools and adults are inclined to complain about the immorality of the young nowadays. In the universities, people sometimes said to us: 'There is too much academic, and not enough moral, teaching. We ought to be teaching a new code of morals, drawn up by the Ministry of Education.' A test of the situation is made by a double question used in the National Public Opinion Research Institute's representative investigation. It concerns *giri*, the basic traditional moral conduct in Japan. It is essential to consider in the first place the description of *giri* given by Ruth Benedict.

The relations between men in society are regulated, that is to say, rules of conduct exist. The Western comment on an individual who does not observe these rules is: 'he does not know how to behave'. What the Japanese often say is: 'he does not know *giri*'. A rough equivalent of this phrase would be: 'he does not know his duty', or 'he does not recognize his obligations'. But *giri* does not mean any kind of obligation and, in particular, it is not a moral obligation, an absolute 'must'. It is the quasi-contractual obligation of a person who has received a favour (an *on*) and who has thus become a 'debtor'. Hence, to act according to *giri* is to discharge a debt, not figuratively but literally; to neglect *giri* means, in a nutshell, failure to honour one's undertakings, the destruction of one's credit, exactly as in bankruptcy. That, at least, is the essence of Ruth Benedict's analysis, though she goes into many fine shades of technical difference.

While praising the penetration of the great American ethnologist, the Japanese have not been sparing of criticism, and have especially taken her to task for selecting too narrow a base for her study, for paying too little attention to the population as a whole, and for relying on documents supplied by intellectuals brought up in the Samurai tradition.[1] The results of the NPORI investigation undoubtedly throw some light on this matter. First and foremost, however, what does the Japanese public think of present-day behaviour in terms of *giri?*

In the Japanese version, the question was put in the following terms: 'Some people say it is a disaster that in the world today, the number of those who do not know *giri* is growing: do you think so, too?' This question can apparently be taken in two different ways: Is it a disaster that people no longer know *giri?* or, is it true to say that the number of people who do not know *giri* is growing? In fact, it is quite clear that the question was understood in the second sense, and the replies are distributed as in Table 55.

This table is very informative. In the first place, it shows the importance which the Japanese attach to *giri:* large numbers of subjects in all categories agree that this moral rule is no longer sufficiently respected. This view is commonest among the older people and also among the rural population, who are the regular champions of tradition. We also see that the young—especially in the towns—more frequently abstain from answering, either because they are more indifferent about this basic moral obligation or because they know less about it. But it is also evident that while a higher rate of abstentions among the young is balanced by a lower percentage of replies in the affirmative (which simply illustrates the elementary arithmetical rule that if one of the terms of a constant

---

1. On this subject, see the special number of *Minzokugaku-Kenkyu (Japanese Journal of Ethnology)*, 1949, 14, no. 4, particularly Kunio Yanagilā's article 'The common man's view of life' (in Japanese).

TABLE 55.

Age-group	Yes	No	No opinion
	%	%	%
Sample as a whole	72	21	7
Urban			
16-19	64	20	16
20-24	60	26	14
25-29	67	24	9
30 and over	77	18	5
Rural			
16-19	61	24	15
20-24	71	24	6
25-29	75	18	7
30 and over	75	19	6

sum increases, the other must decrease), there is no similar decrease in the negative replies. On the contrary, the young tend to assert more frequently than the rest that the number of those who do not know *giri* is not increasing. It is as if they were trying in this way to rebut an accusation levelled particularly against themselves. This is not mere guesswork; it is founded on analogy. For instance, when one invites the public, through an opinion poll, to condemn more or less indirectly a particular social category, judgments implying blame are less frequent in the category incriminated. This is probably the case here.

The second question asked for a definition of *giri:* 'If anyone in your own district says of a man, "He does not know *giri*", what would that be likely to mean?'

Taking the sample as a whole, a third (32 per cent) proved incapable of giving any definition. The percentages in this category were higher in the country than in the towns and higher among the young than among the other age-groups. This combination is rather unusual; it tends to suggest first, that the young are less acquainted with *giri* and less interested in it—thus the concept of *giri* represents a tradition that is growing weaker; and secondly, that this tradition is not essentially popular, that is to say, rural. As an aristocratic tradition it has been more accessible to the towns, either through the schools and through books or as a result of social exchanges.[1]

---

1. Asano's comment, after reading a preliminary version of this report, was that not all of those who refrained from defining *giri* were necessarily ignorant of the term, but that probably some of them could not find the words to express themselves. In its general terms, the justice of this observation is beyond question. It is very likely that difficulty in self-expression is greater in the country than among the urban population. The whole point is whether this

These assumptions are not invalidated by a study of the replies, which also provide us with additional information. The replies were, indeed, so varied that an extremely complicated classification had to be made in the Japanese analytical code. They can be regrouped in five categories: Not knowing *giri* means:

1. Failure to recognize an *on*, i.e. an obligation towards someone, a debt of gratitude. The great majority of those answering along these lines had in mind any conferer of the *on;* some of them, however, explicitly mentioned an *on* received from parents, relatives, or employers but always in cases when specific services had been rendered by these, and not in the sense of a general natural obligation;

2. Failure to discharge one's material debts: not giving back a thing borrowed; failing to remember a person in difficulties who lent one money when one was in a similar position;

3. Failure to fulfil the formal obligations of social life: not replying to an invitation; not thanking the donor for a gift; not replying to congratulations offered on the occasion of some ceremony;

4. Not honouring one's general moral obligations: failure to help neighbours in difficulty; thinking only of oneself; trampling on persons who get in one's way; not keeping promises; not doing what one should;

5. Miscellaneous replies, including lack of tact, lack of consideration for others; speaking evil of people behind their backs; making a distinction between rich and poor in one's social intercourse; failure to understand the principles of democracy.

The distribution of the above replies was as in Table 56.

This table is very interesting and deserves careful study. The replies in the first category correspond more or less with Ruth Benedict's suggested definition. It will at once be seen that the percentages in this column increase with age and also that, within the same age-group, the differences between town- and country-dwellers are here most marked, and are as considerable, though in the reverse order, as the differences

---

invalidates our hypotheses. Nothing in the investigation warrants a definite decision one way or the other.

A detailed analysis of the data does, however, enable us to make certain assumptions (see supplementary analysis of the replies to question 14a, Appendix I, page 258). It regularly happens that difficulty in self-expression liable to make the subject abstain from replying is most frequently found not only among the rural population, as Asano rightly points out, but also among women and elderly people. Hence, if difficulty in self-expression were the determining factor here, we ought to find the highest percentages of abstentions, not only in the rural categories but in the other two as well. A study of the detailed table shows clearly that this is not the case: abstentions are much more frequent among the young of both sexes. It is also noticeable that in all age-groups and both types of habitat the technical answer (1) is not less frequent in the case of the women: indeed, the opposite is true. I therefore feel justified in the absence of proof to the contrary, in standing by my interpretation.

TABLE 56.

Age-group	1	2	3	4	5	Don't know
	%	%	%	%	%	%
Sample as a whole	30	5	10	19	4	32
Urban						
16-19	28	7	8	14	3	40
20-24	30	9	10	18	4	29
25-29	34	7	10	15	3	31
30 and over	36	6	10	20	4	22
Rural						
16-19	19	3	8	12	3	55
20-24	26	4	11	18	3	38
25-29	29	4	10	17	3	37
30 and over	30	3	9	23	3	32

in the percentages of abstentions. The replies in the second category are merely the transfers to the practical sphere of the meanings given to *giri* in Category 1 replies. Here again, the differences shown in the percentages of the urban and rural age-groups are considerable. As regards comparison between age-groups however, by contrast with what occurs in the first column, one gathers the impression that in both types of habitat percentages are inclined to decrease with increasing age, and this is certainly the case if we leave out the youngest age-group. Turning now to the three following columns, corresponding to the replies in Categories 3, 4 and 5, and comparing the percentages by habitat in each age-group, we find that they differ from the two preceding columns and that habitat has practically no influence on the result: for each age-group the percentages of replies are almost identical. One is therefore left with the feeling that the replies in the first category and also the clumsy translation of them in Category 2, are to be explained by a notion of *giri* peculiar to the urban population; or rather, if it is true that *giri* has its origin in the ethics of the aristocracy, by a concept that spread first in the towns and afterwards to the villages, but to a lesser degree. The replies in Categories 3, 4 and 5 belong, on the other hand, to the realm of commonplace morality: according to the interpretation they provide, *giri* means 'doing one's duty' or something equally vague, 'doing what one ought', etc. A particular form of this interpretation is shown in Category 4, where *giri* is understood in the sense of the natural moral obligation towards one's neighbour, as this might have been preached in Asia and Europe by any of the great world religions of an ethical tendency.

Thus, for the purpose of our present analysis, the five categories of replies have been arranged in two groups: a technical and a non-technical interpretation of *giri*. After regrouping the percentages of replies on this

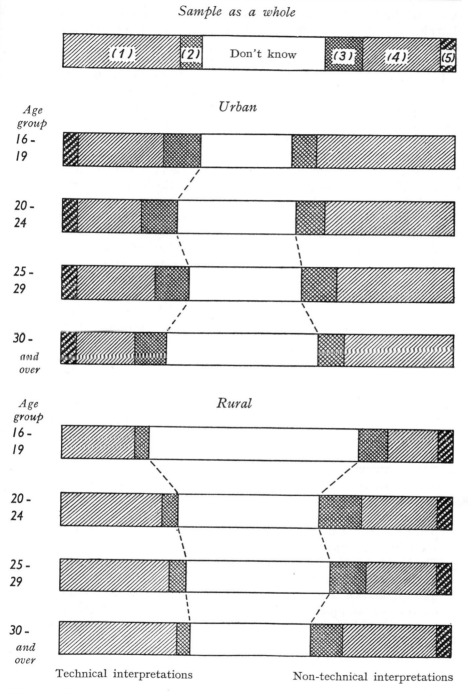

Sample as a whole

(1) (2) Don't know (3) (4) (5)

Age group
16 - 19

Urban

20 - 24

25 - 29

30 - and over

Age group
16 - 19

Rural

20 - 24

25 - 29

30 - and over

Technical interpretations   Non-technical interpretations

Fig. 15. Interpretations of *giri* (see text)

basis, we find that in each habitat, the replies of the 'under-20s' are sharply distinguished from those of the rest, whereas between the other age-groups, the discrepancies are very slight and in any case inconsistent. The general percentage of Group 2 answers, in both town and country, is lowest in the 25-29 age-group. Above all it should be noted that in Group I, which combines the definitions of *giri* contained in Categories I and 2, the percentages according to age-group are very stable from 20 years upwards, in each habitat. The explanation is that from the age of 20 onwards, the low proportion of Category I replies is offset by a higher proportion of Category 2 replies, which are at bottom a crude and perhaps debased version of the replies in Category I. On the other hand, no matter how they are grouped, the replies of the 'under-20s' are always fewer in number than those of the other age-groups.

A hypothesis, not necessarily accurate but taking into account the facts analysed above, could be formulated as follows:

1. The concept of *giri* belongs to the traditional ethics of the aristocracy; it has been disseminated by means of the theatre, literature, and social intercourse, but first in the towns and only afterwards—and to a lesser degree—in the countryside;

2. This concept has been correctly assimilated by about a third of the Japanese public; a slightly lower percentage have heard of it but interpret it in purely material terms;

3. Another third of the population, approximately, are acquainted with the expression but have not the least idea what it means, interpreting it in terms of the various forms of morality they happen to know, ranging from the rules of strict etiquette to the inspirations of loving kindness. As this general morality is common to all classes of society, this kind of interpretation of *giri* is found everywhere to more or less the same extent.

4. Precise knowledge of the meaning of *giri* decreases in direct ratio to the age of the subject interrogated; it is a concept which is in the course of disappearing. The young people now reaching adult status who have still heard of it, usually make the mistake of giving it a purely material meaning. The youngest quite evidently know least about it; the difference is very striking.

5. The ignorance and indifference of the youngest age-group (the 'under-20s'), is not confined to *giri:* the technical meaning of the term being quite unknown to them, they cannot even fall back, as their elders do, on commonplace moral definitions; in this class of replies, too, the difference between the 'under-20s' and the older age-groups is very marked.

Consequently, if we leave aside technical consideration of the nature of *giri* and of the way this concept was disseminated among the Japanese public, we find, as regards the young, in particular, that they show a minimum knowledge, not merely of traditional and limited moral values but even of general morality. Those who have reached adult status betray this shortcoming by their less refined thinking, while among the youngest obvious gaps can be discerned. It is not possible to attempt a forecast on the strength of the evidence so far available. Will subjects who have not yet reached the age of 20 develop, as they grow older, on the same lines as their elders? Or will they advance beyond the point their elders have reached? To answer these questions we should have to know, not only the ethical development of the individuals concerned, but also, without doubt, the direction Japan will take now that the end of the occupation has left her to her own devices.

Despite the fact that the young are in this moral condition, and although they take more interest than their elders in foreign peoples— not only in their technology but also in certain aspects of their artistic and intellectual culture—it would be a grave mistake to imagine that they feel their own culture, as it were, alien to them, or that they have lost their attachment to, and confidence in the national traditions. One tiny fact seems to indicate that the position is quite otherwise: the young are often inclined to ignore minor obligations such as sending new year wishes (a very widespread custom in Japan). Nevertheless, an investigation by the National Public Opinion Research Institute which included a question concerning this custom reveals that it is not only the young who would like to see the tradition relaxed: this point of view is most strongly supported in the 30-50 age-groups, particularly among those who have had a higher education. Neither are the young the most numerous advocates of a strengthening of this tradition: by a clear majority, more than in any other age-group, they are in favour of leaving things as they are.

The Japanese are very attached to their own history. Often, in the course of public opinion investigations, young people have seized the opportunity of making allusions which showed that they both knew and loved it. Of the young people interrogated by Vos, only 29 per cent said they went occasionally to see *Kabuki* performances (Japanese historical drama); half the group (49 per cent) admitted they were *Kabuki* enthusiasts. Japanese find many faults in their own national character. Sofue's investigation, in particular, shows that they blame themselves for being enthusiastic without perseverance, for letting their feelings too easily get the better of them, for making too much fuss over trifles and for retaining a feudal outlook. They accept without question the stereotyped criticism levelled at them by foreigners that they are never punctual and they are obsessed by this idea (an ethnological study of punctuality, the part it plays in the industrialized urban society of the West and its dissemination in other culture, would be worth undertaking). They are also frequently of the opinion that they are too imitative. Against this they can, on occasion, perceive the advantage they derive from their cultural malleability; they know that they are diligent and persevering, that their willpower is strong, that they are skilful, modest and courteous, and have a sense of duty. In short, as we have seen, despite their recent trials, the young are glad and proud to have been born Japanese. Four per cent of the Kyoto students thought the loss of Japan's independence one of the greatest misfortunes which could befall them personally. In the NPORI investigation, 4 per cent of the subjects interrogated mentioned the preservation of Japan's independence as having given them great happiness. The young gave this reply more frequently than the rest. It is also of some interest that replies of this kind are approximately twice as frequent among the rural as among the urban population.

CHAPTER VIII

THE PERSONALITY OF THE YOUNG

PERSONAL VALUES OF THE YOUNG

The analysis of the attitudes of Japanese youth, to which the preceding chapters have been devoted, is in itself a contribution to the description of their personality. People express themselves through their attitudes and one of the commonest ways of defining the personality of an individual is to describe what he thinks and what opinions he holds.

Though suffering from the present economic conditions, and to some extent hostile to authority in the economic sphere, young Japanese show little interest in domestic politics and not much inclination to take an active part in them. They retain the utmost respect for the forms of civil authority and for the person of the Emperor. Verbally, they express certain attitudes of approval regarding the legal changes which have taken place in personal relationships within the family, and in particular, like the rest of the Japanese public but still more emphatically, they profess to welcome the new principles of sex equality and the emancipation of women. But in practice they often accept the inequality and subordination which continue to exist. These attitudes are sometimes, no doubt, subconscious, but when the conscious mind becomes aware of them, we find the young trying to satisfy themselves with rationalizations. Again, some women are loud in their demands for equality of rights and conditions,[1] but many young women spontaneously admit that they would like just as well to keep their former status. Interest in foreign countries is lively and genuine and, in some of its aspects, will certainly outlive the contemporary circumstances which have given it a still stronger impetus; but attachment to Japanese culture is profound, and in essentials, ineradicable. Horror of the lost war is general and all idea of revenge seems to be absent; pacifism and even anti-militarism are widespread. These views, however, are not held completely without reserve and it is foreseeable that, fanned by strong but variable winds, the present attitudes of many young people, especially the girls and the country folk, might as easily veer in another direction.

---

1. See for instance, *The Japanese family system, as seen from the standpoint of Japanese women*, Setsuko Hani, Tokyo, 1948.

In all these attitudes of the young there is no lack of continuity with those of their elders. It is true that the latter often complain that the young are no longer willing to follow their parents and are too ready to listen to the new cry of liberty without being really educated up to it, or being capable of understanding it. Despite this, however, and notwithstanding the impression young people sometimes have that there is a gulf between them and the preceding generations, hardly any 'progressive' tendencies are accepted by the young unless public opinion has first stamped them with the seal of its approval, sometimes less emphatically, but on occasions even more enthusiastically, than the young themselves.

We should accordingly expect to find the other facets of the personality of Japanese youth, particularly its traits of character, simply by extending those of the adults; or rather, to reverse the metaphor, and regarding the new generation not as the continuation of the old but as destined to take its place, many traits of contemporary youth should be recognizably forming and making possible by the processes of natural development personalities which will not be very different from those of the adults of the present day and even of the past.

However, even if such a theory were correct, it would not be easy to prove it conclusively. The young are not adults, and this is to be understood above all in a psycho-social sense: the personality of the young is not the same as the personality of adults. The difference between the two types is essentially covered by the notion of immaturity and, indeed, an analysis of the personality traits of Japanese youth will reveal a good deal of immaturity. Is the presence of this characteristic due to a primarily psychological cause—the fact that the young have not finished their personal development? Or is the cause a social one—the holding of a status which does not yet allow them to behave like adults? It is extremely difficult to say, although the important part their juvenile status plays in the immaturity of the young is hardly to be denied: the less urgent obligation to act, the lighter responsibility, and the fact that some want of initiative on their part is expected and even accepted by adults, are all factors favouring wishful thinking, the entertainment of agreeable illusions, romanticism and a lack of realism. In Japan, however, young people share many of these traits with their elders, so that it is very hard to say whether their presence in the young is in fact a characteristic of immaturity which will disappear with attainment to an adult age or whether it foreshadows an enduring personality structure, often regarded as undesirable.

In any case it is beyond dispute that, as far as we can gather from the evidence collected in the course of investigations, the personal behaviour patterns of young Japanese exhibit not only a fair amount of inexperience but also much vacillation. This is understandable if we bear in mind that, in the circumstances in which they are placed, many choices are not, and so far have not needed to be, made. It must also be said, however, that unless there are decisive structural changes in the culture of contemporary Japan, there is nothing to prevent the process of growing up from bringing the type of juvenile personality observable today nearer to the personality of the contemporary adult.

Before going on to examine the personality traits of Japanese youth, it would seem to be necessary, as a sequel to our study of their attitudes, to specify the values to which young people are attached. Spranger has suggested a list of six groups of values each of which, when dominant, determines a corresponding type of personality. These six groups of values are: values of knowledge and truth, corresponding with the academic type; utility values, corresponding with the economic type; values of beauty and art, corresponding with the aesthetic type; values of affection and sympathy, corresponding with the social type; power values, corresponding with the political type; and lastly religious values (values of unity) corresponding with the religious type. It should be noted that the terms used to describe the various types are technical and it would be an error to interpret, say, the 'social type' or the 'political type' according to the ordinary meanings of those adjectives.[1] No individual ever conforms completely to a particular type but approximates to it more or less according to the values dominant in his personality. The intentions, ambitions, hopes, dominant anxieties, and the things that give maximum satisfaction to an individual enable us to infer these dominant values and to classify the person in question, though not always positively, as belonging to a particular type.

It was quite impossible to put all the subjects interrogated during the National Public Opinion Research Institute's representative investigation the questions used in the West for the assessment of personal values; the chief aims of the investigation were obviously altogether different. Moreover, many of the questions would have been meaningless in a culture so different from that of the West, and would have had to undergo modifications which would have made it impossible to compare the answers. In the present skeleton analysis, therefore, nothing more than the crudest and most general comparison with the results of tests carried out in the West must be looked for. It is to be hoped that in the near future we shall have at our disposal better means of comparison, which will then be of great interest.

Although we might have taken advantage of the more numerous data assembled during the investigation carried out by NPORI, the replies to only two of the questions were used for classifying subjects as belonging to one or other of the above six types. The first question was: 'On what occasions have you felt happy and light hearted?' The second was: 'Is there any particular thing you hope to accomplish in the course of

---

1. C. E. Spranger, *Lebensformen*, Halle, 1929, Other works to which the reader may refer are *A study of values*, by G. W. Allport and P. E. Vernon, Boston, 1931; and *Théorie des opinions* by J. Stoetzel, Paris, 1943.

your life? If so, what kind of thing?' The classification was made in Tokyo by the staff of the National Public Opinion Research Institute after our departure but in conformity with our general instructions.

Since the reactions to two questions only were available for the purpose, the classification of some of the subjects (15 per cent of the sample as a whole) proved risky or impossible. The largest number of those tested were classed under 'social type' (38 per cent) while the 'economic type' also occurred frequently, in 30 per cent of the cases. The 'aesthetic type' accounted for 8 per cent of the subjects interrogated and the 'political type' for 5 per cent, the last two types were very rare—only 2 per cent were of the 'theoretical type' and 1 per cent of the 'religious type'.

The frequent occurrence of the economic type, whose interests are centred on utility values, is not surprising in a modern society with a commercial and industrial basis. The rarity of the religious type is also what might be expected; the Japanese themselves admit that as a people they are very practical and little inclined to mysticism or metaphysics. Nevertheless, it is not impossible that the investigation may have underestimated certain religious tendencies or needs which are perhaps taking shape; but any attempt to get fuller details on this point would have required research on a much more considerable scale than we could have contemplated. We have no specific information about the distribution of the academic type among the peoples of the world, but the probability is that the low percentage found in this case is not exceptional. Despite the spread of popular education, learning is still regarded as a luxury, and this notion made its appearance more or less explicitly, in many of the replies received. The small number of subjects belonging to the 'political type' is probably more indicative of a society which has traditionally tended not to develop the will to power, at least in its individual expression. The comparatively high frequency of the aesthetic type would merit comment but, for lack of familiarity with Japanese culture, any remarks we might feel tempted to add would probably turn out to be mere literary embroidery; it is therefore better to leave this matter to the Japanese themselves. The most striking piece of evidence is probably the very large number of 'social personalities' encountered; this agrees not only with the Western stereotype of Japanese public behaviour[1] but also with many other findings of the investigation, for instance with interpretations 4 and 5 of *giri* (see above Chapter VII, page 195) and also with certain personality traits.

Distribution of the types of personality is as in Table 57.

---

1. Cf. Lafcadio Hearn, *Japan, an interpretation*, 1904.

TABLE 57.

Age-group	Social	Economic	Aesthetic	Political	Academic	Religious	Unclassified
	%	%	%	%	%	%	%
Sample as a whole	38	30	8	5	2	1	16
Urban							
16-19	22	22	23		7	0	19
20-24	29	29	14		3	1	19
25-29	29	32	11	2	3	3	20
30 and over	43	34	5	4	1	2	11
Rural							
16-19	20	24	16	9	4	1	26
20-24	33	26	11	4	2	1	23
25-29	39	29	8	5	1	1	17
30 and over	46	31	3	3	1	2	14

Compared with the others, the young seem at first sight more difficult to classify, and this applies especially to the rural age-group. This circumstance provides us with a recognizable mark of greater immaturity: the young have not crystallized their values to the same degrees as their elders. Moreover, the two types most common in the population as a whole, the social and the economic, are found less often among the young, and that is another unmistakable and very important sign of their immaturity. As they do not yet enjoy the status of adults, they have less responsibility, are less impressed by utility values and have less feeling and taste for relationship with the other sections of society. The more marked individualism, the withdrawal into oneself and the tendency towards introspection which may be inferred from the very considerable difference in the prevalence of the social type among juveniles and among fully developed adults, will reappear in the analysis of certain personality traits of the young. They may perhaps indicate the beginning of a change in the personality structure of the Japanese: in studying the various interpretations of *giri*, we have noted the increasing tendency of the young to conceive less of this notion, either as a philosophic doctrine or as a part of social ethics.

The distribution figures for the religious type are low, and it would therefore be risky to draw any conclusions from them. However, they do nothing to disprove the oft-repeated comment that the young are even less interested in religion than the adults.

On the other hand, the young reveal far more sensitiveness than their elders towards political, academic and aesthetic values. It is undeniable that the young show a stronger will to power: in reply to a question which has not been used for the purpose of the present classification, they showed that they were much more often ready to assume leadership (Cf. Chapter VI, page 148). This strengthens the impression of individualism among the young which we had when considering the distribution of the social type. A more detailed interpretation of the facts is essential and will be attempted later.

The much greater prevalence of the academic and aesthetic types is remarkable. Although far more young people in these two categories are to be found in the towns than in the country, the difference between the youngest and the oldest age-groups tends to be the same for both habitats, and decreases progressively with increasing age. The values of truth and beauty are directly associated with schooling, particularly in countries where education is on classical lines, as in Japan; their presence here may therefore be regarded as a direct consequence of the status of the young, who are not allowed as yet to share in the sordid— or, if you like, the serious—activities of adult life and are relegated to the infantile world of the schoolroom, the library and the theatre, where truth and beauty are the things that matter. But one wonders whether subscribing to these values is not sometimes a sign of escapism: in a world dominated by force and money, art and science may look like havens of refuge to those who, lacking the will to power, hesitate before plunging into the maelstrom of competition; we have seen with what trepidation many young people face the prospect of earning their own living in some trade or profession. In any case, art and science are activities which allow and encourage individual sensitiveness and reflection; the predominance of these values among the young is yet another indication of a possible tendency towards individualism.

Whatever significance we may attach to it and whatever consequences we may envisage, the interest of Japanese youth in cultural values is an unmistakable fact, which the investigations confirm in every respect. The students of Kyoto and Sapporo, when asked what they would do if they unexpectedly received a large sum of money, most often replied that they would spend it on study or on buying books; this reply was made by 24 per cent of the Sapporo students and by 28 per cent of the men and 15 per cent of the women at Kyoto. Asked to name the two

TABLE 58.

Preference	Age-group			
	18-25	*26-35*	*36-45*	*46 and over*
	%	%	%	%
Classical music	45	38	21	6
Light music	48	55	33	21
Plays	60	52	55	45
Variety	48	61	72	80
Stories	32	36	45	53
Humour	52	63	64	74
'Gossip'	23	25	36	32

things they wanted most and did not possess, they mentioned books (Sapporo 18 per cent; Kyoto, men 23 per cent, women 15 per cent, or such things as pianos, gramophones or cameras (Sapporo 35 per cent; Kyoto, men 13 per cent, women 8 per cent). The favourite leisure occupations of the young people interrogated by Vos in Tokyo were music (24 per cent) and reading (21 per cent); sport came only third, with 18 per cent. The investigation carried out by the Dentsu Company between March and June 1951, on radio listening preferences, makes it clear that the most popular programmes are those least favoured by the young, who look rather for broadcasts of a cultural character (Table 58). Lastly it will be recalled that, as the NPORI investigation showed, the young, more frequently than their elders, admire Western science and want Japan to borrow from it; they also show more interest in France on account of her cultural and intellectual achievements.

AMBITION AND OPTIMISM

Thus the youth of Japan differs from its elders in underestimating the economic and social element—not to speak of religious values—and in overestimating the importance of art and science, as well as by its greater will to power. These findings are in accord with the most representative results of the NPORI investigation covering, not only the general attitudes and personality traits of Japanese youth, but, in particular, the growth of ambition in the young, especially as revealed by a hankering after fame. Science and art undoubtedly provide particularly striking examples in this domain; and the need for expansion of the ego and the will to power can easily be canalized in these directions. The question set by NPORI was in the following terms: 'Which of the following comes nearest to being your goal in life? (a) to devote yourself to the service of the public without thought for your own affairs? (b) to achieve material security through your own work? (c) to become wealthy by devoting every ounce of energy to your work? (d) to live light-heartedly for the day, with no thought of the future? (e) to achieve fame by your work and learning? (f) to lead an honest life, regardless of what other people do? (g) to live the life you like without worrying about money or fame?'

The replies made by the sample as a whole and their distribution by age-group and habitat (see Table 59), both deserve extensive comment.

One is immediately struck by the indisputable predominance of the second answer (financial security), indicating the existence of serious economic anxieties among the Japanese—a point that has already been made earlier (Cf. Chapter VI, page 142). It is clear, however, that this worry is considerably less serious among the young. The aim to live an

TABLE 59.

Age-group	Aim in life							
	Public service	Financial security	Wealth	Living for the day	Fame	Honest life	The life one likes	Miscellaneous and no reply
	%	%	%	%	%	%	%	%
Sample as a whole	4	45	3	6	15	17	9	1
Urban								
16-19	6	27	1	6	36	13	11	0
20-24	7	34	1	5	21	15	17	0
25-29	2	47	1	8	16	10	12	3
30 and over	3	53	3	5	10	17	7	1
Rural								
16-19	2	24	4	6	30	20	14	2
20-24	4	37	3	5	22	16	13	1
25-29	6	50	6	6	12	13	7	0
30 and over	5	48	4	6	10	19	8	2

honest life comes second in order of preference; it is stated rather less often in the towns than in the country and is at its lowest in the 25-29 age-group, where it is offset by greater concern for financial security and more lively preoccupation with the struggle for existence. Living the life one likes, without letting oneself be worried by cares of ambition, although not a very general choice, is nevertheless not uncommon and is found more often among the young. The resolution to live from day to day is distributed remarkably evenly over all age-groups and both habitats, and this contrasts with the very uneven distribution of the other aims in life, thereby presenting a problem which may turn out to be highly instructive. The aim to make a fortune is not very widespread but is more prevalent in the country than in the towns. All these attitudes towards life merit much more careful investigation and it is likely that research along these lines would enable us to acquire a better understanding of certain deep-seated traits of Japanese psychology.

But the most striking thing about the above table, if one compares the replies of the young with those of their elders, is the prevalence among young people of the desire to achieve fame. This ambition is by no means exceptional among the older groups, where it is found in one case out of ten. This shows how much the individual, in Japanese society, is affected by the opinions of others and, while it brings out the extremely 'integrative' character of that society, it also reveals how competitive it is. The figures sum up and clarify the impression one gains from a perusal, in the classification code compiled by the National Public Opinion Research Institute, of the innumerable sample replies asserting: 'I want to be the best man in Japan in my line of work'; 'I want to make

our village more advanced than the other villages'; 'I want to devote
my whole energies to success in such-and-such a business'; 'I want to
work out my own special stockraising techniques,' etc. But the longing
for fame is still more marked in the case of the young: it is found three
times as often among the under-20s as among the over-20s. The desire
to make a name for themselves is expressed in their replies by one out
of every three in the under-20 age-group, where answers of this kind
outnumber all the others; they remain very frequent up to the age of 25.

This very frank ambition is accompanied in the young by considerable
self-confidence. This is well brought out by a group of questions in the
Allport-Gillespie test used at Kyoto and Sapporo and in a modified
form by Sofue. Thus the great majority of young people think that they
will 'have more success as leaders in their own field than the average
person of equivalent education' (Table 60).

TABLE 60.

	Kyoto		Sapporo
	Men	*Women*	
	%	%	%
More successful	39	23	35
About the same	56	72	59
Less successful	4	5	6
No reply	1	0	0

Self-confidence is high; an inferiority complex is exceptional and among
the men, at Sapporo and Kyoto alike, almost one in four is sure that he
will excel; the girls have this feeling less often, but at least they are sure
they will not be below average.

To achieve the success on which they reckon, the young count mainly
on their own efforts, far more than on outside help from their family
or relations, as may be seen from their answers to the following questions:
'In general, what will help you most to get ahead, your own ability or
"pull" (that is, personal contacts or influence, through family or friends)?'
(Table 61).

TABLE 61.

	Kyoto		Sapporo
	Men	*Women*	
	%	%	%
Ability	78	65	59
'Pull'	21	34	35
No reply	1	1	6

Young people likewise do not rely on being helped by circumstances, but rather take the view that their future will be determined to a great extent by their own actions. The replies collected by Sofue from young peasants and workmen agree with those of the students (Table 62).

TABLE 62.

Principal factor in determining the subject's future	Kyoto		Sapporo	Sofue's group	
	Men	Women		Men	Women
	%	%	%	%	%
Oneself	67	69	53	67	61
Circumstances	31	30	47	33	39
No reply	2	1	0	0	0

These various groups of results are remarkably consistent, despite the small number of cases on which some of the percentages are calculated (e.g. at Sapporo and in the case of Sofue's group)—that is to say, in circumstances where we might have expected to find considerable fluctuations in the samples. The Sapporo students do, however, appear to be a little less self-confident and this is perhaps no chance variation. Although the results are contradictory, it would also seem that the self-confidence of the women is not so great. However this may be, all the results show a substantial amount of self-confidence. There is therefore nothing surprising in the students' reactions to the following question: 'To what extent do you agree with the following proposition: "The world is a hazardous place in which men are basically evil and dangerous"?' (Table 63).

TABLE 63.

	Kyoto		Sapporo
	Men	Women	
	%	%	%
Agree	11	15	18
Slightly agree	27	26	12
Slightly disagree	25	21	41
Disagree	37	34	29
No reply	0	3	0

Disagreement, slight or complete, is thus clearly the attitude of the majority and it is clear that there are hardly any neurotic or accusatory tendencies.

Another well marked trait in the personality of the young Japanese, which links up with the preceding one, is optimism. We have already seen from the NPORI investigation (Chapter VI, page 144) that the young are more optimistic than their elders when asked whether they think world conditions will get progressively better, and the young people in the towns are even more optimistic than those in the rural areas. Many other data point to the same general conclusions. Similar results were obtained in reply to several of the questions used in an investigation by the newspaper *Asahi* in 1950. For instance, in reply to the question: 'Do you think that the children of today will be better off in 20 years' time than you are now?', 49 per cent of those interrogated answered 'yes', only 5 per cent thought the situation would be worse, and the replies of the young were even more confident about the future. Students also show much optimism. Their replies concerning the way they feel about their own personal future are distributed as in Table 64.

TABLE 64.

| | Kyoto | | Sapporo |
	Men	Women	
	%	%	%
Enthusiastic	26	29	18
Hopeful	37	41	65
Indifferent	7	4	18
Resigned	11	21	0
Embittered	18	1	0
Double answers	1	0	0

The young expect to achieve a better social position than their parents and this is true not merely of the Sapporo students, who are mainly working-class and have embarked on higher education with that object in view, but also of the young people of the middle class at Kyoto and in the group interrogated by Vos in Tokyo. In this last group both sexes are represented and, as at Kyoto, expectation of rising in the social scale is less among the girls than among the men (Table 65).

TABLE 65.

| By comparison with that of their parents, expect that their own social position will be | Kyoto | | Sapporo | Vos's group |
	Men	Women		
	%	%	%	%
Better	42	29	53	36
Same	47	63	35	16
Worse	11	3	6	2
No opinion	0	0	6	46

Two related questions in the Allport-Gillespie list enable us to define the way in which this optimism is applied, and to some extent assess the intensity of the trait itself. The questions were as follows: 1. What are the two worst things that could *conceivably* happen to you during your lifetime? 2. What are the two worst things that are *likely* to happen to you?' The total number of eventualities mentioned in reply to each question by a given group of subjects makes it possible for us to evaluate their capacity for imagining misfortunes, while analysis of the categories of eventualities mentioned reveals the sensitive spots. The replies to these two questions have already been used several times in this report, but a comparison of the replies to the first question with the replies to the second (Table 66) helps us, in addition, to estimate the extent to which the imagined misfortunes are regarded as real or at least potential. As the results prove fairly clearly, the replies to the two questions are far from being entirely unconnected, and this leads us to suspect that subjects have yielded to the promptings of their own imaginations; but optimism consists precisely in resisting promptings of this kind. The replies are analysed below: we have omitted 'miscellaneous' and 'vague' answers which throw no light on the matter, and also the mention by four men from Kyoto of 'the loss of Japan's independence' as an anticipated misfortune, since this eventuality does not figure in the list of imagined evils.

TABLE 66.

	Sapporo			Kyoto					
				Men			Women		
	I	A	D	I	A	D	I	A	D
	%	%	%	%	%	%	%	%	%
National or local disaster	18	0	+18	4	2	+2	7	3	+4
War	18	35	—17	55	57	—2	39	45	—6
Revolution	0	0	0	6	7	—1	2	1	+1
Destitution	6	18	—12	9	6	+3	8	6	+2
Family disunion	6	0	+6	4	3	+1	8	7	+1
Death in the family	24	18	+6	0	2	—2	34	25	+9
Unfaithfulness of the marriage partner, etc.	0	0	0	5	6	—1	5	6	—1
Death of the marriage partner	12	0	+12	7	3	+4	8	8	0
Death of a child	0	0	0	1	2	—1	4	3	+1
Unsuccessful career	6	0	+6	5	17	—12	2	6	—4
Unemployment	0	6	—6	11	8	+3	2	5	—3
Accidental death	0	0	0	18	5	+13	2	3	—1
Calumny	6	12	—6	1	2	—1	0	1	—1
Illness	24	24	0	23	15	+8	14	12	+2
	96	89	+7	149	135	+14	135	131	+4

Note: I = conceivable misfortunes, A = expected misfortunes, D represents the difference between the two percentages. Positive differences indicate an optimistic attitude.

The table shows that on balance there is a tendency towards optimism. The subject about which pessimism is most widespread is war. The young men of Sapporo are also pessimistic about their own financial prospects; among the Kyoto students, this fear is more apt to take the form of anticipated failure in their careers. In the family sphere, and in matters relating to the home, the tendency is towards optimism. The subjects do not really believe they will fall ill or be killed in an accident. Young men are more optimistic than young women, though the latter are also far from being pessimistic.

Sofue found more realism among young men than among girls. When he asked what age they would choose to live in, the present was chosen by more men (54 per cent) than women (29 per cent). Similarly, as we have already seen, women more often want to leave their native village although they are happy enough there. Sofue also found a higher degree of independence among the men, of whom 45 per cent felt no need of anyone's help in solving their personal problems; whereas this attitude was taken by only 19 per cent of the women. Among the men independence was more marked among the villagers of Hokkaido (44 per cent) and among the same class in Kyushu (14 per cent); it attains its maximum in Sofue's group, among the young factory workers of Yawata (54 per cent). At Kyoto, the boys, when they needed a confidant, were more ready to turn to a friend (22 per cent) than were the girls (12 per cent), who were more inclined to confide in their families.

A considerable number of subjects said they were prepared to take an active part in the life of the community. According to the NPORI investigation, the young more often said that they were ready to take a leading part or to make a personal contribution to associations or meetings of interest to them. [1] The distribution of answers is as follows:

---

1. The expressed intentions to play an active part in the life of the community should not, however, be taken at their face value. As we saw earlier in one particular instance (Cf. Chapter VI, page 141), the proportion of women who are members of trade unions does not exceed 50 per cent and the number of women holding office in the unions is only 12 per cent: among the very young subjects, the percentage is even smaller.

   Indeed, among the persons interrogated in the course of the NPORI investigation, the percentage holding office in social organizations was very low, especially in the youngest age-groups.

Group	Seinen-dan		Fujin-kai		Municipal bodies		Professional organizations	
	Urban	Rural	Urban	Rural	Urban	Rural	Urban	Rural
	%	%	%	%	%	%	%	%
Men	1.4	4.2	0.2	0.1	4.3	14.1	1.4	2.9
Women	0.6	6.4	3.1	3.0	1.0	1.4	0.4	0.1
16-19	0.8	3.0	0	0	0	0	0	0
20-24	2.0	8.1	0	0.4	0	1.2	0.7	0
25-29	2.0	7.6	0.7	0.9	0	6.0	0.7	0.9
30-39	0.8	2.6	1.5	3.7	2.3	8.1	0.4	1.7
40-49	0.5	8.8	2.4	0	4.8	12.5	1.0	2.7
50 and over	0	0.4	5.2	3.7	8.1	17.0	3.0	3.0
Sample as a whole	3		3		6		1	

Among the urban age-groups the proportion is 16-19 years, 47 per cent; 20-24, 53 per cent; 25-29, 40 per cent; 30 and over, 35 per cent. For the urban age-groups, 53, 46, 39, and 40 per cent.

Sofue, in his investigations, found in almost all the groups he examined some young people who had at least thought, at some time or other, of embarking on politics; in the sample as a whole, this was the case with 22 per cent of the young men and 13 per cent of the girls and young women.

PASSIVENESS, INSECURITY, ESCAPISM

However, any sketch of the personality of Japanese youth which took into account only the evidence so far presented, or even which limited itself to it and accepted it as it stands, might easily be misleading. Not only can the data themselves be interpreted in more than one way, but the actual mentality of the young is highly ambivalent. The replies to the question mentioned above, from the NPORI investigation, convey the impression of fairly intense social activity, and this also emerges from the answers to another item in the same questionnaire—'Do you feel that you want to do something for the community?' Those answering in the affirmative are distributed as follows: Among the urban age-groups, 16-19, 52 per cent; 20-24, 44 per cent; 25-29, 50 per cent; 30 and over, 48 per cent. For the equivalent rural age-groups the figures are: 50, 49, 53, and 49 per cent.

It would appear, then, that the young are not less active socially than the others.

(Continued from the note on page 213)

In any case it should be noted, in connexion with these data, that active participation in the life of the community tends to be more marked in the country than in the towns, as the table given in the text indeed indicates.

Further, the NPORI investigation shows clearly that readiness to accept office is much commoner among men than among women and increases considerably with a higher level of education.

Group	Willing to accept office	Unwilling	No reply
	%	%	%
Sample as a whole	41	56	3
Men	51	47	2
Women	32	65	3
6-8 years of education	23	73	4
9-11 years of education	40	57	3
12-13 years of education	55	43	2
More than 13 years of education	76	23	1

But the same subjects, interrogated on different lines, exhibit quite other traits. Take for instance the following questions: 'Are you satisfied so long as all the members of your family are in good health and living in harmony, or do you think that other things are also necessary for a good life?'; 'Is there any particular thing you hope to accomplish in the course of your life?' The number of young people who ask no more of the future than the health and harmony of the family tends to be even higher than in the other age-groups, but the young less frequently declare that they have an object in life (Table 67).

TABLE 67.[1]

Age-groups	Subjects asking nothing of the future but the health and harmony of the family	Subjects having an object in life
Urban	%	%
16-19	74	56
20-24	68	68
25-29	70	66
30 and over	71	76
Rural		
16-19	65	52
20-24	74	59
25-29	73	72
30 and over	67	74

Here we get the impression of a great deal of passivity and resignation, traits which are of course fairly general among the Japanese but which are found in this case in nearly three-quarters of the under-20 age-group in the towns and of the 20-30 rural age-groups. Those in the youngest age-group also reveal a considerable lack of imagination: not only do fewer of them state they would like to achieve a particular object during their lives but also, when asked to specify their aims, they are much more frequently unable to reply. This is illustrated by the following figures, which shows the distribution, by age and habitat, of those who said they had an object in life but were unable to give any details about it (percentages are calculated on the basis of the total number of individuals interrogated in the relevant age-group): Urban age-groups, 16-19, 9 per cent; 20-24, 3 per cent; 25-29, 3 per cent; 30 and over, 2 per cent. Equivalent rural age-groups, 6, 5, 1, and 3 per cent.

The greater passivity shown by young people is probably due merely to their youth: as they have not yet found their permanent place in society, they still lack that anchorage for their plans on which adults can rely: as the full table of replies shows, they are able far less often

---

1. This table gives the percentage of replies to two different questions.

than other age-groups to mention among their specific plans a house to be built, land to be exploited or children to be brought up. However, they think no more than the other age-groups of wanting to improve their education. They more often mention taking part in political life (though the proportion doing so is very small); raising themselves in the social scale; contributing to technical progress, and above all doing what they can for their families, that is, the family in which they were born, their relatives, to whom they remain profoundly attached. What they want most from the future, when they desire anything definite, are negative satisfactions: having a little more time to themselves and so on. Such replies become less frequent in proportion as the subjects grow older and, conversely, positive aims, collective or individual, tend to be mentioned more often by the older age-groups.

This evidence discloses a certain element of withdrawal into the self, of antism. Young people take a lively interest in news, though appreciably less than their elders. The Dentsu company's investigation of March 1951 showed that listening daily to radio news bulletins was habitual with 77 per cent of subjects between the ages of 18 and 25 and, with 75 per cent of the 26-35 age-groups, but was the regular custom of 82 per cent of the subjects between the ages of 36 and 45, and of 83 per cent of subjects over 45 years old. Among the women, the younger generation as a whole undeniably shows more interest in public affairs than is to be found in women who have reached middle age and who were already set in the traditional ways when the new principles came into practice, and therefore find it difficult to change their habits. The women in the youngest age-groups, however, display much more ignorance and indifference than their immediate seniors. On this point we have at our disposal data collected by the National Public Opinion Research Institute in 1948 in the course of an investigation—to which we have already referred several times—concerning women in employment. In the course of that investigation a certain number of questions were set with the object of testing the subjects' knowledge of political and administrative affairs. Table 68, which analyses a selection of the replies, shows that the standard of knowledge decreases sharply after the age of 30 and deteriorates still further between 40 and 50, but it reveals, too, that the youngest subjects are also ill-informed:

Sofue investigated in detail the political affiliations of the subjects he interrogated. The most active politically were the Yawata and Bibai trade unionists: out of 13 men, 9 belonged to a political party, 3 had no political affiliations and 1 did not reply; of 11 women, only 4 had definite political views, 5 had no party and 2 did not reply. In T. village in Hokkaido, where the younger people may be regarded as relatively active politically, 4 out of 7 men held party views, compared with 2 out of 11 women. In F. village in Kyushu, only 1 man out of 10 said he had a party preference, though it is true that in this village the women

Table 68.

	Age-groups				
	19 and under	*20-25*	*26-29*	*30-39*	*40 and over*
	%	%	%	%	%
Subjects able to name					
Prime Minister	80	82	86	82	72
President of the United States	77	82	78	67	58
Local M.P.	16	21	22	19	11
Local councillors	7	10	10	12	12
Prefect of Tokyo	24	34	35	25	19
President of the Chamber	20	27	25	19	12
President of the Cabinet Council	11	14	15	12	6

were comparatively active: out of 9 women (3 of whom had jobs in the town of Kagoshima) 4 held party views. Speaking of this village, and commenting on the fact that he found only 5 out of 19 subjects able to say which political party they supported, Sofue writes: 'It is true that five people gave replies, but they expressed themselves so incoherently that I gained the strong impression that they were giving hasty answers and saying the first thing that came into their heads. This is shown by the fact that none of them could answer the question, *Why?* I will quote in full some of the more interesting questions and answers:

'*Subject No. 7* (female). Q. What political party do you support? A. Er . . . (hesitatingly) I belong to the Democratic Party. Q. Fine: What is the Democratic Party? A. (greatly puzzled) Er . . . it's the Democratic Party.

'*Subject No. 6* (female): Q. What party do you support? A. Er . . . (hesitates) I support the Liberals. Q. What makes you support the Liberal Party? A. Well, you know . . . it's because, according to Liberalism, members of the party can do as they please, and that's good.

'Similarly', Sofue continues 'subject F (II) 1 for instance [woman, F. village employed in Kagoshima] gave fairly alert replies to questions about things like the equality of the sexes. When it came to politics, however, she at once became confused. Although she managed to mention the Democratic Party as the one she supported, she gave up the struggle in despair when asked why, and said, "I know nothing about politics". (It may be mentioned, by the way, that more than two weeks before this survey was made, the Democratic Party ceased to exist and a new party, the Progressive Party, had been organized in its place.) We have been dealing with the women but in this locality [F. village] it is practically the same with the men. For instance, one man said offhandedly "Politics don't interest me in the slightest"!'[1]

---

1. Extract from Sofue's report.

This passage from Sofue is extremely valuable because it gives us an excellent insight into one of the mechanisms of juvenile behaviour. The young feel that they ought to take part in the life of the community, that they ought to accept responsibility and show initiative. They 'ought to', not merely because they are reaching the age for doing this but also because they feel, more or less distinctly, that the new watchword of democracy is their concern, that it applies to them just as much as to the other members of the Japanese new order. At the same time, they feel that they are unfitted to undertake this task and it is quite likely, moreover, that the ambivalence of their feelings is matched by the ambiguity of their position, since those around them expect them to do those things while not yet conceding their right or their ability to do them. This state of affairs should not be regarded as confused: it is, in the strict sense of the word, ambiguous. It renders the psychological description more complex but it is never unintelligible in itself. For instance, it may help us to explain the apparent paradox in the answers to several questions asked during the NPORI investigation: young people state more frequently than the others that they want to play their part in the life of the community, but they are more liable to evade the issue when asked for details. This is what happens, for example, with regard to the question described earlier (Chapter VIII, page 214): the young are more apt to say that they want 'to do something for the community'. When asked 'what kind of thing?', they display more embarrassment than anyone else, as may be seen from the following figures, which shows the percentages giving vague answers among those who said they 'had the feeling' they wanted to do something. Urban age-groups: 16-19, 28 per cent; 20-24, 30 per cent; 25-29, 17 per cent; 30 and over, 25 per cent. Equivalent rural age-groups: 34, 29, 30, and 27 per cent.

A situation of this kind is apt to develop feelings of insecurity in in those subjected to it, and that such feelings do, in fact, exist can be discerned from some of the material at our disposal. Thus, in the reactions to Sofue's projective test, an inclination to see the tragic side of life finds ready expression. A good example of this may be found in the reactions to plate 3. This plate was designed with the object of exploring attitudes towards the relations of the grandmother with the rest of the family, especially with her daughter-in-law (who is not shown in the picture). The plate was not tried out sufficiently before the interviews took place and did not produce the expected results. On the other hand, it did provide subjects with an opportunity for giving free expression to their sense of the tragedy of life. Here are two examples, taken from Sofue's report:

'Town of Bibai, woman "Here one senses the misery of the post-war period. This grandmother's son was killed in battle and his wife has to work outside the home as a factory hand. Although the grandmother is absorbed in her work she is worrying about her grandchildren's future." '

'Town of Yawata, man. "The two children lost both their parents in an air raid and so they have been brought up by their grandmother. But she has been driven to utter despair by the hardships of life. The children have noticed her expression and are startled." '

This feeling of despair is expressed in the reactions of 26 per cent of the male and 19 per cent of the female subjects and is more frequent in industrial areas than in the country villages; in Yawata, among the men, it rises to 64 per cent.

Another symptom of insecurity is the fear of illness. Asked what were the two worst things that might conceivably happen to them, 23 per cent of the men at Kyoto and 24 per cent at Sapporo mentioned illness as one of them; this reply was slightly less frequent among the Kyoto girls (14 per cent). Fifteen per cent of the men and 12 per cent of the women at Kyoto, and 12 per cent of the Sapporo subjects, said that this misfortune was likely to happen to them. The views of these young people on their own health also deserve study (Table 69).

TABLE 69.

Estimate of own health	Kyoto		Sapporo
	Men	Women	
	%	%	%
Excellent	28	45	12
Good	56	47	76
Fairly good	13	8	6
Bad	3	0	6

It is possible that the difference in the estimates of the three groups corresponds to the actual facts. But it is also possible that it points to a greater sense of insecurity in the men, particularly the young men of Kyoto.

One is led to take this view—and consequently to suppose that these estimates of their own health are a means whereby the subjects give outward expression to their sense of insecurity—in considering the replies given by the same students to the question: 'What do you think is likely to be the cause of your death?' First and foremost we find a majority of commonplace replies, notably 'illness' and 'old age', which are of no interest for our present purpose.

But some of the subjects have seized the opportunity to give free reign to their sense of the dramatic (Table 70).

It is obviously not possible to decide how far, in these replies, the subject is being serious or frivolous with himself and others. In any case, however, the minds which produce them cannot be entirely at ease;

TABLE 70.

| Cause of death | Kyoto | | Sapporo |
	Men	Women	
	%	%	%
Illness	38	60	47
Old age	32	23	29
Accident	8	3	6
Suicide	3	2	0
Earthquake	0	1	0
War	6	2	0
Execution (shooting)	3	0	0

imagining the macabre and the tragic is a symptom of deep-seated-insecurity and the percentage of such cases is by no means negligible. As an indication of insecurity of a different kind it is also worth mentioning that one of the female subjects at Kyoto answered that she would die in childbed.

The feeling of inferiority is closely linked with insecurity. Although there were hardly any opportunities for giving expression to it, this feeling is not entirely absent from the replies collected at Kyoto and Sapporo, where subjects took advantage of the chance offered them by the question: 'What two things would you most like to have that you don't now have?' Twenty-eight per cent of the men and 18 per cent of the girls at Kyoto, and 6 per cent of the Sapporo subjects, mentioned moral and social qualities such as courage, kindliness, perseverance or sociability. In addition, and still more frequently, the girls indicated their desire for greater intellectual talents than they actually had; 42 per cent, i.e. nearly half of them, gave this reply, against only 23 per cent of the men at Kyoto and no one at Sapporo.

Feelings of insecurity are liable to call into play protective mechanisms, the function of which is to relax the tensions created in the personality. One of the commonest of these mechanisms is that of escape, and certain signs of escapism are clearly discernible in the reactions of Japanese youth in the course of the investigations. Thus, two of the questions in the Allport-Gillespie list asked the subjects to say, first, which period of 10 years out of the next 50 they expected to give them most satisfaction and, secondly, which of these 10-year periods they could picture most clearly. Now, naming as probably one's happiest period in the future a decade which one cannot picture with any clarity is in itself unrealistic behaviour, indicating a tendency towards escapism. This did in fact occur fairly frequently among the subjects interrogated (Table 71).

The taste for what is foreign, the attraction of travel, the notion that people get along better in other countries than they do in Japan, and that those who go abroad will be happier there, may also be an expression

TABLE 71.

Period	Kyoto						Sapporo		
	Men			Women					
	C	H	D	C	H	D	C	H	D
	%	%	%	%	%	%	%	%	%
1952-1961	51	26	+25	53	59	—6	53	24	+29
1962-1971	21	32	—11	24	24	0	6	18	—12
1972-1981	15	29	—14	14	12	+2	18	24	—6
1982-1991	7	6	+1	7	3	+4	6	24	—18
1992-2001	5	4	+1	0	0	0	6	0	+6

Note. *C* signifies *clear* and the figures in these columns indicate the percentages naming the decade in question as the one they could picture most clearly. *H* signifies *happy* and the figures in these columns have the corresponding meaning. *D* signifies *difference*; the figures in these columns represent the difference between the percentage of subjects naming it as the one likely to give them most satisfaction; a 'minus' figure indicates lack of realism in the group concerned.

of latent escapism. This does not mean that everyone who shows interest in some feature of a foreign culture or says that he would like to travel or that he intends to travel, is trying to run away, to escape from reality. One is, however, entitled to think that this may be so in the case of at least a proportion of those who exhibit these attitudes, and indeed, some of the reasons advanced by subjects confirm this assumption: 'All I want is to go somewhere'; '. . . to Switzerland, because it is a peaceful country'; '. . . because it is a country where life is easy'. It will also be remembered that many of the justifications of attitude are only rationalizations of inexpressible or subconscious motivations. Now, as we have already seen (Chapter V), the number of young people who are interested in foreign countries, who would like to travel and who wish they could settle abroad, is considerable;[1] and this indicates, not only a certain malaise in the Japanese nation taken as a whole, but also psychological difficulties in the personalities of the young.

It should be added that the habit of travel on what Westerners would regard as the most flimsy pretexts, is very widespread in Japan. To a foreigner, the Japanese seem to be a nation of travel maniacs. The intention

---

1. The desire to travel is less frequent among women of all age-groups than among the men. According to the NPORI investigation, the distribution according to sex and age of those with an itch for foreign travel is as follows:

Age-group	Men	Women
	%	%
Sample as a whole	80	64
16-19	90	84
20-24	86	76
25-29	85	63
30-39	83	63
40-49	75	58
50 and over	67	44

or the hope of travelling is common among the young. 'Do you expect to be able to travel (at some time during your life) as extensively as you would like to?' the students at Kyoto and Sapporo were asked. At Kyoto 65 per cent of the men and 45 per cent of the women, and at Sapporo 65 per cent of the subjects replied in the affirmative. The women feel less free to move about than the men, but even in their case the percentage desiring to travel is very large. It is possible that this reveals an important psycho-therapeutic element in Japanese culture.

Even more noticeably, leisure activities, recreation and games serve a purpose analogous to that of travel. The constraints felt in the serious affairs of life find their compensation in the freedom easily achieved and enjoyed in leisure time. Setbacks and disappointments in work, family life, and the life of the community in general, are offset by success in games. The feelings of inferiority experienced in the face of reality disappear in situations where activities are recreational, because recreation is organized for that purpose and also because talents which have no outlet in real life and are not appreciated there in a way that satisfies the ego, are given full scope in playtime and count for something then; moreover, the loser in a game can always tell himself that his failure is unimportant, and when he wins, his success does not seem illusory. All societies have institutionalized leisure activities, in order to allow these psycho-therapeutic functions to come into play. Sociological analysis would probably show that this institutionalization is carried even further when frustratiors in a given community are more serious and more obvious. For the young, who are practically excluded from the serious activities of life although they feel sufficiently grown up to take part in them, and who consequently experience feelings of impatience and disappointment, leisure activities assume considerable importance. In some societies, political activity may serve the same psychological purpose for the individual, but this, as we have seen, is hardly the case in Japan today, and leisure activities are therefore the chosen refuge, the favourite means of escape, of the young.

This fact is amply demonstrated by the documents at our disposal. Sofue has established that some young people go to the cinema as often as eight times a month and that the average attendance is two or three times a month; this is a high rate of frequency if we bear in mind that country folk must travel into the towns in order to see a cinema performance. At Kyoto, the girls placed leisure activities second only to family relationships in the list of things likely to afford them most satisfaction, while the young men placed them third, after their family and their job. Nine per cent of the girls and 7 per cent of the men placed leisure activities first and 30 per cent and 21 per cent respectively put them second. They come well before participation in local, national or international affairs, and, of course, before religion, which in other societies might play the same role (see fig. 12, Chapter VII, page 168).

But it is above all the NPORI investigation which reveals the full importance of leisure activities to the young. Whenever there was an opportunity to mention these activities, it was seized far more often by the young than by their elders, and sometimes the disparity is great. Thus, among the things considered necessary for happiness in addition to health, leisure activities were mentioned by the under-20s four times more often in the towns and six times more often in the country than by the over-30s in either habitat. Among the things which the subjects interrogated intended to achieve before their death those connected with some form of recreation were the second choice of the young people in the towns, coming immediately after family relationships. The associations and meetings in which urban youth is most ready to take part are usually recreational in character; in the country, this category meets with competition from cultural societies and youth clubs which, although classified separately in the code, are essentially the same. When asked to mention occasions on which they had felt happy, young people mainly chose incidents connected with their studies, and circumstances to do with their leisure activities came a close second.

Table 72 gives the figures on which these statements are based; percentages are calculated by age-group and habitat for the total number of individuals interrogated. It will be observed that, with few exceptions, there is a gradual fall in the percentages between one age-group and the next. Moreover, recreation seems to correspond to psychological needs that are even stronger in the towns than in the country.

TABLE 72.

Age-group	Leisure necessary for happiness	Leisure an aim in life	Participation in societies and meetings connected with leisure activities	Happiness found on leisure occasions
	%	%	%	%
Sample as a whole	0.7	2	7	3
Urban				
16-19	1.5	6	17	14
20-24	0.7	6	18	7
25-29	0.6	4	6	2
30 and over	0.5	1	7	1
Rural				
16-19	2.5	3	11	8
20-24	0.4	5	8	3
25-29	0.9	1	6	6
30 and over	0.4	2	3	2

Thus an analysis of the personality of Japanese youth, undertaken with means that are still rudimentary, and instruments that can only be regarded as clumsy, enables us to glimpse serious psychological difficulties.

If we study the portrait more deeply and fill in the relief, we find that it changes completely. The optimism and self-confidence of Japanese youth are well-established facts, checked and counterchecked by a whole series of investigations and there is therefore no question of effacing these traits. But they must not be studied by themselves, independently of the whole, since it is there that they take on their real significance. Put back in its place in the complex structure of the personality, optimism is seen to tend towards wishful thinking, to the illusion that what one desires must necessarily be true—characteristic of the personality which has not yet reached maturity. Self-confidence, when placed alongside the other details we have observed, means primarily drawing bills on the future, thinking of the powers one will acquire when grown up, and of the status, quite different from what it is now, to which one will attain. The self-confidence shown by young Japanese is faith in their star, not belief in their present judgment, will power, and efficiency. Sofue asked the following question: 'Do you think you should cling to your opinion in all circumstances if you are convinced that you are right, or is it preferable not to do so in some circumstances?' Seventy-five per cent of the men and 61 per cent of the women answered that it was better to be guided by circumstances.

PERSONAL DEPENDENCE

In reality, one of the traits of personality emerging most clearly from the various investigations is the very marked dependence of Japanese youth. They need to lean on others, they need the other person.

In answer to the question: 'What two things would you most like that you don't now have?' students at Kyoto and Sapporo frequently mentioned persons: 25 per cent of the subjects at Kyoto and 41 per cent at Sapporo gave answers of this kind. Moreover, the replies varied considerably according to the sex of the subject, the girls being even more dependent than the men, especially with regard to their family. At Kyoto, the proportion of male students who gave expression to their need of other persons was 17 per cent; in the case of the girls it was 30 per cent. Need for a friend of their own sex was expressed slightly more often by the girls than by the men (9 per cent against 7 per cent), while need for a friend of the opposite sex was mentioned more frequently by men than by girls—the exact percentages are 9 per cent of the men to 3 per cent of the girls at Kyoto, and 33 per cent to nil at Sapporo. It is above all in relation to the family, however, that the replies differ. At Kyoto 18 per cent of the girls mentioned a brother, sister, father or mother as something they wanted but had not got, whereas among the men only 1 per cent gave answers of this kind.

The range of replies, which are spontaneous and quite unprompted, is wide. When young people are asked whether they would like more friends or a more intimate friend, the frequency of replies naturally increases very considerably. Table 73 shows what happens in that case.

TABLE 73.

| | Kyoto | | Sapporo |
	Men	Women	
	%	%	%
Want more friends	61	55	76
Want a more intimate friend	72	69	65

We lack the data for determining why the young men at Sapporo are more concerned with the quantity than with the intimacy of their friendships. It is clear, at any rate, that at Kyoto fewer girls than men feel the importance of friendship; the reason is that the girls have much stronger family attachments. When asked to name the worst things that could conceivably happen to them, the girls think at once of the possible death of their father or mother (34 per cent; this reply is second in order of frequency, the most frequent answer—given by 39 per cent—was war); they think also of disunity in their family (8 per cent, against 4 per cent of the men). Again, one of the things the girls would do if they received an unexpected sum of money, would be to hand it over to their families (4 per cent; boys, 1 per cent). Above all, girls much more frequently confide in their families. The relevant question was worded as follows: 'If you had a personal problem that worried you (for example, a difficult decision to make), whom would you *prefer* to talk it over with?' A list of choices followed. The replies at Kyoto and Sapporo respectively were as in Table 74.

TABLE 74.

| | Kyoto | | Sapporo |
	Men	Women	
	%	%	%
Immediate family	40	70	65
Other relatives	2	1	0
An expert (doctor, psychologist, etc.)	18	6	18
Others	32	18	6
No one	2	2	12
No reply	6	4	0

The 'others' named were mainly 'an intimate friend' (22 per cent of the men and 13 per cent of the women at Kyoto, and 6 per cent at Sapporo) and 'a teacher' (men 6 per cent, girls 4 per cent at Kyoto). It is obvious, in any case, that the girls are even more dependent on their families than the men are.

This matter of seeking advice (*sodan*) is extremely important in Japan and deserves more detailed study, so as to enable us to reach a fuller understanding of the extent and nature of the personal dependence of the young.

It so happens that this problem was one of those most studied, quantitatively at any rate, during the investigations organized for the purpose of obtaining material for this report. In addition to the question just mentioned, which was set at Kyoto and Sapporo, the problem of consultation was the subject of three questions in Vos's questionnaire, two in Sofue's survey and two in the NPORI investigation. The situation is, however, complicated by two circumstances: the questions were set to different subjects, and they were not worded in identical terms. In order to establish the facts, therefore, it is preferable to proceed analytically and to begin by giving a rough description of the results obtained.

The Kyoto-Sapporo investigation shows that 2 per cent of the men and 2 per cent of the girls at Kyoto, and 12 per cent of the Sapporo subjects do not seek advice when in difficulties. These figures, however, must at once be rejected because the question, as set, assumed that subjects did in fact seek advice, and on that basis sought to elicit their preferences; hence those who said they did not ask advice were evading the question. It follows that we are entitled to assume: (a) That some subjects not in the habit of seeking advice took the question in the spirit in which it was asked and indicated a hypothetical preference in the event—however improbable—of their being led to do so. This possibility would lead to an underestimate of the number of independent subjects. (b) That some subjects, who for some reason or other found the question embarrassing, hit on a way of evading it by replying that they were not in the habit of seeking advice. This at least theoretical possibility would lead to an overestimate of the number of independent subjects. In any case, the results of these two influences are unknown and it is therefore better not to take the answers to these two questions into account; this we can do all the more easily in that we have fairly abundant material from other sources.

The three questions put by Vos and the replies are as follows:

'When you have personal difficulties do you like to discuss them with your father or mother, or with older people, or with a boy or girl friend? Or do you not discuss them at all?'

With parents or older people, 36 per cent;
With parents and friends, 31 per cent;
With friends, 19 per cent;
Do not discuss them, 13 per cent;
No reply, 1 per cent.

'Do you normally take important decisions yourself or do you act on the advice of your father, your mother or your family (e.g. in the choice of a job, political party, etc.)?'

Act on advice of others, 54 per cent;

Sometimes take advice, sometimes not, 15 per cent;

Do not take advice, 29 per cent;

No reply, 2 per cent.

'Do you think that young people ought to take such important decisions by themselves?'

Yes, 21 per cent;

No, 52 per cent;

Up to a point, 22 per cent;

No opinion, 5 per cent.

In Sofue's questionnaire, the first relevant question is the following: 'In your experience, is it better always to stick to your own judgment, or do you think that you would do better always to follow the advice of others, or is it preferable to follow the advice of others sometimes?'

Better always to stick to one's own judgment: men 18 per cent, women 13 per cent;

Better always to follow advice: men 0 per cent, women 0 per cent;

Preferable to follow advice sometimes: men 82 per cent, women 87 per cent;

It is an interesting fact that none of the Yawata subjects gave the first answer (always to stick to one's judgment).

The second question from Sofue's list, separated from the first by a large number of quite different questions, was worded as follows: 'When something worries you, do you settle it yourself, or do you consult other people?'

Settle problem unaided: men 45 per cent; women 19 per cent. The proportion of men who settle their problems unaided is highest at Yawata, where it reaches 54 per cent, in contrast to F. village where it is only 14 per cent.

Lastly we have the two questions set by the National Public Opinion Research Institute: 'When you have personal difficulties do you generally consult your parents, family or friends? When the opinions of the people consulted differ from your own, do you merely take note of them for information or do you usually follow them? If you find this last question difficult to answer, would you say in general that you cling to your own opinion or that you bow to the opinion of others?' The replies can be classified as shown in Table 75.

Several conclusions may readily be drawn from these data: first, that the habit of seeking advice is extremely widespread in Japan, in all

TABLE 75.

Age-groups	No advice sought	Advice sought				
		For information only	And followed	'It all depends'		
				Stick to own views	Inclined to follow advice	Don't know
	%	%	%	%	%	%
Sample as a whole	9	45	25	7	7	7
Urban						
16-19	6	53	19	7	10	5
20-24	9	54	24	4	1	8
25-29	12	54	18	4	6	6
30 and over	13	45	21	6	8	7
Rural						
16-19	5	54	25	5	6	5
20-24	5	49	26	6	7	7
25-29	8	40	28	6	9	9
30 and over	7	40	29	8	8	8

sociological groups and at all ages; secondly, that the young take advice more frequently than the others; and thirdly, that the same is also true of villagers as compared with townsfolk. Is it possible, however, by comparing and discussing these various data, to arrive at something more specific?

The first impression which emerges is one of confusion. Four types of behaviour can be distinguished: (a) seeking no advice; (b) seeking advice without intending to follow it and, in fact, not following it; (c) seeking advice and taking it sometimes but not always; (d) seeking advice and invariably acting on it.

It should also be noted that the various questions approach the problem from two different angles: what the subjects think people ought to do; what the subjects say they do themselves.

Take, for instance, the first type of behaviour, which consists in never seeking advice and consequently represents the most independent conduct: as regards the effective (declared) conduct of the subjects, the NPORI investigation establishes that this type of behaviour is found among the young in proportions varying between 5 per cent and 9 per cent. Among Vos's subjects the corresponding figure is 13 per cent; among Sofue's it is 31 per cent on the average. Moreover, Vos's second question indicates that the first and second types of behaviour combined occur in 29 per cent of cases. As regards the standards accepted as proper by the subjects concerned, the first type of behaviour is favoured by 21 per cent of Vos's subjects and the first and second types combined by 18 per cent of Sofue's. Thus in Vos's group more subjects accept the standard than put it into practice, while in Sofue's group the balance is markedly on the other side. Furthermore, in Sofue's group, it is the least independent subjects who most frequently declare themselves in favour of personal independence whereas none of the Yawata subjects, who give every indication of being exceptionally aggressive and independent, felt able to assert as a general proposition that it is better never to follow any advice.

The apparent disaccord between the results obtained by Vos and those of Sofue seems, therefore, easy to resolve. The emphasis of their two questions is entirely different; it is easy and attractive to maintain that young people should be able to take decisions, even serious ones, by themselves: 21 per cent of Vos's subjects said this, whereas only 13 per cent had the courage to act accordingly. On the other hand, to say that one must persist in one's own opinion in all circumstances is as absurd as to say (which none of the subjects did) that one must always follow the advice of others: the 18 per cent of Sofue's subjects who adopted the first view showed thereby, not a tendency to independence, but their own childishness, and they were in fact drawn from the least autonomous subjects.

Compared with the results obtained by NPORI and Vos, the proportion (31 per cent) of independent subjects in Sofue's group seems high, but the heterogeneous group he investigated was in no sense representative and did not pretend to be. It included a considerable proportion of subjects, the young trade unionists, who were exceptionally biassed in the direction of independence and these unduly inflated the percentage; the proportion of independent subjects for F. village was only 7 per cent, i.e. about the same figure as that given by NPORI for the country areas. Similarly, Vos's 13 per cent is not altogether inconsistent with the NPORI results, if we take into account that the subjects interrogated by him came from Tokyo and included many students, who are particularly independent.

One result of the NPORI investigation which seems astonishing when compared with the others is the very high proportion of subjects (45 per cent on the average) who said they sought advice for information only, that is, without intending to follow it or in fact doing so—the behaviour classified above as Type 2. The other investigations provide no cross check for this item but it will be recalled that Vos's second question gives 29 per cent as the combined figure for the first and second types of behaviour. In addition my colleague and I, in the course of our conversations with young people, frequently had the personal experience of meeting subjects who said that they asked advice, but solely for the sake of information. These subjects generally proved not only to have little independence of character but at the same time to be unconscious of this fact. They were victims of illusions about themselves, trying to convince themselves that they were unaffected by the opinions of other people. One is thus led to regard this kind of reply as possibly pointing to a lack of independence combined with a certain want of perception. It will be noted from the NPORI investigation that the younger the subjects, the more often they give this type of reply.

Finally it appears possible to relate the four categories of behaviour defined above to three overlapping types of personality.

Type I consists of entirely or largely autonomous subjects and would include those giving answers 1 and 4 from the NPORI table, and also the 13 per cent of Vos's subjects who 'do not discuss their problems at all' and Sofue's 31 per cent who 'settle their problems by themselves'.

Type II consists of non-autonomous subjects who are aware of their own characters in this respect. The answer corresponding to this type is number 3 in the NPORI table; the fifth answer in this table has the same significance, as has also the sixth, though to a lesser extent.

Type III consists of subjects who cannot be called autonomous and who may well not be, but are completely unaware of this. Many of the subjects who gave answer number 2 in the NPORI table are of this type. The investigations of Vos and Sofue do not enable us to distinguish between these last two types. We suggest that type III should be designated 'unconscious dependents'.

If this analysis is correct, the table of the representative results of the NPORI investigation can be rearranged as in Table 76.

TABLE 76.

Age-group	Type I	Type II	Type III
	%	%	%
Sample as a whole	16	39	45
Urban			
16-19	13	34	53
20-24	13	33	54
25-29	16	30	54
30 and over	19	36	45
Rural			
16-19	10	36	54
20-24	11	40	49
25-29	14	46	40
30 and over	15	45	40

The habit of seeking advice is very widespread in Japan and personal independence is rare. The two traits, the cultural trait of *sodan* and the psychological trait of personal dependence, are closely interwoven, as often happens, without our being able to say which is cause and which effect. Because it is understood that people do not take serious decisions by themselves and because the normal rule is to seek someone else's advice, the behaviour of the individual tends to be modelled on the views of those around him; conversely, insecurity, self-distrust, and the need for others lead to the development and perpetuation of an institution which enables everyone to open his heart to others concerning his most intimate problems, and expect them to provide a solution. A culture is reflected in the conduct of individuals, but it is through the conduct of individuals that a culture comes into being and survives. An example such as this helps us to realize how purely theoretical is the distinction between sociology and psychology.

As Table 76 clearly shows, the young are even more dependent than their elders. That is a consequence both of their psychological immaturity and of the more limited freedom which their status confers. That the individual's status has a direct, and as it were relative, effect is borne out by the fact that Japanese women appear to be even less independent than the men: this is revealed by a closer analysis of the data collected by NPORI (Table 77).

TABLE 77.

Age-groups	Type I		Type II		Type III	
	Men	*Women*	*Men*	*Women*	*Men*	*Women*
	%	%	%	%	%	%
Sample as a whole	19	11	28	52	53	37
Urban	21	13	23	45	56	41
Rural	27	10	32	55	51	35
16-19	17	5	28	45	57	49
20-24	15	9	25	49	60	42
25-29	17	12	27	52	56	36
30-39	17	11	26	52	57	37
40-49	22	11	29	52	49	37
50 and over	24	17	34	61	42	22

It will be observed that the differences between the sexes are fairly constant between one category and another, as though the various differential factors—age, sex, habitat—were each exercising their influence independently of the others. The only appreciable exceptions to this rule are in the under-20 and the 40-50 age-groups. Differences between the sexes are less where there is heteronomy and greater where there is autonomy; in the case of the under-twenty group the irregularity seems to be due to the young men, who give themselves out to be more independent than would appear to be the case from the way the percentages run; in the 40-50 age-group it is the women who seem to be less than normally autonomous.

There is likewise no doubt that the achievement of a high standard of education does much to encourage independence as a personality trait (type I), or at least makes this trait sought after (type III) (Table 78).

TABLE 78.

Number of years of study	Type I	Type II	Type III
	%	%	%
6-8	14	56	30
9-11	14	40	46
12-13	16	29	55
over 13	21	19	60

The influence of education on personal independence is complicated, but in any case it undoubtedly helps the development of a cultural process whose effects may be discerned alongside the factors already mentioned. The new watchwords of liberty and democracy tend to make personal dependence seem an undesirable trait. This is clearly to be seen in the opinion expressed by 21 per cent of the group studied by Vos that young people should take their important decisions unaided. It is also on this account that personal autonomy seems more widespread in the towns than in the countryside not only do urban living conditions and a higher level of education make independence easier psychologically, but also, as a new cultural trait,was accepted first in the towns. However, personal independence does not come as a gift; it has to be won; 13 per cent of the young people studied by Vos either have, or claim to have, achieved it, whereas 21 per cent, almost twice as many, regard it as desirable. The inference is that the search for independence frequently ends in frustration. Unawareness is precisely one of the protective mechanisms which spare the personality from suffering through its failures. Hence in Japan today we frequently find a lack of personal independence combined with unawareness that anything is wrong. This composition of the personality is relatively less frequent in the countryside (despite the fact that personal autonomy is also less widespread there), because in the country personal dependence is still easily accepted, especially by adults. It is commoner in the urban areas (although autonomous personalities are more numerous there), because in the towns personal dependence is more widely felt to be undesirable. Unconscious heteronomy is particularly widespread up to the age of 30 where it is the personality trait most frequently met with in the domain we are now considering.

Culturally then, the Japanese are evolving towards personal independence. People are more autonomous in the towns than in the rural areas, but the young are not more so than their elders because they find within themselves, and in the small familiar group around them, obstacles which it is difficult for them to overcome. This state of affairs produces unawareness, which is a condition detrimental to the normal functioning of the personality. Thus, the perpetuation of old-established traits, more easily accepted in the country, may well produce a degree of repression and give rise to neuroses, particularly among the urban population. The young seem to be exposed to this danger more than the rest.

IMMATURITY OF THE YOUNG

The most obvious conclusion to be drawn from this attempted analysis of the personality of young Japanese, is their immaturity. The fundamental meaning of many traits thrown into relief by the data collected during the course of our investigations, nothwithstanding the crudity of the instruments used, is that the subjects examined are not adult, either psychologically or socially. This would seem to be the real source of their passivity and introspection, their sense of insecurity, their tendency towards escapism and a lack of realism and their dependence. It is probable that research concentrating on other traits would lead to similar conclusions. Thus an investigation into prostitution carried out in 1949 by the National Public Opinion Research Institute, revealed that the young were in favour of more brutal and radical measures against it: they advocated far more often than the others that prostitutes should be imprisoned, and far less often that they should be fined (Table 79).

TABLE 79.

Age-groups	Prison	Fine
	%	%
20-29	30	25
30-39	28	35
40-49	26	26
50-59	25	32
60 and over	16	31

Another trait typical of an immature personality is inconsistency, lack of synthesis in the various aspects of an individual's behaviour. Sofue examined from this point of view all the different kinds of behaviour elicited by the 10 plates in his projective test. It will have been observed that the reactions to Plates 4-10 are classified according to three types which are the same for each plate, have the same general attitude and exhibit the same philosophy of life. Of the 63 subjects tested, only eight had coherent reactions and were classified throughout as belonging to the same type. Six of them, all males, were from Yawata and two, a youth and a girl, from Bibai; all eight were Type I.

Sometimes, as we have already seen, the young seem to be aware of their own immaturity. For this reason they tend to put off the moment when they will assume responsibilities. Whereas the normal age for marriage appears to be about twenty-six in the case of young men, quite a number of them hope they will not marry before they are thirty. We suspect that the reason why young men think marriage an individual and not a family concern, is generally not so much that they want to choose their partners themselves—the romantic tradition does not seem so very powerful in Japan—as that they want to decide themselves—that is, to postpone—the date when they will marry. That is the impression we received from several of our interviews with them. It is also significant that, at Kyoto at any rate (see above, page 220), the young men take the view that the decade which will afford them most satisfaction is not the one on which they are now entering but the one following. Several 'autobiographies of the future' written by the men students at Sapporo give the same impression, as though the authors sensed more or less clearly that they would not achieve their full personal development for another 10 years. This, at least, seems to be the case as regards the young men; for the girls, personal maturity implies something different and they have less immediate hope of attaining it.

The precise direction in which the young will develop—we must repeat—is far from certain. They have of course been more affected than the older generation by the spirit of the age. They have heard at least as much as their elders about the new watchwords of individualism and liberty and have given them a more favourable reception. If they have not fully grasped the scope and implications of the new ideas, and especially the responsibilities that freedom to behave as one likes brings in its train, it is not altogether their fault: instead of having this explained to them, they have been more often told that freedom must be exercised within specified limits or even that its objectives have already been fixed. Above all, as Sofue has rightly pointed out, for the young, many of the new ideals are still, as it were, floating in the air, carried by strange winds which already blow less strongly than they did, and liable to be scattered by other winds blowing from a different quarter.

It must be borne in mind that, in a given society, the only way the individual can develop unchecked is by conforming to the accepted standards—the institutionalized values. What the young Japanese of today will be tomorrow probably depends less on their present attitudes and personality traits than on the path to which the Japanese society commits itself; and they themselves are still too immature and show too much dependence for us to be able to think that they will have much say in the fresh impulse—in whatever direction it may be—that will be given to that society with the end of the Occupation.

We must also reflect, however, that those who regard themselves as the leaders of a given society cannot do just what they like with it. Economic conditions, and the way these are felt and interpreted by the people, history and tradition, and the ideals and values which social and political events have brought with them and whose traces remain in men's minds, are the factors—varying in importance and difficult to assess, though none of them is insignificant—which determine the cultural and political outlook of a society. In the case of contemporary Japan, it should be added that too frequent and too radical changes may well produce chaotic results and render the future unmanageable. In several of the places we visited, our attention was drawn to a certain element of confusion already existing in Japan today. Several schoolmasters, speaking quite independently of each other, since some were at Kagoshima and the others at Nemuro, pointed out to us that after preaching the military virtues and obedience to the Imperial house and then being obliged to become converts to democracy and pacifism, they must now speak in favour of rearmament. In their view their whole credit with the young is being destroyed and they have twice lost face. At Sapporo, the keen and intelligent head of a youth group confided in us about his fears and disappointments: the young, he said, were being faced with completely incompatible values and institutions, family life had not changed, and the schools taught nothing but the virtues of democracy. The question they all ask is how, in the midst of such confusion, the personalities of the young can possibly develop harmoniously?

These general remarks do not mean, however, that Japanese youth should be imagined as a homogeneous unit. We trust the reader will have perceived, whenever he was given the opportunity, the very considerable differences between the various categories of young people. The limited possibilities of the investigations which supplied the material for this report unfortunately did not enable us to pursue the analysis of these differences as far as we should have liked. It is essential to reflect that young Japanese do not all behave in the same way, and that they not all have the same mental picture of themselves. The replies to a double question in Sofue's questionnaire show this clearly.

The question was as follows: '(a) What famous Japanese and (b) what famous foreigners do you respect?' Although 35 out of the 59 subjects interrogated were unable to answer the first part of the question and 29 the second part, the replies received covered a wide range, including the names of 10 Japanese and 12 foreigners. They are as follows: Japanese —the Emperor, Hideki Yukawa, Sontoku Ninomiya, Takamori Saigô, Yukichi Fukuzawa, Mr. Yoshida (the Prime Minister), Hideyo Noguchi, Gakudô Ozaki, Ikutarô Shimizu, and Hyoe Ouchi;[1] foreigners—

---

1. Hideki Yukawa (born 1907): famous atomic physicist, Professor in the University of Kyoto, Nobel prize winner in 1949. Sontaku Ninomiya (1787-1856): a poor peasant who made a fortune through his tremendous industry: in Japan his name has come to stand for 'hard worker'. Takamori Saigo (1827-77): a samurai from Kyushu who organized an unsuccessful revolt against the Meiji Restoration in 1877. Yukichi Fukuzawa (1834-1901): a pioneer of the new ideas of the Meiji epoch; founded the Keio University in Tokyo and preached a doctrine of personal independence and self-respect based on English utilitarianism. Hideyo Noguchi (1876-1926): born in poverty, became a world-

MacArthur, Lincoln, Florence Nightingale, Gandhi, Eisenhower, Ridgway, Jesus Christ, Churchill, Stalin, Nehru, Helen Keller and Zola. We might attempt to sort these choices into categories: some of them have political implications of a conservative order, or at least relate to persons now in power—the Emperor, Saigo, Yoshida, MacArthur, Eisenhower and Ridgway; those in the second category also have political implications, but of the opposite camp, and evoke ideas of liberty, pacifism, social criticism and socialism—Fukuzawa, Ozaki, Shimizu, Lincoln, Gandhi, Jesus Christ, Stalin, Nehru and Zola; there are also two scientists— Yukawa and Noguchi, while Helen Keller and Florence Nightingale are readily classifiable as the standard-bearers of feminism (the Japanese edition of *Reader's Digest* published an article on both at about the time when the investigation was taking place); finally, it is difficult to know exactly what the three remaining names—Churchill, Ninomiya and Ouchi—mean to Japanese youth and it is better to leave them unclassified.

The distribution of choices over the group as a whole, according to the sex of the subject interrogated, and in the three principal centres of investigation, is as in Table 80.

TABLE 80.

	Sample as a whole	Men	Women	Yawata	F. village	T. village
Political (Conservative)	20	12	8	7	8	4
Political (Progressive)	19	15	4	11	1	5
Scientists	5	2	3	2	2	0
Feminists	4	0	4	3	1	0
Others	6	5	1	2	1	2
No reply						
Famous Japanese	35	11	24	11	7	12
Famous foreigners	29	11	18	2	9	11
Number of subjects	59	28	31	19	15	18

Experience suggests that the replies to questions such as these not only enable us to diagnose the interests of the persons interrogated but also reveal their personal identifications. It will be noted that in the sample as a whole political choices are the most frequent; women are markedly

(Continued from page 235)

famous bacteriologist after studying at American universities. Gakudo Ozaki (born 1854): elected to the first Diet and repeatedly re-elected since, has devoted himself for half a century to the administration of Japan; during the war he took a stand against militarism and supported the idea of world federation. Iukatro Shimizu (born 1907): one of the most famous social critics, is campaigning against rearmament as head of the 'Conference for Peace Affairs', which he founded. Hyoe Ouchi (born 1888): economist, former President of the University of Legal and Political Science, Tokyo; translator, among other works, of Adam Smith's *Wealth of Nations*.

less politically minded and more frequently refrain from answering. The young people of Yawata frequently abstain from naming famous Japanese, as though they wanted to dissociate themselves from their compatriots; on the other hand it is from this group that we get the largest selection of foreign names. When the women choose famous political personages, these are generally of a conservative persuasion; the opposite tendency is shown by the men but there is little difference in the numbers of conservatives and progressives named. The young people of F. village are decidedly conservative while those of Yawata are strongly of the contrary opinion; this is specially true of the men, who mentioned 11 progressives and only 2 conservatives; the young people of T. village are more progressive than those of F. village—three 'progressives' were named by the women.

This example shows the considerable differences that may exist among young people as regards their choice of heroes and their personal identifications. The most striking evidence of these differences, perhaps, is provided by the answers to a question which was put to several groups of young people: 'When you have children of your own, what lesson will you try hardest to teach them?' The question, which was put at Kyoto and Sapporo in writing and probably in a slightly ambiguous translation, was not, as a rule, properly understood. The verbal replies collected by Sofue, however, are significant; the girls in the country areas insist most of all on politeness, that is to say, on the importance of conforming to social tradition; the boys in the same category put most emphasis on health, showing that they took little interest in social matters and giving proof of their passivity and introspection. In Yawata and Bibai both sexes replied that they would develop their children's personalities and inculcate in them a spirit of independence.

APPENDIX I

INVESTIGATION BY REPRESENTATIVE SAMPLING, CARRIED OUT BY THE NATIONAL PUBLIC OPINION RESEARCH INSTITUTE

March-April 1952

GENERAL PLAN OF THE INVESTIGATION

Questionnaire drawn up by J. Stoetzel and discussed with T. Asano, F. Vos acting as interpreter. Tried out at Tokyo and in the Nagano Prefecture. Several weeks' work was needed to arrive at the final version of the questionnaire, in the course of which several successive preliminary versions were produced.

Interviews covered 2,671 persons, selected throughout the country on a percentage basis. They took place in March-April 1952.

The code was prepared and the results were classified accordingly in Tokyo after the departure of Stoetzel, who had been able to give only general instructions. It was then sent to Europe where it was translated into English by F. Vos. As will be seen, each heading in the code is normally followed by samples of replies quoted more or less verbatim.

STATISTICAL AND SOCIOLOGICAL PARTICULARS OF THE SAMPLE

1. Number of cases: 2,671

		%
2. Distribution by sex:	Men	51
	Women	49
3. Distribution by age-group:		
	16-19	12
	20-24	15
	25-29	14
	30-39	23
	40-49	21
	50 and over	14
4. Marital status:	Unmarried	27
	Married (with spouse)	66
	Widowed or divorced	7
5. Number in family:	One	3
	Two	5
	Three-six	55
	Seven and over	37

6. Number of children (married subjects):   %

                None. 10
                One 20
                Two-three 36
                Four-five 25
                Six and over 10

7. Married subjects having children in the following age-groups living at home:

                No children 10
                Up to 5 years 49
                6-11 years 45
                12-19 years 42
                20 and over. 29

8. Administrative experience:

                Seinen-dan 3
                Fujin-kai 3
                Municipal councils 6
                Trade or professional associations . . . 1
                Others 1
                None. 88

9. Travel abroad: (a) Country: Korea, Formosa, Sakhalin, the Kuriles and other formerly Japanese territories 5
                Manchuria 5
                China. 7
                Other countries of Asia. 3
                Europe and America 1
                Never travelled abroad 81
        (b) Reasons for travel: Military service . . 12
                Prolonged stay 6
                Short visit 0.4
                Not clear 0.3
                Never travelled abroad 81

10. Birth-place: In the prefecture where now domiciled . . 84
                In another prefecture 15
                Abroad 1

11. Newspaper reading habits:

                Regular readers 71
                Occasional readers 20
                Non-readers 9

12. Listeners to radio: Yes 77
                No 23

13. Social and economic status:

                High. 6
                Average 48
                Below average 34
                Low 12

14. Standards of education for the sample as a whole, and by age and habitat combined:[1]

	(E)	(1)	(2)	(3)	(4)	(5)	(6)	(7)	(8)
6 years minimum	23	9	3	10	29	2	7	13	36
7-9 years	49	46	45	47	45	61	61	59	45
10-12 years	23	41	41	29	19	36	29	24	15
13 years or more	5	4	11	14	7	1	3	4	4

15. Occupations of subjects interrogated, for the sample as a whole, and by age and habitat combined:

	(E)	(1)	(2)	(3)	(4)	(5)	(6)	(7)	(8)
Agriculture, forestry, fisheries	14	—	1	4	4	5	7	13	30
Private industry and commerce	9	1	2	13	19	3	2	5	9
Exercising official functions	1	—	—	—	2	1	—	—	1
Liberal professions	1	—	1	1	2	—	1	1	2
Workmen	16	34	29	26	17	15	19	12	8
Office workers	11	11	23	18	12	6	16	12	8
No occupation	23	16	30	33	38	17	16	16	16
Students	3	26	5	—	1	21	—	—	—
Domestic servants	20	12	9	5	5	31	37	38	23
Others	2	—	—	—	—	1	2	3	3

RESULTS OF THE INVESTIGATION[2]

QUESTION 1. *Do you think that living conditions in the world will become progressively better?*

	(E)	(1)	(2)	(3)	(4)	(5)	(6)	(7)	(8)
1. Better	39	56	48	46	36	49	46	46	32
2. Worse	23	14	17	13	25	16	15	24	28
3. No change	23	14	18	21	22	21	25	17	26
4. Don't know	15	16	18	20	17	15	15	13	14

QUESTION 2. *What are you most worried and unhappy about at the present time? (We don't mind whether it is something personal or otherwise.)*

	(E)
1. Housing (no house: worrried about accommodation)	3

---

1. All answers to questions will be shown as percentages both of the sample as a whole and of the various age-habitat groups. The number of cases in the different categories are as follows:
   (E) Sample as a whole: 2,671
   (1) Urban 16-19 age-group: 133
   (2) Urban 20-24 age-group: 145
   (3) Urban 25-29 age-group: 158
   (4) Urban 30 and over: 607
   (5) Rural 16-19 age-group: 200
   (6) Rural 20-24 age-group: 255
   (7) Rural 25-29 age-group: 224
   (8) Rural 30 and over: 954
2. In the following tables, the figures express percentages. The sign * indicates results below 0.5 per cent.

2 Economic worries (stabilization of living: the trials and tribulations of (E)
life: 'taxes are heavy') 21
3. Education (education of children; 'what are social and formal education going to be like from now on?'; 'it would be better if they did not
change the school textbooks every year') 5
4. Health ('I can't keep going unless I am in good health'; 'my husband's
illness'; ('where my own family is concerned, I have made health my
watchword') 5
5. Occupation (worries about poor salary; the problem of getting a job: in
the case of a person employing others, worry about his own inadequate
knowledge) 7
6. Marriage (misgivings about the marriage of a son; 'own marriage') . . 2
7. Rearmament ('we shall be invaded, if rearmament is not carried
through quickly'). 6
8. War (third world war) 11
9. Thought and ideas (the spread of communist-tainted ideas; freedom
of thought; the growth of communism) 3
10. Slackening of moral fibre (the *'apuregeru'* [après la guerre] attitude of
youths and girls; the desire of the young to be real democrats but without
having to accept personal responsibilities; horse-racing and car-racing) 2
11. The social order (the maintenance of public order in the country from
now on; worries about disturbances of the world's peace by communism;
worries about the atmosphere created by the chaotic state of society) 1
12. Problem of unemployment (worry about the growing numbers of
unemployed) 1
13. The national economy (inflation; hope that there will not be too many
economic fluctuations; 'everyone will have to live in straightened
circumstances because Japan has become smaller') 1
14. Internal administration (growth of parochialism; State officials live
like old-time village headmen *oshoya*; the reconstruction of Japan after
the conclusion of peace; the problem of social security) 1
15. The international situation (the state of affairs between the United
States of America and the U.S.S.R.; anxiety about whether—as things
now are—the world will become peaceful or not; the world situation) . 3
16. Miscellaneous (worries about people without money falling sick; the
prisoners of war who are not yet back from Siberia; the population
problem) 4
17. Vague, and worries about children (whether to have children; whether
children are being properly brought up; whether children, when they
grow up should do something for the State) 6

Distribution of answers by habitat and age-groups

	(1)	(2)	(3)	(4)	(5)	(6)	(7)	(8)
1. Housing	1.5	4.8	9.1	4.6	1.5	0.7	2.6	2.0
2. Economic worries	10.5	11.7	23.5	26.0	9.5	16.0	17.8	24.9
3. Education	7.5	2.7	2.6	6.7	2.0	2.3	3.5	5.6
4. Health	3.0	4.1	3.2	5.7	3.0	4.3	7.5	4.7
5. Occupation	11.2	3.4	3.2	7.0	11.5	5.8	5.8	5.8
6. Marriage	1.5	4.8	1.3	1.1	4.0	1.9	0.4	1.9

	(1)	(2)	(3)	(4)	(5)	(6)	(7)	(8)
7. Rearmament	11.2	11.7	2.6	2.9	10.5	9.4	7.1	5.1
8. War	12.0	13.7	16.3	13.0	11.0	12.9	10.2	8.3
9. Thought and ideas	—	—	2.6	1.9	0.5	0.7	2.6	5.0
10. Slackening of moral fibre	3.0	3.4	2.6	2.8	1.0	1.1	0.8	2.4
11. The social order	1.5	1.3	1.3	0.9	1.5	1.1	1.3	1.4
12. The problem of unemployment	0.7	1.3	—	0.5	1.0	0.3	—	0.8
13. The national economy	1.5	—	1.9	1.6	0.5	0.7	0.8	1.3
14. Internal administration	0.7	2.7	1.9	1.3	2.5	1.1	1.7	2.4
15. The international situation	4.5	4.1	3.9	2.1	4.5	5.8	1.7	2.9
16. Miscellaneous	1.5	3.7	2.6	3.4	4.0	5.8	6.2	3.7
17. Vague: worries about children	3.0	2.6	5.1	8.2	2.0	2.6	6.1	7.8

Alternative classification

	(E)	(1)	(2)	(3)	(4)	(5)	(6)	(7)	(8)
1. Matters concerning the subject alone	9	21	15	8	7	20	13	7	5
2. Worries about children	12	2	3	7	17	2	3	9	18
3. Worries about the family	29	14	16	31	37	16	24	28	31
4. Public affairs	32	37	39	36	29	31	33	33	32
5. Miscellaneous and vague	1	2	2	2	1	1	1	*	1
6. No reply	17	24	24	16	9	30	26	23	13

QUESTION 3. *On what occasions have you felt happy and light-hearted? (There are probably many different ways of answering this question.)*

(E)

1. Harmony in the family ('when the whole family was fit and in work'; 'the joy of seeing the children growing up'; 'when all members of the family could live happily and comfortably') 13
2. Filial piety (the joy of seeing the children growing up; 'when I accomplished something my parents had wanted and bidden me do'; 'although our children are about 20 years old now, they still behave very lovingly towards their parents') 0.2
3. The end of the war ('when I had the joy of seeing the end of the war and the return of real peace') 2
4. Demobilization, repatriation ('when I was demobilized'; 'when I was repatriated to Japan') 7
5. Marriage (marriage of eldest son; 'when I got married') 3
6. Vague: period of childhood and youth ('the period between my school-days and my marriage was happy'; my childhood; when I was in Manchuria in my youth). 1
7. Occasions connected with schooling ('when I learnt that the school had accepted me as a pupil'; 'when the *roku-san* system (6 years primary school and 3 years middle school) was introduced and everyone could go to middle school'; 'when I graduated') 6
8. Child-birth (birth of a boy). 2
9. Leisure activities (sightseeing in Kyoto; 'when I took part in a physical training competition'; study tour) 3

10. Occupation, craft ('when I was farming'; 'when I was working in a ^(E) factory'; 'when my salary was raised because of my diligence as an official') 9
11. Material well-being (post-war inflation kept the farm kitchens busy; 'when adequate quantities of food became available, commodity prices were properly controlled and it was possible to lead a pleasant life'; 'I am happy because my parents help me with my expenses') . 3
12. Housing (building a new house; finding a house of one's own after having to share one with other people; 'when I got my own house') . 1
13. Vague: a hope fulfilled ('when my plans worked out as I had hoped'; 'when I had finished all my work'; 'when things turned out as I had hoped'; 'when I was able to buy something I wanted very much') . . 2
14. Social relations—friendship, harmonious relations outside the family ('when I was given a kindly welcome to the village'; 'the time I was nursed when ill in bed'; 'when I was in love') 3
15. Service to or gratitude from others ('when I acted as a go-between and helped others in other ways'; 'when I was working for the sake of someone else'; 'when little children thank me for a gift or generally when people show me they are grateful') 0.3
16. Religious ecstasy ('when I came to believe in salvation—through the power of Amida'; 'during periods of meditation'; 'when I got a close view of His Imperial Majesty, the Emperor'; 'when I felt the dawn of Buddhism upon me') 0.4
17. Health, escape from danger, preservation of life (good bodily health; 'when I was cured of an illness and thus narrowly escaped death'; 'when the war ended, I thought they would kill me but I was set free') 4
18. Japanese independence—conclusion of peace; national resurgence (ratification of the peace treaty; now that it is again allowed to sing the *Hinomaru no Hata* [The Flag of the Rising Sun] and the *Kimi ga Yo* [Japanese national anthem]; when the peace treaty was signed through the brilliant diplomacy of Mr. Yoshida] 4
19. International friendship ('after the war America's behaviour was not cruel: this was unexpected and I was happy about it'; the friendly attitude of the army of occupation; good treatment of Japanese troops by the Western Powers) 1
20. Assistance to bereaved families ('I don't think the assistance given to bereaved families is enough, but I can manage'; the passing by the Diet of the Act for the assistance of bereaved families) 0.2
21. Public services ('transport arrangements are now convenient'; 'there is a bus stop near our house now'; when the gaps in the transport network were filled) 0.7
22. Miscellaneous (sex equality; 'I got a paper about the protection of life'; the disappearance of militarism and the army) 3

Distribution of replies by age-habitat groups

	(1)	(2)	(3)	(4)	(5)	(6)	(7)	(8)
1. Harmony in the family	9.7	8.2	7.8	16.4	5.0	6.2	10.7	15.7
2. Filial piety	—	—	—	0.8	3	0	0.4	0.1
3. End of the war	0.7	2.0	0.6	3.4	1.5	1.9	1.3	1.6

	(1)	(2)	(3)	(4)	(5)	(6)	(7)	(8)
4. Demobilization	1.5	1.3	5.8	8.2	2.5	2.7	8.9	8.2
5. Marriage	—	1.3	1.2	4.2	0.5	4.7	3.1	2.7
6. Vague: childhood memories	3.0	1.3	0.6	1.6	0.5	0.7	1.3	0.7
7. Connected with schooling	15.7	6.8	2.6	5.7	18.5	3.5	2.6	5.0
8. Child-birth	0.7	1.3	3.2	1.9	0.5	2.3	3.1	2.2
9. Leisure activities	14.2	6.8	1.9	1.1	7.5	3.1	5.8	1.7
10. Occupation, craft	9.0	9.6	9.8	9.7	8.5	10.9	9.3	7.8
11. Maternal well-being	2.2	2.0	3.9	4.4	0.5	3.1	2.2	3.9
12. Housing	0	1.3	2.6	1.1	1.0	0.3	0.4	1.6
13. Vague (hope fulfilled)	1.5	1.3	1.3	1.3	3.5	2.7	0.8	1.4
14. Social relations	5.2	4.8	5.8	2.1	5.5	6.2	0.4	2.3
15. Service to, or gratitude from others	0.7	0	1.3	0.1	0	0.7	0	0.3
16. Religious ecstasy	0	0.6	0	0.3	0.5	0.3	0.4	0.5
17. Health, escape from danger, preservation of life	3.0	2.0	1.9	1.3	5.5	4.3	5.8	4.6
18. Japanese independence	0.7	2.0	4.5	3.6	4.0	3.5	3.5	3.7
19. International friendship	0	0	1.3	0.3	0	1.5	0.4	1.7
20. Assistance to bereaved families	0	0	0	0.3	0	0.3	0.4	0.3
21. Public services	1.5	2.0	0.6	0.3	0	0	2.2	0.8
22. Miscellaneous	2.2	6.2	1.9	2.8	2.0	3.9	4.0	3.1

QUESTION 4. (a) *Are you satisfied so long as all the members of your family are in good health and living in harmony, or do you think that other things are also necessary for a good life?* (b) *If you think other things are necessary, how would you set about creating a good life and what kind of things would you want to do?*

Replies (a)

	(E)	(1)	(2)	(3)	(4)	(5)	(6)	(7)	(8)
Satisfied	69	74	68	70	71	65	74	73	67
Don't know	1 ⎫								
Not satisfied	30 ⎬	26	32	30	29	35	26	27	33

Replies (b)[1]

(E)

1. Study ('I would like to give my children proper schooling'; 'I think it is important to aim at raising intellectual standards'; 'I would like to let my children study abroad') 5
2. Ethics ('knowing the way of the world is a necessary part of education'; 'the enjoyment of leisure depends on a healthy world situation'; 'community spirit [helping one another] must be enhanced'; I hope my children will grow up 'sincere' [*makoto* [2]]) 1
3. Religion ('I should like to live a pious life with Buddha as its centre'; 'I'd like to spread religion [Buddhism; religion in general]'; 'we find joy in our faith) 0.4

---

1. Percentages based on the numbers of those answering 'Not satisfied'.
2. For the implications of *makoto*, translated by 'sincere', see Ruth Benedict, *The Chrysanthemum and the Sword*, pp. 215-19.

4. Respect for the individual (understanding between the members of the (E) family based on acknowledgment of each other's individuality; 'I'd like people to acknowledge the freedom of human beings') 0.4

5. Social position 0.2

6. Occupation ('I think I shall be satisfied if my children can make a living at a job which comes up to their desires'; 'I should like to take up a job with a future'; 'I'd like to work: at present our livelihood is precarious and I am accordingly applying for a job in a company, but how will it turn out?') 5

7. Leisure, recreation ('I'd like to live for hobbies—sports, reading, etc.'; 'I'd like to give my whole time to being an amateur of films and other forms of entertainment'; 'the whole family would like to travel about together freely—and such things') 2

8. Happiness ('I think happiness means a happy family life') 0.3

9. Social intercourse ('there should be friendly relations between all in the neighbourhood and in the hamlet [*buraku*]'; 'I should like to be a good neighbour to the people I meet daily'; 'I'd like to be a good friend to orphaned children') 0.8

10. Security and the achievement of a better life ('I think daily self-examination about one's work is necessary'; 'I should like to live the life of a rich man'; 'I should like to leave a little money at least to my children') 36

11. Service to the community (co-operation for the benefit of the community in general; 'if we co-operate, society as a whole will improve'; 'I should like to increase my knowledge by mixing with other people in society and then employ all my powers for the good of all'; 'first and foremost, we must place production on a solid basis so that Japan does not perish') 6

12. Relief ('I should like to plan for the well-being of the poor'; 'I'd like to help the unfortunate, say, helping peasants in their work'; 'when I have achieved happiness myself, I should like to do good to others') . . . 1.6

13. Peace (exerting oneself to secure peace in the community; working for peace within the hamlet and village) 7

14. Vague: things that cannot be achieved by oneself: mutual assistance ('I should like people generally to have more leisure'; 'I want to see higher standards of well-being in the community: with poor, orphans and war cripples before my eyes I cannot be happy or content'; 'families want, of course, to co-operate with their neighbours') . . . 24

15. Social institutions ('I should like to create a government in which the Ministers were paid a working man's wage, below the middle class standard'; improvement in the accident insurance system; 'I want the working classes to bear the cost of compulsory education') . . . 2

16. Miscellaneous (problem of emigration and safeguarding of food supplies; 'we must have values for which we stand as a people') . . 0.7

17. Reduction of taxes 0.4

Distribution of replies by habitat and age-group combined [1]

	(1)	(2)	(3)	(4)	(5)	(6)	(7)	(8)
1. Study	5.8	2.1	4.3	4.0	4.3	1.4	0	7.3
2. Ethics	2.9	0	2.1	1.1	0	0	0	1.6
3. Religion	2.9	0	0	0.5	0	0	1.6	0.3
4. Respect for the individual	2.9	0	0	0	1.4	1.4	0	0.3
5. Social position	0	2.1	0	0.5	0	0	0	0
6. Occupation	8	2.1	6.5	6.3	5.7	2.9	8.4	3.8
7. Leisure	5.8	2.1	2.1	1.7	8.6	1.4	1.6	1.2
8. Happiness	0	0	0	0.5	0	0	0	0.6
9. Social intercourse	2.9	0	0	0.5	0	4.4	1.6	0.3
10. Security and the achievement of a better life	29.4	30.4	39.1	35.8	36.2	39.7	47.4	34.6
11. Service to the community	0	8.6	2.1	5.2	5.7	13.2	6.7	6.0
12. Relief	0	4.3	2.1	2.3	0	1.4	1.6	1.2
13. Peace	2.9	10.8	8.6	7.5	4.3	5.8	6.7	7.3
14. Vague	26.4	26.0	23.9	23.6	21.7	17.6	15.2	26.6
15. Social institutions	0	4.3	0	4.6	0	0	1.6	2.5
16. Miscellaneous	0	0	2.1	0	0	2.9	0	0.9
17. Reduction of taxes	0	0	0	0.5	0	0	0	0.9

Alternative classification [2]

	(E)	(1)	(2)	(3)	(4)	(5)	(6)	(7)	(8)
1. Things done for other people	38	29	41	43	35	32	37	32	42
2. Reliefs (negative satisfaction)	39	44	37	39	41	45	40	39	36
3. Positive individual projects	8	6	2	7	7	10	7	10	8
4. Collective projects in which subject has a part to play	9	11	13	4	12	1	9	12	10
5. Don't know	6	9	7	7	4	12	7	7	4

QUESTION 5. *Do you feel that you want to do something for the community?*
  (a) *If so, what kind of thing?*

	(E)	(1)	(2)	(3)	(4)	(5)	(6)	(7)	(8)
1. Yes	49	52	44	50	48	50	49	53	49
2. No	48 }								
3. Don't know	3 }	48	56	50	52	50	51	47	51

Replies 5 (a). Sample as a whole [3]

(E)

  1. Relief of war victims ('I should like to devote myself to the interests
     of those killed and wounded in battle'; 'I should like to help war
     orphans, but it seems impracticable for me'; protection of refugees) .   7

---

1. Percentages based on the number of subjects replying that health alone is
   not sufficient.
2. Percentages calculated on the same basis as above.
3. Percentages relate to the total number of subjects answering yes to Question 5.

2. Relief of the destitute ('I should like to give at least a little help to (E) those in distressed circumstances'; 'as there are unhappy people, I should like to teach them to live happily together'; 'I should like to assist the destitute in a more positive way') 4

3. Aid to victims of natural catastrophes (earthquakes, fires, etc.) . . 0.2

4. Collecting for charity: literally *feathers*, so called from the feathers worn in the collector's badge ('I should like to contribute to public utility undertakings'; 'I should like to collect for the community chest'; 'I should like to collect for the Red Cross') I

5. Social welfare work—often vague ('I want to work for society, for others'; 'I want to give moral support and also make a physical contribution, e.g. to the welfare of the community, to work that is of value to society, etc.'; 'I want always to do whatever I am asked to do so long as it is beneficial to the community', 'I want to help in child welfare work'). 9

6. Roads, irrigation, etc. (piping in drinking water; road repairs; 'I want to work on roads for opening up forest areas and on road improvements in agricultural areas'). 4

7. Parks, playgrounds ('I want to build playgrounds for children'; 'I want to drain ponds which are no longer needed when there is an adequate supply of piped water, and convert them into children's playgrounds'; 'I should like to buy land and turn it into a park with animal and bird sanctuaries') 6

8. Public nurseries ('I have worked in a public nursery and would therefore like to help children'; 'I should like to create more institutions for small children'; 'I am thinking of taking charge of children at peak periods in the farming year'). 3

9. Homes for the aged ('I want to give unhappy old people loving care and I want to work for the establishment of an old people's home'; improvement of treatment of the inmates of old people's homes; 'I want to help old people, who have no one else to help them, to find places in a home for the aged') I

10. Employment offices (establishment of a suitable employment exchange) 0.2

11. Social movements—peace, reform, revolution (social movements for the protection of human rights; world peace movement; '. . . something in the political line, because that is my dream'; 'I should like to carry through agrarian reforms'). 2

12. Development of self-governing community organizations ('I want to make the village a better place to live in'; 'I want to develop industries in agricultural villages, e.g. by a scheme for *udon* [macaroni] factories'; in village administration, projects affecting the village as a whole—expansion of the *komin kan* [village institute], organization of a library) 4

13. Organizational activities in connexion with local self-governing bodies, municipalities, etc. (meetings of neighbourhood associations [*tonari-gumi*]; using the volunteer fire brigade [*shopo-dan*] for village improvement work) 2

14. Women's associations [*fujin-kai*] ('as a member of a women's associa- (E)
    tion I want to do my utmost to improve the conditions of everyday life';
    'I want to work hard to secure friendly relationships in the women's
    associations') 2
15. Young men's associations (*seinen-dan*) ('I want to do something for the
    benefit of boys and young men'; 'I want to launch a young men's
    movement which is wholesome and positive in its outlook') 1
16. Miscellaneous associations ('I want to join the parents' association and
    take an active part in its work'; 'I want to work for my union' or
    'my professional association'; 'I want to work in a society for revering
    the old [*keirokai*]'; 'as I am now helping Unesco, I should like later
    to join those who are working with it') 2
17. Religion ('I want to save men's hearts by religion'; 'I want to give reli-
    gious instruction'; 'I hope to be a priest or a teacher') 2
18. Education, thought, study, ethics (community [*komin-kan*] move-
    ments; 'society is in a state of ethical confusion and I want to set it
    right'; 'I want to study the culture of my native province'; 'I want to
    promote education'; 'the young people of today have warped ideas and
    I want to do my utmost to see that my children do not grow up like
    that') 11
19. Art, culture (raising the standard of culture; enriching people's culture;
    devoting oneself to cultural matters) 1
20. Amenities of life (belonging to a recreational society) 1
21. Health and hygiene ('I want to help improve economic conditions in
    country villages and also the food supply') 1
22. Improvement of living conditions ('I want to secure a larger life for the
    country villages'; 'I want to discuss methods for improving living con-
    ditions and clothing and then work to achieve these aims'; 'I want to
    buy articles and tools in common use and then allow everyone to make
    use of them free of charge'; 'I want to serve the public by improving
    living conditions') 3
23. Assistance through the medium of the subjects's own occupation
    ('all my time is taken up by my work as a teacher so that I have no
    energy left for anything else, but I want to work still harder at my
    regular job'; 'through the medium of my present occupation, I want to
    devote the little strength I have to enable the people around me to
    live a little better'; 'as I am a servant of the community [revenue offi-
    cer] I want to do what I can through the medium of my work') . . . 7
24. Action in connexion with people's work (raising industrial production;
    endeavouring to bring the agricultural techniques of the farmers up
    to a satisfactory level; 'I should like to see an improvement of
    agricultural plans on rational lines') 5
25. Miscellaneous ('I want to make children stronger physically'; 'I'd like
    to work on land improvement projects or on the construction or
    repair of roads through forests and in the farming districts'; 'I should
    like to bear splendid children') 2
26. Hazy and unformulated ('I will do anything if it is for the good of
    others'; 'things within my capacity'; 'I haven't thought of anything
    definite') 27

Distribution of answers

	(1)	(2)	(3)	(4)	(5)	(6)	(7)	(8)
1. Relief of war victims	8.6	12.1	12.9	9.6	5.9	3.2	6.7	4.8
2. Relief of the destitute	5.7	7.5	6.4	6.5	3.9	3.2	2.5	2.7
3. Aid to victims of natural catastrophes	—	3	—	—	—	—	—	0.2
4. Collecting for charity, etc.	1.4	—	—	0.3	0.9	0.8	0.8	1.0
5. Social welfare work	17.3	9.0	11.6	8.3	7.9	8.0	9.2	9.5
6. Roads, water supplies, etc.	2.8	3.0	5.1	1.3	3.9	1.6	2.3	5.3
7. Parks, playgrounds	—	1.5	—	1.0	—	0.8	0.8	1.0
8. Public nurseries	4.3	1.5	3.8	6.2	1.9	4.0	1.6	2.1
9. Homes for the aged	1.4	1.5	—	1.3	—	0.8	—	0.8
10. Employment offices	—	—	1.2	—	—	—	—	0.4
11. Social movements	2.8	—	3.8	1.7	4.9	2.4	4.2	1.6
12. Development of self-governing community organizations	1.4	3.0	—	3.8	3.9	3.2	5.8	5.9
13. Activities in connexion with local self-governing bodies	—	1.5	3.8	2.0	0.9	0.4	4.2	1.6
14. Women's associations	—	—	2.5	2.0	1.9	0.4	2.5	2.7
15. Young men's associations	1.4	1.5	—	0.3	3.9	6.4	0.8	0.4
16. Miscellaneous associations	—	4.5	—	3.4	2.9	0.4	1.6	1.0
17. Religion	1.4	—	2.5	2.0	0.9	—	0.8	2.3
18. Education, thought, study, ethics	7.2	9.0	12.9	10.3	7.9	10.4	10.0	12.7
19. Art, culture	—	3.2	2.5	—	3.9	1.6	1.6	1.0
20. Amenities of life	1.4	—	2.5	1.3	—	1.6	0.8	0.4
21. Health and hygiene	—	1.5	1.2	0.6	—	1.6	2.5	0.8
22. Improvement of living conditions	5.7	—	2.5	0.6	1.9	9.6	1.6	4.4
23. Assistance through the medium of the subject's own occupation	2.8	6.0	9.0	9.6	4.9	6.4	5.8	7.6
24. Action in connexion with people's work	4.3	6.0	6.4	5.1	4.9	5.6	5.0	3.1
25. Miscellaneous	4.3	—	1.2	2.0	1.9	3.2	—	2.9
26. Hazy and unformulated	27.5	30.3	16.8	24.9	34.0	28.8	30.2	26.9

Distribution of the replies into broad categories by habitat-age group[1]

	(1)	(2)	(3)	(4)	(5)	(6)	(7)	(8)
Charity, welfare, social work	11	12	12	11	6	6	6	6
Community tasks	1	2	3	1	2	1	2	3
Social movements, local organizations and associations	3	5	5	6	9	7	10	6
Cultural and spiritual undertakings	5	5	9	6	6	6	7	8
'Social action'	9	4	6	4	4	4	5	5
Material improvements	5	3	5	3	3	8	5	4
Not clear	14	14	8	12	17	14	16	13
Occupational } Miscellaneous }	4	2	6	6	3	5	4	5

---

1. Percentages relate to the total number of subjects interviewed.

QUESTION 6. *If a society or a meeting of any kind interested you, would you be inclined to take the lead in it or to make a personal contribution to the proceedings?*
  (a) *If the answer is yes, what kind of society or meeting have you in mind?*

	(E)	(1)	(2)	(3)	(4)	(5)	(6)	(7)	(8)
1. Yes	41	47	53	40	35	53	46	39	40
2. No	56 }								
3. Don't know	3 }	53	47	60	65	47	54	61	60

Replies 6 (a). Sample as a whole

(E)

1. Education, ideas (of or about the young) ('I would like to organize societies to investigate young men's ideas about rearmament and other subjects'; 'societies concerned with children's education, particularly the parents' association') 4
2. Culture, religion (meetings of a spiritual or religious character; meetings dealing with questions of religious faith; meetings of a cultural nature; reading circles or something on the lines of a film club) . . 4
3. Youth associations (*Seinen-dan*) (young men's associations; societies concerned with children, or showing children *kami-shił ai* [picture show] or for telling them stories; children's societies; girls' clubs) . . 4
4. Women's associations (*fujin-kai*) ('I should like something resembling the League of University Women'; meetings for the improvement of home life) 5
5. Amusement, recreation (organizing play activities for children; 'I should like to do this if it took the form of an amateur dramatic club'; sports, e.g. volley-ball matches) 7
6. Social (social gatherings of graduate associations; municipal social functions; 'societies that do not pursue private interests, or which enrich human life, preferably those where all the members are on friendly terms with one another and have no axe to grind') 4
7. Societies of benefit to the community (vague) ('I can't undertake anything important in the prefecture, but I think I can perform small tasks and there I will do anything'; material aid for societies; 'societies such as those for helping bereaved families') 4
8. Trade or professional associations (associations of small and medium businesses, etc.; societies for the defence of common interests, e.g. taxpayers' associations; 'I should like to help create solidarity by forming a plasterers' association') 6
9. Political (including trade unions) 1
10. Indefinite ('if it is a society that answers to my ideals, all right'; 'it doesn't matter much what society'; 'so long as it is something for women, any kind of society will do') 4

	(E)	(1)	(2)	(3)	(4)	(5)	(6)	(7)	(8)
1. Education, ideas	4	2	4	5	3	4	1	3	5
2. Culture, religion	4	7	6	7	3	11	5	4	4
3. Youth associations	4	4	8	3	3	12	9	6	2
4. Women's associations	5	3	6	4	3	3	8	4	7
5. Amusement, recreation	7	17	18	6	7	11	8	6	3

	(E)	(1)	(2)	(3)	(4)	(5)	(6)	(7)	(8)
6. Social	4	5	2	3	5	3	3	3	4
7. Societies of benefit to the community (vague)	4	3	3	3	5	3	2	2	4
8. Trade or professional societies	6	3	2	5	4	4	6	7	8
9. Political	1	0	2	2	1	0	0	2	1
10. Indefinite	4	6	6	7	4	6	5	4	4

QUESTION 7. *Which of the following comes nearest to being your goal in life?*
1. To devote yourself to the service of the public without thought for your own affairs?
2. To achieve financial security through your own work?
3. To become wealthy by devoting every ounce of energy to your work?
4. To live light-heartedly for the day, with no thought of the future?
5. To achieve fame by your work and learning?
6. To live an honest life regardless of what other people do?
7. To live the life you like without worrying about money or fame?

	(E)	(1)	(2)	(3)	(4)	(5)	(6)	(7)	(8)
1. Public service	4	6	7	2	3	2	4	6	5
2. Financial security through own efforts	45	27	34	47	53	24	37	50	48
3. Wealth	3	1	1	1	3	4	3	6	4
4. Living for the day	6	6	5	8	5	6	5	6	6
5. Fame	15	36	21	16	10	30	22	12	10
6. Honest life	17	13	15	10	17	20	16	13	19
7. The life one likes	9	11	17	12	7	14	13	7	8
8. Miscellaneous and indefinite	1	—	—	3	1	2	1	—	2

QUESTION 8. *Is there any particular thing you hope to accomplish in the course of your life?*
    (a) *If so what kind of thing?*

	(E)	(1)	(2)	(3)	(4)	(5)	(6)	(7)	(8)
1. Yes	70	56	68	66	76	52	59	72	74
2. No	26 }	44	32	34	24	48	41	28	26
3. Don't know	4 }								

Replies 8 (a). Sample as a whole

                                                        (E)

1. Social contributions ('I want to make our village more advanced than other villages'; social work: 'there are many unhappy people in the world and I want therefore to devote my energies to them', 'I want to look after children for people who cannot go out to work if their children are at home') 9
2. Money ('I want security in my old age'; 'I want to accumulate savings through my work'; 'being an impoverished farmer myself, I should like to leave some property to my children and grandchildren and let them have an easy life') 17

3. Houses and other real estate ('I want to repair my house'; house building; 'I should like to build a house and to buy a paddy field and a dry field') 20
4. Bringing up children ('at the very least I want to give my children a first-class upbringing and make them into people who will exert themselves for the benefit of society'; 'if I have children, I want them to live their lives as free individuals who are not dominated by their surroundings'; 'all I want is to make my children straightforward and honest people') 34
5. Marriage ('I want to arrange perfect marriages for my children'; 'all I want is for my elder brother to get married quickly') I
6. The home, filial piety (' I want to spare no pains to be a good child to my parents'; 'I want my parents to die with an easy mind about me'; I, want to make my family life harmonious') 5
7. Technical skills, craftsmanship ('I want to attain sufficient skill in tailoring'; 'I want to raise the living standards of the farmers by rationalized methods of management'; 'I should like to try to work out my own special stock raising techniques') 4
8. Occupation ('I want to be the best man in Japan at my line of work'; 'I want to make my career in a job that I thought about myself'; 'I want to follow in the footsteps of my adopted father') 11
9. Social position ('when I die I want people to say of me: "He was a good man and will be a great loss" '; 'I want to reach a position in the company where I work in which I am neither pushed around nor push other people around'; 'I have been taken on by a company: I want to become a foreman with them') 2
10. Relations with others ('I am under a moral obligation to the people who have moulded my character: I want to discharge it to the last farthing'; 'some of my relatives have lost two sons in the war: I want to do something for them'; 'I have been helped by my parents, brothers and sisters; I want to repay their kindness') . . . . *
11. Education, learning ('I want my children to have the best possible education'; 'I want to improve school equipment'; 'I want to start a nation-wide network of school libraries') 18
12. Ideas . . . . *
13. Inventions, discoveries i.e. creative work ('before I die, I want to have written a book which will bring about an improvement in Japanese society'; 'I want to try to produce a well written treatise or something of the kind'; 'a work of art'; 'I want to stage a good play and have many people come to see it') I
14. Hobbies, amusements (physical training: 'I should like to play table tennis'; 'I should like to grow hothouse flowers of all kinds'; 'I want to enjoy life') 3
15. Self-improvement ('I want to correct my shortcomings vigorously'; 'I want to improve my mind') I
16. Religion ('my faith is extremely weak and I want it to become strong'; 'I want to win more people to the *Tenri-kyo* [the Teaching of Divine Reason, a faith-healing Shinto sect]'; 'I want to spread the life of Christian love in the world') I
17. Others ('I want to be healthy') I

18. Political ('when I am rich, I want to do something to assist the village administration'; 'I want at least to institute a system of government which will ensure that no one is unable to support his own wife and children'; 'as I am a woman I cannot become Prime Minister, but I want to take part in politics') I

20. Don't know 3

	(E)	(1)	(2)	(3)	(4)	(5)	(6)	(7)	(8)
1. Social contributions	9	10.8	8.1	5.9	9.0	7.6	5.9	9.2	9.7
2. Money	17	5.4	13.2	10.9	23.5	5.7	10.0	17.2	17.9
3. Houses and other forms of real estate	20	6.7	7.1	16.8	14.9	15.2	21.3	23.4	25.4
4. Bringing up children	34	9.4	12.2	26.7	41.2	7.6	17.9	34.5	44.1
5. Marriage	1	0	0	0.9	1.9	0	1.9	0.6	1.4
6. The home, filial piety	5	12.1	6.1	2.9	2.8	11.4	5.3	5.5	3.9
7. Technical skill, craftsmanship	4	9.4	7.1	4.9	1.5	18.1	6.6	3.0	1.1
8. Occupation	11	8.1	17.3	22.7	12.9	14.2	11.3	11.1	6.5
9. Social position	2	2.7	4.0	0.9	1.5	2.8	1.9	1.8	1.7
10. Relations with others	*	0	2.0	0	0.6	0	1.3	0	0
11. Education, learning	18	20.2	20.4	17.8	19.2	15.2	13.3	24.6	17.6
12. Ideas	*	0	0	0	0	0	1.9	1.2	0.6
13. Inventions, discoveries	1	1.3	2.0	5.9	0.8	0	1.3	0	0.2
14. Hobbies, amusements	3	10.8	9.1	5.9	1.3	4.7	8.6	1.2	2.2
15. Self-improvement	1	0	2.0	0	1.9	1.9	0.6	0.6	0
16. Religion	1	0	0	1.9	1.0	0	0.6	1.2	0.8
17. Others	1	2.7	1.0	0	1.0	0	2.6	1.8	0.4
18. Political	1	2.7	4.0	0.9	1.3	0.9	0	1.2	0.9
20. Don't know	3	9.4	3.0	2.9	1.7	5.7	4.6	0.6	3.4

Classification of subjects by their combined answers to questions 3 and 8

	(E)	(1)	(2)	(3)	(4)	(5)	(6)	(7)	(8)
Social type	38	22	29	29	43	20	33	39	46
Economic type	30	22	29	32	34	24	26	29	31
Aesthetic type	8	23	14	11	5	16	11	8	3
Political type	5	7	5	2	4	9	4	5	3
Academic type	2	7	3	3	1	4	2	1	1
Religious type	1	0	1	3	2	1	1	1	2
Unclassified type	16	19	19	20	11	26	23	17	14

QUESTION 9. *When you have personal difficulties, do you generally consult your parents, family or friends? When the opinions of the people consulted differ from your own, do you merely note them for information or do you usually follow them? If you find this last question difficult to answer, would you say in general that you cling to your own opinion or that you bow to the opinion of others?*

	(E)	(1)	(2)	(3)	(4)	(5)	(6)	(7)	(8)
1. Don't ask advice	9	6	9	12	13	5	5	8	7
2. Do ask advice but only for information		45	53	54	54	45	54	49	40	40

	(E)	(1)	(2)	(3)	(4)	(5)	(6)	(7)	(8)
3. Ask advice and usually follow it	25	19	24	18	21	25	26	28	29
4. Ask advice; may or may not follow it but more inclined to stick to own views	7	7	4	4	6	5	6	6	8
5. Ask advice; whether I follow it depends on circumstances but more apt to follow it	7	10	1	6	8	6	7	9	8
6. Ask advice; whether I follow it or not depends on circumstances; can't say more	7	5	8	6	7	5	7	9	8

QUESTION 10. *Asked their views about this or that, women often say: 'I know nothing about it because I am a woman'. Are they right to take this attitude?*

	(E)	(1)	(2)	(3)	(4)	(5)	(6)	(7)	(8)
1. No	88	89	85	88	86	90	93	91	88
2. Yes	8	4	12	7	11	4	5	9	9
3. Can't say	4	7	3	5	3	6	2	*	3

QUESTION 11. *Do you think it better that the eldest son should inherit the houset as was formerly the case?*

(a) *Do you think it better to concede a special position to the eldest son and no, to treat him exactly like his brothers?*

	(E)	(1)	(2)	(3)	(4)	(5)	(6)	(7)	(8)
1. Yes	66	53	51	54	64	56	63	68	76
2. No	31	45	48	42	34	37	33	28	22
3. Don't know	3	2	1	4	2	7	4	4	2

QUESTION 11 (a)

	(E)	(1)	(2)	(3)	(4)	(5)	(6)	(7)	(8)
1. Better to concede him a special position	48	35	39	39	50	37	40	46	56
2. Better to make no distinction	49	64	59	57	48	55	55	50	42
3. Don't know	3	1	2	4	2	8	5	4	2

QUESTION 12. *Do you think that the number of children who pay no attention to their parents has increased recently? What is the position in your area?*

(a) *Do you think there is no harm in children obeying their parents implicitly?*

(b) *Is this still the case when children have become independent?*

	(E)	(1)	(2)	(3)	(4)	(5)	(6)	(7)	(8)
1. Yes	66	64	65.5	66	67	66	64	64	66
2. No	28	24	27.5	22	24	29	31	31	29
3. Don't know	6	12	7	12	7	5	5	4	5

255

Replies 12 (a), 12 (b)

	(E)	(1)	(2)	(3)	(4)	(5)	(6)	(7)	(8)
1. No harm in it in any circumstances	12	8	16	8	11	11	13	14	12
2. No harm in it but different when they have become independent	33	35	31	33	38	19	27	31	35
3. No harm in it once they have become independent, don't know	5	4	4	5	3	7	8	7	6
4. Don't know	50	53	49	53	47	64	52	48	47

QUESTION 13. *Do you think the choice of a husband or wife is a matter for the person concerned or for his or her family?*

	(E)	(1)	(2)	(3)	(4)	(5)	(6)	(7)	(8)
1. Exclusively the business of the two families concerned	14	17	10	12	14	14	13	15	14
2. The family should have the most say in it	4	2	2	2	5	1	2	5	7
3. The individual concerned and the family should have an equal say	15	9	12	8	13	12	14	13	19
4. The individual should have the most say	20	13	22	21	21	16	23	18	21
5. A matter for the individual exclusively	44	51	49	53	45	49	47	47	37
6. Don't know	3	8	5	4	2	8	1	2	2

QUESTION 14. *Some people say it is a disaster that in the world today the number of those who do not know* giri *is growing. Do you think so, too?*

	(E)	(1)	(2)	(3)	(4)	(5)	(6)	(7)	(8)
1. Yes	72	64	60	69	77	61	71	76	75
2. No	21	20	26	23	18	24	23	18	19
3. No opinion	7	16	14	8	5	15	6	6	6

QUESTION 14 (a) *If any one in your own district says of a man: 'He does not know* giri', *what would that be likely to mean?*

(E)

1. Not recognizing an *on* (individual cases) (forgetting an old *on*; harming a person who has done one a kindness; 'when one has received help in a difficult time, forgetting all about it when things go well again') . 28
2. Not recognizing the *on* to one's parents, brothers, or sisters ('at the end of the war, when food was short, we took care of our relatives in the town, but now, although conditions are difficult for us here, our relatives behave as if they knew nothing of it'; 'when there are all kinds of trouble between members of a family'; 'when someone brought up in a loving home goes to the bad when he grows up') . . 1
3. Other kinds of *on*—towards one's superior, one's employer ('taking advantage of post-war confusion to steal one's employer's customers, without a qualm of conscience at having practically ruined him';

'going elsewhere for higher wages despite the fact that one's former (E) boss looked after his employees well'; 'forgetting assistance received from one's superior and repaying the *on* with evil') . . . . .   *

4. Lack of humanity or kindness 'Although the neighbours are in trouble, not giving it a thought'; not consoling one another; 'if young people do not give up their seats in a public conveyance when they see an old woman of 70 standing'; 'not having the habit of kindly and sympathetic behaviour')   4

5. Egoism ('headstrong self-will'; 'thinking only about oneself in good times and bad'; 'thinking only about one's own well-being without concern for that of others')   11

6. Lack of moral sense ('people who don't follow the right path as human beings; 'people who tread others underfoot'; 'lack of ethical principles')   1

7. Questions of 'sincerity' (*makoto*), duty, keeping promises (failure to keep promises; 'wanting to return goods to the supplier two or three years after they were bought'; 'not doing things one ought to do') . .   3

8. Lack of consideration for others ('not using one's head'; 'being a nuisance to others'; 'when parents behave as though children who are kind and affectionate to them were trying to borrow money') . . .   2

9. Courtesy in social intercourse (failure to answer invitations; lack of manners; 'people who do not know how to behave in society') . . .   6

10. Obligations concerning the borrowing and lending of things and money (borrowing a thing and keeping it indefinitely; not returning a thing in the state in which it was borrowed; failure to repay a loan of money received when in difficulties from a friend when the friend in turn is in difficulties and asks for it)   5

11. Exchange of gifts, courtesies, or past favours received (failure to acknowledge congratulations offered on ceremonial occasions; failure to acknowledge a gift; 'non-attendance at a funeral when one has been greatly helped by the bereaved family')   4

12. Calumny ('making trouble in a neighbourhood where relations are friendly'; speaking evil of people behind their backs; taking pleasure in speaking evil of others)   1

13. Making a distinction between rich and poor in one's social intercourse.   1

14. Others (misconception of democracy)   1

15. Don't know   32

	(E)	(1)	(2)	(3)	(4)	(5)	(6)	(7)	(8)
1. Not knowing *on* (individual cases)	28	27.0	28.9	30.7	33.4	18.5	23.5	27.6	28.5
2. Same (towards parents, brothers, etc.)	1	0	0.6	1.9	1.8	0.5	1.9	0.4	1.2
3. Same (other instances: towards employer, etc.)	*	1.5	0.6	1.3	0.8	0.5	0.7	0.4	0.4
4. Lack of humanity or kindness	4	3.0	4.1	5.2	5.2	2.0	3.1	4.9	4.2
5. Egoism	11	6.0	9.6	5.8	10.3	4.5	10.5	8.9	14.1
6. Lack of moral sense	1	0	0.6	1.3	1.3	1.0	1.1	1.3	2.0
7. 'Sincerity', good faith, duty	3	4.5	3.4	3.2	3.6	4.0	2.7	1.7	2.6
8. Lack of consideration	2	1.5	2.0	1.9	2.1	1.5	0.3	0.8	1.6

	(E)	(1)	(2)	(3)	(4)	(5)	(6)	(7)	(8)
9. Courtesy in social intercourse	6	6.7	5.5	5.2	6.5	4.5	6.6	4.4	5.2
10. Obligations in connexion with borrowing and lending	5	6.7	8.9	6.5	5.9	3.0	3.5	4.0	3.1
11. Acknowledgment of gifts, favours, etc.	4	1.5	4.1	5.2	3.9	3.5	4.3	5.8	3.2
12. Calumny	1	1.5	0.6	0.6	1.1	0.5	0.7	1.3	0.5
13. Distinguishing between rich and poor in social relations	1	0	0	0	0.6	0	1.5	0	0.7
14. Others	1	0	1.3	0	0.9	1.0	0.4	1.3	0.6
15. Don't know	32	40	30	31	22	55	39	37	32

Additional analysis of replies according to sex[1]

	(1)		(2)		(3)		(4)		(5)		No reply	
	M	W	M	W	M	W	M	W	M	W	M	W
Sample as a whole	30	31	5	4	10	9	21	17	4	4	30	35
Urban age-groups, total	33	34	8	6	11	9	20	17	4	5	24	29
16-19	32	25	6	8	9	8	14	12	0	6	39	41
20-24	28	33	11	7	10	10	21	15	7	1	23	34
25-29	30	38	5	8	9	12	18	14	4	1	34	27
30-39	35	31	9	4	11	5	22	20	5	8	18	32
40-49	29	37	7	6	17	11	28	21	3	6	16	19
50 and over	50	45	7	2	7	14	12	15	4	2	20	22
Rural age-groups, total	27	29	4	3	10	8	22	18	4	3	33	39
16-19	19	20	3	3	8	8	11	11	3	4	56	54
20-24	26	26	5	2	14	8	20	15	2	4	33	44
25-29	33	25	5	3	7	13	17	17	5	2	33	40
30-39	25	30	2	3	15	7	26	17	3	5	29	38
40-49	28	32	4	3	8	9	27	24	5	2	28	30
50 and over	32	37	4	3	7	5	26	19	4	1	27	35

QUESTION 15. *People sometimes say: 'nagai mono niwa makareru' (never contradict a superior) or words to that effect; have you ever heard that saying? Do you think this is a bad attitude, or do you think that it cannot be helped?*

	(E)	(1)	(2)	(3)	(4)	(5)	(6)	(7)	(8)
1. Not good	41	33	35	46	42	31	35	40	45
2. Unavoidable	32	13	34	35	44	17	21	22	33
3. Don't know the saying	27	54	30	19	13	52	44	38	22

QUESTION 16. *Do you think that people examined by the police are all of doubtful character, or are some of them different?*

	(E)	(1)	(2)	(3)	(4)	(5)	(6)	(7)	(8)
1. All bad characters	20	15	17	20	22	12	15	18	23
2. Some are different 3. Don't know	} 80	85	83	80	78	88	85	82	77

1. For code of replies see text, Chapter VII, page 195.

QUESTION 16 (a). *Do you know anything about the recent incident at Tokyo University? If so, what do you think of the attitudes of the students and the police respectively? Which of the two explanations seems to you the more acceptable?*

	(E)	(1)	(2)	(3)	(4)	(5)	(6)	(7)	(8)
1. The students' explanation is the more credible	15	17	25	24	16	13	13	15	10
2. The explanation of the police is the more credible	17	11.5	12	15	17	17	15	15	17
3. Don't know enough details	11	11.5	14	14	10	7	10	14	10
4. Don't understand	17	16	25	19	18	17	14	12	15
5. Don't know	41	44	24	28	39	46	48	44	43

QUESTION 17. *We turn now to an entirely different subject: Whether or not you know anything about current events in foreign countries.*

   (a) *Do you feel that what happens abroad might adversely affect your own way of life?*

   (b) *Do you not want to know what is going on in foreign countries?*

   (c) *What kind of things would you be interested to know about?*

Replies 17 (a) and (b)

	(E)	(1)	(2)	(3)	(4)	(5)	(6)	(7)	(8)
1. Cannot have the slightest adverse effect on me personally	9	9	7	8	9	8	7	8	12
2. Will probably have little effect	11	13	5	11	13	5	12	9	11
3. Cannot affect me adversely but I should still like to know about them	15	13	19	16	15	18	14	13	14
4. Can harm me but I am still not interested	12	9	8	9	12	11	13	17	12
5. Can harm me and I want to know about them	53	56	61	56	51	58	54	53	51

Replies 17 (c)[1]

                                (E)

1. Politics (general administration) 10
2. Economics (mechanism of the economy; fluctuations in commodity prices). 16
3. International affairs (in so far as they affect Japan; what effect will the peace treaty have on the attitudes and policy of foreign countries?) 5
4. Trade (import and export trade; 'I would like to know about trading organizations') 4
5. Military (the development of the Korean problem; European rearmament; nature of the next war; can war be avoided?) 9
6. Industry ('we hear about planning of production to keep supply and demand in line and about harnessing atomic energy for peaceful purposes; I should like to know more'; 'I should like to know about agricultural methods'; 'industrial economics') 6
7. Social behaviour (ethics; national traits; customs) 2

---

1. Percentages based on those wanting to know about happenings abroad.

(E

8. News (current problems) 4
9. Education (educational methods; methods of training children) . . 4
10. Science, learning 5
11. Culture, ideas ('I should like to know about the psychology, ideologies, etc. of young people of about my own age'; 'higher cultural standards') 9
   I
12. Health and hygiene I
13. Sports 0.4
14. Spare time activities, recreation I
15. Etiquette (punctuality, 'because Japanese always arrive late at meetings, etc.'; social relations between men and women) I
16. Fashion ('beauty culture') 2
17. Household matters (modern kitchens, home training of children; daily routine and methods of housewives). 7
18. Living standards and conditions (clothing, diet and housing; raising of living standards; 'standard of living of the workers'; routine of daily life) 17
19. The situation in foreign countries (social conditions; 'home affairs'; the problem of the local communist parties) 6
20. International situation (the problem of the relations between the United States of America and the U.S.S.R.; 'I should like to know what is really going on in the U.S. and Soviet blocs') 12
21. Others ('I want to learn English'; 'I want to know about Japanese interned in communist China'; 'religion in foreign countries') 3
22. Emigration (the emigration problem, 'because the population of Japan is increasing'). I
23. Condition of women (women's occupations; 'what is the position of unmarried girls in everyday life?') 2
24. Don't know II

	(1)	(2)	(3)	(4)	(5)	(6)	(7)	(8)
1. Politics	15.2	8.6	9.9	9.9	9.9	9.1	7.4	7.8
2. Economics	15.2	10.4	14.5	19.0	13.9	10.9	14.9	17.6
3. International affairs	3.2	3.4	4.5	5.6	1.9	4.0	6.1	4.5
4. Trade	3.2	2.6	3.6	3.4	3.9	3.4	3.4	5.4
5. Military	5.4	13.0	9.0	8.4	5.2	10.9	10.8	9.1
6. Industry	2.1	6.0	6.3	4.2	5.9	5.7	13.6	6.9
7. Social behaviour	6.5	1.7	1.8	2.4	1.3	3.4	0.6	1.4
8. News	5.4	2.6	2.7	5.9	3.3	1.1	2.7	4.1
9. Education	6.5	4.3	2.7	7.4	2.6	2.2	2.0	2.8
10. Science, learning	11.9	8.6	2.7	4.4	9.2	5.7	7.4	3.2
11. Culture, ideas	10.8	12.1	9.9	8.1	11.2	7.4	8.8	7.2
12. Health and hygiene	—	0.8	—	0.9	—	0.5	—	0.9
13. Sports	3.2	—	0.9	0.4	—	0.5	0.6	0.1
14. Spare time activities, recreation	3.2	2.6	—	0.2	0.6	1.7	0.6	—
15. Etiquette	—	—	0.9	1.4	0.6	1.7	—	0.1
16. Fashion, beauty culture	3.2	2.6	4.5	2.7	3.3	1.1	0.6	0.9
17. Household matters	6.5	7.8	9.0	6.4	11.7	4.5	8.1	5.9
18. Living standards and conditions (diet, housing)	21.7	20.8	18.1	12.6	23.8	20.6	22.4	13.6

	(1)	(2)	(3)	(4)	(5)	(6)	(7)	(8)
19. Situation in foreign countries	4.3	5.2	2.7	6.9	3.3	13.2	6.8	5.7
20. International situation	8.6	12.1	12.7	12.6	4.6	5.1	12.9	13.9
21. Others (learning English, religion abroad)	2.1	1.7	2.7	2.9	4.6	5.1	2.7	2.8
22. Emigration	—	1.7	—	0.2	—	—	0.6	1.1
23. Condition of women	2.1	2.6	0.9	1.7	2.6	4.0	2.0	2.2
24. Don't know	11.9	6.9	9.9	12.1	7.2	8.0	4.7	14.1

QUESTION 18. *Which foreign countries are, in your opinion, ahead of Japan?*

	(E)	(1)	(2)	(3)	(4)	(5)	(6)	(7)	(8)
1. United States of America	81	84	86	82	79	89	79	80	79
2. Great Britain	18	30	23	23	21	19	18	21	13
3. France	7	9	15	15	7	8	7	7	4
4. Germany	6	10	10	8	7	5	3	6	5
5. U.S.S.R.	5	12	10	8	6	5	4	4	4
6. Switzerland	2	3	4.1	1.3	2.4	4.0	2.3	3.5	1.6
7. Italy	0.2	0	0	0.6	0.3	0	0	0	0.3
8. Sweden	0.7	0	1.3	1.3	0.6	0.5	1.5	0.4	0.6
9. India	0.3	0	0.6	0.6	0.1	0.5	0.7	0	0.3
10. Denmark	1.5	0	0.6	0	0.9	1.5	1.5	2.6	2.3
10b. Australia	0.03	—	—	—	—	—	—	—	0.1
11. Every other country	0.8	—	0.6	1.3	0.4	0.5	0.3	0.8	1.2
12. All countries in Europe and America	0.5	0.7	1.3	0.6	1.1	0	0	0	0.5
14. Canada	0.007	0.7	0	0	0	0	0	0	0.1
16. Brazil	0.03	0	0	0	0	0	0	0	0.1
17. China	0.2	0	0.6	0.6	0.4	0	0	0.4	0.2
18. Norway	0.1	0	0.6	0	0.1	0	0	0.4	0.2
19. Netherlands	0.1	0	0	0	0.1	1.0	0	0	0.2
20. Don't know	13	11	6	9	15	8	12	12	15

QUESTION 18 (a). *In what respects are they ahead of Japan?*

(E)

1. Science (medicine; dye-stuffs) 34
2. Machinery, technology, industry (precision machine tools; industrial 'know how'; heavy industry) 24
3. Inventions, discoveries (inventive power) 0.6
4. Commerce, economic power, wealth of natural resources ('they have goods of all kinds in abundance'; 'in the economic field, they have planning, organization and capital'). 7
5. Agricultural techniques ('agriculture has been mechanized'; 'they have a planned agriculture') 5
6. Civilization — in the sphere of industry. 7
7. Politics ('their territory is vast but united'; 'far ahead of us in their handling of foreign affairs'; 'maintenance of public order') 5
8. Education (standards generally higher). 4

261

9. Philosophical and social doctrines (democracy; respect for human rights). . . . . 4 (E)
10. Culture, art (in literature; in level of knowledge; in the arts proper—e.g. fine arts and music) II
11. Daily life: clothing ('they wear Western clothing which is simple and does not hamper movement') I
12. Daily life: diet . . . . *
13. Daily life: housing (their architecture is far ahead of Japan's) . . . I
14. Standard of living: domestic arrangements; rationalization of housework ('life has been made scientifically efficient in the kitchen, etc.'; standard of living is high; 'they have mechanical household appliances') 15
15. Manners and customs ('they are kind, humane') 2
16. 'Breeding', education, social morality ('their sense of public duty is attractive'; 'they are cultured and well bred'; high ethical standards) 5
17. Strength of character—perseverance, etc. ('they are a resolute people') I
18. Means of transport (cars, traffic, shipping). 3
19. Social system (thorough-going democracy; full acceptance of equal rights for women both in theory and in practice; 'although differences between rich and poor exist, their social welfare system provides security at all levels'). 3
20. Social institutions (social service; welfare of the old, homes for the aged, etc.; 'they are taking practical action for the reclamation of juvenile delinquents'). I
21. Military matters (scientific production of the A-bomb, etc.; tactical superiority) 4
22. Peaceful outlook ('the people love peace and are taking practical steps to ensure it') I
23. All respects 5
24. Others (sports) . . . . *
25. Health and hygiene (chemo-therapy, drugs, etc.). 2

Replies classified by habitat-age groups

	(E)	(1)	(2)	(3)	(4)	(5)	(6)	(7)	(8)
1. Science	34	42	29	38	32	38	36	37	32
2. Machinery, technology, industry	24	19	20	22	28	18	24	24	23
3. Inventions, discoveries	0.6	1.7	0.7	0	0.9	0.5	0.4	1.1	0.3
4. Commerce	7	9	9	8	8	8	4	8	6
5. Agricultural techniques	5	1	3	1	1	8	9	6	8
6. Civilization	7	9	12	9	8	6	5	8	6
7. Politics	5	8	5	9	5	8	5	5	4
8. Education	4	2	2	4	5	3	1	3	4
9. Philosophical and social doctrines	4	3	5	7	4	3	3	5	4
10. Culture, art	II	13	12	9	II	13	10	12	10
11. Daily life, clothing	I	0.8	5.1	2.9	1.5	0.5	1.8	1.5	0.4
12. Diet	*	0	0	0	0.3	0	0.9	0	0.4
13. Housing	I	0.8	0.7	0.7	0.9	0.5	0.4	1.0	0.1

	(E)	(1)	(2)	(3)	(4)	(5)	(6)	(7)	(8)
14. Standard of living: domestic arrangements	15	15	18	15	16	19	18	14	12
15. Manners and customs	2	3.4	2.1	2.9	2.1	2.1	1.8	1.0	1.7
16. Breeding, education	5	4	6	1	5	3	4	6	5
17. Strength of character	1	0	2.9	3.6	1.7	0.5	0	2.0	0.7
18. Transport	3	0	1.4	2.1	2.7	4.3	3.1	4.5	2.0
19. Social system	3	5	2	7	2	3	4	4	2
20. Social institutions	1	0	0.7	0.7	2.1	0.5	2.2	1.5	0.8
21. Military matters	4	4	5	5	3	1	4	2	5
22. Peaceful outlook	1	0.8	1.4	0	0.7	0.5	0.4	1.5	0.3
23. All respects	5	3.4	5.1	5.0	5.6	2.1	5.0	7.1	6.4
24. Others (sports)	*	0	0	0	0	0.5	0.4	0.5	0.4
25. Health and hygiene	2	0	0.7	0.7	1.9	1.6	0	3.5	2.2

New codification and supplementary analyses: (a) Relation of the new code (Roman numerals) to the old (Arabic numerals).

I.   Science and technology 1, 2, 3, 6, 18, 21
II. Intellectual values. 8, 9, 10
III. Standard of living 11, 12, 13, 14, 25
IV. Political evolution. 7, 19, 20, 22
V.   Economic evolution 4, 5
VI. Spiritual values 15, 16, 17
VII. Others 23, 24

(b) Reclassification of replies on the above basis and breakdowns by sex, age and sex combined, length of education, and percentages ascribing superiority, in the fields indicated, to specific countries

	I	II	III	IV	V	VI	VII	No reply
Sample as a whole	53	14	15	8	10	7	5	7
Men								
Total	64	17	14	12	14	8	5	4
16-19	82	22	22	19	20	9	1	5
20-24	63	15	17	11	15	9	5	3
25-29	72	18	16	18	15	7	6	4
30-39	62	18	15	13	14	6	11	3
40-49	64	22	11	10	15	10	5	4
50 and over	60	11	9	7	13	9	7	8
Women								
Total	43	11	17	4	6	5	6	10
16-19	55	14	17	7	7	4	4	8
20-24	46	10	20	5	7	3	5	11
25-29	44	11	19	6	4	7	6	7
30-39	41	11	23	3	6	6	5	10
40-49	39	13	14	3	8	4	5	11
50 and over	37	8	9	2	4	5	9	11

Years of education	I	II	III	IV	V	VI	VII	No reply
6-8	40	7	7	4	6	3	7	12
9-11	57	11	16	7	10	5	6	7
12-13	58	24	23	13	13	10	2	4
Over 13	54	31	19	21	16	16	1	1

Superiority ascribed to:

	I	II	III	IV	V	VI	VII	
United States of America	71	14	18	7	11	5	6	
Great Britain	55	23	16	22	11	14	3	
France	38	55	19	10	7	7	4	
Germany	77	17	18	3	8	11	2	
U.S.S.R.	63	14	5	19	14	5	3	
Switzerland	42	12	14	29	15	6	0	
Denmark	26	10	12	14	67	2	0	

QUESTION 19. *In what respects—as regards their way of life or anything else you can think of—could the Japanese learn from foreign countries?*

(E)

1. Science (medicine). 5
2. Industrial and technological development (precision machines; manufacturing methods—i.e. methods of mass production; industrial techniques). 6
3. Inventions, discoveries . . . . *
4. Commerce (economic power, abundance of goods) 1
5. Agricultural techniques (management of mechanized farming; labour-saving through electrification; scientific agricultural techniques) . . 3
6. Civilization (thinking about the material aspects of culture; industrialization). 2
7. Politics (parliamentary democracy; legislation for the relief of destitution; 'government based on public opinion') 2
8. Education (the educational system, educational methods from infancy to adolescence; student life). 3
9. Philosophical and social doctrines (respect for the individual—i.e. for human rights; individualism in the good sense; 'democracy'). . . . 4
10. Culture (learning). 2
11. Daily life: clothing (simplification of clothing: ease in laundering; 'active' clothes: 'Western clothes are better adapted to active movement than Japanese clothes'; skill in introducing new fashions) . . . 4
12. Daily life: diet (inclusion of more vegetables in the diet; bread; simplification and rationalization of diet) 3
13. Daily life: housing (fire proof buildings; healthy houses—dry, light and hygienic; the refinements of modern architecture). 2
14. Domestic organization (efficiency based on mechanical aids in the home—contribution of science to domestic life, rationalization of kitchen utensils; electricity in the home, easing housework and saving the housewife time; improvements in the kitchen). 19
15. Manners and customs of the nation (the family system—'the atmosphere of the home is usually cheerful and harmonious with all the members of the household sharing in the work'; respect for women;

'relations between the two sexes are on a satisfactory basis'; 'open- (E)
heartedness'). 5
16. Good breeding, moral training, social ethics (strict respect for time;
    proper civility in social intercourse; gentlemanly behaviour; scrupulous
    training in public morality). 11
17. Strength of character, perseverance, etc. ('they are persevering';
    'they stand by their fellow countrymen'; 'they carry a righteous
    struggle through to the end') 1
18. Transport (excellence of the roads). 1
19. Social system (equality of men and women; the English social system) 3
20. Social institutions (excellence of social welfare institutions; excellence
    of public institutions, e.g. libraries) 1
21. Armaments . . . . *
22. Peace . . . . *
23. Everything 1
24. Others (sports; foreign languages) 1
25. Health and hygiene (better medicines; clean and hygienic way of life;
    'excellent hygienic arrangements'). 4
26. Don't know 31

Replies by habitat-age groups

	(E)	(1)	(2)	(3)	(4)	(5)	(6)	(7)	(8)
1. Science	5	11	6	6	5	6	5	4	5
2. Industrial and technological development	6	6	3	8	8	3	5	5	5
3. Inventions, discoveries	*	0	0	0	0.5	0	0	0	0
4. Commerce	1	1	1	2	3	1	1	1	*
5. Agricultural techniques	3	0	1	1	1	7	4	3	4
6. Material aspects of culture	2	2	2	3	2	4	2	1	2
7. Politics	2	2	1	4	1	3	1	2	1
8. Education	3	4	2	5	2	3	3	1	3
9. Philosophical and social doctrines	4	5	6	4	3	2	5	6	4
10. Culture (learning)	2	4	1	1	2	1	2	3	1
11. Clothing	4	0	3	3	5	4	2	2	5
12. Diet	3	1.5	6.2	3.2	3.4	2.5	0.7	5.8	3.5
13. Housing	2	3.7	4.8	1.3	2.8	1.0	0.7	4.0	1.9
14. Domestic organization	19	17	24	21	18	20	20	22	17
15. Manners and customs	5	4	8	10	8	4	3	5	4
16. Good breeding, moral training, social ethics	11	11	16	10	12	9	8	12	10
17. Strength of character, perseverance, etc.	1	1.5	2.0	0.6	0.9	0.5	0.4	0.8	0.9
18. Transport	1	1.5	0.6	0.6	0.8	1.5	0.4	0	0.4
19. Social system	3	5	1	5	2	3	4	3	2
20. Social institutions	1	2.2	0.6	0.6	0.9	0.5	0.4	0.4	0.7
21. Armaments	*	0	0.6	0	0	0.5	0	0	0.3
22. Peace	*	0	0	0	0	0	0.4	0	0
23. Everything	1	1.5	0.6	0	0.8	0.5	1.1	1.3	1.0

	(E)	(1)	(2)	(3)	(4)	(5)	(6)	(7)	(8)
24. Others (sports)	I	0.7	1.3	0.6	0.8	1.5	1.5	0.8	1.6
25. Health and hygiene	4	5	4	5	4	4	4	4	4
26. Don't know	21	32	24	26	31	31	30	28	34

QUESTION 20. *Conversely, what features of foreign life do you not want to imitate?*

(E)

1. Too high an esteem for women (debasement of the status of men; equal rights for men and women; 'lack of gentleness in women'; 'they make too much of women') 3
2. Relations between men and women (walking arm in arm or hand in hand; 'social relations between men and women are too crude, i.e. too free'; 'the kind of things that go on between Occupation troops and Japanese girls'; 'girls behaving like prostitutes') 8
3. Women's fashions and their luxury, extravagance and gaudiness (adoption of fashions which do not suit Japanese women; stupid slavery to fashion; heavy make-up; [too much lipstick; lacquered nails]; clothes of primary colours; 'they are gaudy') 5
4. Permanent waves. I
5. Dancing 5
6. Kissing ('kissing in the presence of others'). 6
7. Unrestricted choice in marriage (marriages between different nationalities). . . . . *
8. Birth control. . . . . *
9. Divorce ('divorce has become too easy and generally speaking too frequent'; 'they get divorced again and again') 2
10. Strip-tease. . . . . *
11. Addiction to pleasure ('foreigners are frivolous—without serenity or depth'; 'they cannot control their feelings'—i.e. they show them too openly, give way to them too much; 'their lives are showy and luxurious'). I
12. Casual behaviour ('eating nonchalantly while walking'; 'foreigners are continually chewing in the street and at work—they are chewing gum all the year round'; 'table manners are appalling'; 'they perch casually on desks, etc.') 4
13. Gangsterism, in real life and in films ('daylight bank robbery by army deserters'; gangster films a bad influence on children; 'they commit perfect crimes') 2
14. Slackness of the family bond ('it is customary for parents and children in due course to go their own separate ways: the family does not live together'; 'they do not take care of their parents, have no sense of filial duty'; 'the bond between parent and child is weak—they do not love their children much') 5
15. Materialistic outlook ('foreigners attach too much importance to money'; 'they depend too much on science and mechanical civilization'; 'they measure spiritual values in terms of material advantages') . . . I
16. Individualism, liberalism, democracy ('I should not like to imitate such things after they have been introduced into Japan in a form different from what they really are'; selfishness i.e. excessive individualism). . 2

17. Imperialism, aggressiveness (having no compunction about invading other nations' territories) . . . . (E) I

18. Communism, dictatorship ('what might, in a sense, be called the "reign of terror" in Soviet Russia and communist China'; 'the brute force and the deeds of communism'; 'all communist politics are detrimental to the nation') 5

19. Education. I

20. Christianity . . . . *

21. Others (borrowing from foreign languages; racial prejudice; Summer Time) 2

22. Excessive sense of public duty (concentration on public duty [probably in the sense of overdoing this, to the detriment of family duty]; inhumanity; 'calmly throwing things out of the windows of railway carriages, and other public conveyances') I

23. Strikes (general strikes) . . . . *

24. Internal disturbances, civil wars (revolutions; the struggle with the Chinese communists in China) . . . . *

25. No. Don't know ('we must not copy them wholesale') 53

Replies by habitat-age groups

	(E)	(1)	(2)	(3)	(4)	(5)	(6)	(7)	(8)
1. Too high esteem for women	3	2	2	5	4	2	2	3	2
2. Relations between men and women	8	2	6	8	12	2	3	7	9
3. Women's fashions	5	7	4	3	8	5	4	4	4
4. Permanent waves	1	1	0	0	1	0	*	1	3
5. Dancing	5	2	2	3	7	2	2	3	6
6. Kissing in public	6	5	3	4	8	4	3	4	7
7. Unrestricted choice in marriage (marriage between different nationalities)	*	0	1	0	1	1	*	*	*
8. Birth control	*	0	0	0.6	0	0.5	0	0.4	0
9. Divorce	2	2	4	7	1	1	2	1	1
10. Strip-tease	*	0	0	0.6	0.3	0.5	0.4	0.4	0.6
11. Addiction to pleasure	1	2.2	2.7	1.9	1.6	2.0	0.7	0.8	0.6
12. Casual behaviour	4	.8	6	7	3	6	4	4	2
13. Gangsterism	2	1.5	1.3	2.6	1.4	1.5	1.1	2.2	2.6
14. Slackness of the family bond	5	2	3	5	6	4	4	4	7
15. Materialistic outlook	1	1	2	3	1	0	0	0	1
16. Individualism, liberalism, democracy	2	1	2	1	2	1	*	*	2
17. Imperialism, aggressiveness	1	1	1	0	1	1	1	1	1
18. Communism, dictatorship	5	4	3	2	3	5	6	6	7
19. Education	1	1.5	0.6	0	1.3	0.5	0	0.4	1.2
20. Christianity	*	0	0	0.6	0	0	0.3	0	0.2
21. Others	2	1.5	0	3.9	2.1	1	2.7	0.8	0.2
22. Excessive sense of public duty	1	0.7	1.3	0.6	0.9	1.5	0.7	0.8	0.4
23. Strikes	*	0.7	0	0	0	0	0	0.4	0.5

	(E)	(1(	(2)	(3)	)4)	(5)	(6)	(7)	(8)
24. Internal troubles, civil war	*	0.7	0	0	0	1	0.7	0	0.4
25. No. I don't know. We must not imitate wholesale	53	60	59	47	43	65	63	59	51

QUESTION 21. *If you could go abroad freely now, would you like to do so?*
(a) *If so what country would you like to visit first of all?*
(b) *Why?*

	(E)	(1)	(2)	(3)	(4)	(5)	(6)	(7)	(8)
1. Yes	72	87	83	80	70	87	79	71	64
2. No	27 }	13	17	20	30	13	21	29	36
3. Don't know	1 }								
1. United States of America	48	54	50	43	45	59	53	53	46
2. Great Britain	6	8	6	11	7	8	5	3	5
3. France	8	21	21	17	7	13	11	5	4
4. Germany	3	4	3	6	3	3	1	2	2
5. U.S.S.R.	3	4	8	3	3	1	2	2	3
6. Switzerland	3	3	4	3	3	7	3	4	2
7. Italy	1	0	0	1	1	0	*	0	1
8. Sweden	0,3	0	0	1	0	1	1	*	*
9. India	1	0	1	0	1	2	*	*	1
10. Formosa	0.4	0	0	1	1	0	*	*	*
11. Manchuria	1	1	0	1	*	0	*	1	1
12. China	2	2	4	3	2	1	1	2	3
13. Korea	0.07	0	1	0	0	0	0	0	*
14. Sakhalin, Kuriles	0.07	0	0	0	0	0	*	0	*
15. Philippines	0.5	0	0	0	*	1	*	*	1
16. Australia	0.2	0	0	0	*	0	*	*	*
17. Java	0.3	1	1	1	*	0	0	1	*
18. Borneo	0.1	0	0	1	*	1	0	0	0
19. Sumatra	0.07	0	0	1	0	0	0	0	0
20. Hawaii	2	6	2	3	1	2	3	1	1
21. Brazil	2	2	2	3	2	1	*	3	1
22. Norway	0.1	0	1	0	0	0	*	0	*
23. Denmark	1	0	0	1	*	3	2	1	2
24. Netherlands	0.2	0	0	0	*	1	0	0	*
25. Argentina, Chile	0.3	0	1	1	*	0	*	0	*
26. Thailand	0.1	2	0	0	0	0	0	*	0
27. Spain, Portugal	0.07	0	1	0	*	0	0	0	0
28. Indo-China	0.2	0	0	1	*	0	0	1	*
29. Canada	0.1	0	0	0	*	1	*	*	0
30. Burma	0.1	0	0	0	0	0	1	1	0
1. High civilization	18	20	21	20	17	22	16	18	17
2. Fine country	7	11	8	7	7	11	6	7	5
3. To study the country	19	20	23	14	16	16	24	21	20
4. Sightseeing	17	26	20	20	17	25	21	14	12
5. For educational purposes	2	2	3	2	2	4	4	2	1

	(E)	(1)	(2)	(3)	(4)	(5)	(6)	(7)	(8)
6. Business, employment	2	2	1	3	2	2	1	2	1
7. Personal reasons	2	0	1	4	2	2	1	2	3
8. Links with Japan	2	3	1	5	1	2	2	0	2
9. Others	*	0	0	0	0	0	0	0	*
10. Don't know	4	5	4	6	4	5	4	4	2

QUESTION 22. *Do you think that war could be stopped by human effort or is war inevitable in the sense that it is determined by the march of history?*

	(E)	(1)	(2)	(3)	(4)	(5)	(6)	(7)	(8)
1. Avoidable	39	49	43	42	33	48	41	41	38
2. Unavoidable	52	45	54	53	59	45	45	50	52
3. Don't know	9	6	3	5	8	7	14	9	10

QUESTION 23. *With regard to public affairs, do you think that it would be better for private persons to refrain from intervening or would it be better for them to express their opinions as far as possible?*

	(E)	(1)	(2)	(3)	(4)	(5)	(6)	(7)	(8)
1. Better to express their opinions	70	81	82	78	71	76	69	65	64
2. Better not to intervene	25	14	16	18	23	21	27	30	30
3. Don't know	5	5	2	4	6	3	4	5	6

QUESTION 23 (b). *In recent years it has become a basic assumption that public affairs are the concern of everybody in the country and all have the right to discuss and criticize them from every angle, as you do when a building is being put up. How will this work out in practice? In the case of unusually complex and technical questions, do you think it is unavoidable that these should be left entirely to the authorities concerned?*

	(E)	(1)	(2)	(3)	(4)	(5)	(6)	(7)	(8)
1. Unavoidable	75	76	81	72	81	69	71	70	72
2. They should not be left to the authorities alone	25	24	19	28	19	31	29	30	28

RESPONSES TO THE PROJECTIVE TESTS USED BY SOFUE

Two examples extracted from Taka Sofue's report

EXAMPLE I. TOWN OF YAHATA (MALE)

Plate 1

'He is a workman, isn't he? He's a factory worker who has been off for the last two or three days because of illness. A girl from the same shop, with whom he is in love, has come to visit him. She appears happy to find him in better spirits than she had expected; but the man seems hesitant about letting her see his face for fear she will notice how haggard and ill he looks. He would certainly look cheerful for her if he could.'
  'How old are they?'
  'The man may be 26 or 27 and the woman about 20.'
  'Is there anything else to say about the picture?'
  'Nothing in particular.'

Plate 2

'Three labourers are at their work in the fields. It is a hot day and they were going to take a rest in the shade of the tree when their boss turned up. Two of them have hurried to greet him as they are in the habit of flattering him. The man in the shade of the tree is thinking that it is reasonable enough for them to take a rest and there is no reason to fuss because the boss has come along. The children are laughing at the two men because they are overdoing the civility and making themselves ridiculous.'
  'How old are these various people?
  'The two bowing to the boss are about 30. The one under the tree may be 25 or 26. The children are still very young.'

Plate 3

'This is a scene in the home of a poor family. The man of the house has lost his wife. He is at work in a factory and his old mother, at her needlework, is wondering when he will get home. The children are the man's sons. They have been brought up by their grandmother and are the hope of her old age. They are lonely children because they have no mother; however, the children of the neighbourhood are their friends and they also console each other. I should say their grandmother has been a mother to them all their lives. She seems to have suffered much. At present she is so worried about her son not coming home that she has no heart for her sewing. The children are looking at her and wondering what it is all about.'

'How old is the old woman?'

'About 60.'

'How about her son?'

'Possibly 27 or 28.'

'What did his wife die of?'

'I should say an illness of some kind. She died two or three years ago. Anyhow this is a gloomy picture, isn't it?'

Plate 4

'I should say that what this picture was about was what we call the superiority of men over women. I think the people are the master of the house, his wife and their children. The man's view is that as he is the family breadwinner he deserves to be treated as such. The wife finds her life humiliating but reluctantly submits to her husband's authority. The husband makes it a rule to dine sumptuously, but the wife and children have to be contented with a simple diet. I can see the difference in the picture. Because of the father's overbearing attitude the children don't seem to like him much. But they love their mother, don't they?'

'How old are the various people?'

'I think the husband is 40 or so and his wife 35 or 36.'

Plate 5

'This looks to me like a picture of a scene in a railway station with a conscript being seen off in wartime. I think it probably is wartime, don't you? I think I am right in guessing that the two men in the foreground are related in some way to the soldier going to the front. I should say that in spite of the war they are progressives and they are undoubtedly very sorry to see him leave. They find the sight and sound of the excited crowd shouting nonsense heart-rending, and are sorry for them because they don't realize the truth and are going out of their way to give him a cheerful send off. We must never repeat such folly, but must resist with all our might—that's all. You know it's awfully hard to say all one feels.'

'How old are the two men?'

'They are both about 30.'

Plate 6

'Yes, this is another horrible wartime scene. It makes you shiver! [Subject picks up the plate and looks closely at it.] The photograph is not very clear, but I think this man is General Tojo and I feel I have seen the one who looks like a platoon or company commander before. Boys like him have been brought up to believe blindly in the military spirit and have been warped by their education. In other words the platoon or company commander is a dupe. Tojo

PLATES

Plate I

Plate 2

Plate 3

Plate 4

Plate 5

Plate 6

Plate 7

Plate 8

Plate 9

Plate 10

on his horse looks as though the only thing that interested him was his own position and distinctions.'

Plate 7

'This shows the send-off of a special attack flight. These three men also look sad. It must strike them as tragic that they should be in a position in which death is inevitable. They are thinking of their families, mother, brothers, sisters. I fancy the man in the background on the right is saying a few words of praise which he does not mean and that his real ideas are entirely selfish. All three fliers are young lads straight from school.'

Plate 8

'Prime Minister Yoshida is saying: "We leave everything to America". He intends to commit Japan's future to the United States of America. He is smiling as he shakes hands but Japan seems to be running headlong into difficulties. After all, with a cabinet as reactionary as the papers and wireless show that Yoshida's is, I think this handshake may be profoundly significant. I can only think that he is proposing to reduce Japan to a colony.'

Plate 9

With a sneer: 'Our precious Emperor is showing himself to the crowd. A lot of old grannies who will never get out of the old ways are doing reverence to him as the Living God. The children in the foreground have the conventional attitude to him but those in the background seem to have a grudge against him for the death in battle of their fathers or brothers.'
    'How old are the women?'
    'Perhaps between 45 and 50.'
    'How old is this boy?'
    'I should say about junior secondary school age.'

Plate 10

This shows trade unionists on strike. Although the maintenance of minimum standards of living is guaranteed under the Constitution, the men can hardly live and have come out on strike, which is the only way workers can fight for their rights. The police have turned up to coerce them.
    It's quite clear from the picture that the police are following the line laid down by officialdom and against the spirit of the times. My view is that democratic police cannot beat people or push them about like this. Though the workers are fighting to enforce legitimate claims of their own, the police take it for granted that they are acting on Communist instigation.'

EXAMPLE II. F. VILLAGE (PEASANT WOMAN)

Plate 1

'Let's see: what's it all about? [A long pause] Well, I think they are husband and wife and have had a quarrel. The picture shows that they live in separate rooms and the woman seems to have just come in to the room without making any noise.'
　'How old are they?'
　'The man is about 27 or 28 and the woman 24 or 25.'
　'What did they quarrel about?'
　'Well, . . . I can't say.'

Plate 2

'It looks to me as though some great man has turned up unexpectedly. The people are surprised to see him but are bowing politely. The man under the trees doesn't seem to know what is going on.'
　'Who do you think the great man is?'
　'Well, I can't see clearly, but it's pretty certain that he is the Emperor.'
　'How old are the men bowing and the man under the trees?'
　'The two men bowing are probably about 40. The man under the trees is about 20. That's all.'

Plate 3

'It seems to be a picture of an old woman sewing in a room. I should say the two children are brother and sister and her grandchildren. They are going to play some prank on her aren't they? She may be looking out of the window. [Subject looks closely at the picture for some time.] No that's wrong: the children are looking out of the window in surprise. The grandmother, too, is surprised at what she sees outside. I suppose something has happened out of doors.'
　'What do you mean by "something"?'
　'Well I can't say.'
　'How old is the old woman?'
　'About 70.'

Plate 4

'I think the man is the father. He is at supper and is taking a drink to refresh himself after his day's work. His wife wants to give him nice food to make him feel less tired. The children also hope their father will get a good dinner. The atmosphere in which they are having supper strikes me as friendly and relaxed.'
　'How old are the parents?'
　'The father is about 50 and the mother about 30.'

Plate 5

'This is a picture of a conscript leaving home. People round him are waving flags, and are glad that he is going to the front to fight for his country. A big crowd has come to see him off. Some of them may be sad to think that he is going, but the man will go off bravely to offer his life for his country, since he has so many well-wishers.'

'What are the two men on this side? What do they feel? Tell me what you think about them.'

'Let me see: as they are standing apart from the rest they can't be related to the conscript. They are looking on cheerfully, thinking that they will be seen off in the same way if they are ever drafted.'

'How old are the two?'

'They are young, perhaps 20 or so. The scene reminds me of past days.'

Plate 6

'A picture which reminds me of wartime. This man may be someone distinguished. There are many soldiers and he seems to be keeping his eyes on them. I am not against smartness and activity like that. [Stammers a little] The soldiers are standing too stiffly.'

'Who's the man on horseback? The photograph is not very clear. Look at him. Who do you think he is?'

[Subject looks intently at the photograph and thinks awhile.] 'I can't really say. Is it Mr. Yoshida? I can't identify him at once, though he seems to be a commander. If so, the man with his back towards the commander, making the soldiers stand in a straight line, must be a company commander.'

'Well what are they all thinking? Tell me anything that comes into your mind.'

'Let me see. The soldiers are keyed up. They feel that since they have been selected for the army they should do their best to defend Japan. The commander seems very glad to see his men. The man straightening the line is trying as hard as he can. I have nothing else particular to say.'

Plate 7

'An inspiring scene: a special attack flight is about to take off. The men are drinking a glass of wine, thinking to themselves that it is a farewell drink before they die. Their last wish is to do their duty to Japan by smashing as many enemy ships as possible. I think they are all just over 20.'

'Who is the man over on the right?'

'The commander.'

'What is he thinking?'

'Well, he is hoping that the men will go into action in high spirits, and that they will succeed in ramming the enemy warships. I've nothing more to say.'

Plate 8

'General MacArthur and Mr. Yoshida have been talking something over for a while and are glad to find that they hold the same views about Japan's future. Both are peace-lovers, concerned for democracy in Japan. But I cannot understand why General MacArthur still looks so serious. Oh yes, no doubt it is a picture of MacArthur leaving for America. He is going reluctantly and is anxious about Japan. Mr. Yoshida is trying to comfort him, saying: "Don't trouble about things here after you are gone".'

'You say they have been talking together. What about? Will you give me an example?'

'Well I can't say.'

'Anything that comes into your mind will do.'

[Subject thinks and hesitates.] 'I can't think of anything in particular, though they will have been talking about democratizing Japan thoroughly.'

Plate 9

'The man is our present Emperor, isn't he? I should say it was a post-war scene. The people are watching him pass and have resolved, by working together, to make Japan much better than before, in spite of her defeat. The people in the bottom half of the picture look angry. I should say they have a grudge against the Emperor for Japan's defeat. The Emperor looks modest with his hat in his hand, doesn't he?'

'How old are the women in the top part of the picture?'

'I should say about 50. No, they may be younger—perhaps 30 or so.'

'What about the men in the lower part of the picture?'

'They are 27 or 28 or maybe younger. They may be children, though I am not sure.'

Plate 10

'Are they working men? It looks like a riot. They are workmen from a company on strike and the police have appeared. The men are asking for a rise in their basic wage, or something of the sort. But the position of the company employing them makes it impossible for it to agree, and their demand has been rejected. So they have gone on strike because they cannot work for such low wages. I think they would have done better not to have taken such action.'

'Tell me what the policemen think about it.'

'They are asking the labourers to calm down and not make trouble. They wish they were rather less aggressive. No special comment about the picture.'

AUTOBIOGRAPHIES OF THE FUTURE

Students at Sapporo

HARUKO KINOSHITA[1]

Up till now I never thought of making plans for my life during the next 50 years—besides, it is a peculiar question—therefore I am now suddenly making plans for my life in my mind and making them at short notice, so they will not be very hard and fast.

I am a girl aged 22 [= 21] and I graduated from high school two years ago. As to my future, I can think about it in two ways. First, there is the way I have always wanted ever since I was a child—to devote my life to helping small children, not only for the sake of experience but because I love them. Second, I might marry and lead a domestic life.

As for institutions which provide help for small children, there are kindergartens, primary schools, day nurseries, orphanages, infant hospitals and so on; but I would especially like to work in an establishment like a day nursery, to which working mothers bring their children—thus I would help the children and indirectly, the grown-ups as well. To achieve this I need a special type of education (so-called dry nurse training) for two years in preparation for the task, and must at the same time secure the necessary qualifications and basic knowledge. I shall be on duty in day nurseries in places where working women are comparatively numerous—factory zones, farming villages and mountain villages. In those places the equipment is still inadequate; the institutions are poor and only just large enough to accommodate children, and there are only one or two really capable teachers. I, who have no ability for management shall first work there as an assistant for three years.

Of course, the first task will be the training of the children's character; but, as children develop their own lives, I want to establish some system for stimulating their creative imagination and to prepare them to live entirely free lives.

My idea is that a day nursery shall be not merely a place where children play with their teachers and receive education, but a place where they lay the foundations for a good life. I shall ask the administrative authorities to help me improve the equipment and ensure that it shall be clean and efficient.

When I am 27 I shall go abroad for three years to undertake further studies either in England, where social institutions are so well developed, or in Europe generally. My work there will be not only theoretical, through observation, but also practical and I shall be able to exchange knowledge and experience.

---

1. All names are, of course, fictitious.

On my return to Japan I shall go to different regions, each time for a period of three years—not as an assistant, but making my own plans and trying to put them into practice. Working in each day nursery for three years, I shall have experience in three places. In each place I shall compile data about the administrative and educational methods, the results of the teaching, etc., in the form of biographies of the children.

By that time I shall be nearly 40; I shall establish an educational institute, on lines which my own experience tells me are the best.

For the next 10 years I shall continue this work. When I am 50, I shall hand over my task to the younger generation, and act as an adviser, being called 'grandmother' by the children.

When I am 54 years old, it will be 1984; I don't know how society and the world will have changed by then, but my work will never be finished, as working women and children will always exist.

Although I would like to finish my life at the age of 50, unfortunately I might live on. After I am 60, I'd like to live in a home for old people (a very comfortable one) and write some memoirs of a dry nurse's life; then my existence will be finished.

Now I will speak about the second way. I have not so far spoken of marriage —not because I intend to be a spinster, but because my work comes before all else. I should like to marry someone who, despite his interest in his own work, would be interested in my work too and would constantly advise me. Thus I should follow the two paths at the same time and that is why I did not deal with my married life in the first place.

During the next few years I shall have many opportunities of thinking about marriage or talking about love and marriage with girls and men. I shall get married either between 23 and 25 or much later. I cannot say clearly how my marriage will come about. It may sound strange—it will not be because of love or by marriage arrangement, but when I find a man in my environment of the type described above I shall ask my parents' advice. I shall marry after a good period of engagement. If I cannot find such an opportunity, I shall meet someone introduced by my parents, but I shall take the decision myself.

If I marry then, say, at the age of 24, my husband will be a Christian. We shall take as our motto in life—'to try to build a Christian home like the one we were brought up in'. Every two years I shall have a baby, and we shall have four children altogether. I should like to have six children, but we shall have to think of our social and economic position. So I shall have two boys and two girls, and we will do our best to create an atmosphere in which our children can develop their personalities. They could choose their own way of life, as I did myself. From our standpoint of father and mother we shall try to make our children happy, so that they have a pleasant youth, loving each other and living in their own way. After five years of planning we shall build our own house. Then I shall devote myself to domestic life, but at the same time, take part in the work of women's organizations, or in meetings generally. In that way I want to show my interest in, and express my opinions about, the development of children and of myself. But I shall not take part in social life in the narrower sense. When I am 40 my life will be greatly changed, because my husband will have died. I shall then have to bring up my children myself. I shall become a secondary school teacher or, like my cousin, devote myself to social work. I shall have to think of my salary then, because I shall be working for that.

If my children want to go to a university I shall encourage them, and I shall continue to work until I am 50. Once my children are independent, I would like to enter a Christian home for old people and become a good friend to women who have difficulties in their spiritual lives.

One of my children will be a teacher, another a diplomat, the third will marry and found a good household, and the fourth will be a scientist; they all will have faith in their own lives.

In 2002 I shall finish my 72 years of life, happy in the feeling that I have done my best as a housewife, a mother and a human being, despite the sad fact that my husband died so early.

YOSHINOSUKE SATÔ

1952: 20 years old, student in the Faculty of Arts, Hokkaido University.

1962: 30 years old; residence, Tokyo; office, Ministry of Labour; family, 5 persons.

At the age of 22 I shall graduate from the university; I shall then enter the hall of graduate studies and make a special study of sociology. I am in fact interested in journalistic sociology and population sociology. Because of my poor talents as a linguist, I am always toiling hard. As I hold extremely realistic views as regards womanhood and marriage, I have no experience in love.

At the age of 24 I shall graduate from the hall of graduate studies, and by recommendation of the professors I shall obtain a position in the Ministry of Labour.

In pursuance of my long cherished desire to go abroad, I shall take an examination for students who are candidates for study abroad; but I shall fail.

Both in the free and in the Communist countries, the development of industries using atomic energy is spurred on; the world is facing a critical situation.

At the age of 25, the problem of love arises. My partner is an office girl working in the same section. She has a round face and is 5 *shaku*, 2 *sun* and 5 *bu* (about 1.57 m.) tall. She is lively and has talent for music and dancing. At 23 she is at her best. Her mother and relatives, however, object to our free relations, and a *miai* (formal confrontation with a view to marriage) is arranged. The reason is that the girl was born in the same region as myself, and is an accomplished young lady who has attended college. In the same year (1957) there is a report that Stalin seems to be ill; but as this is reported so often, the world is not very much surprised. In America, the Republican Party gradually strengthens in power.

Twenty-six years old. I marry the girl mentioned above, in the traditional way. Japan's population surplus becomes ever greater, and the country now has nearly 100 million inhabitants.

Suddenly Stalin dies. The cause of his death is a special kind of heart desease in an acute form. As a result of this, insurrections break out in the U.S.S.R.

The countries of Eastern Europe seize the opportunity, and escape from Soviet pressure; insurrections occur; in Eastern Germany and Czechoslovakia, liberal governments are already established.

Thus, at the time when I am 30 years old, Stalin's successor can do nothing but ward off an internal collapse by instituting a reign of terror which is even worse than the previous one. The fact that the countries of Eastern Europe join the free countries of the world alters the balance between the two camps, Democracy and Communism. Simultaneously, in all countries the Communist Parties are becoming less active.

We already have one son and one daughter; and relations between my wife and myself are very good. I have become accustomed to my work in the office. In the evening, I and the whole family enjoy looking at the TV after dinner.

1972: 40 years old. I have been promoted head of section. In material respects I am also blessed. My family consists of my wife, three sons and one daughter—six persons in all. In Japan, Shôwa Tennô has passed away, and it is the era of Emperor Ginin (Righteousness-Benevolence). In Russia an internal revolution has occurred; the people who have suffered during the Stalin period when Communism was in full swing have, under the banners of democracy, established a government with modified capitalist tendencies. The former Russian Communist leaders have for the most part sought refuge in Communist China. In the southern part of Africa and in the Middle East all 'colonial' territories have become fully independent and freed themselves from the rule of such countries as England, France and the Netherlands; under United Nations supervision they have all taken their first steps forward in their new life, for the establishment of a free and peaceful world.

Here in Japan the nation has acquired much greater powers of organization than before.

Flights to the moon by rocket, which have been planned for several years now, have at last succeeded. It had already been claimed that rockets without a crew had reached the moon world. The discharge designs of these rockets have been sent from America, by television, to all countries of the world; furthermore, the form of the globe as seen from the extremities of the earth's sphere of gravity has now been photographed in natural colour television, and has amazed the peoples. There are reports that flights of rockets to the moon complete with crew have been planned, and that eminent scientists from all countries have assembled in America and are studying this project.

These last years there have been quarrels between myself and my wife, because I am much occupied with my work and often stay away from home; consequently I am very seldom in the household, which does not seem to be good for my children.

These, of whom the eldest is 13 years old, are all now at school; their marks are not surprisingly good, simply average.

1982: 50 years old. My health is none too good—maybe owing to excessive drinking? I have a feeling of weakness in my bones. I have four sons and two daughters. Originally I thought that three sons and two daughters would be enough, but as I grew older I realized that it would be better to have more children. My eldest daughter is married, and I have two grandchildren.

In the office I have—thanks to my own character—few enemies, so relations with my colleagues and others (superiors and inferiors) are very smooth. The critical period in the relations with my wife has also passed, and there are no more difficulties.

Japan has not escaped the effects of the recent world-wide disturbance in sexual morality, so that we, as parents of adolescent children, are very much worried about their future.

In these last 10 years the people of Communist China have gradually become discontented with their government. After an unsuccessful attack upon the Nationalist Army in Formosa, the Communists lack the strength to recover and are in process of collapse. A new government has now been established in Nanking with the aid of the Nationalist Army. The disastrous end of Communist China has been accelerated by the general situation throughout the world. There is no single country which could now be called Communist; at the same time, hardly any imperialist countries are to be found. The progress in methods of transport is formidable and, thanks especially to the utilization of atomic energy, the world has become exceedingly small. School attendance has risen, and standards of learning and knowledge have everywhere become higher.

1992: Sixty years old. At the end of this year I am supposed to retire from the office, but personally I'd like to continue work. My children have all grown up; as a doctor, musician, official, etc. they have all made good use of their individual talents. I have about ten grandchildren. I am living with my eldest son, his wife, his two children, my old wife and my own last child—a household of seven persons.

Thanks to the progress in medicine, the death-rate has declined and, in general, there is a striking tendency towards longevity. Radical methods of treating diseases which have long afflicted mankind have recently been discovered, and this is a source of great hope for the whole world. Despite the great progress of medical science, however, when I think of my own body I am more and more aware of the decline in my physical strength, and somehow I have the feeling that a sense of loneliness is tormenting my brain. Particularly when I think of the time of my youth, when I recall the springtime of my life to which I shall never return, I cannot help feeling in my brain the loneliness of human life and the transitory nature of all things. My greatest pleasure is in the growing up of my children and grandchildren.

The world is already escaping from the inconsistencies of capitalism and is progressing in a Socialist direction; these changes have begun on a world-wide scale.

2002: 70 years old. I retired from my office about ten years ago. Day after day I read books, and my companions are the plants and small birds. The world, which two years ago passed from the twentieth into the twenty-first century, has changed enormously. In the year 2000 the world held celebrations in which all countries took part, the people shouting: 'Long live mankind!' I, too, felt extremely happy that I could witness this historical event. On entering the twenty-first century, people have started to think about a language common to all the world, and it is reported that this idea will soon be translated into fact. Movements for the establishment of a 'world government' are active; such a government, with the United Nations as its core, will abolish racial prejudice, class distinctions and similar relics of the past. It is the hope of mankind, the more so since it is thought that the problem of surplus population, which has exercised the world ever since the nineteenth century, cannot be solved without a world government. All countries are exerting themselves for the happiness of mankind; nearly all of them are following the principles of Socialism. Monarchies now exist in only five or six countries, including Japan and England.

Someone like myself, who has had such wretched experiences as the burning down of his home in World War II, has now, about 60 years later, an unchanged feeling of hatred for war. Even though one tells the young people of today about World War II, they seem unable to understand it; but that, I suppose, is natural, as it is more than thirty, indeed nearly forty, years since wars ceased to exist in this world. At present, the stories of that time are just tales, nothing more. Every time I meet young people who are so sanguine in their expectations of life, I draw a comparison with the period in which I was born, and am amazed at the change.

How many years more shall I live? Every extra minute is like a gift, I think, but my mind is at present entirely at peace. I am ready to be called to Heaven at any moment and at any place. I have no special hopes for this particular year; but if it were possible I should like to become 20 years old again, and look at the world for the next fifty years with my present eyes.

MINORU ÔTANI

Wenn Morgen nun Heute wird, alles ist nach wie vor.

The passage of one day in the calendar does not seem to bring any great change, but, if we consider an interval of one year, it seems possible to look into the future. As I think, however, that such an attempt will be much influenced by my state of health, I shall try to record the autobiography of my future in relation to my illness. Nevertheless, my illness will not weaken my will, or curb my thoughts as products of a free spirit.

The people at home are expecting my graduation next year. I become a teacher at a high school in some mining town. My new duties take me daily to and from the school and my rented room in an attic. The lessons allotted to me are 'history and social thought' and economics, and in the evenings I study the theories of revolution with my students and the miners. Marx, Lenin, Stalin and Mao Tse Tung become our comrades. Days illuminated by the sun of progress follow one another. But after two years my illness, which has given little trouble for some time, takes a sudden turn for the worse. I am sent to a sanatorium. My 'plastic surgery' lung has been contracting fast. In the struggle with my illness I seek self-confidence, since, while it is a time for retrospection into the past, it is also a time for speculation as regards the future. At this time, too, I discover that I am drawn towards a comrade of the opposite sex by ties stronger than purely comradely ones. I marry this girl after two years of sanatorium life. I am then 30 years old.

The great event of my marriage is accompanied by other factors implying, for me, radical changes; movements in the development of history. It has been proved historically that the cold war of 1952 was the last 'pawing' of capitalism. Europe has been progressing along the road to socialism; the peoples of Asia have, out of the colonial struggles, discovered the way to socialism. In America, which stood isolated on the globe, the revolutionary forces have also been steadily growing.

It is 1957. Japan, America's colony, has at last realized that she has fallen behind the rest of Asia in the race for progress. My duty, in view of these historical events, is to form broad unions of workers and peasants, For literary activities, lectures and meetings I must again mingle with the masses. I anticipate a 'revolution by peace'.

In 1958 I have become a father. Without knowing why, I form the idea that I want to make my child into a musician. Wiping the dust from it, I take out the music for the violin which I played in my student days. . . . With a strong feeling that 'he should avoid the charm of the Romance in F. Major,'[1] I set this music aside for my child. I myself am grappling with the classics of Marxism again in connexion with the theoretical development of socialist economic science.

In the summer of 1959, in a troubled situation, the revolution suddenly breaks out. A people's army has succeeded in building itself up, and, with the soldiers of the regular army who changed sides, has achieved the revolution at a single stroke. In the following January a people's government is established. The liberated masses celebrate this event with much rejoicing.

While I am glad that there have been but few victims of the revolution, I celebrate with my wife the fact that I have become the father of a second child in that same year, 1960. But, with the coming of spring, my health deteriorates again. The part I took in the revolutionary struggle made me believe strongly in 'supplementing the flesh with the spirit', but this process has certainly not been of long duration. Sanatorium life has been resumed. It is as if I can only here, in the sanatorium, find days of rest, and only here take pleasure in the growing-up of my children. This life is to continue for three years.

In 1964 I become a father again. A free society has, in every respect, been achieved. We can talk with each other freely; there is also freedom of publication. Economic and legal freedom have been promised for the future. I had decided that my duty as a teacher called upon me to engage in social education, but the improvement in my health is not long sustained.

I want to make artists of my children; one must become a violinist, the other a painter. In my own life, thirst for beauty has taken the form of the pursuit of social harmony. My children will probably express that harmony in music and painting. This was something for which the people of the earlier period suffered, and it had to be achieved even at the risk of our lives.

The sounds of the hammers, with the establishment of socialist society in 1966, becomes my funeral march. I am expecting to 'live on' forever in the future life of my wife and children.

According to the announcement of the concert held in 1979 in commemoration of the twentieth year of the revolution, my child has received the prize of honour for his composition and violin playing. There was unity in his work,

---

1. A literary quotation.

despite the complicated expression; even the *fortissimo* passages contained beautiful melodies; and in his loud wailings there was harmony. It reminded me of the songs I once sang in the midst of suffering; it also gave expression to the wailing of the masses. In my grave I was absorbed in contented listening to his music. I was also delighted to discover the same features in the paintings of my second child, shown at the exhibition of paintings in the same year.

With the completion of the fifth five-year plan in 1984, private ownership of land entirely vanished from Japan. Mechanization has been achieved in all branches of agriculture and industry.

Unemployment caused by machines has become a thing of the past, incomprehensible to the younger generation. Electrification enterprises have rendered possible a cultured life for the masses. A five-hour working day is increasing the resources of individual existence.

In 1994, Socialist society is gradually evolving towards Communist society; with the completion of the seventh five-year plan, the theory of value in production and consumption has been finally discarded, and a completely free society has been established. 'Man as the master of history' has become a fact, within the lifetime of my children. The first page in a new history of mankind has been turned.

In 2002, the joy of labour and the freedom of virtually unlimited consumption have created 'paradise on earth'. 'War' has been deleted from the dictionaries, and all the people of the earth are free from materialistic fetters.

YOSHISABURŌ HIROTA

I have been asked to write my autobiography for the next 50 years, but the more I think of it the more difficult it becomes to express my thoughts. Not to mention the changes in the world situation which certainly will be most marked, I shall, as a member of a certain family, undoubtedly be affected in my life by certain transformations. Further, we don't know what natural calamities will overtake us today or tomorrow. Particularly in a small country like Japan, where so many people live, individual lives will be much affected by change. Therefore I will start to write my autobiography honestly, assuming that the material situation so far as I am concerned will not alter during the next 50 years.

I take 1952 as my starting point. I shall finish my university studies in 1953. In a certain sense I might say that that year will be a decisive one in my life. At present my parents are in good health, so I would like to continue my studies for some years more. As I said before, when I think of 1954, 1955 and 1956, I cannot envisage what my future will be, since I cannot believe that the material situation will never change. The fate of human beings is always conditioned by some struggle.

After 10 years, in 1962, I may have found some way to my future; and after another 10 years, in 1972, when I am 40, I might perhaps find some meaning in human life.

When I am 50, in 1982, I shall cling to my dreams about my children and be interested in their development, as parents are; and I shall start to think about having a quiet and peaceful existence. during the last part of my life, in the country. I could imagine, too, that I would devote myself to my work without thinking about my children and my rest.

When I am 60, I shall, during the next 10 years, have no cause for any dreams about my future. I shall look, sentimentally, back on my past. Fifty years from now I shall be simply on old man waiting for death, living on day by day without anything happening. Still, I should like to work on, with a passion that will be always alight.

I have forced myself to set down, in this way, my autobiography for the next 50 years. I cannot think of anything else to say. I myself am surprised— the next 50 years of my life have no sense, but I cannot work up an interest in my future in the same way as others of my generation do.

I don't know whether this report will meet your expectations, but I hope it will.

TOSHIO NISHIMURA

March 1952: While I am studying in the Sociological Department of the Faculty of Arts, Hokkaido University, my home is in Tokyo and I have a job in Tokyo too. I am helping in the economic division of a trading company which was established by my family. In the university vacations, I have to go back to Tokyo and to my work. At present I am working and studying at the same time.

In March 1954 I shall finish my university life and have a post in some press enterprise. By that time my family's trading company will be firmly established. I shall devote some of my time to advising on the accountancy of my family's company. Meanwhile, in 1952, the Korean conflict will have been settled by a treaty, but in French Indo-China Red China is helping the army of Ho Chi Minh. As the Communist forces become stronger, the United Nations will mediate between them and the French at the request of the French Government. The United Nations will fail and cannot but recognize Ho Chi Minh's army and the territories occupied by it. Japan, having regained her independence, will return to her former status by rearming. A large part of the Japanese population will complain about the government's diplomacy and its autocratic policy. This resistance will be supported not only by the Leftists, but by the Liberal Party. In the election of 1953 the Liberal Party will, unexpectedly, obtain many seats in the Diet and form the Cabinet again; but they cannot, as before, obtain most of the seats, and the political situation will be disturbed.

The rearmament policy will fail in face of the peace policy of the U.S.S.R. The future for American capital will be dark, as it will be unable to find channels of investment to replace the armament industries. American help to underdeveloped areas will 'lose caste' in face of the people's supreme movement for independence. The capitalist countries can no longer reconcile the inconsistency between their social service policy and their negative financial policy. There can be no doubt that the socialists will exploit these troubles for the purpose of the class struggle and will lead the way to planned economic policy and positive democracy. Internationally, they (the socialists) will sweep away the dust of imperialism, and should bring about harmony in international trade between all countries—a harmony based on the equality of men. Or should we choose war? I, personally, want to believe in the intelligence of men.

In 1954 the Soviet Union will do away with her revolutionary principles and find a way to a rapprochement between the United States of America and themselves; that, at least, is my hope.

In 1954, too, we shall construct collective residences for the entire family; I shall move there, and leave the administration of my work to someone else. In November of the same year, at the age of 27, I shall marry.

In April 1956 a baby (boy) will be born. In the autumn of the same year the draft of my Theory of the Economic System will be completed, but I have no intention of publishing it; it is a work in which I shall assemble my personal ideas.

In December 1957 my second son will be born.

In June 1959 a daughter will be born. Thus I shall be the father of two sons and one daughter. I am opposed to the use of birth control methods; I simply observe temperance in sexual matters.

In 1960 my Sociological Observations on Economic Phenomena (draft) will be completed.

1962: It is peace. Under planned economy, the world has become three times wealthier than it is now. Nevertheless, free economy is not entirely ruled out. National economy and individual economy reflect the different methods of planned economy and free economy, but they are preserved on the same plane. Deep down within each person the free *homo economi* will always remain, and individual desires for self-preservation will conflict with the trend towards management of the people as a whole, which is rooted in the principle of men's equality and of equal justice for all. Complete harmony between the 'self' as a member of society and the individual 'self' has not yet been attained. A revolution can compel an individual to obey the whole, but I don't like it. Proceed slowly! Social life should be reformed in a rational way, account being taken of facts, possibilities, and human nature.

Internationally, the barriers between the States have not yet been removed entirely. Tendencies toward 'cliques' still persist. There are still more capitalist elements in international than in national economy.

In 1962 I am 33 years old. I am very busy with the press company and my wife, looking after our children of 6, 5 and 3, will be waiting for me till late in the evening. She therefore spends some of her time at the next house where my parents, with my brother and his wife, are living. Nevertheless, I believe that my home is peaceful. When we have finished dinner early, my wife sings some nursery songs for the children. The eldest one sings with her, while the others listen contentedly. I smoke a cigarette, sitting in a chair beside them. Sometimes I draw pictures for the children, or work in my study. After the children have gone to bed, my wife will read some book beside me, or knit for the children. On holidays I take the children to the moors or to the river. At home I may scold them sometimes, teaching them the difference between right and wrong, but then on holiday I take them into the fresh air and let them play as much as they want with me and my wife; both of us are enjoying the spring of our life.

In 1962 the Japanese planned economy might be deadlocked. With her poor resources Japan will face an uneasy situation. What she needs is the resources of Manchuria. It is irrational that a certain State should occupy certain regions as colonies. Originally colonies were acquired by waging war upon the native population. What should a small country, over-populated and short of resources, do? Wage war?

The way to avoid war is to abolish national borders and open up new territory. Having this feeling, I shall perhaps enter active politics.

In 1963, if it is possible, I shall go to Germany to study, and after that to Moscow, Paris, London, Rome, the Near East, and India; I shall observe the feelings of the people of every country, from a sociological and historical standpoint.

In 1965 the draft of my Theory of World Government will be complete. In the meantime, immigration restrictions will be abolished and, at government expense, large numbers of emigrants will go to South America, Australia, the United States of America, China, and South-East Asia.

In 1972 the economic scene will have changed. Completely free economy will be the rule in the distribution process; in the production process, economists everywhere will be discussing projects for raising the living standards of all peoples. One will have to conform with the decisions of the economic conference at which the economists will express their views. Everyone will have to bow to the general opinion. Even labourers may attend such meetings and have a share in the national economy. Nobody will be compelled, however, to do heavy labour. Every person will be free to choose his own occupation, according to his ability. Only one thing will be prohibited—the interference of private profit with public profit. The international economic conference (or council) will plan measures for each country, according to the latter's resources and circumstances.

In 1972 I am 43 years old. My eldest child is 16. I treat him like a grown-up man. Nevertheless, I am still responsible for protecting him, so we will discuss the question of what a human being should be. I like to encourage my children to be accomplished in music and painting. My idea is that children can best start with such things when they are 7 or 8 years old, because they can then find happiness by consoling themselves, in difficult times, by the expression of their feelings in art.

I cannot think that in 1972 our social life will have become an ideal one, despite external conditions. The most important thing for mankind is spiritual, not political or economic, life. Politics and economics create certain conditions for spiritual life; and wealth and leisure bring with them the danger of leading people to indulge in enjoyment.

Even in 1972, the 1940 existentialism of Kierkegaard, Heidegger, Jaspers and others may continue to exist; people will not make God and the world belong to them. Sexual intercourse will take place without any sense of guilt; possibly people will control it 'rationalistically', but they will forget to restrain it in a spiritual way.

I would like sometimes to invite my children's friends to come, and talk with them about many things. I would like to explain to them the character of young men and young women who are growing up, and their relation to nature. When my children have attained the age of 18, they are completely independent. They have their own life, and stand on an equal footing with me. I have to regard them as 'personalities', rather than from the standpoint of a father.

If I am frank with them, they will not mind my faults. Human life has several stages, so that a fault or defect may improve one's personality sometimes. But if they think that life consists of nothing but personal enjoyment, I certainly aim to give them advice. Anyhow, I like to have good children. If they are not good, I shall be desperate.

1982: My eldest child has entered social life. My daughter is married. As a father I shall feel somewhat lonesome, because my responsibilities are at an end. I shall, however, continue to work with my children. I have to work in a practical way for the nation and the world.

Nations should not be sovereign, as they used to be. Sovereignty should belong to the world government. National frontiers should not exist, for they cause people to wage wars.

In 1982, world government might be established completely. Meanwhile, I shall write essays on the 'spirit of man'; the development of the spirit of man goes hand in hand with political and economic development. After I am 60, I don't want to work in society any longer, but shall like to observe society. I shall write stories, for children, mysterious and very beautiful.

2002: 73 years old. I shall live in a small house beside a mountain lake, waiting for death, which will come soon.

The whole world has become one nation. People will explore the moon and discover what it is really like. Transportation to Mars may still be impossible, but it is the heavenly bodies that are of most interest to people.

While watching a TV broadcast of classical Russian dances from the U.S.S.R., I look back at the past. The history of mankind has gone through many dangerous stages. Human beings have their limitations, and are stupid. They know what material things are, but they don't know anything about life. There are no living things on the moon; but I know that something is living on it, as a spirit. From here I can go to meet that spirit. Perhaps I shall go to Mars too. If the soul of human beings were not polluted, one could go anywhere. Although I shall no longer be bound by material civilization, I shall be on this world from time to time, to watch the life of my grandchildren.

Limited human beings, *sayônara* (farewell)!

As I loved mankind, I shall die peacefully.

SHIGEO MATSUDA

1952: I am studying sociology as a student in the Department of Philosophy, Faculty of Arts, Hokkaido University. I shall take, as a subject for my graduation thesis, a study of the co-operative associations in the Japanese farming villages. The reason for this is as follows: In practice the democratization of Japan is very behindhand, and the Japanese farming villages are repositories of the feudalistic dust of Japan's backwardness. The post-war land reform and the democratization of the farming village were only partial. Thus, even though the farming villages are at present modernized and 'capitalistic', the relations between the landowner and the tenant, between the rich and the poor farmer, are the same as they were in the Middle Ages. The special features of capitalist society are to be seen in the process. The suffering and the aspirations of the poor farmers who form the lowest class of this society (these feelings are similar to those of the labouring class under the capitalist system) can only be dealt with in a positive sense if these farmers form co-operative associations in a logical way, based on economic science. Such associations must then play their rightful part. What is the position of existing co-operative associations in Japan? What are their traditions? What are their special features? What have the poor farmers at present to hope for from these co-operative associations? Sociology is the only practical means of dealing with them.

I shall therefore visit two or three farming villages this summer, and make a survey of the situation. I shall not overlook the smallest detail, in the hope that the poor farmers will take control of the associations and that these will become the cultural centres of the villages.

At that time I shall withdraw from the students' newspaper group, as I have to work for my thesis and know that it is impossible to do two things at the same time: studying, and engaging in cultural activities. For three years I have been editing the student newspaper, but the reaction against this paper (which is called *Heiwa wo sakebu*—'We call for peace') will now become progressively stronger.

Even if the paper is suppressed entirely, I shall continue to cry: 'Why is it wrong to call for peace?' 'Where is freedom of speech?' and 'Defend the independence of the schools!'

The problem is rooted in the promotion of rearmament by the Yoshida Cabinet, which is abolishing every element of democracy in Japan. Once more they will send youths to the battlefield!

If the rearmament plans were based on public opinion, there would be no reason for the government to promote them so strongly; if the greater part of the people really wanted rearmament, it would be no problem at all.

Personally I am opposed to rearmament, but I object still more to a government which, illogically and undemocratically, is promoting it. The age in which non-politically minded people were called 'excellent' is past. The raising of our daily life to a higher level has to be done politically, by politics in the most modern sense.

Unless at the general election this autumn the conservative powers lose and the progressive powers win, Fascist pressure will continue.

1962: I have just married. Of course it is a love marriage, but we have no child as yet. I am working in a motion picture company as a scenario writer. The reasons why I joined this company are as follows: In order that happiness may be brought to Japan, which has been so backward during recent times (owing, of course, to economic and social conditions), the people must, firstly, not be intimidated by illogical customs and laws. The day must come when we shall do our own thinking and act on our own responsibility. In order that people shall live according to the democratic tradition and way of thinking, art and literature must flourish.

When we compare films and literature, we find that films are the most modern and comprehensive form of art; they can move, say, some 3 million. And I, personally, like films very much.

Those are my reasons for devoting my life to the cinema. The years between 1952 and 1962 will be the most difficult. Between 1942 and 1952 I was afraid of militarism. Between 1952 and 1962 all Japanese, including myself, were able to win their individual freedom. The revolution by peace *(heiwa ni yotte no kakumei)* has been achieved, but a few reactionaries still exist. The question now is, how can we create the new social life of which we have been dreaming.

1972: I already have three children. My wife and I wanted one daughter and two sons, and . . . there they are! Now I am director of the motion picture company.

At present the real democratic government is carried out by representatives of each occupation group. No monopolistic capitalists are left. All nations are bound together by mutual trust, and Unesco is the centre of this movement. The cold war between the United States of America and the U.S.S.R. has already become a thing of the past. Among the old stories the most famous one is that of the 'disposal' of the A-bomb—in the middle of the Pacific. Nowadays armies have become unnecessary. On the basis of these facts I have written several stories.

The development of civilization through the use of atomic energy is remarkable. Cinema techniques have made enormous progress. There are no more black and white movies; and the movies' enemy, TV, of which there was already question in 1962, has appeared. Picture planning now includes TV, and we deliver films to the TV companies.

This splendid cultural achievement is a natural one, but it is also due to the following reasons: Everybody's democratic 'life experience' has already been established, therefore everybody respects the personality of others and recognizes their good points. People have no inferiority complex, and develop their own abilities in freedom.

Novels appeared in which the reformed, democratic circumstances of life were described. Human beings are again being described, but there is no more 'anxiety about life' or 'anxiety about death'; such thoughts have become a thing of the past. The delights and sorrows of living are portrayed in these novels.

1982: I begin to write essays. Undeveloped areas of the earth are brought under cultivation.

1992: My creative power has not yet disappeared, but I have started to find delight in the growth of my children; my wife, also, is in good health.

2002. I am leaving this world. The new age belongs to my children.

NOBORU HAYASHI

Since I entered the university and started studying sociology, already six months have passed. I have not yet got an answer to the question 'What is sociology?' and I cannot make any decisions about my future. Now, I have to write an autobiography taking me to my seventieth year: it will be a 'monologue of a madman'.

1954, Spring: I graduate from the university, go back to my place of birth, and become a teacher in a high school. For about five years I shall lead the simple life of a country school-teacher, in company with my 75-year-old father and 68-year-old mother. I cannot say that these five years will be a 'plus' in my life, but I shall have time for introspection and can care for my shattered health.

1956: My relatives and brothers advise me to marry, but I will stick to my life with my parents. It is my view that when one wants to devote oneself whole-heartedly to one's work, a wife and children are often obstacles.

1959: My father dies at the age of 80. My eldest brother comes back to our home and my mother goes to the next eldest brother, who is living in Osaka. I, who have become independent, go to Sapporo and enter a timber company which is managed by a friend of my university days. Thus I shall start my career as a business man, the most suitable profession for me.

1960: 8 April will be the day of my 'rebirth'. This company was established in 1952, when I was a student (I helped, in a planning capacity, in its establishment). At that time, many medium-sized and small enterprises were destroyed by the forces of big capital; and their numbers gradually declined. The director of this company has first-class talent for business, and is very careful in his management of projects. We can thus maintain our company in the period when small enterprises are disappearing, and obtain capital, because of increasing trust in us. Nevertheless, our company is still a small-scale one when compared to great enterprises with big capital. Its production methods are not yet fully mechanized. I shall devote myself to this, advise the director and achieve mechanization. As a result, there will be shorter working hours for the operatives; five hours' work a day will leave them considerable leisure time.

1965: As a result of five years of effort, our small company has made remarkable progress in the industrial world. I shall build two houses. One of them I will give to a 70-year-old teacher of my high school days. The other I will present to my eldest sister, who lost her husband and is now living with a very strict mother-in-law, bringing up two children. I shall live in the new house with her.

1967: Without taking any holiday, I start to work in a second enterprise. It is concerned with the development of the fishing industry, which has many resources in Hokkaido and for which I intend to make use of atomic energy.

1968: The successful use of atomic energy in peaceful industries creates a second revolution in production all over the world. My company, which is ready to apply these new methods of production, will be safe. The company's products may be seen, not only in Japan, but in every market of the world.

1973: I shall invest my savings in the building of a home for old people, a sanatorium or some other establishment of a social nature. Such enterprises cannot be carried out in a short time, so I shall have to work about ten years on this one.

1982: Gradually I see the realization of half of the hopes I harboured from the start. The director of the company dies and I become director.

1985: This is the last plan. I start to administer a mine. This enterprise seems difficult by comparison with my former ones. It is impossible to estimate results for fixed periods.

Being at the beginning of my old age, I feel my physical condition growing less and less sound; often I cannot move my hands and feet.

1988: October. Before I see my sixty-first birthday I get a stroke and die. I, who have no wife and children, look upon my beloved enterprises as my wife and children; and, when I cannot work any longer, death will lay upon me a coverlet of feathers.

TARÔ SUZUKI

1952: At present I am a student of sociology at the Faculty of Arts in Hokkaido University. This April my last year of study starts. The three points I am most interested in are: what kind of graduation thesis I shall write; what kind of occupation I shall choose after my graduation; what kind of woman I shall marry. Socially, my question is: towards which of the two political powers in the world will Japan incline? I hope that the reactionary powers will disappear as soon as possible, and that the progressive powers will succeed in all respects. I hope so because in that case, if a third world war begins, Japan will be outside the struggle and sustain no war damage. Nevertheless, my attitude towards life is divorced from those hopes. I am really quite alone; this does not mean that I have no family, but nobody helps me with my education expenses. Yet I never pity myself. I have suffered much, and nearly all my tears have already been expended. These sufferings of the past may still be reflected in my face, for my friends often tell me that my face bears a shadow of sadness. At present, however, I have a feeling of contentment. Sometimes, in the past, my heart suffered painfully but it seems that I have the strength to recover from past experiences which stunned me. I thus take a comparatively optimistic view of my future. True, my present principles should incline me away from a hopeful view as to what is to happen. But if I have an honest belief, a belief like iron, in the 'now' of the present, and if I think and act in the best way, there will, I feel, be no misfortune in the future. For the world and for society there are at present few encouraging propects. As I am now, I intend to study with a youthful outlook, enthusiasm and humanity, and to enjoy myself.

1962: The hopes of my student days seem to be achieved. I am 33 years old. I have a wife, but no children. I shall never have one, for reasons of principle, which I will state later.

The world has entirely changed. Once the United States of America and the U.S.S.R. were struggling against each other, and caused us to fear a third world war: but that difficult situation has gradually been resolved. Relations between the United States of America and the U.S.S.R. seem, to outside observers, to be very good. Together with my wife, whom I married three years ago, I have visited the place of my birth, Karafuto (Sakhalin), crossing the Sōya-kaikyō (between Hokkaido and Karafuto). My present occupation is that of a senior official in the Hokkaido administration. Although I became a civil servant as soon as I graduated, I don't like that kind of life too much; but I do not intend to change. My wife and I love each other very much, and she is very beautiful, at least I think so. My wife wants a child, but I don't want one, because I do not wish my children to experience a life so full of contradictions. Even if we had children I could not, I think, love them if they did not subscribe to my ideals.

As for social phenomena, there are, despite apparent peace, deep clefts beneath the surface. I cannot think that there are really many unemployed, but the numbers of the 'habitually unemployed' is growing. Although they graduated from a university, these people complain they cannot get a job! In the educational system of America, too, we can see bad points; America seems gradually to be becoming 'colonized'.

My classmates in the university, Marxists, have always said: 'The revolution will take place in 10 years' time; it will not happen now'. In our neighbour country, China, the revolution has made considerable progress; internally it seems complete. Many tensions between revolutionaries and reactionaries will, be better than our present life. In the United States of America, too, the power of labour has increased, and the struggle between labour and capitalism seems to be violent, even cruel.

I am acting as a committee member for the Officials' Association in the Hokkaido administration. I have been thrown into prison several times. My humane feelings impel me to agree with the rules of the Marxists, in view of the conflicts within a capitalist society. My wife is a progressive woman. If I give a hint, she can respond immediately; she is a woman with an elastic nature. Even after quarrels, I go to bed with her and in the night we can love as before. She graduated from the university and is a novelist, but a second-class one. Her income is much larger than mine. Thus I can have a luxurious life. I have indeed got a wonderful wife! Often pale-faced young literary men visit her, but she is considerate of my feelings and likes me to be present at the same table. I, however, don't mind such small things; I am broadminded. I would not mind, even if my wife spent a night having intercourse with someone else. My future hope for marriage is Communist marriage, which developed originally on an idealist basis. Surely the system of 'one husband, one wife' will become pointless.

1972: I am already a middle-aged man of 43. I am now an official in the Department of Foreign Affairs. I have been in the United States of America, England and the U.S.S.R. as a diplomat. Japan has feared a revolution; but it is now relieved of these fears, because relations between the United States of America and the U.S.S.R. have become less strained. This improvement of Russo-American relations is due to American socialization within a short period. The advance of the working class pushed the capitalists back without their being able to resist. England, France, Germany, and indeed most countries have turned Socialist. In Japan, political power is with the left wing of the Socialist Party. The Liberal and other conservative parties have less seats in the Diet than the Socialist and Communist parties. As a member of the Socialist Party, I am working for a peaceful revolution

The period of planned economy has begun. Work never brings worry. The Japanese population, which has always presented a serious problem, now amounts to less than 90 million because of an energetic birth control campaign. Class struggles, however, are becoming more violent as the conservative influences stage their last resistance. But time is not on their side. Revolution by violence is unlikely, as the parliaments are made up everywhere of members of the working class.

Atomic energy has been utilized for peaceful production, and reforms have been carried out in all fields. Had I been born 50 years later, I should have had a happy life. Sometimes I talk to my wife about it. Nevertheless, I cannot but rejoice over such a period of change.

Sometimes I feel rather lonely, because there are only two of us. I began to think I would have done better to have children. But when I am working I have no feelings about it; I rather enjoy the quietness.

Recently women have tended to have less children, two at the most; I think this is better for a cultural life.

1982. I am 53, and my wife is 50. Both of us are in good health. She looks comparatively young, because of her never having borne children. I am well, live like a young man, and enjoy our married life. Recently I started dancing every day as a sport. My dancing progressed, so that now I can instruct others. In present-day Japan the working class has absolute authority. During the last 10 years there have been some struggles between the working class and the capitalists, but each time labour has gained in strength. The bloodless revolution has in fact already been completed by the working class. I am an important member of the Government. The whole of youth is looking forward to a happy future. In America, too, the working class is in authority; America is, in fact, a Socialist nation. All countries are looking in the same direction; history is going to be as described by Marx.

Nevertheless, I and my wife are worried. Admittedly, economic problems have been solved. All contradictions in social life have been removed. Soon, heaven will come to earth. But how will human beings seek a higher development of their spirit?

Imagining all kinds of things about the future world, I finish my fifty-third year, embraced in the arms of my tender wife.

INVESTIGATION CARRIED OUT
AMONG STUDENTS

The instrument used was the Allport-Gillespie questionnaire ('Autobiography: from now to A.D. 2000', Part II).

The test was given to the Kyoto subjects in Japanese and to those at Sapporo in English (cf. Chapter I, page 29).

DISTRIBUTION OF SUBJECTS

By Establishments

Kyoto: A. Faculty of Education, University of Kyoto 18
          B. Sociology Section, University of Kyoto 24
          C. Osaka Women' College 50
          D. Momoyama Secondary School 122

                                               214

Sapporo E. Sociology Section, University of Hokkaido 17

By Sex and Age (combined per establishment)

	A		B	C	D		Kyoto		Sapporo	
Age	Men	Women	Men	Women	Men	Women	Men	Women	Men	Women
15	0	0	0	0	17	16	17	16	0	0
16	0	0	0	0	17	23	17	23	0	0
17	0	0	0	0	18	18	18	18	0	0
18	0	0	0	32	1	10	1	42	0	0
19	0	0	0	13	0	1	0	14	0	0
20	5	0	5	2	0	0	10	2	1	0
21	7	1	4	2	0	0	11	3	2	1
22	1	0	4	0	0	0	5	0	0	0
23	2	0	5	0	0	0	7	0	1	0
24	2	0	4	0	0	0	6	0	2	1
25	0	0	1	0	0	0	1	0	3	1
26	0	0	0	0	0	0	0	0	2	1
27	0	0	0	0	0	0	0	0	0	0
28	0	0	0	0	0	0	0	0	0	0
29	0	0	0	0	0	0	0	0	1	1
Un-known	0	0	1	1	1	0	2	1	0	0

Marital Status

	[K, m]	[K, w]	[S, m]	[S, w]
Unmarried.	88	188	11	4
Engaged	4	1	1	0
Married.	0	0	0	1
Not known.	3	0	0	0

ANSWERS[1]

QUESTION 1. *What two things would you most like to know about the future up to A.D. 2000?*

	[K, m]	[K, w]	[S, mw]
International situation, industrial progress of the world, etc..	79	58	76
National, political and social affairs	20	24	47
Personal questions: marriage, job.	42	53	24
Others.	52	52	12

QUESTION 3. *To what socio-economic class would you say that the family in which you were reared belonged?*

	[K, mw]	[S, mw]
Upper class.	3	0
Middle class	85	41
Working class	9	53
Lower class.	2	6
No reply.	1	0

QUESTION 4. *What two things would you most like to have that you don't now have?*

	[K, m]	[K, w]	[S, mw]
Money	35	15	35
Material possessions			
House.	9 ⎫	14 ⎫	6 ⎫
Car.	7 ⎪	1 ⎪	0 ⎪
Bicycle.	4 ⎬ 39	0 ⎬ 34	6 ⎬ 47
Piano, gramophone, camera.	13 ⎪	8 ⎪	35 ⎪
Others.	6 ⎭	11 ⎭	0 ⎭
Cultural objects, books.	23	15	18
Time to oneself.	6	0	0
People			
Brothers, sisters, father, mother	1 ⎫	18 ⎫	0 ⎫
Friend.	7 ⎬ 17	9 ⎬ 30	18 ⎬ 41
Friend of opposite sex	9 ⎭	3 ⎭	23 ⎭

1. The numbers correspond to those of the questions in the Allport-Gillespie Test. The answers to certain questions have not been analysed, usually because the question was misunderstood.

	[K, m]	[K, w]	[S, mw]
Moral and social qualities	28	18	6
Good health	5	2	o
Intellectual gifts.	23	42	o
Talent.	o	5	o
Other things.	15	24	29
No reply	6	14	o

QUESTION 5. *What is your present state of health?*

	[K, m]	K, w]	[S, mw]
Excellent.	28	45	12
Good	56	47	76
Fair	13	8	6
Poor	3	o	6

QUESTION 6. *What three situations or events in your past life do you regard as the most important or significant? That is, what three events in your past have had the greatest effect upon your present life?*

	[K, mw]	[S, mw]
The second world war.	71	65
Situation arising from the war (occupation, inflation, agrarian reform, co-education, etc.)	20	29
Death of parents	21	24
Sickness, accident	15	18
Events at school	22	65
Love affairs.	10	18
Others	79	24
No reply.	50	6

QUESTION 7 (c). *Do you expect to enter:*

	[K, m]	[K, w]	[S, mw]
The same occupation as your father or guardian?	12	6	6
The same occupation as your mother?	1	7	6
A closely related occupation?	19	13	18
A different occupation?	68	74	71
No reply	o	1	o

QUESTION 7 (i). *What is your attitude toward careers or occupations outside the home for unmarried women?*

	[K, m]	[K, w]	[S, mw]
I approve of full-time careers	79	82	53
I approve of part-time occupations	15	15	47
I disapprove of any career or occupation outside the home	6	3	o

QUESTION 7 (j). *What is your attitude toward careers or occupations outside the home for married women?*

	[K, m]	[K, w]	[S, mw]
I approve of full-time careers	44	31	6
I approve of part-time occupations	34	43	53

	[K, m]	[K, w]	[S, mw]
I disapprove of any career or occupation outside the home	22	25	41
No reply	0	1	0

QUESTION 7 (k.) *Do you favour military service for men?*

	[K,m]	[K, w]	[S, mw]
Yes	14	5	6
No	84	89	94
No reply	2	2	0

QUESTION 7 (l.) *Do you favour military service for women?*

	[K, m]	[K, w]	[S, mw]
Yes	5	2	6
No	95	98	94

QUESTION 8. *Do you expect to marry sometime or other?* (In this, as in other questions, you may have no definite expectation, but even so you are asked to make a guess.)

	[K,w]	[K, w]	[S, mw]
Yes	97	97	94
No	2	3	6
No reply	1	0	0

QUESTION 9. *If so, at what age do you expect to marry?* (The figures indicate the number of subjects.)

	[K, m]	[K, w]	[S, m]	[S, w]
20	0	0	0	0
21	1	1	0	0
22	0	5	0	0
23	2	25	0	0
24	4	30	0	1
25	10	24	0	1
26	14	6	1	0
27	14	7	0	1
28	8	7	3	0
29	4	1	1	0
30	25	3	4	1
31	1	0	0	0
32	3	0	1	0
33	2	0	0	0
34	0	0	0	0
35	1	0	1	0
Average.	27 years	23.8 years	29 years	25.9 years

QUESTION 10. *Do you consider it at all likely that you will be married more than once?*

	[K, m]	[K, w]	[S, mw]
Yes.	15	12	0
No.	84	86	88
No reply	1	2	12

QUESTION 11. *Do you think it at all possible that you will be divorced at any time?*

	[K, m]	[K, w]	[S, mw]
Yes.	12	13	12
No.	86	85	76
No reply.	2	2	12

QUESTION 12. *If you marry, how many children do you expect to have?* (The figures indicate the number of subjects.)

	[K, m]	[K, w]	[S, m]	[S, w]
One	5	7	0	0
Two	32	24	0	1
Three.	38	52	4	2
Four	8	27	1	1
Five	5	6	2	0
More than five	3	1	3	0
None	3	1	1	1
No reply	1	1	1	0
Average	2.87	3.04		

QUESTION 13. *If you marry, how many children would you like to have?* (The figures indicate the number of subjects.)

	[K, m]	[K, w]	[S, m]	[S, w]
One.	4	2	0	0
Two	31	35	0	0
Three.	45	70	6	1
Four	4	12	1	1
Five	3	0	2	1
More than five	2	0	1	1
None	2	0	1	1
No reply	1	0	1	0
Average	2.74	2.62		

QUESTION 14. *How old do you expect to be when your first child is born?* (The figures indicate the number of subjects.)

	[K, m]	[K, w]	[S, m]	[S, w]
22.	1	0	0	0
23.	0	3	0	0
24.	2	10	0	0
25.	2	29	0	0
26.	9	22	0	0
27.	8	13	1	1
28	14	14	0	0
29.	9	6	0	0
30.	10	7	1	2
31.	10	1	3	0
32.	10	2	3	1
33.	6	2	1	0

	[K, m]	[K, w]	[S, m]	[S, w]
34.	I	o	o	o
35.	5	o	o	o
36.	o	o	o	o
37.	2	o	I	o
No reply	6	7	I	I

QUESTION 17. *Which one of the following qualities do you regard as the most important in a good wife or husband?*

	[K, m]	[K, w]	[S, mw]
Shares my own opinions and beliefs.	18	19	18
Intelligence, common sense.	13	11	29
Pleasant disposition—a good companion	68	68	47
No reply or double reply.	I	2	6

QUESTION 18. *If you get married and have a family, who do you expect will be more influential in the direction and control of the affairs of the family?*

	[K, m]	[K, w]	[S, mw]
Myself.	21	7	12
My wife (or husband)	13	16	o
Both equally.	66	75	82
No reply	o	2	6

QUESTION 19. *Would you like to live the main part of your life in:*

	[K, m]	[K, w]	[S, mw]
Country of birth.	79	84	82
Other countries	21	16	18
United States of America	3	6	
France.	4	3	
Great Britain	2	0	
Switzerland.	4	3	
Germany	2	1	
Brazil	I	1	
China	3	1	
Japan[1]	I	1	
Not specified	I	0	

QUESTION 20. *Do you expect to be able to travel (at some time during your life) as extensively as you would like to?*

	[K, m]	[K, w],	[S, mw]
Yes.	65	45	65
No.	35	55	35

---

1. Both subjects born in China.

QUESTION 21. *If you were able to travel, what three foreign countries would you like most to visit?*

	[K, m]	[K, w]	[S, mw]
France	60	76	65
United States of America	70	66	53
Switzerland	22	50	18
Great Britain	31	29	35
U.S.S.R.	39	12	41
Germany	14	13	12
China	14	9	29
Italy	7	11	18
India	6	2	12
Sweden	3	2	6
Denmark	5	2	—
Egypt	5	1	—
Greece	0	5	—
Other countries (percentages below 5%)	13	8	6
No reply or vague	11	14	5

QUESTION 23. *What do you think is likely to be the cause of your death?*

	[K, m]	[K, w]	[S, mw]
Illness	38	59	47
Childbirth	0	1	0
Old age	32	22	29
Accident	8	3	6
Earthquake	0	1	0
War causes	6	2	0
Execution (by shooting, etc.)	3	0	0
Overwork	0	3	0
Suicide	3	2	0
Vague and no reply	15[1]	9	18

QUESTION 24. *If you had a personal problem that worried you (for example, a difficult decision to make), whom would you prefer to talk it over with?*

	[K, m]		[K, w]		[S, mw]	
Members of your immediate family	40		70		65	
Relatives outside your immediate family	2		1		0	
Some trained person (e.g. doctor or psychologist)	18		6		18	
Others					6	
People of reputation	2		2			
Christian mission	1		1			
Teacher	6		4			
Intimate friend	22	32[2]	13	18[2]		
Fiancé(e)	4		1			
An older person	1		0			
Not specified	1		0			

1. Five men gave two causes each.
2. Six men and two women specified two people.

	[K, m]	[K, w]	[S, mw]
No one.	2	2	12
No reply	6	4	0

QUESTION 25 (a.) *Would you like to have more friends than you now have?*

	[K, m]	[K, w]	[S, mw]
Yes	61	55	76
No	39	45	24
No reply	0	0	0

QUESTION 25 (b.) *Would you like to have some friend more intimate than you now have (i.e., in whom you can confide, on whom you can rely)?*

	[K, m]	[K, w]	[S, mw]
Yes	72	69	65
No	28	30	35
No reply	0	1	0

QUESTION 26. *Concerning your own personal future, would you say that in general you feel:*

	[K, m]	[K, w]	[S, mw]
Enthusiastic.	26	30	18
Hopeful	37	41	64
Indifferent	7	4	18
Resigned.	11	21	0
Embittered	18	4	0
Double answers	1	0	0

QUESTION 27. *Of the following activities, which are the three from which you expect the greatest satisfaction? (Only the first choice is noted here.)*

	[K, m]	[K, w]	[S, mw]
Your career or occupation.	21	13	35
Family relationships.	36	63	24
Leisure, recreational activities.	7	9	0
Participation as a citizen in the affairs of your community	5	0	0
Participation in activities directed toward national or international betterment.	25	6	24
Religious beliefs and activities.	1	3	18

QUESTION 28. *Looking ahead to A.D. 2000 which of the five 10-year periods between now and then do you expect to give you the greatest satisfaction in living?*

	[K, m]	[K, w]	[S, mw]
1952-1961.	26	59	24
1962-1971.	32	24	18
1972-1981.	29	12	24
1982-1991.	6	3	24
1992-2000.	4	0	0

QUESTION 29. *In terms of standard of living (income) how do you expect your own future standard to compare with that of the family in which you were brought up?*

	[K, m]	[K, w]	[S, mw]
Higher standard.	42	29	53
About the same .	47	68	35
Lower standard .	11	3	6
No reply .	0	0	6

QUESTION 30. *Looking ahead to A.D. 2000, which of the five 10-year periods between now and then seems clearest to you in your imagination as you think about them?*

	[K, m]	[K, w]	[S, mw]
1952-1961.	51	52	52
1962-1971.	21	24	6
1972-1981.	15	14	18
1982-1991.	7	7	6
1992-2001.	5	0	6
No reply .	1	3	12

QUESTION 31. *In general, what will help you most to get ahead, ability or 'pull' (that is, personal contacts or influence, through family or friends)?*

	[K, m]	[K, w]	[S, mw]
Ability.	78	65	59
'Pull' .	21	34	35
No reply .	1	1	6

QUESTION 32. *What are the two worst things that could conceivably happen to you during your lifetime?*

	[K, m]	[K, w]	[S, mw]
National or local disaster .	4	7	18
War .	55	39	18
Revolution .	6	2	0
Destitution .	9	8	6
Family disunion.	4	8	6
Death in family.	0	34	24
Deception by fiancé(e), wife .	5	5	0
Death of spouse.	7	8	12
Death of child .	1	4	0
Unsuccessful career.	5	2	6
Unemployment .	11	2	0
Accidental death.	18	2	0
Calumny .	1	0	6
Illness.	23	14	24
Others.	11	8	12

QUESTION 33. *What are the two worst things that are likely to happen to you during your lifetime?*

	[K, m]	[K, w]	[S, mw]
National or local disaster	2	3	0
War	57	45	35
Revolution	7	1	0
Loss of Japan's independence	4	0	0
Destitution	6	6	18
Family disunion	3	7	0
Death in family	2	25	18
Deception by fiancé(e), wife	6	6	0
Death of spouse	3	8	0
Death of child	2	3	0
Unsuccessful career	17	6	0
Unemployment	8	5	6
Accidental death	5	3	0
Calumny	2	1	0
Illness	15	12	12
Others	19	7	24

QUESTION 34. *To what extent would you agree with the following propositions?*
   (a) I would approve of an expansion of the idea of trial marriage, *i.e., of greater sexual freedom among young people, so as to enable them to discover whether they are compatible as marriage partners.*
   (b) 'The world is a hazardous place, in which men are basically evil and dangerous'

Replies to 34 (a)

	[K, m]	[K, w]	[S, mw]
Agree	17	3	6
Slightly agree	23	18	29
Slightly disagree	17	16	12
Disagree	43	61	53
No reply	0	2	0

Replies to 34 (b)

	[K, m]	[K, w]	[S, mw]
Agree	11	15	18
Slightly agree	27	26	12
Slightly disagree	25	21	41
Disagree	37	35	29
No reply	0	3	0

QUESTION 35. *Do you expect to be more interested in:*

	[K, m]	[K, w]	[S, mw]
The local affairs and problems of your own community? . .	9	26	12
National affairs and problems?	31	24	12
International affairs and problems?	59	49	76
No reply and confused replies	1	1	

QUESTION 36. *Do you expect to be more successful as a leader in your own field than the average person of equivalent education?*

	[K, m]	[K, w]	[S, mw]
More successful .	39	23	35
About the same.	56	72	59
Less successful .	4	5	6
No reply .	1	0	

QUESTION 37. *To what extent do you expect members of your present family and your future in-laws to be of assistance to you in life?*

	[K, m]	[K, w]	[S, mw]
Constantly available and indispensable.	26	17	12
Available, whenever needed, for assistance, mainly financial	45	52	53
Emergency economic assistance only.	22	26	12
Of no assistance at all.	7	2	23
No reply .	0	3	0

QUESTION 38. *If you should get a large sum of money five years from now, what would you do with it?*

	[K, m]	[K, w]	[S, mw]
Live more comfortably.	12	11	6
Build a house.	20	20	24
Buy a car/motorcycle	2	1	0
Buy clothes .	1	1	0
Spend on study, schooling.	28	15	24
Buy piano/gramophone records.	1	3	6
Get married; dress well.	1	7	0
Travel abroad.	7	9	29
Make gift to father and mother	1	4	0
Make donation to worthy public object .	13	18	12
Bank it .	7	7	6
Buy shares .	8	3	0
Others.	4	3	0

QUESTION 41. *Do you expect your destiny to be:*

	[K, m]	[K, w]	[S, mw]
Determined by yourself?	67	69	53
Determined by external circumstances? .	31	30	47
No reply .	2	1	0

QUESTION 42. *Will there be another world war between now and A.D. 2000?*

	[K, m]	[K, w]	[S, mw]
Yes, within 5 years.	31	24	18
Yes, within 15 years.	45	55	35
Yes, within 30 years.	10	12	6
Yes, within 50 years.	0	3	0
No .	13	5	41
No reply .	1	1	0

QUESTION 43. *If there should be another world war, what would be its effect on the world as we now know it?*

	[K, m]	[K, w]	[S, mw]
Civilization would be destroyed.	52	50	59
World progress would be very seriously retarded	38	45	23
Things would go on much as before	10	5	12
No reply	0	0	6

QUESTION 44. *By the year 1975, for what purposes do you expect atomic energy to be more widely used?*

	[K, m]	]K, w]	[S, mw]
Constructive (e.g., industrial) purposes.	40	29	82
Destructive (e.g., wartime, belligerent) purposes.	59	68	18
No reply	1	3	0

QUESTION 45. *Do you think war is:*

	[K, m]	[K, w]	[S, mw]
Needless and preventable	72	58	88
A necessary evil.	16	37	6
Sometimes a good thing.	8	4	6
No reply	4	1	

QUESTION 47. *Would you like to see greater equality between white and coloured races within your lifetime?*

	[K, m]	[K, w]	[S, mw]
Yes	98	97	82
No	2	3	6
No reply	0	0	12

QUESTION 48. *Do you expect to see greater equality between white and coloured races within your lifetime?*

	[K, m]	[K, w]	[S, mw]
Yes	59	44	82
No	39	56	0
No reply	2	0	18

QUESTION 49. *Democracy is often defined in the words of Abraham Lincoln as 'government of the people, by the people, and for the people'. If you were forced to do so, to which of the two conceptions would you personally give greater emphasis?*

	[K, m]	[K, w]	[S, mw]
By the people.	43	36	35
For the people	57	64	59
No reply	0	0	6

QUESTION 50. *Do you feel that you require some form of religious outlook or belief in order to achieve a fully mature philosophy of life?*

	[K, m]	[K, w]	[S, mw]
Yes	36	37	47
No	26	14	35
Doubtful	38	49	18

F. VOS'S INVESTIGATION

For the conditions under which this investigation was carried out, see above, Chapter I, pages 28-29. Only those questions are given here for which F. Vos has made a complete analysis of answers; they have been renumbered consecutively. The sample consisted of 100 subjects.

QUESTION 1. *If later on you have children of your own, do you want to give them the same sort of education you have had yourself, or would you give them a better one, or do you think that a less elaborate education would be quite as good?*

The same 14
The same or better. 15
Better 67
Whichever the child wants . . 1
No opinion 3

QUESTION 2. *Would your children be free to choose their own line of studies and their own jobs?*

Yes 66
No 1
Up to a point 7
No opinion 26

QUESTION 3. *Do you like the work you are doing now, or would you prefer something different?*

Yes 48
Would like to change. . . . 29
Don't care 3

QUESTION 4. *Do you earn enough money to live on or are you obliged to do another job 'on the side'?*

Earn enough 55
Do not earn enough 23

QUESTION 5. *Do you like your present subject of study or would you prefer something different?*

Like it 25
Would like to change. . . . 10

QUESTION 6. *If you are a student, is your allowance sufficient or do you have to earn extra money to pay your tuition fees?*

Sufficient 5
Insufficient. 28

QUESTION 7. *Do you read newspapers, and if so which?*

No 7
Most popular papers:
  Asahi. 46
  Mainichi. 33
  Tokyo Shimbun. . . . 27
  Nippon Keizai 23
  Yomiuri. 21

QUESTION 8. *Do you like reading books?*

Yes, very much. 62
Fairly well. 16
No 18
No opinion. 4

QUESTION 9. *Do you read magazines? If so which do you read regularly?*

Seldom or never 18
Most popular magazines:
  Bungei Shunju 32
  Sekai. 11
  Ridazu daijesuto (Reader's Digest) 9
  Fujin Koron. 8
  Shufu no Tomo 7
  Chuo Koron 6

QUESTION 10. *Is your main reading magazines or books?*

Magazines 26
Books 52
No reply or various 22

QUESTION 11. *Do you read foreign books or newspapers?*

Never 41
Yes 38
No reply. 21

QUESTION 12. *If you go to the pictures, which films do you like best?*

Foreign. 12
French 11
Japanese. 7
American 7
English. 7

Musicals. 17
Westerns 9
Love. 6
Psychological 5
Human interest. 3

QUESTION 13. *Do you go to the kabuki (Japanese classical drama)?*

Never 24
Seldom 49
Occasionally 22
No reply 5

QUESTION 14. *Do you like kabuki?*

Yes 49
Not much 28
No 6
No reply. 17

QUESTION 15. *If you listen to the wireless, what kind of programmes do you prefer?*

Music of all kinds. 61
News. 36
News commentaries 20
Radio plays. 17
Story programmes ('fountain
   of stories') 10
Quizzes. 10

QUESTION 16. *Do you consider that girls ought to have more or less the same education as boys with the general idea of fitting them for a job, or do you think that a girl ought to work in the house and be an ornament of the home?*

They should have the same
   education. 53
They should work in the home . 7
Other views. 27
No reply. 13

QUESTION 17. *Do you like sports? Which?*

Baseball. 40
Tennis 20
Swimming 12
Volley ball. 11
Table tennis. 10
Skiing 9

QUESTION 18. *Do you prefer to take part yourself or to be a spectator?*

Take part 48
Spectator 32
Both. 13
No reply. 7

QUESTION 19. *Have you any hobbies? What are they?*

Music of all kinds. 24
Reading. 21
Sports 18
The cinema. 9
Drawing, painting 7
Photography 5
Hiking 5
Tea ceremony 5
Shogi (Japanese chess) . . . 5

QUESTION 20. *When you have personal difficulties, do you like to discuss them with your father or mother, or with older people, or with a boy or girl friend? Or do you not discuss them at all?*

With parents or older people . . 36
With parents and friends . . . 31
With friends 19
Do not discuss them 13
No reply 1

QUESTION 21. *What do you think of the traditional marriage arrangement?*

Bad	27
Needs modification to some extent	45
Good	10
Not bad but don't like it	8
The practice of 'arranged' marriage and freedom of choice are equally good	2
No opinion	8

QUESTION 22. *It is necessary for girls and women to have the same rights as youths and men or do you feel that men should take precedence over women because it is a law of nature and/or of the essence of Japanese culture?*

They should have the same rights	88
Their status should be different	10
No reply	2

QUESTION 23. *What do you think about the positon of the mother-in-law and her attitude towards her daughter-in-law?*

No objections	2
Changes advocated	41
Wrong	30
No opinion	27

QUESTION 24. *Do you normally take important decisions yourself or do you act on the advice of your father, your mother or your family (e.g. in the choice of a job, political party, etc.)?*

Act on advice of others	54
Sometimes take advice, sometimes not	15
Do not take advice	29
No reply	2

QUESTION 25. *Do you think that young people ought to take such important decisions by themselves?*

Yes	21
No	52
Up to a point	22
No opinion	5

QUESTION 26. *Do you think that our social position will be better, worse, or about the same as that of your father?*

Better	36
Worse	2
Same	16
No opinion	46

QUESTION 27. *Do you profess a religion?*

Yes	31
No	69

QUESTION 28. *If you do, is it the same as that of your parents or family?*

Different	9
Protestants	5
Roman Catholics	2
Shintoists	1
Buddhists	1

QUESTION 29. *Do you reverence the family shrine or do you not pay much attention to it?*

Reverence it	58
Disregard it	38
No reply	4

QUESTION 30. *Do you regard the emperor as the symbol of the Japanese nation or not?*

Yes 74
No 16
No opinion. 10

QUESTION 31. *What do you think of Emperor-worship?*

Good. 46
Bad. 37
No opinion. 17

QUESTION 32. *Do you think that generally speaking the older generation acted as it should have done?*

Yes 21
No 33
Up to a point 20
No opinion. 26

QUESTION 33. *Do you feel that there is a deep gulf between the older generation and your own?*

Yes 50
No 27
Not very deep. 14
No opinion. 9

QUESTION 34. *The great transformation of Japan from an agricultural to an industrial country and from a nation of merely regional significance to a world power took place without democracy as conceived in Great Britain, France and the United States of America. Do you think that a democratic regime such as that of these countries would be suitable for present-day Japan or not?*

Suitable. 22
Unsuitable. 53
Suitable up to a point. . . . 10
No opinion. 15

QUESTION 35. *Do you think that the ideas of Japan's military and political leaders between 1930 and 1940 were basically correct, in spite of the fact that these leaders were not able to achieve their aims?*

Basically correct 15
Wrong 49
Correct up to a point. . . . 26
No opinion. 10

QUESTION 36. *If you could study or work abroad, to which country would you like to go?*

France 30
England. 14
Germany 14
United States of America. . . 11
U.S.S.R. 8
China 5

QUESTION 37. *Was the influence of the* zaibatsu *good or bad?*

Good. 20
Bad. 38
Good in certain respects . . . 26
No opinion 16

APPENDIX VI

BIBLIOGRAPHY ON YOUTH AND THE FAMILY[1]

PSYCHOLOGY

USHISHIMA, Yoshitimo. *Seinen no Shinri* (Psychology of youth), 1940.
Deals mainly with the growth, development, differentiation and socialization of awareness of self, and with its rebuilding in the deepening and broadening of social consciousness. Elucidates the emotional, idealistic and occupational problems of youth, as well as young people's feeling of isolation and their sexual and political problems, based on cases, investigations and statistics.

TAKE, Masatarô. *Saishin-hattatsu Shinri-gaku* (Psychology in its latest developments), 1950, vol. II.
Deals with the development of awareness of self and intellectual, emotional, social and religious existence in the life of youth, based on investigations, statistics and studies hitherto made in Japan.

KATSURA Hirosuke. *Seinen Shinri-gaku* (Psychology of youth), 1950.
Based upon many years of study and investigation in regard to young people, it deals with the development of family relationships and relationships between friends; intellectual and cultural interests; the development of a joy in life; and the social groups formed by young people. It describes the form of young people's spiritual life.

NOGAMI, Toshio. *Seinen no Shinri to Kyôiku* (Psychology and education of youth), 1937.

YODA (or YORITA), Arata. *Seinen no Shinri* (Psychology of youth), 1950.

AOKI, Seishirô, *Kaitei Seinen Shinri-gaku* (Psychology of youth, revised), 1950.

NOBECHI, Masayuki. *Chûgakusei no Shinri to Kyôiku* (Psychology and education of secondary school pupils), 1950.

MOCHIZUKI, Mamoru. *Seinen Shinri-gaku* (Psychology of youth), 1949.
Deals with the various types of behaviour in young people; argues that light can be thrown upon the behaviour of youth only by envisaging it as social behaviour, and not merely from the standpoint of individual conduct.

ATTITUDES TOWARDS AUTHORITY

KUBO, Yoshihide. *Chûgakkô Seito Issemmei no Rensô Kensa* (Investigation into the association of ideas in a thousand male secondary school students), *Jidô Kenkyû-sho Kiyô*, vol. 10, 1927.

---

1. Prepared by Professor Usui.

KUBO, Yoshihide. *Jogakkô Seito Issemmei no Rensô Kensa* (Investigation into the association of ideas in a thousand female secondary school students), *Nippon Shinri-gaku Zasshi*, 1923.

MASUDA, Kôichi. *Kôtô-gakkô Seito no Rensô Keikô* (Tendencies in idea association among high school students), *Jidô Kenkyû-sho Kiyô* vol. 14, 1932, *Shinri-gaku Rombun-shû*, 3rd compilation, 1931.

NOGAMI, Toshio and *Satô*, Kôji. *Seinen Shidô-sha no Shinri-gaku-teki Kenkyû* (Psychological studies of youth leaders: teachers of ideals as seen by youth), *Shinri-gaku Rombun-shû*, vol. 4, 1933.

AKAKURA, Takeshi. *Waga Kuni Seinen-sô ni okeru Shidô-sha no Jinkaku Kôzô* (The character building of leaders among the youth of our country), *Shinri-gaku Kenkyû*, vol. 15, 1940.

ÔTAKE, Kiyoshi. *Shinrai-shin ni kan-suru Ichi-kôsatsu* (Studies on feelings of confidence), *Kyôiku Shinri Kenkyû* vol. 10, 1935.

MORI, Hiroshi. *Seinen-ki ni okeru Dôkei no Shinri* (The psychology of adoration in adolescence), *Shinri-gaku Kenkyû*, vol. 17, 1943.

KUBO, Yoshio. *Seinen-ki okeru Shibo no Nasake ni tsuite* (On vague yearning in adolescence), *Jidô Kenkyû-sho Kiyô*, vols. 14-16, 1932-34.

YODA (or YORITA), Arata. *Seishun-ki ni okeru Hankô* (Defiance in puberty), *Kyôiku Shinri Kenkyû*, vol. 15, nos. 1 and 6.

MAMIYA, Takeshi. *Seinen-ki no Hankô* (Defiance in adolescence), *Seinen Shinri*, vol. 1, no. 2, 1950.

NISHIHIRA, Naoyoshi. *Seinen-ki no Rettô-sei Kanjô* (Inferiority complex in adolescence), *Seinen Shinri* vol. 1, no. 3, 1950.

MARUYAMA, Ryôji. *Shakumei wo mochiiru Seishun-ki no Shinri* (Puberty psychology in the use of nicknames), *Kyôiku Shinri Kenkyû*, vol. 13, no. 7, 1938.

SUZUKI, Michita. *Oya to Kyôshi e no Kôgi* (Complaints against parents and teachers), *Seinen Shinri* vol. 2, no. 4, 1951.

KATSURA, Hirosuke *Scinen to Ryôshin* (Youth and parents), *Jidô Shinri*, vol. 3, no. 3.

TAMAKI, Osamu. *Kyôshi no Seito ni oyobosu Eikyô no Chôsa* (Investigation into the influence exerted by teachers upon pupils), *Kyôiku Shinri Kenkyû*, vol. 14, 1939.

OTAKE, Kiyoshi. *Chûtô Gakusei no Kami no Gainen ni tsuite* (On the concept of the gods in secondary school pupils), *Kyôiku Shinri Kenkyû*, vol. 11, 1936.

OKA, Michikata. *Shudô-jûdô-sei to Shûkyô-sei* (Leadership, obedience and religious feeling), *Shinri-gaku Rombun-shû*, vol. 5, 1935.

TANAKA, Kanichi. *Dôtoku Handan ni kan-suru Tûkei-teki Kenkyû* (Statistical studies concerning moral judgment), *Shinri-gaku Kenkyû*, vol. 1, 1926.

AWAJI, Enjirô and USHISHIMA, Yoshitomo. *Dôtoku Ishiki no Hattatsu ni kan-suru Kenkyû* (Studies concerning the development of ethics), *Shinri-gaku Rombun-shû*, vol. 2, 1929.

INTEREST IN POLITICAL PROBLEMS

Aoki, Seishirô, *Sôtei no Shisô Keikô ni tsuite no Chôsa* (Investigation concerning the ideological tendencies of young people), *Kyôiku Shinri Kenkyû*, vol. 6, 1931.

Masuda, Kôichi, *Shisô-teki Dôkô Kôsatsu no Kokoromi* (An attempt at the observation of ideological tendencies), *Shinri-gaku Kenkyû*, vol. 7, 1932.

Homma, Sakae and Ushishima, Yoshitomo. *Gakusei Seinen no Shisô Keikô ni tsuite* (On the ideological tendencies of students and young people), *Ôyô Shinri-gaku Kenkyû*, vol. 2, 1935.

Takata, Shirô, *Genka Jikyoku ni tai-suru Kinrô Seinen no Shisô Chôsa* (Investigation on young workers' ideas about the present political situation), *Kyôiku Shinri Kenkyû*, vol. 14, 1939.

Ômuro (or Ôya), Teiichirô. *Gakusei Undô no Senzen to Sengo* (The pre-war and the post-war periods in student movements), *Seinen Shinri*, vol. 2, no. 2, 1951.

Abe, Magoshirô, *Shakai-teki Kinchô to Seinen no Fuan* (Social tensions and the unrest of youth), *Seinen Shinri*, vol. 2, no. 2, 1951.

Koga, Yukiyoshi. *Sensô ka Heiwa ka—Seinen Gakusei no Taido no Kenkyû* (War or peace?—a study of the attitudes of young students), *Ôyô Shinri-gaku Kenkyû*, vol. 4, 1936.

Inui, Takeshi. *Seinen to Seiji* (Youth and politics), *Seinen Shinri*, vol. 2, no. 2, 1951.

SOCIAL ACTIVITIES

Kamitake, Shôji. *Seinen Gakusei Shûdan ni okeru Tôsotsu Genshô ni kan-suru Ichi-kenkyû* (A study concerning leadership phenomena in young people's and students' groups), first report, *Kyôiku Shinri Kenkyû*, vol. 14, 1939.

Ônishi, Kemmei. *Gakkyû Shinri no Mondai, I: Chûgakkô Seito no Yûjin Kankei;* (a) *Sono Genshô-teki Kenkyû* (Problems of educational psychology, I: Relations of friendship among secondary school pupils; (a) Studies of the relevant phenomena), *Jikken Shinri-gaku Kenkyû*, vol. 5, 1939.

Hasegawa, Mitsugi. *Seito-kan no Taikô Ishiki ni tsuite* (On the consciousness of antagonism between pupils), *Kyôiku Shinri Kenkyû*, vol. 15, 1940.

Kobayashi, Sae. *Jidô oyobi Seinen no Kôyû—Toku ni Naka no yoi Tomodachi ni tsuite* (Friendships among children and young people, especially close friendships), *Shinri-gaku Kenkyû*, vol. 17, 1942.

Aoko, Seishirô. *Jidô Kôgai Seikatsu Shûdan no Tôsotsu-sha ni tsuite* (Group leaders in children's out-of-school life), *Seishônen Shakai Seikatsu no Kenkyû —Nippon Seishônen Kyôiku Kenkyû-sho Kenkyû Hôkoku*, 1942.

Muraishi, Shôzô. *Kazoku ni okeru Sôgô Izon Kankei no Seiritsu* (The formation of relationships of mutual dependence within the family), *Seinen Shinri*, vol. 2, 1951.

Matsumoto, Yô. *Shakai-teki Eikyô—Tôron ni tsuite* (Social influence; on discussions), *Shinri-gaku Kenkyû*, vol. 7, 1932.

315

Koga, Yukiyoshi. *Kyôgo ni kan-suru Taido no Sokutei* (Assessment of competitive attitudes), *Shinri-gaku Kenkyû*, vol. 9, 1934.

Take, Masatarô and Gotô, Iwao. *Kenka no Shinri* (The psychology of quarreling), *Shinri-gaku Rômbun-shû*, vol. 5, 1935.

Oka, Michikata. *Sekkyoku-teki oyobi Shôkyoku-teki Settoku ni okeru Zengo Inshi* (Determinant factors in positive and negative persuasion), *Ôyô Shinri Kenkyû*, vol. 4, 1936.

Oka, Michikata. *Joshi Seinen Settoku no Sho-inshi* (Various factors in the persuasion of girls), *Kyôiku Shinri Kenkyû*, vol. 13, no. 2, 1938.

Toki, Chû. *Gakkyû-nai no Shidô Jûsoku Kankei* (Relations between those in and those under authority in a given school class), *Shinri-gaku Kenkyû*, vol. 10, 1935.

Tsuru, Hiroshi. *Seinen-ki no Yûjin Kankei* (Friendships in adolescence), *Jidô Shinri*, vol. 3, no. 8.

Kaneko, Chûgai. *Jidô no Gakkyû-nai ni tsukuru Yûjin Kankei* (Friendships formed by children in class), *Seishônen Shakai Seikatsu no Kenkyû—Nippon Seishônen Kyôiku Kenkyû-sho*, 1942.

Tazaki, Jin. *Seinen Shinri to Seinen Undô* (Youth psychology and youth movements), *Seinen Shinri*, vol. 1, No. 2, 1950.

Munakata, Seiya. *Seinen Undô* (Youth movements), *Kyôiku Jiien*, 1938.

Nishitani, Kendô. *Yûjin ni tsuite* (On friends), *Shinri-gaku Kenkyû*, vol. 16, 1941.

ATTITUDES TOWARDS FOREIGNERS

Tachibana, Hirosuke. *Nichibei Gakusei no mitaru Nippon Minzoku no Tokusei* (Characteristics of the Japanese people as seen by Japanese-American students), *Ôyô Shinri Kenkyû*, vol. 4, 1936.

Tachibana, Hirosuke. *Minzoku Kôsei Hintô no Kenkyû* (Studies on the nature of friendly attitudes in the different races), *Shinri-gaku Kenkyû*, vol. 16, 1941.

Sakamoto, Ichirô. *Gendai Seinen no Gaikoku Sûhai* (The cult of foreign countries among modern youth), *Seinen Shinri*, vol. 2, no. 3, 1951.

Satô, Kôji and Nakane, Fuyuo. *Sengo ni okeru Seinen Gakusei no Minzoku Kôo* (Like and dislike for other nations among post-war student youth), Satô Kôji's *Shinri-gaku no Kiso* (Foundations of psychology), 1948.

SOCIOLOGY AND LAW

YOUTH AND YOUTH GROUPS

Nakayama, Tarô. *Nippon Wakamono-shi* (History of Japanese youth), 1930.

Deals with the historical background and the organization of the young men's groups *(wakamono-gumi)* which appeared spontaneously in the rural villages during the Tokugawa period (1603-1868); describes the ceremonies of admission and withdrawal from them, their operation, discipline, financing and general resources. It is the first work, on this subject, to be based on a systematic nation-wide survey of the varying fortunes of young men's institutions in the light of ethnographic material found in the archives of the districts and villages.

DAI-NIPPON RENGÔ SEINEN-DAN. *Wakamono Seido no Kenkyû* (Study on young men's organizations), 1936.

YAMAURA, Kunihisa. *Nagano-ken Seinen-dan Hattatsu-shi* (History of the development of *Seinen-dan* in the prefecture of Nagano), 1935.

SHIZUOKA-KEN SHAKAI KYÔIKU-KA. *Waka-renjû ni kan-suru Bunken* (Bibliography concerning youth groups).

SEGAWA, Kiyoto. *Wakamono-gumi to Musume-nakama* (Young men's groups and girls' groups), 1937.

IMANO, Ennosuke. *Wakamono-gumi Musume-gumi* (Young men's groups girls' groups), 1949.

SEGAWA, Kiyoko. *Wakamono-nakama to Nakôdo* (Youth groups and intermediaries), 1947.

ARIGA, Kizaemon. *Wakamono-nakama to Konin—Mura no Seikatsu Soshiki ni kanrenshite* (Youth groups and marriage; in relation to the organization of rural life), *Nippon Konin-shi Ron*, 1938.

KOMADA, Kinichi, SATÔ, Kôji and YOSHIDA, Noboru. *Seinen Kyôiku* (The education of youth), 1951.

KINOSHITA, Mosaburô. *Nippon Seiken to Seinen Undô* (Youth movements and the reconstruction of Japan), 1946.

KINOSHITA, Mosaburô. *Atarashii Seinen Undô* (New youth movements), 1949.

KUMAGAI, Tatsujirô. *Seinen Soshiki Kôsô* (Plans for the organization of youth), 1948.

KOMORI, Bunkei. *Seinen-dan no Seikaku to Unei* (Features and activities of the *Seinen-dan*), 1948.

SAIKÔ SAIBAN-SHO JIMU-KYOKU KATEI-KYOKU, *Shônen Hogo wo meguru Seinen Gakuto no Undô* (Youth and students' movements concerned with child protection), 1949.

SUZUKI, Chûrô. *Atarashiki Seinen-dan no Sho-mondai* (Various problems of the new *Seinen-dan*), 1949.

SEINEN BUNKA SHINKÔ-KAI, *Tachi-agaru Seinen Undô* (Rising youth movements).

FAMILY

KAWASHIMA, Takeyoshi. *Nippon Shakai no Kazoku-teki Kôsei* (The family structure of Japanese society), 1948.

KOJIMA, Toshio. *Kazoku Keitai to Nôgyô no Hattatsu* (The form of the family and the development of agriculture), 1947.

TAMASHIRO, Hajime. *Nippon Kazoku Seido no Hihan—Han-hôken-teki Kazoku Seido no Honshitsu* (Criticism of the Japanese family system—the essence of the semi-feudal family system), 1949.

TAMASHIRO, Hajime. *Kazoku-ron* (Treatise on the family), 1947.

ARIGA, Kizaemon. *Nippon Kazoku Seido to Kosaku Seido* (The Japanese family system and the tenancy system), 1937.

TANABE, Toshiyori, ed. *Shakai-gaku Taikei* (Outline of sociology), vol. I. *Kazoku* (The family). 1948. Contents:
TODA, Sadazô. *Kozaku no Kôsei to Kinô* (The structure and function of the family).
MAKINO, Sen. *Kazoku no Ruikei* (Types of families).
ARIGA, Kizaemon. *Nippon Kodai Kazoku* (The Japanese family in ancient times).
KOYAMA, Takashi. *Nippon Kindai Kazoku* (The Japanese family in modern times).
NAKAGAWA, Zennosuke. *Kazoku Seido* (The family system).

TODA, Sadazô. *Kazoku no Kenkyû* (Studies on the family), 1926.
——. *Kazoku Kôsei* (The structure of the family), 1937.
——. *Ie to Kazoku Seido* (The 'home' and the family system), 1944.
——. *Kazoku to Konin* (The family and marriage), 1934.

HOZUMI, Shigetô. *Rikon Seido no Kenkyû* (Studies on the divorce system), 1924.

ARIGA, Kizaemon. *Nippon Konin-shi Ron* (Treatise on the history of Japanese marriage), 1948.

YANAGITA, Kunio. *Senso no Hanashi* (Stories about our ancestors), 1946.
——. *Konin no Hanashi* (Stories about marriage), 1949.
——, ed. *Sanson Seikatsu no Kenkyû* (Studies on mountain village life), 1937.
——, ed. *Kaison Seikatsu no Kenkyû* (Studies on coastal village life), 1949.

FUKUTAKE, Naoshi. *Waga Kuni Nôson ni okeru Kazoku Shugi* (The family system in the rural villages of our country), 1947, *Kikak Daigaku*, no. 2.

ISODA, Susumu. *Kazoku Seido to Nôson Shakai Kôsô* (The family system and social structure of rural villages), *Kikan Daigaku*, no. 2, 1947.

WATANABE, Yôji. *Nôson to Shin-sôzoku-hô* (Rural villages and the new laws of inheritance), *Hôritsu Jihô*, vol. 28, no. 1, 1951.

MIYAZAKI, Kôjirô. *Mimpô Kaisei to Yoron* (Public opinion and the revision of the Civil Code), *Hôritsu Jihô*, vol. 28, no. 1, 1951.

KOIKE, Motoyuki. *Nôgyô Keisai ni okeru Kazoku Rôdô to Koyô Rôdô* (Family labour and non-family labour in agriculture), *Mitta Gakkai Zasshi*, vol. 37, no. 10.

KOYAMA, Takashi. *Gyoson Kazoku no Teichaku-sei ni tsuite* (On the fixity of residence of families in fishing villages), *Gendai Skakai-gaku no Sho-mondai*, 1949.

OKAZAKI, Ayanori. *Nippon Jinkô no Jisshô-teki Kenkyû* (Factual studies on the Japanese population), 1950.

OKAZAKI, Ayanori. *Kekkon to Jinkô* (Marriage and population), 1942.

ÔKAWA, Terue. *Joshi no Mikon Zanson-ritsu ni tsuite* (On the proportion of girls remaining spinsters), *Jinkô Mondai Kenkyû*, 1941.

TATE, Minoru. *Waga Kuni Haigû-sha Kankei no Kansatsu* (Survey on the relations between couples in our country), *Jinkô Mondai*, 1944.

WATANABE, Yôji. *Gaishô no Shakai-gaku-teki Kenkyû* (Sociological study of prostitutes), 1950.

HOZUMI, Shigetô and NAKAGAWA, Zennosuke. *Kazoku Seido Zenshû* (Complete collection of studies on the family system), Kawade Shobô, 1937, 10 vols. Composed of:

FIRST PART: *Historical Treatises*

VOL. I: *Marriage*

NAKAGAWA, Zennosuke. *Kekkon-shi Gaisetsu* (Treatise on the history of marriage).
TANAKA, Kôtarô. *Shizenhô-teki Konin oyobi Rikon-ron* (Natural law marriage and the problem of divorce).
ÔMACHI, Tokuzô. *Nippon Nekkon Fûzoku-shi* (History of Japanese marriage customs).
MIKI, Kiyoshi. *Ippu-ippu-sei Ron* (Treatise on the system of monogamy).
TAMAKI, Hajime. *Tsuma* (The wife).
MIYAZAWA, Toshiyoshi. *Fujin to Seiji* (Women and politics).
TAOKA, Yoshikazu. *Fujin no Kokusai-teki Hogo* (The international protection of women).
ISHIZAKI, Shôichirô. *Tsuma no Shotoku no Hogo* (The protection of the wife's income).
HANAOKA, Shirô. *Soviêto Konin-hô Hensen* (Changes in the Soviet marriage laws).
KIMURA, Kensuke. *Furansu ni okeru Naien Mondai* (The problem of concubinage in France).
HAYASHI. *Kekkon Yûsei-gaku* (The eugenics of marriage).

VOL. 2: *Divorce*

NAKAGAWA, Zennosuke. *Rikon-shi Gaisetsu* Treatise on the history of divorce).
HASEGAWA, Nyozekan. *Jiyû Rikon-ron* (Treatise on free divorce).
SUENOBU, Sanji. Igirisu no Bekkyo Seido (Judicial separation in England).
ISHIZAKI, Shôischirô. *Furansu no Bekkyo Seido* (Judicial separation in France).
HOZUMI, Shigetô. *Seishim-byô Rikon Genin Ron* (Treatise on the causes of divorce: mental illness).
———. *Sôtai-teki Rikon Genin Ron* (Treatise on the causes of divorce: mutual consent).
MIYAKE, Shôtarô. *Rikon-fu to Mibôjin* (Widows and divorced wives).
KIMURA, Kameji. *Fujin Hanzai to Konin* (Marriage and criminal offences by wives).
NAKAGAWA, Zennosuke. *Kantsû oyobi Jûkon* (Adultery and bigamy).
HOZUMI, Shigetô. *Rien-jô to Enkiri-dera* (Bills of divorcement and divorce proceedings).
TAMASHIRO, Hajime. *Konin Rikon Tôkei-ron* (Statistical studies of marriage and divorce).

VOL. 3: *Parents and Children*

ARAKI, Masamichi. *Ketsuen-ron* (Treatise on consanguinity).
AOKI, Seishirô. *Shônen Hanzai Shinri* (The criminal psychology of children).
MORIYAMA, Takeichirô. *Shônen Hogo Mondai* (The problem of child protection).
YANAGIDA, Kunio. *Oyakata-Kokata* (Quasi-paternal relationships).
HOSOKAWA, Kameichi. *Kyûri-Kandô* (Absence and inheritance).
NAKAGAWA, Zennosuke. *Yôshi Seido-ron* (Treatise on the system of child adoption).
TAKIGAWA, Yukitoki. *Shiseiji Mondai* (The problem of illegitimacy).
YAMAZAKI, Iwao. *Bosei Hogo* (The protection of motherhood).
KIMURA, Kameji. *Danshu to Datai* (Sterilization and abortion).
YOKOTA, Kisaburô. *Jidô no Kokusai-teki Hogo* (The international protection of children).

HANAOKA, Shirô. *Soviêto ni okeru Ko no Hogo* (Child protection in Soviet Russia).
FURUBATAKE, Tanemoto. *Oyako Hôi-gaku* (Medical jurisprudence regarding parents and children).

VOL. 4: *Family*

TSUNETÔ, Kyô. *Kazoku Seido-ron* (Treatise on the family system).
ARAKI, Masamichi. *Kazoku Kôsei-ron* (Treatise on the family structure).
HONDA, Kiyoji. *Boken to Bokei* (Matriarchy and matriheritage).
FURUNA, Kiyondo. *Kodai Kazoku* (The family in ancient times).
WAGATSUMA, Sakae. *Kindai ni okeru Kazoku no Kyôdô Seikatsu* (The cohabitation of the family in modern times).
TAKIGAWA, Masajirô and TAMASHIRO, Hajime. *Nippon Kazoku-shi* (History of the family in Japan: Takigawa—Pre-Meiji; Tamashiro— Post-Meiji).
NAKAGAWA, Zennosuke. *Tai-kazoku to Bunke* (Extensive families and junior branch families).
MOGAMI, Kôkei. *Dôzoku Ketsugô* (Grouping of extensive families).
OKAZAKI, Ayanori. *Gendai Nippon Setai Jôkyô* (Domestic conditions in present-day Japan).
SHIMIZU, Morimitsu. *Shina ni okeru Dôzoku Buraku* (Family arrangements in China).
NAKAGAWA, Zennosuke. *Suisu ni okeru Ie to Kachô* (The family and heads of families in Switzerland).

VOL. 5: *Inheritance*

KONDÔ, Eikichi. *Sôzoku-shi Gaisetsu* (Treatise on the history of inheritance).
HOZUMI, Shigetô. *Kasan Seido* (On the system of family property).
NAKAGAWA, Zennosuke. *Sueko Sôzoku* (On the inheritance rights of the last-born child).
AOYAMA, Michio. *Chôshi Sôzoku* (On the inheritance rights of the eldest son).
YAGI, Yoshinosuke. *Isshi Sôzoku* (On inheritance rights of the only child).
NAKAGAWA, Zennosuke and SHIODA, Sadaichi. *Ane Katoku* (On the house headship of the eldest sister).
FUJITA, Tôzô. *Chôsen Sôzoku Seido no Taikan* (General survey of the inheritance system in Korea).
TAKAYANAGI, Kenzô. *Eikoku Sôzoku-hô Kôyô* (Outline of the English law of inheritance).
KÔBE, Masao. *Sôzoku-zei to Kazoku Seido* (Inheritance tax and the family system).
OKAZAKI, Ayanori. *Kazoku Seisaku* (Family policy).
MAKINO, Eiichi. *Kazoku Seido no Ichi-hôritsu-kan* (Legal aspects of the family system).

SECOND PART: *Law*

VOL. 1: *Marriage*

NAKAGAWA, Zennosuke. *Konin-hô Gaisetsu* (Treatise on marriage law).
HIROHAMA, Yoshio. *Yuinô* (Betrothal gifts).
AOYAMA, Michio. *Kekkon Dôi* (On marriage consent).
ISHIDA, Bunjirô. *Tsuma no Munôryoku* (On the incapacity of the wife).
NEMOTO, Matsuo. *Nichijô Kaji Dairi-ken* (On the right of representation in everyday household affairs).

KOISHI, Toshio. *Naien* (On informal marriage).
SUEKAWA, Hiroshi. *Shissô to Konin* (Marriage and desertion of the family).
ÔMORI, Kôta and *Saitô*, Hideo. *Konin to Soshô* (Marriage and legal process, I: *Ômori*, Outline of marriage litigation; *Saitô*, Divorce procedure).
EGAWA, Hidebumi. *Kokusai Konin-hô* (International marriage law).
HOZUMI, Shigetô. *Mimpô Kaisei Yôkô Kaisetsu* (Explanation of the main features of the revision of the Civil Code. I: Introduction; Marriage).

VOL. 2: *Divorce*

NAKAGAWA, Zennosuke. *Rikon-hô Gaisetsu* (Treatise on divorce law).
MIYAZAKI, Kôjirô. *Kyôgi Rikon-ron* (Treatise on divorce by mutual consent).
HOZUMI, Shigetô. *Otto no Kantsû* (On the adultery of the husband).
KATSUMOTO, Seikô. *Rikon no yoru Songai Baishô* (Compensation for damages in divorce).
FUKUSHIMA, Shirô. *Rikon-go no Fuyô Gimu* (On the obligation of maintenance after divorce).
AOYAMA, Michio. *Rikon to Ko no Kango* (Divorce and guardianship of the children).
ÔMORI, Kôta and *Saitô*, Hideo, *Konin to Soshô* (Marriage and legal process, II: *Ômori*, Outline of marriage litigation; *Saitô*, divorce procudure).
EGAWA, Hidebumi. *Kokusai Rikon-hô* (International divorce law).
HOZUMI, Shigetô. *Mimpô Kaisei Yôkô Kaisetsu* (Explanation of the main features of the revision of the Civil Code, II: Divorce; Adoption).

VOL. 3: *Parents and Children*

NAKAGAWA, Zennosuke. *Oyako-hô Gaisetsu* (Treatise on the legal relationship tionship between parents and children).
YASUDA, Kanta. *Jisshi* (Children by consanguinity).
TONOOKA, Mojûrô. *Yôshi* (Adopted children).
AOYAMA, Michio. *Shiseij Ninchi* (On the recognition of illegitimate children).
WAGATSUMA, Sakae. *Oyako no Zaisan Kankei* (Paternity relationships between parents and children).
SUEKAWA, Hiroshi. *Shinken no Seigen oyobi Hakudatsu* (Limitations and cessation of parental authority).
KANEKO, Hajime. *Oyako Kankei no Kakunin* (Establishment of paternity relationships).
SANEKATA, Masao. *Kokusai Oyako-hô* (International law and paternity relationships).
KAINÔ, Michitaka. *Kôken-hô* (The law on guardianship).
HOZUMI, Shigetô. *Mimpô Kaisei Yôkô Kaisetsu* (Explanation of the main features of the revision of the Civil Code: III: Parental authority and children by consanguinity).

VOL. 4: *Family*

NAKAGAWA, Zennosuke. *Kazoku-hô Gaisetsu* (Treatise on family law).
MURASUGI, Toshio. *Ie no Kôsei* (Structure of the family).
FUNABASHI, Shunichi. *Bunke* (Junior branch families).
NAKAJIMA, Tamakichi. *Koshu-ken Ron* (Treatise on family headship).
KONDÔ, Eikichi. *Inkyo* (Retirement).
SUEHIRO, Gantarô. *Kadan-ron* (Treatise on family groups).
KOISHI, Toshio. *Shinzoku-kai* (Family councils).

NEMOTO, Matsuo. *Koseki* (Civil status).
WADA, Uichi. *Fuyô Gimu* (Duties of maintenance).
HOZUMI, Shigetô. *Mimpô Kaisei Yôkô Kaisetsu* (Explanation of the main features of the revision of the Civil Code, IV: The family, family councils and the duties of maintenance).

VOL. 5: *Inheritance*

NAKAGAWA, Zennosuke. *Sôzoku-hô Gaisetsu* (Treatise on the law of inheritance).
KAINÔ, Michitaka. *Hôtei no Suitei Katoku Sôzoku-nin* (The heir presumptive to the headship of the family as permitted by law).
FUNABASHI, Shunichi. *Sôzoku-nin no Haijo* (Exclusion from the succession).
ISHIDA, Bunjirô *Isan no Kyôdô Sôzoku* (Joint inheritance of estate).
KONDÔ, Eikichi. *Gentei Shônin* (Acceptance of estate without liability to debts beyond assets descended).
TANIGUCHI, Chihei. *Iryû-bun* (Legal portions).
KAWASHIMA, Takeyoshi. *Sôzoku Kaifuku* (Recovery of succession).
SANEKATA, Masao. *Kokusai Sôzoku-hô* (Succession in international law).
KAJIURA, Hikoomi. *Yuigon no Hôshiki* (Testamentary forms).
YASUDA, Kanta. *Yuigon no Shikkô* (The execution of wills).
HOZUMI. Shigetô. *Mimpô Kaisei Yôkô Kaisetsu* (Explanation of the main features of the revision of the Civil Code. V: Inheritance and wills).

LIST OF BOOKS AND PUBLISHED MATERIALS
TO WHICH REFERENCE IS MADE IN THE TEXT

ALLPORT, G. W. and VERNON, P. E. *A study of values*, Boston, 1931.
ARIGA, Kizaemon, 'Benedict's conception of hierarchy in the Japanese social system', *Minzokogaku-Kenkyu* (Japanese journal of ethnology), 1949, 14, no. 4, 13-22 (in Japanese).
Ashi Shimbun. Research on international problems, Tokyo, 1950 (text and tables in Japanese; summary in English).
Asahi Picture News. Number dated 6 August 1952 (in Japanese).
BARRET, F. *L'Evolution du Capitalisme Japonais*. Paris, 1945-47, 3 vols.
BENEDICT, Ruth. *Patterns of culture*. Boston, 1934.
——. *The chrysanthemum and the sword*. Boston, 1946.
BRUNER, Jerome S. *Mandate from the people*. Mew York, 1944; French translation *(Ce que pense l'Amérique)* by Didier Lazard, Paris, 1945.
CANTRIL, Hadley, (ed.). *Public opinion 1935-1946*. Princeton, 1951.
Dentzû (Nippon Dempo Tsushinsha). *Radio research*. Tokyo, 1951, 2 roneographed booklets (in Japanese).
EMBREE, John F. *Suye-Mura, a Japanese village*. Chicago, 1939.
GORER, Geoffrey 'Themes in Japanese culture', Transact. New York Acad. of Sciences, 1943, 5, 106-24.
HAGIWARA, Tôru. *Taisen no Kaibô* (Analysis of the second world war: American and British strategy up to the defeat of Japan), Tokyo, 1950 (in Japanese).
HANI, Setsuko. *The Japanese family system*. Tokyo, 1948 *(Pacific studies series)*.
HARING, D. G. 'Aspects of personal character in Japan', *Far Eastern Quarterly*, 1946, 6, 12-22.
HEARN, Lafcadio. *Japan, an interpretation*, 1904, French translation *(Le Japon)* 3rd. ed., Paris, 1914.
Hiroshima and the Atomic Bomb. Tokyo, 1952, photo album (in Japanese).
HOZUMI, Shigetô. 'The "Tonari-gumi" of Japan', *Contemporary Japan, a review of east Asiatic affairs*, 1943, 12, no. 8, Tokyo; reproduced in German in 'Das *Tonari-gumi* in Japan', *Nippon, Zeitschrift für Japonologie*, 1944, 10, 1, 25-29.
NATIONAL INSTITUTE FOR PUBLIC OPINION RESEARCH (Kokuri-tsu-Yoron-Chosajo), Tokyo. Various pamphlets in Japanese: *Attitudes towards prostitution* (1949), *Problems of women wage earners* (1948), *Attitudes towards population problems and birth control* (1950), *The postal services* (1951).
Japan Statistical Yearbook 1950. Tokyo, 1951.

KAWASHIMA, Takeyoshi. 'Appreciation and criticism of *The chrysanthemum and the sword*', *Minzokugaku-Kenkyu* (Japanese journal of ethnology), 1949, 14, no. 4, 1-8 (in Japanese).

KEIM, Jean A. *Mon Japon du demi-siècle*. Paris, 1952.

KLINEBERG, Otto. *Tensions affecting international understanding*. New York, 1950.

LA BARRE, Weston. 'Some observations on the character structure in the orient: the Japanese', *Psychiatry*, 1945, 8, 319-42.

MATSUSHIMA, Shizuo. 'Characteristics of the *oyabun-kobun* among the miners', *Shakai-gaku Hyoron* (Japanese sociological review), 1950, 1, 61-7 (in Japanese).

MOMBU-SHÔ (Japanese Ministry of Education). *Progress of education reform in Japan*, Tokyo, 1950.

OKASAKI, Ayanori. 'The demographic problem and policy in Japan', *Population*, 1952, 7, 207-26.

OKUBO, Genji. *The problems of the emperor system in post-war Japan*. Tokyo, 1948 *(Pacific studies series)*.

OTA, Takashi. 'The reform of educational methods', *Shakai-gaku Hyoron* (Japanese sociological review), 1950, 1, no. 2, 17-23.

OUCHI, Hyoye. *Financial and monetary situation in post-war Japan*. Tokyo, 1948 *(Pacific studies series)*.

RAMMING, M. *Japan-Handbuch*. Nachschlagewerke der Japankunde, Berlin, 1941.

RAPER, Arthur F., TSUCHIYAMA, Tamie, PASSIN, Herbert and SILLS, David L. *The Japanese village in transition*. Tokyo, 1950.

REISCHAUER, Edwin O. *Japan, past and present*. New York, 1951.

SAKAI, Atsuharu. *Japan in a nutshell*. Yokohama, 1949.

SANSOM, G. B. *Japan, a short cultural history*. French translation *Le Japon, histoire de la civilisation japonaise*, Paris, 1938.

SCAP (Supreme Commander of the Allied Powers). *Post-war developments in Japanese education*, Tokyo, 1952, 2 vols.

SPRANGER, E. *Lebensformen*. Halle, 1929.

TEXTOR, Robert B. *Failure in Japan*. New York, 1951.

UENODA, S. *Calendar of annual events in Japan*. Tokyo, 1951.

UNITED STATES EDUCATION MISSION TO JAPAN. *Report*. Washington, 1946.

WAGATSUMA, Sakae. 'Democratization of the family relation in Japan', *Washington Law Review*, 1950, 25, 405-26.

WATSUJI, Tetsurô. 'Some doubts as to the scientific value of Benedict's book', *Minzokugaku-Kenkyu*, (Japanese journal of ethnology), 1949, 14, no. 4, 23-7 (in Japanese).

YAMAGUCHI, Shinrokuro. *Some aspects of agrarian reform in Japan*. Tokyo, 1948 *(Pacific studies series)*.

YANAGITA, Kunio. Life in the eyes of the ordinary man', *Minzokugaku-Kenkyu*, (Japanese journal of ethnology), 1949, 14, no. 4, 28-35.

YANAIBARA, Tadao. *Religion and democracy in modern Japan*. Tokyo, 1948 *(Pacific studies series)*.

YOSHIDA, K. and KAIGO, T. *Japanese education*. Tokyo, 1937.

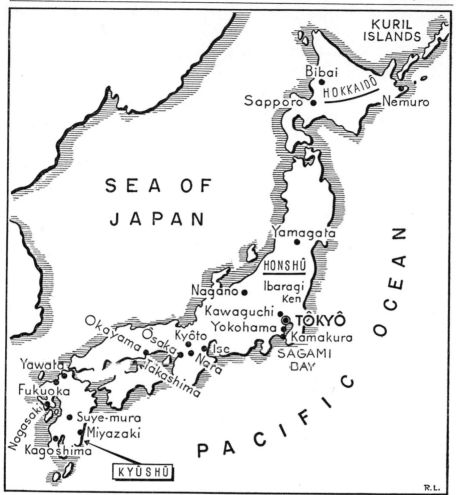

Fig. 16. Map showing localities named in the text.

INDEX OF NAMES

SUBJECT INDEX

A

Adopted son, *see* Son.
Adultery, 96.
Advice-seeking (*sodan*): practice of, 226 *et sqq.*;
frequency in youth, 228.
Ainu, 44.
see Marginal groups.
Allport-Gillespie test, 24, 29-30, 167, 185, 191, 209, 211, 220, 295.
Ambition of youth, 143, 207-9.
America, *see* U.S.A.
Ancestor-worship, 48, 57.
reform of, 94, 95.
Anthropology, anthropometric data, 44.
Associations:
equalitarian (*humi*), 61-2, 75.
neighbourhood (*tonari-gumi*), 61.
of youth, 75-6; membership of, 213n; reform of, 106-8.
Authority: attitude of youth towards, 150 *et sqq.*
in the family, *see* Father.
Autobiographies of the future, 29, 40, 110, 135, 140, 143, 144, 160, 234, 277.

B

Behaviour: methods of studying, 17; planes of, 30.
cultural, 125 *et sqq.*, *see also* Recreation.
Birth control, 145.
Books, *see* Reading.
Buddhism, 48.
Bunke, *see* Extended family.

C

Career, preoccupation of youth with, 142-3, 167, 169.

Children, 65.
number wanted, 190.
proportion of population, 69.
upbringing of, 77-8, 79.
attitude of youth towards, 166, 171.
Chinese: classics, study of, 101.
immigrants, 47.
influence on Japanese society, 48, 58.
Christianity, 49, 191.
Cinema, 126.
frequency of attendance, 222.
Civil Code:
concerning family, 94-6;
concerning laws of inheritance, 95, 97-8.
concerning women, 96-7.
Co-education, 96, 101.
attitude of youth towards, 175, 176.
Cold war, attitude of youth towards, 135-7.
Communism, 108.
attitude of youth towards, 136, 137-8.
Confucianism, 48, 96.
Constitution, 91-3.
ambiguity of, 93.
attitude towards, 131-2.
Country-dwellers:
age of marriage, 183.
associations of, 61.
attitudes towards:
authority, 151, 153, 155; equality of sexes, 174; foreign countries, 124; freedom in family, 172; inheritance, 53, 172; international affairs, 110; morality (*giri*), 195-6; rearmament, 132; relations between sexes, 189; war, 130.
dependence of, 232.
family hierarchy among, 54, 57, 60.
in enquiry, 21.

Music, 126.
Myths, in relation to Japanese history, 46-7, 105.

N

Name, family, *see* Family name.
Newspapers, *see* Reading.

O

Obligation (*on*), 58, 193, 195.
On, *see* Obligation.
Optimism, 85-6.
    in youth, 144, 210-13; significance of, 224.
Overpopulation, 59, 85, 144-5.
    fear of, 190.
Oyabun-Kobun, *see* Quasi-father-son system.

P

Pacifism, 19, 128, 134.
    limits of, 133.
    in youth, 130, 132.
Passivity, in youth, 215-16.
Patriarchal units, *see* Family name.
Patriarchal system, *see* Quasi-father-son system.
Peace treaty, 128.
Peasants, *see* Country-dwellers.
People, sovereignty of the, *see* Sovereignty of the people.
Personality:
    types of, 203-5; in youth, 147, 205-6.
    See also Ambition, Dependence, Escapism, Immaturity, Inferiority, Insecurity, Optimism, Passivity, Self-confidence.
Police, 152-5.
Politics:
    interest of youth in, 147-9, 214, 216-17.
    See also Communism, Constitution, Democracy, Emperor, Foreign countries, International affairs.
Population, 44.
Public affairs, *see* Politics.

Q

Quasi-father-son system (*oyabun-kobun*), 54-5, 60.

R

Reading, 125-6.
Rearmament, 19, 129, 235.
    attitude of youth towards, 132.
Recreation, as escapism, 222-3.
Red Cross, Junior, *see* Junior Red Cross.
Reforms:
    post-war, 90.
    See Ancestor-worship, Associations, Constitution, Education, Extended family, Family in limited sense, Inheritance, Land reform, Language, Marriage, Women. *See also* Meiji reforms.
Religion:
    attitude of youth towards, 191-2, 204.
    See also Ancestor-worship, Christianity, Shintô, Sun-worship.
Rescript, imperial, *see* Imperial rescript.
Resignation, *see* Passivity.
Resources, of Japan, 44-5.
Rural population, *see* Country-dwellers.

S

Salaries, 59, 73-5, 89,
Samurai, 36, 47.
Schools, *see* Education.
Script, ideographic, *see* Language.
Seinen-dan, 76.
    See Associations (of youth).
Self-confidence, in youth, 209-10; significance of, 224.
Service, military, *see* Military service.
Sexes:
    difference of treatment of in family; 78-9.
    equality of, 166, 175 *et sqq.*; attitude of youth towards, 176-8; obstacles to, 179; *see also* Women (inferior position of).
    relations between, 186-9; attitude of youth towards, 189.
Shintô, 75, 76, 86, 191.
Shizoku, *see* Family in limited sense.
Shôgun, 47, 48.
Social mobility, 57, 143, 211.
Social structure, 57.
    reforms of, 86.
    See also Family in limited sense, Hierarchy.
Social studies, teaching of, 104-6.

UNESCO PUBLICATIONS ON THE RACE QUESTION

What is Race?

Attractively presented, clearly written, this publication gives by means of coloured pictographs and simple texts, essential information about the biological aspects of race. $1.00

RACE AND SOCIETY (series)

Racial Equality and the Law
MORROE BERGER $ .50

Race and Class in Rural Brazil
CHARLES WAGLEY $1.25

THE RACE QUESTION IN MODERN THOUGHT (series)

The Catholic Church and the Race Question
REV. YVES M. J. CONGAR $ .40

The Ecumenical Movement and the Racial Problem
W. A. VISSER 't HOOFT $ .40

Jewish Thought as a Factor in Civilization
LEON ROTH $ .40

THE RACE QUESTION IN MODERN SCIENCE (series)

The Race Concept $ .50

Race Mixture
HARRY L. SHAPIRO $ .25

Racial Myths
JUAN COMAS $ .25

Race and Culture
MICHEL LEIRIS $ .25

Race and Psychology
OTTO KLINEBERG $ .25

Race and Biology
L. C. DUNN $ .25

Roots of Prejudice
ARNOLD M. ROSE $ .25

Race and History
CLAUDE LÉVI-STRAUSS $ .25

The Significance of Racial Differences
G. M. MORANT $ .25

Race and Society
KENNETH L. LITTLE $ .25

Obtainable in the U.S. from the Unesco National Distributor:
COLUMBIA UNIVERSITY PRESS
2960 BROADWAY, NEW YORK 27, N.Y.

"... *Rapid changes in the industrial or social structure in any country are apt to lead to unforeseen disturbances even when such changes are initiated or supervised by nationals of that country. When men and women with technical skills set out to help in shaping new developments in a country or culture other than their own, there are clearly many more possibilities of producing unfortunate consequences.*"

J. R. REES, Director
World Federation for Mental Health

CULTURAL PATTERNS AND TECHNICAL CHANGE

edited by
MARGARET MEAD

A manual prepared by the World Federation for Mental Health which examines the implications of technical change for mental health and investigates planned change in which the emphasis is on educationa and preventive measures rather than upon clinical and corrective ones.

CONTENTS:

Introduction; The International Setting of Technical Change; Studies of Whole Cultures: Burma, Greece, The Tiv of Nigeria, Palau, The Spanish Americans of New Mexico, U.S.A.; Cross-Cultural Studies of Aspects of Technical Change: Agriculture, Nutrition, Maternal and Child Care, Public Health, Industrialization, Fundamental Education; Specific Mental Health Implications of Technical Change; Principles Involved in Developing Mental Health during Technical Change.

348 pages
Cloth bound $2.50 13/6 650 fr.

A UNESCO PUBLICATION

Obtainable through bookshops or direct from the Unesco Distributors (see list).

UNESCO PUBLICATIONS:
NATIONAL DISTRIBUTORS

ARGENTINA
Editorial Sudamericana, S.A.,
Alsina 500,
BUENOS AIRES.

ASSOCIATED STATES OF CAMBODIA, LAOS AND VIET-NAM
Librairie Nouvelle
Albert Portail,
Boîte Postale 283,
SAIGON.
Sub-depot:
Librairie Albert Portail,
14 avenue Boulloche,
PHNOM-PENH.

AUSTRALIA
Oxford University
Press,
346 Little Collins St.,
MELBOURNE.

AUSTRIA
Wilhelm Frick Verlag,
27 Graben,
VIENNA I.

BELGIUM
Librairie Encyclopédique,
7, rue du Luxembourg,
BRUSSELS IV.

BOLIVIA
Librería Selecciones,
Av. 16 de Julio 216,
LA PAZ.

BRAZIL
Livraría Agir Editora,
rua México 98-B,
Caixa postal 3291,
RIO DE JANEIRO.

CANADA
University of Toronto
Press,
TORONTO.
Periodica Inc.,
5112 avenue Papineau,
MONTREAL 34.

CEYLON
Lake House Bookshop,
The Associated Newspapers of
Ceylon Ltd., P.O. Box 244,
COLOMBO I.

CHILE
Librería Lope de Vega,
Calle Estado 54,
SANTIAGO DE CHILE.

COLOMBIA
Emilio Royo Martin,
Carrera 90, No. 1791,
BOGOTA.

COSTA RICA
Trejos Hermanos,
Apartado 1313,
SAN JOSE.

CUBA
Unesco Centro Regional
en el Hemisfero
Occidental,
Calle 5 No. 306 Vedado,
Apartado 1358.
HAVANA.

CYPRUS
M. E. Constantinides,
P.O. Box 473,
NICOSIA,

CZECHOSLOVAKIA
Artia Ltd.,
30 Ve smečkách,
PRAGUE 2.

DENMARK
Ejnar Munksgaard
Ltd.,
6 Norregade,
COPENHAGEN K.

ECUADOR
Casa de la Cultura
Ecuatoriana,
avenida 6 de Diciembre 332,
QUITO.

EGYPT
La Renaissance
d'Égypte,
9 Adly Pasha Street,
CAIRO.

ETHIOPIA
International Press Agency,
P.O. Box 120,
ADDIS ABABA.

FINLAND
Akateeminen Kirjakauppa,
2 Keskuskatu,
HELSINKI.

FORMOSA
The World
Book Co. Ltd.,
99 Chung King Rd.,
Section I,
TAIPEH.

FRANCE
Unesco Bookshop,
19 avenue Kléber,
PARIS-16e.

GERMANY
Unesco Vertrieb für Deutschland,
R. Oldenbourg,
MUNICH.

GREECE
Elefthéroudakis,
Librairie internationale,
ATHENS.

HAITI
Librairie
'A la Caravelle',
36 rue Roux,
Boîte postale III-B,
PORT-AU-PRINCE.

HONG KONG
Swindon Book Co.,
25 Nathan Road,
KOWLOON.

HUNGARY
Kultura, P.O.B. 149,
BUDAPEST 62.

INDIA
Orient Longmans Ltd.,
Indian Mercantile
Chamber,
Nicol Road,
BOMBAY.
17 Chittaranjan Ave.,
CALCUTTA.
36-A Mount Road,
MADRAS.
Sub-depots:
Oxford Book and
Stationery Co.,
Scindia House,
NEW DELHI.
Rajkamal Publications Ltd.,
Himalaya House,
Hornby Road,
BOMBAY I.

INDONESIA
G.C.T. van Dorp and Co.,
Djalan Nusantara 22,
JAKARTA.

IRAQ
McKenzie's Bookshop,
BAGHDAD.

ISRAEL
Blumstein's Bookstores, Ltd.,
35 Allenby Road,
P.O.B. 5154,
TEL AVIV.

ITALY
Libreria Commissionaria G.C.
Sansoni,
via Gino Capponi 26,
Casella postale 552,
FLORENCE.

JAMAICA
Sangster's Book Room,
99 Harbour Street,
KINGSTON.
Knox Educational
Services,
SPALDINGS.

JAPAN
Maruzen Co. Inc.,
6 Tori-Nichome,
Nihonbashi,
TOKYO.

JORDAN
Joseph I. Bahous and Co.,
Dar-ul-Kutub,
Salt Road,
AMMAN.

LEBANON
Librairie Universelle,
Avenue des Français,
BEIRUT.

LIBERIA
J. Momolu Kamara,
69 Front and Gurley
Streets,
MONROVIA.

LUXEMBOURG
Librairie Paul Bruck,
33 Grand-Rue.

MADAGASCAR
La Librairie de Madagascar,
TANANARIVE.

MALAYAN FEDERATION AND
SINGAPORE
Peter Chong and Co.,
P.O. Box 135,
SINGAPORE.

MALTA
Sapienza's Library,
26 Kingsway,
VALETTA.

MEXICO
Difusora
de las publicaciones de la Unesco,
Artes 31, int. bajos,
MEXICO, D.F.

NETHERLANDS
N.V. Martinus Nijhoff,
Lange Voorhout 9,
THE HAGUE.

NEW ZEALAND
Unesco Publications Centre,
7 De Lacy Street,
DUNEDIN, N.E.2.

NIGERIA
C.M.S. Bookshop,
P.O. Box 174,
LAGOS.

NORWAY
A/S Bokhjornet,
Stortingsplass 7,
OSLO.

PAKISTAN
Ferozsons,
60 The Mall,
LAHORE.
Bunder Road,
KARACHI.
35 The Mall,
PESHAWAR.

PANAMA
Argencia Internacional
de Publicaciones,
Apartado 2052,
Plaza de Arango No. 3,
PANAMA, R.P.

PERU
Librería Mejia Baca,
Azangaro 722,
LIMA.

PHILIPPINES
Philippine Education Co.,
1104 Castillejos,
Quiapo,
MANILA.

PORTUGAL
Publicaçoes Eurôpa-América,
Ltda.,
Rua das Flores 45, 1°,
LISBON.

PUERTE RICO
Pan-American Book Co.,
SAN JUAN 12.

SENEGAL
Librairie
'Tous les Livres'.
30 rue de Thiong,
DAKAR.

SPAIN
Aguilar, S.A. de Ediciones,
Juan Bravo 38,
MADRID.

SURINAM
Radhakishun and Co. Ltd.,
(Book Dept.),
Watermolenstraat 36,
PARAMARIBO.

SWEDEN
A/B C.E. Fritzes Kungl.,
Hovbokhandel,
Fredsgatan 2,
STOCKHOLM 16.

SWITZERLAND
Librairie Antoine Dousse,
Ancienne Librairie de l'Université,
Case postale 72,
FRIBOURG.
Europa Verlag,
5 Rämistrasse,
ZÜRICH.
Sub-depot:
Librairie Payot,
Place Molard,
GENEVA.

SYRIA
Librairie Universelle,
DAMASCUS.

TANGIER
Centre International,
20 rue Molière,

THAILAND
Suksapan Panit,
Arkarn 9,
Rajdamnern Ave.,
BANGKOK.

TUNISIA
Victor Boukhors,
4 rue Nocard,
TUNIS.

TURKEY
Librairie Hachette,
469 Istiklal Caddesi,
Beyoglu,
ISTANBUL.

UNION OF BURMA
Burma Educational
Bookshop,
551-3 Merchant Street,
P.O. Box 222,
RANGOON.

UNION OF SOUTH AFRICA
Van Schaik's Bookstore(Pty)Ltd.,
P.O. Box 724,
PRETORIA.

UNITED KINGDOM AND
N. IRELAND
H.M. Stationery Office,
P.O. Box 569,
LONDON, S.E.1.

UNITED STATES OF AMERICA
Columbia University Press,
2960 Broadway,
NEW YORK 27, N.Y.

URUGUAY
Unesco,
Centro de Cooperación
Cientifica para América Latina,
Bulevar Artigas 1320,
MONTEVIDEO.

VENEZUELA
Libreria Villegas Venezolana,
Madrices a Marrón N. 35,
Pasaje Urdaneta,
Local B,
CARACAS.

YUGOSLAVIA.
Jugoslovenska Knjiga,
Terazijc 27/II,
BELGRADE.

UNESCO BOOK COUPONS

Unesco Book Coupons can be used to purchase all books and periodicals of an
educational, scientific or cultural character. For full information please write to:

Unesco Coupon Office, 19 avenue Kléber, Paris-16e, France